DUMITRU STANILOAE

ORTHODOX SPIRITUALITY

A PRACTICAL GUIDE FOR THE FAITHFUL
AND A DEFINITIVE MANUAL FOR THE SCHOLAR

Translated from the original Romanian by
Archimandrite Jerome (Newville)
and
Otilia Kloos

Foreword by
Alexander Golubov

St. Tikhon's Seminary Press
2003

PUBLISHED WITH PERMISSION OF LIDIA IONESCU-STANILOAE
ALL RIGHTS RESERVED.
COPYRIGHT © 2002 ST TIKHON'S ORTHODOX THEOLOGICAL SEMINARY PRESS,
SOUTH CANAAN, PENNSYLVANIA, 18459
ENGLISH TRANSLATION COPYRIGHT © 2002 ARCHIMANDRITE JEROME (NEWVILLE) AND OTILIA KLOOS.

FIRST PRINTING – 2002
SECOND PRINTING – 2003

ISBN: 1-878997-66-1

Approved for publication.
+ Herman
Archbishop of Philadelphia and Eastern Pennsylvania

Library of Congress Cataloging-in-Publication Data

Staniloae, Dumitru.
 [Spiritualitatea ortodoxa. English]
 Orthodox spirituality : a practical guide for the faithful and a definitive manual for the scholar / Dumitru Staniloae ; translated from the original Romanian by Archimandrite Jerome (Newville) and Otilia Kloos ; foreword by Alexander Golubov.
  p. cm.
 Includes bibliographical references and index.
 ISBN 1-878997-66-1
 1. Spiritual life—Orthodox Eastern Church. 2. Orthodox Eastern Chruch—Doctrines. I. Title.

BX382.S7313 2002
248'.088'219—dc21

2002017832

CONTENTS

Foreword 1

Introduction 21
1. The Goal of Orthodox Spirituality 21
2. The Meaning and Possibility of Union with God 30
3. Orthodox Spirituality and our Neighbor 40
4. The Holy Trinity — the Basis of Christian Spirituality ... 46
5. The Christological, Pneumatological,
    and Ecclesiastical Character of Orthodox Spirituality 56
6. The Major Steps of the Spiritual Life 69

PART ONE: PURIFICATION

A. About the Passions

7. The Essence of the Passions 77
8. The Natural and Unnatural Passions 84
9. The Basic Causes of the Passions and their Effects 90
10. The Passions and the Faculties of the Soul 96
11. How the Passions are Aroused, according to Traditional
    Orthodox Teaching 109
12. The Passionate State and Care 115

B. Purification of the Passions by the Virtues

13. The Order of Purification and Patristic Spiritual Methods 119
14. Faith, the Basic State for Purification 124
15. The Fear of God and the Thought of Judgment 130
16. Repentance 135
17. Self-control 148
18. The Guarding of the Mind or of Thoughts 158
19. Longsuffering, the Patient Endurance of Troubles 168
20. Hope 177
21. Meekness and Humility 180
22. Dispassion or Freedom from Passion 185

PART TWO: ILLUMINATION

23. The Gifts of the Holy Spirit 195
24. The Contemplation of God in Creation 203
25. The Spiritual Understanding of Scripture 224
26. The Negative and Apophatic Knowledge of God in General 230
27. The Steps of Apophaticism 237
28. Negative and Positive Theology: a Dynamic Relationship............ 245
29. Pure Prayer 255
30. Methods for the Facilitation of Pure Prayer 262
31. To Jesus: by what is Deep Within us 283
32. Mental Rest: the First Step of Stillness 294

PART THREE: PERFECTION

33. Love and Dispassion: the Steps of Love 303
34. Love as a Factor of Perfect Union and as Ecstasy 310
35. Love, Knowledge and the Divine Light:
    I. The Role of the Mind in the Vision of the Divine Light... 327
36. Love, Knowledge and the Divine Light:
    II. The Vision of the Divine Light: a Knowledge beyond
    Knowledge 341
37. Deification: Deification in a Broad Sense 362
38. Deification: Deification in a Strict Sense 368

Bibliography 377
Index 385
Postscript 395

Translators' Note:

In translating this work from the original Romanian, it was our intention to preserve and relay, as much as possible, Fr. Staniloae's tendency towards an informal, conversational style of exposition, despite certain commonly accepted conventions of academic writing. Thus, for example, the contractions *isn't, didn't, can't,* and so on, appear throughout this work, instead of the more formal *is not, did not, cannot, etc.* Additionally, the names of individual Fathers, such as Maximus the Confessor, are often given in the latinized form by which they are more commonly known in the West. — *Translators*

ORTHODOX SPIRITUALITY

FOREWORD

Spirituality in an Orthodox Perspective

Underlying the publication in English of Fr. Dumitru Staniloae's extensive study of Orthodox spirituality, originally written in Romanian and intended primarily as a text for Orthodox theological schools, are several substantive issues that are not, perhaps, immediately evident, but which, nonetheless, require some comment. It is important that the reader properly understand these issues as they are particularly refracted in the Orthodox perspective.

The first of these is mostly one of theological language— the propriety, or even the legitimacy, from the standpoint of a traditional Orthodox approach, of appropriating the modern term "spirituality" to a descriptive academic study of the principles and contours of Christian spiritual life. Questions of theological language, however, always arise within a particular context, and are fueled primarily by the need to articulate a message and to define its contents. Thus a second issue immediately arises— that of the larger frame of reference in which the message is to be heard: the context. A message that is poorly articulated, presented in a language that fails to engage the context, is, at best, meaningless. At worst, if improperly articulated or presented outside the intended context, the message itself becomes a source of misapprehension or confusion.

From the larger Christian perspective, the need both to articulate the message and to engage the context is originally framed as a categorical imperative, in terms of the universality both of message and context: "Go into all the world and preach the gospel to every creature" (Mark 16:15). The universality of the Good News not only about a "new way of life," but also about a radical "newness" of life, in other words, is not to be preserved in some comfortable cultural or perceptual ghetto, or, what is worse, in some museum of Christian antiquities,[1] but is to be

---

[1] Of a certain prevailing cultural attitude, or tendency, to reduce the Church to the parameters of a medium for preservation of ancient rites and rituals, Fr. Georges Florovsky remarked: "We glory in the legacy which has been left to us by our forefathers, but I'm afraid that we deal with this legacy in a rather lazy way. It is, of course, a great treasure, but is it the proper way of showing our respect for the treasure to put it aside, to put it in a safe, as it were, to deposit it in a bank or to store it in a treasury like something very delicate, very fragile, which cannot be used and which must be preserved under glass or some other kind of cover? One is tempted to say, he puts the treasure aside because it is a very sacred thing. I suspect that one does so because he does not know very well what to do about it and prefers to adapt to the conditions of the surrounding life and to keep the treasures elsewhere as in a safe" ("To the Orthodox People: The

preached to the whole world, not only in a theological language the "world" can understand, but also with a convincing purposefulness that will allow the world to be overcome and converted. It is not by chance that the issue of comprehensible theological language, in fact, already surfaces as a major component of the events and experience of Pentecost. Not only were the disciples themselves "all filled with the Holy Spirit and began to speak with other tongues, as the Spirit gave them utterance," but also the multitude to which they spoke "came together, and were confused, because everyone heard them speak in his own language. They were all amazed and marveled, saying to one another... how is it that we hear [them], each in our own language in which we were born... speaking in our own tongues the wonderful works of God" (Acts 2:4, 6, 7-8, 11).[2] The results, indeed, were admirable: "and that day about three thousand souls were added to them" (Acts 2:41).

The original context for Staniloae's *Orthodox Spirituality* was the living historical reality of the confessing Orthodox Church sojourning in twentieth-century Romania. There, as in most Eastern European countries of the former communist bloc, fenced in by the Iron Curtain and controlled by a rigid, state-enforced atheist social ideology, the tacit, if not always open, ideological opposition of Christian spirituality to official Marxism was, at best, only marginally tolerated, and any official publication of religious texts subjected to rigid censorship. In that context, the symbolic message of spirituality was not without significance for those who taught and those who learned: the authentic "Orthodox spirituality" of the Church, in a very real sense, stood in understated opposition to an all-encompassing pressure of a patently "false spirituality"[3]

Responsibility of the Orthodox in America," *Ecumenism 1*, Collected Works, vol. 13, pp. 175-176).

[2] The importance of comprehensible theological language is later again emphasized by St Paul: "Unless you utter by the tongue words easy to understand, how will it be known what is spoken? For you will be speaking into the air. There are, it may be, so many kinds of languages in the world, and none of them is without significance. Therefore, if I do not know the meaning of the language, I shall be a foreigner to him who speaks, and he who speaks will be a foreigner to me" (1 Corinthians 14:9-11). Patristic tradition informs us that the Fathers did not hesitate, in many cases, to appropriate terminology prevalent in the pagan world and to imbue it with Orthodox meaning. As we learn from the example of the historical battle over the single iota in the words *homoiousios vs. homoousios*, to a significant degree, the patristic doctrinal struggle for "Orthodox theology" was, indeed, a struggle for theological language.

[3] Of the consuming "anti-spirituality" of the Russian revolution, for instance, the virtually unnoticed Russian religious thinker and philosopher Ivan Il'yin wrote: "Our generations are confronted by a horrifying, mystical emanation [of a diabolical] elemental force, and we still are not able to put our life experience into precise words. We could describe this elemental force as 'black fire.' We could define it as eternal resentment, as unquenchable hatred, as belligerent banality, as shameless falsehood, as absolute immodesty and absolute lust for power, as debasement of spiritual freedom, as thirst for universal destruction, as joy in the annihilation of the best people, as antichristianity. A human being who acquiesces to this elemental force loses spiritual-

propagated by the social and religious doctrine of Marxist scientific atheism, a battle standard, as it were, that permitted not only resistance and survival in a hostile environment, but also inspired the inner struggle for victory. Today, after the meaningful political events of the last decade of the twentieth century, both those who taught and those who learned, not only in Romania, can properly, with some profound satisfaction, repeat the words of the Beloved Disciple: "Whoever is born of God overcomes the world. And this is the victory that has overcome the world—our faith" (1 John 5:4).

To the careful observer it is evident that certain aspects of our own context have much in common with Staniloae's Eastern Europe, manifesting a worldview that is effectively ignorant of apostolic *kerygma*. "Our contemporary world, atheistic and ridden with unbelief," ponders one of the most significant Orthodox theologians of the twentieth century, Fr. Georges Florovsky "is it not comparable in a sense with that pre-Christian world, renewed with all the same interweaving of false religious trends, skeptical and anti-God?"[4] Indeed, it would seem that the circumstances of profound spiritual and cultural crisis reach to the very roots of our civilization. "We would contend," observes Florovsky, "that it is precisely the modern Retreat from Christianity, at whatever exact historical date we may discern its starting point, that lies at the bottom of our present crisis. Our age is, first of all, an age of unbelief, and for that reason an age of uncertainty, confusion, and despair. There are so many in our time who have no hope precisely because they lost all faith."[5] Yet it is here, in this world, in our own age, that Christian theology is called to purposefully engage the context and articulate the message, without an undue pessimism that is not supported by the message itself.

> It is precisely because we are already engaged in the apocalyptic struggle that we are called upon to do work as theologians. Our task is to oppose the atheistic and anti-God attitude, which surrounds us like a viscosity, with a responsible and conscious profession of Christian truth…. Unbelieving knowledge of Christianity is not objective knowledge, but rather some kind of anti-theology. There is in it so much passion, at times blind, often obscure and malignant…. Here again, theology is called not only to judge, but also to heal. It is neces-

---

ity, love and conscience; spiritual decomposition and corruption set in, he submits to conscious iniquity and thirst for destruction; he finishes with impudent sacrilege and ruthless torture of other human beings" ("K istorii d'iavola" [Towards a history of the devil]), *Nashi Zadachi* 1:32 (Paris, 1956), pp. 60-61.

[4] Georges Florovsky, "The Ways of Russian Theology," *Aspects of Church History*, Collected Works, vol. 4, p. 207.

[5] Florovsky, "Faith and Culture," *Christianity and Culture*, Collected Works, vol. 2, pp. 9-10.

sary to enter into this world of doubt, illusion and lies, in order to answer doubt as well as reproach. But we must enter into this world with the sign of the Cross in our heart and the name of Jesus in our spirit, because this is a world of mystical wanderings, where everything is fragmentized, decomposed and refracted as if through a set of mirrors.[6]

It should be remembered, especially in the Western context, that the roots of Christian theology are not only Western, but reach deeply into the theological mind and the living Christian experience of the Orthodox East. Before the medieval political and cultural schism between the Latin and Greek worlds and the subsequent Protestant Reformation, the Christian West was itself, in fact, Orthodox, part and parcel of one united, albeit admittedly bi-polar, Byzantine Commonwealth.[7] In our own time, as Western culture once again gradually comes to recognition of the "Eastern" Orthodox Church as being existentially part of its own root tradition, the imperative of discovering common ground and defining a common frame of reference relative to essentials of Christian spiritual life arises as a matter of some urgency. At the same time, as Orthodox theology engages the Western context, there also arises, once again, the imperative to speak in a comprehensible language, and thus to define a common methodology and lexicon. In this sense, "faithfulness to patristic tradition" may also mean courage to appropriate language, and to imbue it with Orthodox content. Here, too, spirituality as concept acquires layers of meaning and significance not simply as descriptive terminology applied to the topography of Christian life, or as designating a particular field of academic inquiry and a formative goal of the seminary curriculum, but also as a significant commonality bridging the cultural fissure between Christian East and Christian West.

Unfortunately, in our contemporary world a degree of confusion commonly abounds as to what "spirituality" actually means, or even as to what it should mean. This confusion is not necessarily resolved by a glut of attempted formal, often flawed, definitions in a multitude of con-

---

[6] Florovsky, "Ways of Russian Theology," *Aspects of Church History*, Collected Works, vol. 4, pp. 206-207.

[7] The estrangement between Christian East and Christian West, suggests Florovsky, speaks more to the loss of cultural memory than to an insurmountable breach of cultural unity. "This mental divorce of the East and the West was never complete. The common ground was never lost. What really happened was much worse. It was forgotten that there was a common ground. And very often what was in fact common was mistaken for something peculiar and distinctive.... The total outcome of this age-long estrangement was the inability, on both sides of the cultural schism, to ascertain even the existing agreements and the tendency to exaggerate all the distinctive marks." Despite the estrangement, however, Florovsky argues, "there is no reason to believe that these differences or varieties are ultimately irreconcilable and cannot or could not be integrated or rather reintegrated into the fullness of the Catholic mind." "Faith and Culture," pp. 9-10.

temporary publications written from a host of religious and quasi-religious perspectives, definitions that may not always be helpful, or even meaningful, outside their particular context.

In the very busy marketplace of contemporary "quests for meaning" entered into or undertaken in an atmosphere of creeping secularity and affluent materialism, compounded by what the Russian lay theologian Paul Evdokimov has termed "organic atheism,"[8] or "latent atheism" of ordinary believers,[9] the word "spirituality" has nowadays acquired an almost faddish quality. It is glibly used in many different, often contradictory, contexts to point to, or describe, certain aspects or modes of human "being," as represented by beliefs and practices that are deemed to be of a "spiritual" nature, but which most often do not easily fall into the comfortable frameworks either of so-called "institutional religion" (as elements, properly, of religious belief or religious doctrine), or, alternatively, of an essentially secular-humanist, rational and empirical mindset that tends to negate religiosity on principle, as something vaguely old-fashioned and retrograde, thus inappropriate for modern public consumption, and tends to see the primary locus of spirituality as being somehow situated apart from, or in opposition to, religion.[10] In this respect, almost anything even hazily evocative of such aspects or modes of "spiritual" being—from astrology and Tarot cards to the drug-induced visions of Carlos Castaneda; from New Age beliefs in cross-channeling and the power of crystals to credence in so-called "UFO phenomena" and allegedly resulting "encounters of the third kind"; from a naïve and sentimental fascination with spurious gurus and "elders" or the syncretism of so-called "natural religion," to a superficial and

---

[8] "Far from seeming to be a neurosis of civilization, it appears to express a certain health, a psychic state free from all metaphysical unease, fully occupied with the world, insensitive to religion. Such 'profaneness,' such a contented cold skepticism neither struggles with anything, nor any longer asks a simple question about God. To be intelligent today means to understand everything, and believe in nothing" Paul Evdokimov, *Ages of the Spiritual Life* (Crestwood, NY, 1998), p. 16.

[9] "There is the mediocrity of the faithful, who take themselves far too seriously and impose on others their mentality, formed by edifying discourses and sermons characterized by empty formulas and verbal excess. A religious life that has been domesticated, socialized, democratized, has the least attractive appearance. Its intellectual content is quite low, imprisoned by old-fashioned spiritual manuals with their limited ideas and apologetics no longer accepted today." *Ibid.*

[10] "Especially among adherents to established religion," observes Evdokimov, "anything religious provokes in sincere souls an immediate response of boredom, with services and ceremonies performed in an archaic language, or with childish hymns proclaiming a joy devoid of meaning, boredom with a closed symbolism, the key to which is lost forever." *Ibid.* See, in particular: Wade Clark Roof, "The Religious and the Spiritual," *A Generation of Seekers: The Spiritual Journeys of the Baby Boom Generation* (San Francisco, 1993), pp. 76-79.

essentially self-focused "care of the soul" psychologism,[11] or, by way of an incipient curiosity about the teachings of the great Christian and non-Christian mystical and ascetic traditions, both Eastern and Western, to the various outward expressions of Orthodox culture as seen through the prisms of Orthodox liturgy, architecture, iconography or literature (*i.e.*, the "writings of the fathers") all of these, indeed, can easily fall into loosely construed denotative and connotative categories of this fuzzy and slippery word.

This fuzziness of meaning derived from questionable usage, however, does not, of itself, invalidate the word. While Staniloae himself, as is evident from the title of his book, does not see any particular need either to amplify the term "spirituality," or to discuss the ambiguities of its usage,[12] and thus freely appropriates and accepts it as a given, directly relating the essential "matter" of "spirituality" to the fields of Christian moral and mystical theology, it is hardly surprising, in view of the above, that the propriety of the usage of the term in an Orthodox context is not always or universally shared, and has, in fact, been brought into question by such established Orthodox theologians as Fr. Stanley Harakas and Giorgios Mantzarides.

These theologians, and others of like mind with them, reject outright the suggestion that the word "spirituality" can properly or usefully be applied to our understanding of the traditional elements or precepts of Orthodox spiritual life. Thus, remarks Harakas, "Precisely as an Orthodox theologian, I am not confident that I understand what 'spirituality' is. As an Orthodox theologian the term has not been part of my vocabulary."[13] "Spirituality," he further notes, "as contrasted to such terms and phrases as 'the spiritual life' or 'life in the Holy Spirit,' or 'spiritual living,' has a reified, objectified and 'substance-like' connotation. It seems to be a 'thing' which is to be captured and held, but which can also be taken away, and perhaps lost and retrieved. The parallel between 'spirituality' and grace understood as 'created,' an objective substance which is 'conveyed' by the sacraments, is too obvious to need documenting. It is no accident that a theological milieu accustomed to the understanding of divine grace as a created substance which was capable of being dis-

---

[11] The perspective of this "widespread form of atheism…tends to regard every religious sentiment as a function of the soul, a subjective psychological given. It thus reduces religion to a causality which produces particular ends or to the sublimation of instinct." Evdokimov, p. 17.

[12] He does note, however, with reference to prayer, "the abstract spirituality of some of Western Christianity is unnatural." See Chapter 29, p. 260.

[13] Stanley Samuel Harakas, "Spirituality: East and West," in: *The Legacy of St Vladimir: Byzantium. Russia. America. Papers presented at a Symposium commemorating the Fiftieth Anniversary of St Vladimir's Orthodox Theological Seminary* (Crestwood, NY, 1990), p. 179.

pensed or withheld by the official Church, could in a quite analogous way, create the term 'spirituality' and live comfortably with it."[14]

Mantzarides is even more categorical. He pointedly observes that "the term 'spirituality,' which is unknown in the biblical and patristic tradition, derives from Western theology, and presents the ethico-religious life of the faithful in opposition to the life of the worldly or of those without faith. In this way, a theological tendency is expressed which, even though it does not characterize itself as an ideology because it is clear that Christianity cannot be reduced to ideology, is not in reality something very different."[15] And thus, he somewhat imperiously concludes, "Spirituality is an abstract concept which has no place in the tradition of the Orthodox Church. Spirituality is the mother of materialism, together with whatever distorts and dissolves the universality of the truth of Christianity. Therefore, the concept 'Orthodox spirituality' must be abandoned."[16]

The profound discomfort with the term "spirituality" evidenced by Harakas and Mantzarides is not, however, limited to the Orthodox. It is, indeed, shared by all who have acutely felt a certain disjuncture between the academic study of "theology" and so-called "religious studies."

Beginning in the early and mid-1960's, a series of discussions by theologians and historians of religion engaged similar issues,[17] and explored with some depth the historical and lexical aspects of the term. In a seminal article written on the basis of such discussions, as well as on

---

[14] *Ibid.*, p. 181. "Reification" and "objectification" of meaning, it would seem, are not exclusively the provenance of the non-Orthodox theological milieu. In fact, apropos, one wonders if it is not, indeed, such an "understanding of divine grace as a created substance which is capable of being dispensed or withheld," for instance, that perhaps underlies the peculiar "theology of gracelessness" that has arisen of late in the milieu of certain fundamentalist Orthodox "traditionalists," who speciously proclaim themselves to be "in resistance" to the official Church and generally hold that in adopting or permitting a revised Julian calendar virtually contiguous with the Gregorian, as well as "in recompense," as it were, for engaging in ecumenical dialogue with non-Orthodox Christian churches and confessions, the official Church herself has somehow entered an "objectified" state of "gracelessness" through an alleged Divine "withholding" of "reified" grace.

[15] Giorgios I. Mantzarides, *Orthodox Spiritual Life* (Brookline, MA, 1994), p. 8.

[16] *Ibid.*

[17] See, in particular: Louis Bouyer, *Introduction a la vie spirituelle* (Paris: 1960), reviewed by Jean Danielou, "A propos d'une introduction a la vie spirituelle," *Etudes* 94 (1961), pp. 170-174; Bouyer's reply, *ibid.*, pp. 411-415; and Maurice Giuliani, "Une introduction a la vie spirituelle," *Christus* 8 (1961), pp. 396-411; also Gustavo Vinay, "'Spiritualita': Invito a una discussione," *Studi medievali* 2 (1961), pp. 705-709; and the response by Jean Leclercq, "Spiritualitas," *Studi medievali* 3 (1962), pp. 279-296; also Hans Urs von Balthasar, 'The Gospel as Norm and Test of all Spirituality in the Church,' in *Concilium* 9 [Spirituality in Church and World] (1965), pp. 7-23; and F. Vandenbroucke, "Spirituality and Spiritualities," in *Concilium,* 9 [Spirituality in Church and World] (1965), pp. 45-60; and J. Sudbrack, "Vom Geheimnis christlicher Spiritualität: Einheit und Vielfalt," *Geist und Leben* 39 (1966), pp. 24-44.

the basis of his own work at the University of Toronto, the Canadian theologian Walter Principe[18] has with admirable depth studied historically and documented the use of the term "spirituality" in patristic and medieval Latin, in French and in English, and has suggested a three-tiered approach to a comprehensive understanding of the concept: first, spirituality on the *real* or *existential* level, understood as the "lived quality" of a life, in terms of "the way some person understood and lived, within his or her historical context, a chosen religious ideal in sensitivity to the realm of the spirit or the transcendent"; second, as the *formulation of a teaching* about the lived reality, in terms of "traditions or schools of spirituality by reason of differing teachings or emphases in teachings"; and third, a *study* by scholars of the first and especially the second levels of spirituality.[19] Theological study of any spirituality, Principe proposes, should examine the broad context: all theological aspects, whether explicit or implicit, taking into consideration the contribution of all relevant human sciences.

From a theological perspective, the history of spirituality, though broad and deep in scope, essentially differs from the history of religion in that different methodologies are used by the disciplines of "theology" and "religious studies." A theologian, Principe suggests, seeks to examine and judge the results of his research "in the light of theological principles— this theology itself being derived from a community or ecclesial experience of faith responding to a revelation accepted as normative." The religious studies scholar, on the other hand, seeks to produce "a description of different spiritualities ... derived from the sources, widely conceived, that have been studied ... without reference to an accepted belief or theological system." Herein lies the essential difference in their approach: While the theologian "has developed principles of interpretation and judgment within a faith-oriented discipline," the philosopher, psychologist or sociologist of spirituality is "using principles of interpretation and judgment derived from human reason alone as developed, often hypothetically, within the respective disciplines."[20] The implications for theological study of spirituality are palpable.

On the basis of the foundational scholarship of Principe and others,[21] it becomes possible for us to come to a deeper theological under-

---

[18] Walter Principe, "Toward defining spirituality," *Studies in Religion/Sciences religieuses* 12, no. 2 (1983), pp. 127-141.
[19] *Ibid.*, p. 136.
[20] *Ibid.*, p. 140.
[21] It is not my intent to offer here a comprehensive bibliography of writings on spirituality, which would, in any case, very evidently require much more space than is appropriate in a footnote. Apart from the citations given elsewhere in this Foreword, I have found the following to be particularly helpful for understanding contemporary approaches to Christian, especially

standing not only of the wider principles and contours of spirituality, but also to further sort through and elucidate aspects or elements of spirituality that would generally be considered "Christian," or then, specifically and intrinsically "Orthodox." At the root, it seems clear that in a very fundamental way, "spirituality" refers to that aspect, or element, of human "being" that is termed "spirit," however it may be defined, and that a very fundamental definition of "spirituality" could indeed be derived from this concept.

The Roman Catholic theologian Ewert Cousins, for instance, broadly defines "spirit" as the "inner dimension of the person," "the spiritual core" that is "the deepest center of the person. It is here that the person is open to the transcendent dimension; it is here that the person experiences ultimate reality."[22] Very evidently, however, openness to a "transcendent dimension," or a subjective experience of "ultimate reality," does not, of itself, necessarily postulate the existence of, or faith in, the personal Triune God of traditional Christian belief. Indeed, in this broad sense, "life in the spirit," or "spiritual life" can easily be construed in explicitly non-Christian, or even non-religious terms, as "the way in which a person understands and lives within his or her historical context that aspect of his or her religion, philosophy or ethic that is viewed as the loftiest, the noblest, the most calculated to lead to the fullness of the ideal or perfection being sought."[23]

Alternatively, definition of "spirit" from a specifically Orthodox and patristic point of view suggests no substantive difference in broad patterns of understanding, as A. I. Osipov, of the Moscow Theological Academy, explains:

> By the word 'spirit' the holy Fathers mean the moral force in man, the content of which is defined by the mind, and, first of all, by an understanding of the final, highest goal of life. This goal can be God and eternal life in Him; but it can also be riches, power, glory; it can also be various delights and interests: physical (*cf.* 'whose god is their

---

Western Christian, spirituality: *Women's Spirituality: Resources for Christian Development*, Joann Wolski Conn, ed., 2nd ed. (Mahwah, NJ, 1996); Lawrence S. Cunningham and Keith J. Egan, *Christian Spirituality: Themes from the Tradition* (Mahwah, NJ, 1996); Michael Downey, *Understanding Christian Spirituality* (Mahwah, NJ, 1997); *Modern Spirituality: An Anthology*, John Garvey, ed. (Springfield, IL, 1985); *The Study of Spirituality*, Cheslyn Jones, Geoffrey Wainwright, Edward Yarnold, SJ, eds. (New York, 1986); John Macquarrie, *Paths in Spirituality*, 2nd ed. (Harrisburg, PA, 1992); Metropolitan Emilianos Timiadis, *Toward Authentic Christian Spirituality* (Brookline, MA, 1998).

[22] Ewert Cousins, "Preface," in *Christian Spirituality: Origins to the Twelfth Century*, ed. by Bernard McGinn and John Meyendorff in collaboration with Jean Leclercq (New York, 1988), p. xiii.

[23] Principe, p. 136.

belly,' Philippians 3:19), aesthetic (music, art), intellectual (philosophy, science). As man's god is, so is his spirituality.[24]

Numerous attempts have been made at constructing working definitions of "Christian" spirituality. On the surface, at least, it would seem that an acceptable definition could easily be formulated on the basis of the Christian faith, centered either on the historical person of Jesus Christ, or more abstractly, on a living out of the moral principles of the Christian gospel. Asking the obvious question, however, Principe underscores the inherent complexity of such an undertaking:

> Is there not for Christians only one spirituality, that of the gospel lived after the pattern of Christ's own life, death and resurrection? If some have held this, students of the history of spirituality have countered that in fact there have been many variations in the way Christians have interpreted and lived the Gospel. They have identified schools or traditions of spirituality labeled Pauline, Johannine, Oriental, Western, Benedictine, Franciscan, Dominican, Jesuit, lay, clerical, Lutheran, Calvinist, Anglican, etc., each of which seeks to live the gospel but stresses different aspects or groups of components while leaving others in a less prominent position.[25]

Among the more workable and comprehensive definitions of Christian spirituality that I have come across, formulated from a Western perspective, but allowing for wider meaning, is one framed by Sandra Schneiders.[26] In fact, her formulation, derived from a historical understanding of the life of the Christian community, and thus bringing together various significant elements of normative Christian spiritual life, comes closest to Orthodox understanding— at least on the basis of "practical," or "applied" theology— and is useful to us precisely as a sounding board, as it were, for testing aspects of Christian spirituality understood specifically from the Orthodox perspective.

Christian spirituality, then, as summarized in Schneiders' formulation, is "personal participation in the mystery of Christ begun in faith, sealed by baptism into the death and resurrection of Jesus Christ, nourished by the sharing of the Lord's Supper [*i.e.*, Eucharist], which the community celebrated regularly in memory of Him who was truly pre-

---

[24] A. I. Osipov, "Osnovy dukhovnoi zhizni: doklad na iubileinoi bogoslovskoi konferentsii Russkoi Pravoslavnoi TSerkvi [Foundations of spiritual life: A paper presented at the Jubilee theological conference of the Russian Orthodox Church]," *Vstrecha*, 3/13 (2000), p. 44. For a particularly lucid discussion of the larger aspects of patristic teaching on the inner makeup of human nature, see St Theophan the Recluse, *The Spiritual Life and How to be Attuned to It* (Platina, CA, 1996), especially Letters 5-12, pp. 45-76.
[25] Principe, p. 136.
[26] Sandra M. Schneiders, "Scripture and Spirituality," in McGinn, *Christian Spirituality*, pp. 1-2.

sent wherever his followers gathered, and was expressed by a simple life of universal love that bore witness to life in the Spirit and attracted others to the faith."[27] Distilling Schneiders to the essentials, it may be said that Christian spirituality is essentially concerned with a "personal participation in a mystery" which is "begun," "sealed," "nourished," and "expressed" relative to Christ and to certain larger "themes" of Christian living: faith, baptism, resurrection, Eucharist, community, celebration, memory, life, love, Spirit. And indeed, such are the broad "contours" of Christian spirituality that are still exhibited and experienced at the level of the "average" parish community not only in the Christian "West," but also in the Christian "East." All the essentials, it would seem, are in place. So what is it that is lacking, that still needs to be articulated and brought to the forefront of attention? And even—what are the questions that still need to be asked?

Herein lies a third major issue in a focused study of spirituality—the theological context of the discussion, as well as the dangers of facile formulaic definitions taken out of such context. As theologians, we understand that spirituality is both formed and informed by theology. And thus, the very first question to be asked is: What is the theological meaning of all that so fluently has been described by Schneiders? What is the significance of "personal participation in the mystery of Christ," or "baptism into the death and resurrection of Jesus Christ?" Why is there a need for a "sharing of the Lord's Supper," or "bearing witness to the life of the Spirit"? Why live "a simple life of universal love," or even "attract others to the faith"? To what end, or purpose? In all fairness to Schneiders, it must be said that theologically sound and adequate answers to these questions are, indeed, given in her broad treatment of the topic. But in contexts wherein definitions of spirituality, such as the one given above, stand on their own merit, absent a larger framework of discussion, inevitable confusion arises about implicit theological assumptions standing behind such definitions.[28]

The stark realization, ultimately, is that an externally descriptive approach to Christian spirituality is, at best, meaningless, absent the dimensions of theological definition and evaluation, appropriation and understanding of inner goals and purposes. Indeed, if one were to treat

---

[27] *Ibid.*, p. 2.
[28] Cunningham and Egan, for example (*see* note 21, above), offer a most helpful and useful compilation of various definitions and descriptions of Christian spirituality, including the one I cited, by Sandra Schneiders. These definitions and descriptions, however, when taken out of the particular contexts in which they were originally framed, especially by MA/MDiv and senior undergraduate collegiate students who were the original inspiration for Cunningham and Egan's text, typically generate the larger questions and issues which I have pointed out (*see* Cunningham and Egan's *Appendix: Some Definitions/Descriptions of* Christian *Spirituality*, pp. 22-28).

Schneiders' definition on a stand-alone basis, with respect to the Person of Jesus Christ, the central question of Mark 8:29, "Who do you say that I am?" would remain unanswered. Thus, in turn, the theological meaning of the phrase "personal participation in the mystery of Christ" would necessarily be obscured—wherein lies the "mystery"? Is He Savior? Or Redeemer? Or just a mystical philosopher or teacher? Just how does one "personally participate" in this mystery? Through "knowing Him?" Or through "keeping His commandments (*cf.* 1 John 2:2-5)?" Is there need to enter into a personal relationship with Him? And does this, in fact, constitute "redemption?" Or "salvation?" Reference to these concepts, however oblique, is lacking in the stand-alone definition, as if these concepts have nothing to do with Christian living. Do they? What is the ultimate meaning of a Christian spirituality which in its very definition fails to pose or answer these questions? Where does the average reader, or even the average divinity student, who often lacks the requisite academic training and the proper resources to check original sources, find the answers? It can be argued, of course, that the answers are implicit in the definition of "Christian." Are they?

Absent from such a purely descriptive approach, it appears, is also a quintessential understanding of the realities of human nature and the need for transformational inner struggle *(metanoia)* of "putting off" the "old man," which is corrupt through the lusts of the flesh, and being "clothed upon" and "renewed" after the image of "new man," in accordance with apostolic understanding (Ephesians 4:21-23).[29] Is spiritual metamorphosis, or transfiguration, a noteworthy component of Christian spirituality? Or is it that "a simple life of universal love" is somehow (how—magically?) to be attained without need for any internal striving or struggle *(askesis)* implicit in Christian living, without the necessity of self-denial and crucifixion of the self, as implicit in the injunction "If anyone desires to come after Me, let him deny himself, and take up his cross, and follow Me" (Matthew 16:23-25; Mark 8:34-38; Luke 9:23-26)? And is there, in fact, in "coming after," or "following" Christ, a "way"

---

[29] The tasks and goals inherent in the "working out" of human salvation in Christian living, as also the purpose of Baptism itself, are succinctly expressed in the Prayer of the Blessing of Water in the Rite of Baptism: "Thou hast bestowed upon us from on high a new birth through water and the Spirit. Wherefore, O Lord, manifest Thyself in this water, and grant that s/he who is about to be baptized therein may be transformed; that s/he may put away from her (him) the old man, which is corrupt through the lusts of the flesh, and that s/he may be clothed upon with the new man, and renewed after the image of Him who created her (him): that being buried, after the pattern of Thy death, in baptism, s/he may, in like manner, be a partaker of Thy Resurrection; and having preserved the gift of the Holy Spirit, and increased the measure of grace committed unto her (him), s/he may receive the prize of her (his) high calling, and be numbered with the first-born whose names are written in heaven, in Thee, our God and Lord, Jesus Christ." See: *Baptism*, ed. Fr. Paul Lazor (New York, 1983), p. 52.

to be traveled, a "spiritual journey" to be undertaken? Is there any movement, development, growth, direction on the way, or a goal that is to be achieved at the end of the journey?

And finally, still in a rhetorical manner, we might ask: Is it not the higher purpose and role of theology, as an ancillary discipline, to bring the dimension of intention to spirituality understood precisely as "Christian living," or even to lay the conceptual foundation for such living? The answer seems self-evident: Indeed so.[30] It is, in fact, theology, as intentionally engaged in the process of ongoing theological reflection, that directly imparts both meaning and direction to authentic spirituality, not only in the active categories of speaking or informing, but also in passive terms, as hearing and appropriating, or even in seeking deeper theological understanding.

From this perspective, then, beyond exhibiting the inherent weakness of a purely "descriptive" approach to spirituality, there is implicit in stand-alone definitions of Christian spirituality a certain theological naïveté that speaks, perhaps, to a larger failure of theological understanding; it is here, in fact, that we meet up, once again, with the difficult issues of Christian living that have been identified and raised by Evdokimov and Florovsky. Perhaps in this regard, the insight of Philip H. Pfattlicher explains it best: "Too often we are satisfied with stunted and underdeveloped lives because of a lack of vision and hope. Many devout people remain for a lifetime at the beginning of the way, content to be like children, blind to possibility and promise."[31]

Implicit in authentic Christian spirituality, indeed, are not only Christian vision and hope which arise out of the events of the Incarnation and Resurrection, but also the possibility and promise which arise out of the events of Pentecost and the outpouring of the Holy Spirit. Informed by Christian theology and visibly expressed through the various aspects of Christian living, these events exemplify and bring to the surface the essential relationship between God and man, forming the fabric, as it were, and the goal of, authentic Christian spiritual life, thus of spirituality.

---

[30] "In Christianity," writes Archbishop Ilarion Troitsky, "there are no purely theoretical tenets. Dogmatic truths have moral significance, and Christian morals are founded on dogma.... The Church is that point at which dogma becomes moral teaching and Christian dogmatics become Christian life. The Church thus comprehended gives life to and provides for the implementation of Christian teaching. Without the Church there is no Christianity; there is only Christian teaching which, by itself, cannot renew 'the fallen Adam'" See Archbishop Ilarion (Troitsky), *Christianity or the Church* (Jordanville, NY, 1985), p. 17. See also John D. Zizioulas, *Being as Communion: Studies in Personhood and the Church* (Crestwood, NY, 1985).
[31] Philip H. Pfattlicher, "Towards a Definition of Spirituality," in *Liturgical Spirituality* (Valley Forge, PA, 1997), p. 6.

Conversely, outside a proper theological understanding and grounding of its goals and purposes, Christian spirituality loses authenticity. Enervated and robbed of purposefulness and intentionality, reduced to mysterious (at times, even "magical")[32] mimicry of the external rituals of an allegedly "ideal spiritual life," especially in a shallow self-help approach, Christian spirituality is ultimately degraded to the level of insipid morality, or, what is even worse, to some self-serving "alternative" but "meaningful" "life-style" lived within an acquired and artificial subculture, a life-style that neither saves nor redeems,[33] but, like some magic potion, is avidly and profitably promoted in the consumer marketplace as a panacea for lack of meaning and personal fulfillment. Small wonder, then, that this type of naïve and emotional[34] spirituality fails to redress with any convincing degree of sincerity the existential uncertainty, confusion, doubt and despair of our civilization.

What, then, are some of the theological presuppositions that form the basis, or the foundation, of a Christian spirituality that is authentically "Orthodox"? The following affirmations are not meant to be definitive or exhaustive, but, rather, suggestive of the larger contours of an integrative approach:

a. A priori, (from "the Beginning," as in Genesis 1) there exists a relationship between God and man that is derived from the fact that the One God, "the Ground of all Being," glorified and worshipped in the Holy Trinity— Father, Son and Holy Spirit—

---

[32] The essence of magic is to be found in the casting of spells through an intentional and correct repetition of incantations and ritual performances, in accordance with some pre-determined ritualistic formula (*ex opere operato*). This is alleged to confer power and control over the elements of nature, indeed, over God Himself (!), and to influence human or natural events, which thereby, it would seem, involuntarily submit to the power and control of the magician. The dubious implications and value of such an approach to Christian life and spirituality, it would seem, are self-evident.

[33] One cannot escape the implications of the "narrow gate" parable in Luke 13:23-30: "Then one said to Him, 'Lord, are there few who are saved?' And He said to them, 'Strive to enter through the narrow gate, for many, I say to you, will seek to enter and will not be able. When once the Master of the house has risen up and shut the door, and you begin to stand outside and knock at the door, saying, 'Lord, Lord, open for us,' and He will answer and say to you, 'I do not know you, where you are from,' then you will begin to say, 'We ate and drank in Your presence, and You taught in our streets.' But He will say, 'I tell you I do not know you, where you are from. Depart from Me, all you workers of iniquity.' There will be weeping and gnashing of teeth, when you see Abraham and Isaac and Jacob and all the prophets in the kingdom of God, and yourselves thrust out. They will come from the east and the west, from the north and the south, and sit down in the kingdom of God. And indeed there are last who will be first, and there are first who will be last."

[34] Of the naïve brand of specifically Russian 19th century spirituality it has been said that it was very *dushevnaia* ("soul-ful"), but little *dukhovnaia* ("spiritual"), thus directly contributing to the historical plunge of Russia into the deep spiritual abyss and national catastrophe of the Russian revolution.

is the Divine Author of, and Provider for, all human life ("Let Us make man in Our image, according to Our likeness," Genesis 1:26), and thus the Supreme Lawgiver;

b. While man's substance is derived from "the dust of the ground," *i.e.,* from physical elements common to all creation, the Trinitarian "Image of God" embedded in every human person endows the person with soul *(psyche)* and spirit, together with the possibility of eternal life in a direct and personal relationship with God; conversely, without this life-imparting relationship, man is reduced to "dust";[35]

c. Every human person is created autonomous and free, in the Image of God, in order to become, through intentional acquisition of His Likeness, a child and heir of His eternal Kingdom; while the "Divine Image" is freely given to every human as a Divine gift, the acquisition of the "Divine Likeness," being man's primary spiritual vocation, is wholly dependent on man's free choice, and constitutes the immediate task of his spiritual life on earth;

d. God, through His Divine *philanthropia* ("love for man"), desires the welfare and salvation of all humans, "that not one of them may perish, but that all may come to the knowledge of Truth"; this Divine *philanthropia* is manifested in a most generous and all-encompassing fashion, allowing for the exercise of human spiritual freedom to the fullest degree, without any imposed preconditions or prerequisites, including the existence, or the content, of man's faith in God;

e. The human race in itself, from times primordial, proved inadequate to the task of living out human life to the fullness of embedded Divine potential and spiritual freedom, in accordance with the Divine precept; but through defiance and disobedience willfully altered human nature as originally created, entering, instead, into a fallen state of disintegration, corruption, and bondage to sin, being "wedded unto death";[36]

---

[35] Genesis 3:19; *cf.* Job 34:14-15: "If He should determine to do so, if He should gather to Himself His spirit and His breath, all flesh would perish together, and man would return to dust," and Psalm 146:4: "His spirit departs, he returns to the earth; in that very day his thoughts perish."

[36] For a fuller discussion of this and related issues from an Orthodox perspective, see my article: "Rags of Mortality: Original Sin and Human Nature," *Sourozh* 64 (May, 1996), pp. 23-32.

f. Despite the present fallen state of human nature, on a profound ontological level, in both the personal and corporate dimension, the totality of human life remains a lived-out response to the creative Divine *fiat* ("let it be") which originally called man out of non-being into being; but it is only in rising to conscious awareness that the transcendent purpose and goal of life is to be found in God that human experience, *sua generis*, becomes the type of authentic "spiritual experience" through which man arrives at profound understanding not only of the depths of human imperfection and brokenness, but also of an abiding need for effectual deliverance and redemption;[37]

g. Since in its fallen state human nature, at its very core, is darkened and corrupt through a pervasive "sin-sickness" that is both self-inflicted and systemic, humans are organically incapable of extricating themselves out of their fallen state and living up to their full "divinely-human" potential, in the perfection of the Image and Likeness of God; they are thus in need of Divine forgiveness and reconciliation, through a healing reintegration of their relationship with God and with each other (*i.e.*, "redemption" and "salvation");

h. God "so loved the world," that He Himself, in accordance with His promise, "in the fullness of time" initiated the process of human redemption and salvation,[38] sending for this purpose His only-begotten Son, "through Whom He has made the ages," who through His Divine kenosis and perfect obedience, "even unto death on the Cross," becomes the only Redeemer and Savior of mankind; through the Incarnate God-Man *(theanthropos, bogochelovek)* Jesus Christ, "who enlightens and sanctifies every person who comes into the world," God immanently

---

[37] This awareness, in fact, already marks one of the "high points" of the Old Testament Hebrew religion. One of the most hauntingly beautiful passages of the Old Testament, found in the Book of Job, is both illustrative and paradigmatic:

"I know that my Redeemer lives,
And He shall stand at last on the earth;
And after my skin is destroyed, this I know,
That in my flesh I shall see God,
Whom I shall see for myself, and my eyes shall behold, and not another.
How my heart yearns within me!" (Job 19:25-27).

[38] The "fullness of time," we might note, was to a significant degree contingent on man's own capabilities and growth in faith, hope and understanding. It was manifested on both the "horizontal" plane, through objective historical processes in the development of Roman law, Greek philosophy, Old Testament Hebrew religion, and the "initiatory mysteries" of the East; as well as on the "vertical" plane, in the qualitative ethical ripening of human potential and willingness to receive, as directly revealed in the circumstances of the birth and life of Her who Herself was to become "the Living Altar of the Living God."

speaks not only to mankind as a whole, but also individually to each human person, calling for repentance, and offering forgiveness, healing and "re-perfecting" of human nature in the observance of His commandments and ascendance, once again, to the lost image of Divine Glory;

i. Human yearning for salvation and redemption, which springs out of knowledge of the depths of human "dis-integration" and brokenness, responds to Divine kenosis, flowing out of Divine philanthropia, and comes to focus on the Person of Jesus Christ, the Incarnate Son and Word of God. It is from here, in one's personal recognition of Christ as the unique Savior and Redeemer of the world, that faith, indeed, becomes possible, and that an intentional and inspired Christian spirituality becomes a purposeful and integrative inner journey to the ultimate healing of the "old" and "fallen" human nature, through perfect union with the "resurrected," hence "re-imaged" and "glorified," divinely-human *(theanthropic, bogochelovecheskaia)* nature of Christ.

It is precisely the theological challenge— and the promise— of such perfect union that properly constitutes, from the perspective of the Orthodox pastoral and ascetical tradition, both the point of departure and the objective goal of authentic "Orthodox spirituality," which is neither a theological abstraction of Christian doctrine, nor a reification of Christian living or practice that can be "captured" or "taken away." It is not, indeed, an ideology, but, rather, a theologically-informed discipline of living which can be taught, learned, and applied, whether in life or in the academy, in precisely the same manner, for example, that we teach and learn the disciplines of Dogmatic or Liturgical Theology, while understanding, at the same time, that such teaching and learning are not yet the fullness of the "celebration," *Eucharistia*, which itself becomes both the application and the consummation, not only of all Christian teaching and learning, but also of Christian living.

Alternatively, in metaphorical and sensory terms,[39] "spirituality" can be understood as a magnificent multi-colored tapestry of human life,

---

[39] There are those, indeed, who would seek the "spiritual" in sensory deprivation, *i.e.,* in a certain "sense-less-ness." In fact, however, Orthodox doctrine generally holds that in the Church the spiritual is conferred through what is sensory and tactile, in the conjoining, by the grace of the Holy Spirit, of the Divine to the human. This is as true for the Church herself, as also for the sacraments (herein, in fact, lies the "mystery"), especially the sacraments of Baptism, Chrismation, and the Eucharist. Thus, of Holy Chrism, St Ephraim the Syrian writes: "Christ and chrism are conjoined; the secret with the visible is mingled; the chrism anoints visibly—Christ seals secretly, the lamb is newborn and spiritual, the prize of his twofold victory; for He engendered it

18   FOREWORD

richly patterned and thickly textured, woven, experienced and lived out in response to the Divine creative act. The invitation to "taste and see that the Lord is good" is applicable, after all, not only to partaking of the Presanctified Mysteries during Great Lent, but, indeed, to all of Christian life. Thus, while the purely academic task of Orthodox spirituality (Principe's second and third levels) remains to externally observe and describe the tapestry, wholly or in part, its ultimate "meaning" is to be found not in its "hanging" on some professorial library wall, but in the "living," or in the "tasting" (Principe's first level).

Understood symbolically,[40] Orthodox spirituality is experienced *sub specie aeternitatis* ("from the perspective of eternity") and lived out holistically,[41] with inherent purpose and meaning, as a symbolic journey, or a spiritual quest,[42] in accordance with the commandments of the Gospel, through personal appropriation of the living and authentic experience of the ecclesial community ("Holy Tradition"), leading to the

---

of the chrism, and He gave it birth of the water." ("Hymns for the Feast of Epiphany," 1, *NPNF*, 2nd series, vol. 13, p 269).

[40] The essential meaning of "symbol" here is to be found in its integrative function, as that which brings together into one many different layers and aspects of meaning, in the very same way that the Nicene Creed becomes for us the "Symbol of Faith." Opposed to the "symbolic," which integrates, is the "diabolic," *i.e.,* that which tears apart, or dis-integrates, and deprives of totality or fullness of meaning.

[41] That is, with *sophrosyne*, in healthy sobriety and "wholeness" ("wholesomeness") of mind; in Slavonic, *"tselomudrenno."* There is, unfortunately, no exact equivalent in English of either the Greek or Slavonic. Thayer's *Greek-English Lexicon of the New Testament* gives meanings of "soundness of mind," as opposed to mania; "sanity," "soberness," "self-control", and relates to the verbs *sophroneo*—to be of sound mind, right mind; to exercise self-control, to put a moderate estimate on oneself; to think of one's self soberly; to curb one's passion (in Mark 5:15 and Luke 8:35, said of the Gadarene man now in his right mind; 2 Corinthians 5:13, God will say whether Paul is in his right mind; Titus 2:6, exhorting men to be discrete, soberminded;1 Peter 4:7, be soberly watchful since the end is near); and *sophronizo*—to make one *sophron* (wise); to restore to the senses; to moderate, control, curb, discipline; to hold one to his duty; to admonish; to exhort earnestly. In 1 Timothy 2:15 *sophrosyne* is one of the saving qualities of a woman— faith, love, holiness, and sophrosyne: temperance (NEB), sobriety (KJV), modesty (RSV), and discreteness (Greek-English NT).

[42] In this frame of reference, Christians are "strangers," "sojourners" and "pilgrims on earth," who have no "continuing city" or "homeland" here, but instead "seek one to come," prepared by God in a "heavenly country" (Hebrews 11:13-16; 13:14). Alternatively, they are a "chosen generation, a royal priesthood, a holy nation, His own special people," who are "called out of darkness into [Christ's] marvelous light" (1 Peter 2:9-11). It is, in fact, to our capacity for symbolic understanding as seekers of "the way," that the Lord Himself directly appeals, not only in instructing how the Heavenly city is to be entered ("Enter by the narrow gate; for wide is the gate and broad is the way that leads to destruction, and there are many who go in by it. Because narrow is the gate and difficult is the way which leads to life, and there are few who find it" Matthew 7:13, 14), but also in revealing Himself as "the Way" ("'Where I go you know, and the way you know.' Thomas said to Him, 'Lord, we do not know where You are going, and how can we know the way?' Jesus said to him, 'I am the Way, and the Truth, and Life. No one comes to the Father except through Me.'" John 14: 4-6).

ultimate reality of deification *(theosis)*[43] and Life Everlasting in the Eternal Kingdom[44] of which Christ Himself is both Lord and King.

Alexander Golubov
St Tikhon's Orthodox Theological Seminary
Great Lent / Pascha, 2001

---

[43] For a fuller exposition of the doctrinal aspects of theosis, see: Giorgios I. Mantzaridis, *The Deification of Man: St. Gregory Palamas and the Orthodox Tradition*, trans. Liadain Sherrard (Crestwood, NY, 1984).

[44] In his exegesis of the words "Thy Kingdom come" in the Lord's Prayer, St Gregory of Nyssa suggests, on the basis of early Christian belief and a variant text of St Luke, that "the Kingdom" is, indeed, the Holy Spirit Himself. "When Thy Kingdom comes, the pangs and sighs of sorrow vanish, and life, peace and rejoicing enter instead. Perhaps the same thought is expressed more clearly for us by Luke, who, when he desires the Kingdom to come, implores the help of the Holy Spirit. For so he says in his Gospel; instead of Thy Kingdom come it reads 'May Thy Holy Spirit come upon us and purify us'.... For what Luke calls the Holy Spirit, Matthew calls the Kingdom.... The creature's property is to serve; and service is not kingship. But the Holy Spirit is kingship.... If therefore the Holy Spirit is kingship, how do they refuse to acknowledge His sovereignty—those people who have not even learned how to pray? They do not even know who it is that purifies what is defiled; who is endowed with the authority of kingship. 'May Thy Holy Spirit come,' he says, 'and purify us.' Therefore the proper power and virtue of the Holy Spirit is precisely to cleanse sin; for what is pure and undefiled needs no cleansing." Sermon 3, "Hallowed be Thy Name, Thy Kingdom come," *St Gregory of Nyssa, The Lord's Prayer. The Beatitudes, ACW*, vol. 18, pp. 52-53.

In the light of St Gregory's exegesis, St Seraphim of Sarov's alternative understanding of theosis as "the acquisition of the Holy Spirit" makes perfect sense. On this, in particular, see: I. M. Kontzevich, *The Acquisition of the Holy Spirit in Ancient Russia* (Platina, CA, 1988).

INTRODUCTION

General and special Christian Moral Theology describes analytically the conditions of Christian moral life (the moral law, conscience and freedom) as well as doctrine. Sins and virtues are viewed as certain unrelated states. Orthodox Spirituality, on the other hand, presents the process of a Christian's progress on the road to perfection in Christ, by the cleansing of the passions and the winning of the virtues, a process which takes place in a certain order. In other words, it describes the manner in which the Christian can go forward from the cleansing of one passion, to the cleansing of another, and at the same time to the acquiring of the different virtues. Thus a certain level of perfection is reached and culminates in love; this is a state that represents the cleansing of all the passions and the winning of all the virtues. As man climbs toward this peak, he simultaneously moves toward union with Christ and the knowledge of Him by experience, which also means his deification.

In the light of Orthodox spirituality, Christian morality no longer appears as the simple fulfillment of duties imposed by God's commands, duties that in this life lead nowhere, but only assure him of salvation as an exterior reward in the next life. The Christian grows in God, even in the course of this life because response to these commands brings about a step by step transformation in his being; he is filled more and more with the working presence of God.

1. The Goal of Orthodox Spirituality

Orthodox spirituality aims at the perfection of the faithful in Christ. This perfection can't be obtained in Christ, except by participation in His divine-human life. Therefore the goal of Orthodox spirituality is the perfection of the believer by his union with Christ. He is being imprinted to an ever-greater degree by the human image of Christ, full of God.

So the goal of Christian Orthodox spirituality is the union of the believer with God, in Christ. But as God is unending, the goal of our union with Him, or of our perfection, has no point from which we can no longer progress. So all the Eastern Fathers say that perfection is unlimited.

Our perfection, or our union with God, is therefore not only a goal, but also an unending progress. On this road two great steps can be distinguished: first, the moving ahead toward perfection through purification from the passions and the acquiring of the virtues and secondly a life progressively moving ahead in the union with God. At this point, man's work is replaced by God's. Man contributes by opening himself up receptively to an ever-greater filling with the life of God.

From what has been said, we find the following features of Christian Orthodox spirituality:

1. The culminating state of the spiritual life is a union of the soul with God, lived or experienced.
2. This union is realized by the working of the Holy Spirit, but until it is reached man is involved in a prolonged effort of purification.
3. It takes place when man reaches the "likeness of God." It is at the same time knowledge and love.
4. Among other things, the effect of this union consists of a considerable intensification of spiritual energies in man, accompanied by all kinds of charismas.

The East also uses the daring word "deification," or participation in the divinity, to characterize the union with God. So the goal of Christian Orthodox spirituality is none other than living in a state of deification or participation in the divine life. This experience, strikingly expressed as a state of deification, includes first of all two general teachings:

1. It represents the ultimate step of man's perfection; so this supreme phase of the believer's earthly life or the goal of his whole life is also called perfection.
2. Deification is realized through the believer's participation in the divine powers, by flooding him with boundless divine things.

Because this experience represents the highest step of perfection on earth, it means the normalization and supreme realization of human powers: knowledge, love, and spiritual force. Experienced by the believer, this state exceeds the limits of his powers; it is fed by divine power.

The culminating state of the spiritual life is when the believer is raised higher than the level of his own powers, not of his own accord, but by the work of the Holy Spirit. "Our mind goes outside itself and so unites with God; it becomes more than mind," says St. Gregory Palamas.[1]

---

[1] St. Gregory Palamas, "For the defense of the holy hesychasts" 1.3.47 [in Greek], *The Greek Fathers of the Church,* Panayiotis Hristou, ed. (Thessalonika, 1982), vol 54, p. 249, hereafter referred to as *The Defense.* See also a condensed version, *Gregory Palamas, The Triads,* in "Classics of Western Spirituality", John Meyendorff, ed. (New York, 1983).

It wouldn't be able to see what it sees "...only because it has a mental sense, just as a person's eye wouldn't be able to see without a perceptible light exterior to it and distinct from it."[2] During this vision of God, the mind goes beyond its own self and all its mental operations receive a boost from God.[3]

If the goal of Christian spirituality is a mystical life of union with God, then the path to it includes the ascent that leads to this peak. As such, this path is different than the peak; yet it is organically connected to it, in the same way as the ascent of a mountain is to the peak. Only by prolonged effort, by discipline, can the state of perfection and mystical union with God be reached. Efforts that don't contribute to this crowning, this final moment of ascetic discipline, or to the mystical union with God, seem to be without purpose.

The connection between ascetical discipline and the mystical union with God is also closer than that between the path and the goal. Even though the living of that union is realized at the final end of all ascetical efforts, its aura begins in the soul beforehand, along with them.

Christian perfection therefore requires a whole series of efforts until it is attained. The Apostle Paul compares these strivings with the training that athletes employ to get in shape in order to win. Without referring to the word asceticism, St. Paul[4] used the image of the ancient physical exercises to characterize the efforts made by the Christian to reach perfection. Clement of Alexandria[5] and Origen later introduced the terms of asceticism and ascetic. Little by little in the East they gained a monastic coloring. Monasteries are called *askitiria,* places for physical training. The *askitis* (the ascetic) is the monk who strives to obtain perfection by observing all the rules of restraint or temperance through cleansing from the passions. Origen calls zealous Christians ascetics; they are disciplining themselves to mortify the passions and develop good habits that lead to perfection.[6]

St. Neilos the Ascetic in his *On Asceticism* gives us a detailed comparison of the spiritual ascetic with the athlete in the arena.[7] Asceticism then is that part of spirituality that deals with the rules and efforts that

---

[2] *Ibid.,* 1.3.46, p. 247.
[3] *Ibid.,* 2.3.48, p. 503.
[4] 2 Timothy 2:5.
[5] Clement of Alexandria, *The Tutor* 1, p. 7, where he calls Jacob an ascetic, after his struggle with the angel. *ANF* vol. 2, p. 223.
[6] Origen, *Homilies on Jeremiah* 19.7, *PG* 13.517.
[7] *The Philokalia: the complete text compiled by St. Nikodemos of the Holy Mountain and St. Makarios of Corinth* (London, Boston, 1979), vol. 1, pp. 243-4. (Hereafter, the English language translation of *the Philokalia* will be referred to as *Phi,* the original Greek, as *GrPh,* and Fr. Staniloae's Romanian translation, as *RoFil. trs*)

bring man to the first step of the ascent to perfection, to contemplation and union with God. Asceticism is the active part of the spiritual life, the self-coercion and cooperative part that God requires of us. Yet the mystical union with God is also a result of the passive bearing of the work of grace in us. Now God takes the initiative. We have only to follow. It belongs to Him alone.

This doesn't mean that ascetical efforts aren't aided by grace nor that passivity in the phase of union is inertia. It simply means that a culminating spiritual experience doesn't have its source in human spiritual powers, but exclusively in God. Ascetical efforts however, are due to an active contribution from the power of man's soul. I. Hausherr, speaking about activity and passivity in connection with active and passive purification has this to say:

> Active or passive are two more unclear or false ideas. In accounting and maybe in mechanics they can be safely used, because liabilities are clearly distinguished from assets, and the blow given from the blow received. But in psychology? The man who doesn't react in anyway is a corpse, and to react is to act. So a pure passivity doesn't exist. How much more in morality and in spirituality—the single human act is moral or immoral, deserving or not. Divine action doesn't sanctify without human acceptance; and to accept isn't only to tolerate, but also to actively receive. For an adult therefore a purely passive sanctification doesn't exist, neither a purely passive purification. But neither a purely active purification! The creature has no absolute initiative, even in nature. In the realm of grace we must repeat with St. Irenaeus: 'To create is proper to the kindness of God, but to be created is proper to man.'[8] Where psychology sees only the action and the state, metaphysics and theology know suffering and reception first.[9]

Asceticism is the "slaying of death" in us, to liberate our nature from its bondage, as St. Maximus the Confessor points out.[10] There are really two deaths: The first is produced by sin and is the death of our nature. The second is a death like Christ's, which is the death of sin and the death produced by it. However, the death of our nature, through the decomposition produced by sin, doesn't come only at the final moment; rather it nibbles away for a long time like a worm. So too the death of death, or of sin, isn't something momentary, but must be prepared for through long ascetical mortification. Asceticism is the gradual elimina-

---

[8] St. Irenaeus, *Against Heresies* 4.64. This quotation wasn't found in the place cited. *trs*
[9] I. Hausherr, "Do Easterners [*Les Orientaux*] know the 'nights' of St. John of the Cross?" [in French], *Orientalia Christiana* 12 (1946), pp. 1-2, 9-10.
[10] St. Maximus the Confessor, *Questions to Thallasios* 61, *PG* 90.613-636D.

tion of the poison that leads to decomposition, to corruption. It eliminates the sickness that kills our nature and therefore is its fortification. Asceticism is a life giving mortification *(zoopoios necrosis)*, as St. Simeon the New Theologian calls it. It is the gradual slaying of sin and all tendencies toward it.

According to the current use of the word, asceticism has a negative connotation. It means a negative holding back, a negative restraint, or a negative effort. This is because the sinful tendencies of our nature, the habitual things that lead to its death, have come to be considered as the positive side of life. Ascetical striving, though negative in appearance, confronts the negative element in human nature with the intent to eliminate it by permanent opposition.

In reality, asceticism has a positive purpose. It seeks the fortification of our nature and its liberation from the worms of sin that gnaw at it and hasten its ruin. In place of the passions, asceticism plants the virtues, which presuppose a truly strengthened nature. The ultimate goal of asceticism is to free our nature not only from the movements of sinful appetites, but also from the ideas that appear in the mind after the cleansing from the passions. This is only to gain its independence from created things, which have enslaved our nature by the passions, and to make it long more for God.

It is true that asceticism, on the last step of its efforts, must also prepare a pure mind for God, emptied of all impressions of things created, of all earthly preoccupations. But this "emptiness" is not something totally negative. As much as the passivity of the human factor under the work of divine glory is talked about, nowhere is it said that this passivity is the equivalent of inertia, with a total minus. The "emptiness" of the mind offered to God, represents in a positive way a thirst exclusively for Him.[11] Much experience has convinced it of the corruption of all passionate preoccupations and of the relativity of all intellectual preoccupations oriented toward created things. As a result, it has rejected them in order to receive God in their place.[12]

---

[11] We consider then that this positive element of the supreme "thirst" for God, this "emptiness" doesn't banish every created element from the spirit and every sentiment of the created, in order to be only God, as Eckhart believes, according to his pantheistic mysticism.

[12] The journey of the mind through the reasons, the *logoi* [see note 1, ch. 3] of created things was not in vain, because even if it now leaves their present memory, because of them it is left with a wisdom, with increased understanding, so that the virtues have fortified it in such a way that now it can be a medium by which the work of the Holy Spirit is carried out. St. Maximus the Confessor says: "Just as the sun, coming up and enlightening the world, shows itself and the things that it is illuminating, so too the Sun of righteousness, rising in the pure mind, also shows itself as well as the *logoi* of all things that have been made or will be made by Him." *Chapters on Love* 1, p. 95, *GrPh* 2, p. 13; *cf. Phi* 2, p. 64.

Human nature shows its weakness, according to the holy Fathers, by its lack of firmness, by its instability. This instability is manifested by the ease in which it is attracted by pleasure and defeated by pain. It doesn't have the force to stand up to them, but quivers in a cowardly way, like a reed pounded by the wind. Its will and proper judgment, two of the essential elements of our nature, lose their power completely. Our nature becomes like a ball in the hands of the passions, thrown here and there by every circumstance and impression. It no longer stands firm in its freedom; it has reached a spiritual weakness that bears all the signs of corruption. In no way does it show an incorruptibility that would assure it of eternity.

The slaying of this weakness of death that has penetrated our nature, and fortifying it through asceticism, is possible by the mortification and life creating death of Jesus Christ. Divine power helped Him to conquer the love of pleasure and the fear of the death of His nature, thus making it steadfast. Now the mystical relationship, which the nature of any human hypostasis has potentially with the human nature of His divine-human hypostasis, becomes— by living and working faith— an ever more effective relationship. This causes the regained force of Christ's human nature to also be communicated to the nature of the other people who believe in Him.

Ascetic efforts are the means by which human nature— which each of us bears— participates more and more in the force of His human nature, because our efforts also contain the force of the human nature of Christ. The potential tie with Christ is made effective by faith in Him, and His force becomes our force.

Therefore our asceticism is a gradual death with Christ, as a development of power, a death of the old man, an extension of baptism by will. It is not only an imitation of Christ as in the West, but a heroic mortification with Christ and in Christ. We are united with Christ already in the prolonged process of our mortification even before the culminating state of mystical union with Him. We are not only raised with Christ, but we also die with Him. We can't be resurrected with Christ if we don't first die with Him.

The resurrection with Christ follows as a continuation of mortification, or of death, not as a change in direction. It's true that, in union with Christ in death, His presence isn't visible; but this is because while the old man dies gradually within us, Christ also dies with us. Yet His death is a humbling too, an eclipse of glory. Christ isn't seen in the state of mortification, but He is present and it is known that He is. Now the establishment of our certainty regarding His presence in us, by faith and not by sight, makes clear once again the heroic character of the ascetic phase.

The holy Fathers, Mark the Ascetic and Maximus the Confessor, point out this presence of Christ, as an unseen force, when they say that Christ is the essence, the being of the virtues. If virtue means manliness, strength, and the essence of this strength is Christ, it's evident that the power of Christ is working in our asceticism.

The fact that the object of asceticism isn't only the cleansing of the passions, but also the simultaneous acquiring of the virtues, shows once again that asceticism isn't something negative, but a fortification of our nature. In the course of asceticism, by prolonged endeavor, vicious habits are suppressed and virtuous ones planted in our nature; and much tenacity is needed to stop our old ways from springing up again and to consolidate good, new habits.[13]

In this general characterization of asceticism, we should also mention one of its formal aspects. Asceticism follows a definite road, an order and a series of steps which must not be overlooked. It is a precise discipline which takes into consideration the laws of the normal development of the spiritual life, as well as the principles of faith. Such a battle according to law means that its road is established according to a well grounded logic. This fact also sheds light on the final phase of the spiritual life.

The mystical union with God, which asceticism leads to, does not stand at the beck and call of everybody at any given time. It's something altogether different from the confused emotional states one can get himself into by choice or chance.[14] After traveling the ascetical road where each moment is placed, not without reason, in its place, the mind must go through the stage of the knowledge of the *logoi* of created things, as St. Maximus the Confessor says. Only after it has gone through this phase, assimilating its created *logoi* and surpassing them, does it enter into the light of mystical union and knowledge. This phase of the knowledge of the existent *logoi* and of the surpassing of them is also itself a rung on the ladder of asceticism. It is evident that the mystical union with God, situated at the very top of this ascent, is not

---

[13] Leonce de Grandmaison, *Personal religion*, transl. by Algar Thorold (London, 1929). See the chapter "Asceticism," pp. 75-103.
[14] The mystical union with God is beyond present psychological emotion. I. Hausherr writes: "In fact, mysticism ends by going beyond suffering and human joy, beyond that which is called common consolation and spiritual desolation, to a region where human words lose more and more their original meaning, in order to no longer keep but a value of analogy. There doesn't exist only an apophaticism for intellectual knowledge, but also one for mystical psychology, when to put it the way Diadochos does, a unity of spiritual feeling is reestablished." *Op. cit.*, p. 38.

something irrational, but suprarational. It's not a state won as a result of the debilitation of reason or of an ignorance of the reasons of things, the *logoi*, but after the surpassing of all the possibilities of reason; it is brought to its supreme force and insight, as well as to the complete knowledge of the rational meanings of things.

Asceticism is a way of the most rigorous reason practicable and the fullest knowledge of the reasons of things. It is proof that the living union with God isn't reached by surpassing reason, but by the use, from the start, of all its possibilities, that by this too our nature might be joined to a supreme capacity to become a vessel of superhuman understanding, communicated by the grace of the Holy Spirit. God is the supreme Reason, the Logos, and the source of the *logoi* of all things. The mind which is elevated, in the phase of union with God, to the direct contemplation of this Logos, must be ready for the understanding of this womb of all reasons; it must know as many of them as possible, even though the more than unlimited One, which it now knows, puts the way of previous knowledge in the shadows.

Christian asceticism isn't an artificial and one-sided technique, which by itself produces the living of the mystical union with God. Such a false asceticism has as a consequence a false coronation that is characterized by the following signs:

1. It implies no moral condition whatsoever, but is a matter of temperament.
2. Ecstasy is sought for its own sake, as a supreme purpose.
3. This kind of ecstasy is sterile, if not degrading; a person doesn't come out of it either more instructed, or better (morally).
4. This ecstasy is like "a hand reaching into a void, and coming out with nothing."

The primary cause of this erroneous conception of asceticism and of its culmination in union with God is the false idea that man has in his possession all the means which can take him to the supreme spiritual level—that it depends only on a certain training, more or less ingenious, to bring these means to the surface.

In contrast with this false conception, Christianity considers that the direct vision of God can't be reached without the grace given by Him; the reception of this grace requires a moral perfection of the whole of human nature by ceaseless divine help. A purely human training to awaken some unknown "sleeping power" isn't enough. In Christianity, God doesn't have a nature like an object which we can conquer by a human foray directed by clever tactics. He is a Person and as such, without an initiative on His part, He can't be known. For this self-revelation of God in a mystical union we have to make ourselves worthy by being sincere, clean, and good; because He is above an offensive which uses force or slyness. So Christian asceticism is a road illumined not only by reason, but by faith too, and by prayer and the help of God. It's a road along which our whole nature is purified from sin and is morally fortified.

2. The meaning and possibility of union with God

Christian union with God realizes the true sense of this union. It is perverted when it tends to identify man and God, when it leans toward the actualization in the consciousness of an identity which is thought to have existed previously and substantially, as the case is in all pantheist religions and philosophies.

Some Protestant theologians understand the mystical union with God as nothing but this identification and don't admit the possibility of a direct, immediate contact with God, which isn't a substantial identification. Thus they reject on principle any mystical union whatsoever and go to the opposite extreme of an irreducible separation between man and God. Between these two poles, according to them, no transmission, no immediate contact whatsoever is possible; thus they say that God avails Himself exclusively through the word in order to establish, ironically, a relationship between Him and us. "The fact that God chooses the terrestrial form of verbal communications," says a Protestant theologian, "excludes the immediate relation in which we should be to God if we were not strangers from Him."[15] Or as the same theologian says further on, "If God did come near us— we who find ourselves with our whole being against Him— in the indirect form of the word, thus in a form in which He remains nevertheless hidden, we would be spared, mercifully, because we could not bear the immediate presence of God."[16]

Protestant theologians of the dialectical school reject any mystical union with God. As we have said, they subscribe to the Hindu, or Eckhartian idealistic concept or in general to any religious or philosophic pantheism. For them there is an "uninterrupted continuity," an evolutionary ascent, unhindered by any abyss; man is in essence and becoming in actuality, god, by the development of one or the other of his powers.

Christian teaching, however, is a total stranger to the tendency of pantheistic identification of man with God. Nevertheless, it asserts with courage the possibility of a "union" of man with God, of a direct "vision" of Him, of a "participation" in Him, through grace.

Protestant theologians don't see, however, how such a "union" with God can be conceived or how it can be understood except as a more or less total identification.

---

[15] Karl Heim, *Jesus the Lord, The sovereign authority of Jesus and God's revelation in Christ*, trans. D.H. van Daalen (Edinburgh and London, 1959), p. 153.
[16] Karl Heim, *Jesus der Herr* (Berlin, 1935), p. 183.

THE POSSIBILITY OF UNION WITH GOD

So it's good for us to dwell more on the Christian meaning of "union" with God and of an unmediated "vision" of Him, as well as on the possibilities of this mystical fact. Of course we're not going to analyze here the culminating moment of this union.[17] It's anticipated, albeit somewhat less intensively, even on the first steps of the Christian life lived in a spirit of piety. So we will be content to point out just the meaning and possibility of a direct contact with divinity. Once the possibility of such a contact is proven in principle, regardless of its intensity, the possibility of "union" with God on the peaks beyond the limits of human powers is also proven implicitly.

In more general terms we have seen that Christian teaching adopts a middle position between the mysticism of identity and the irreducible separation between man and God. The justification of this position will be made clear from a description of these two extremes.

Christian teaching rejects both identification and absolute separation, because of the creaturely character of man and of the whole world; their creaturely character is a necessary consequence of the absolute character of the Supreme Being. If God is the reality whose power can't be surpassed by any other power whatsoever, this power, not limited by any other power superior to it, must also show itself in God's connection with the world. For Him the world can't be a necessary destiny, an ever changing train, which He must bear forever. It can't be an emanation or an involuntary unfolding of His being. Because then how could He show His sovereignty over any necessity or law?

So the world must be a free production of His will. The more powerful a being is, the less it puts external material, or its being, into the production of something. It follows that God in making the world would have demonstrated the highest form of power conceivable to us; He wouldn't have needed any exterior contribution, neither the push of His shoulder nor the sweat of His brow. He would have brought it forth from nothing by His word, as the manifestation of His being, not as an emanation of particles from Him. Thus nothing of the being of God, as supreme reality, enters into the constitution of the world nor into that of man either. He isn't— and the mind can't admit that He is— an object carried along by the torrent of a power or of a law superior to Him. Now the created character of the world excludes an identity— no matter how small— with God. Created reality can't become uncreated by any evolution.

But, on the other hand, the word God used to create the world, as a manifestation of His will, was in some way an expression of power. God

---

[17] The author will do that further on. *trs*

did not mix His power with the nature of the world. Nevertheless, without the descent of His power into the nothingness from which He took it, it couldn't have been produced; and without the presence of His power around it and even in the immediate intimacy of everything in it, the world wouldn't be able to sustain itself and develop. Without the power of God, in the final analysis, the world would be reduced to the nothingness which has no power whatsoever to sustain it. It could be said that it was enough that God manifested His will from a distance, to make the world appear, just as it's enough now to do the same for the world to be sustained and develop. But this will, in order to have its effect on the world, must somehow reach, as a presence of power, the point where the effect is produced. Wherever the effect of power is produced, the force producing the effect of that power must be present. Thus everything in the world has, intimately within it, the immediate presence of a working power of God.[18]

By this working power each of us from the beginning find ourselves in an immediate "union" with Him; due to it we exist and we develop.[19]

The attainment of this union, Christian spirituality teaches, is only by gradual growth and an understanding of it by the consciousness. Does man have this capability? The holy Fathers say yes: It requires the cleansing of the soul and the mind from worldly preoccupation. More on that later.

Our nature isn't only organic or inorganic, but also has a soul endowed with mind and will. In its mind there is a tireless impulse for knowledge. This impulse can't be understood without the previous certitude of an external reality which must be known.

N. Hartmann,[20] following the Christian thinker S. L. Frank,[21] has formulated a more striking truth. The mind has, he says, before the explicit knowledge of a reality, a general consciousness of it. Then the mind has the consciousness that, beyond it, the trans-object can be found. The mind has a previous knowledge of a general order of a reality which falls constantly beyond the ray of its direct observation. Blondel believes that the mind hasn't only the previous evidence of a transobjective reality in general, but evidence of an infinite realty.[22] It

---

[18] This is the teaching of St. Gregory Palamas: The nature of God is inaccessible, but His energies descend to us.
[19] St. Paul the Apostle said on Mars Hill, in Athens: "In Him we live, and move, and have our being." Acts 17:28.
[20] N. Hartmann, *Grundzüge einer Metaphysik der Erkenntnis* (Berlin, Leipzig, 1925).
[21] S. L. Frank, *Connaissance et Etre* (Paris, 1931).
[22] "Because in regard to objects and the truths which it [the mind] knows, the thought which is worked out in us doesn't fulfill its discursive work whether it be scientific or metaphysical, except by having with it and by following the transcendental truths of all the partial objects of

has the consciousness, more or less explicit, that its thirst for knowledge won't be quenched, that no finite object whatsoever will satisfy it. Confused, it realizes that this thirst could last forever— reality has an infinity of relative objects; or it could come to rest, by being nourished eternally, in the knowledge of an integral reality, infinite in its own self, of a nature other than all that is finite. The first thesis, of an eternal thirst, scares it with a perspective of an unending toil which never finds rest in supreme, complete, unlimited, satisfaction. So the alternative, the hope of gaining rest, which confronts the mind in a general way, looks brighter and more convincing.

The created mind comes into the world with the impulse to know, and to know the infinite One; this is proof that it is made for the infinite, that He exists before it, if from the first moment of its awakening it presupposes that He exists. Somewhere it must find a reality to know that is much greater than itself, an infinite reality; if an aspiration so burning for knowledge is in it and if no finite objects can satisfy it, but rather delays its quest and disillusions it, it must find this reality. The mind is made to seek God; and finite realities, one by one attained and surpassed, can't have, as objects of knowledge, the negative purpose of continuously deluding, of making fun of this impulse; rather they should have the positive one of preparing it successively for that great encounter, for the understanding of Him who stands at the final end of all things.

But let's analyze for a moment the nature of this impulse to know God and of this certainty which the mind has about Him. Can it be understood from the thesis that there is a clear cut separation between God and man? It would be impossible to understand this impulse as being enclosed in a mind completely separated from the infinite universal reality, and from external reality in general. It can't be sustained except by an intense source. The first cause of creation, and the ultimate purpose of knowledge must exercise an impulsive and attractive influence on the mind. The mind has the certainty of an intelligible infinite reality, when it doesn't know it; the certitude which sustains this impulse of knowledge, shows that, before the mind sees, it somehow feels the reality, which it has to know. It shows that it is already in a kind of direct relationship with it, felt as in a kind of darkness.[23]

---

discursive knowledge. And it is in this sense that St. Thomas could say that any distinct thought and knowledge implies a secret affirmation of God; hence this definition of intelligence and of it finality: It is *capax Entis, capax Dei* [capable of being, capable of God]." Maurice Blondel, *L'Action. An essay on a critique of life and on a science of the practical* [in French] (Paris, 1936), vol. 1, p. 368.

[23] *Ibid.*, p. 235. "This presence within the conscious and free agent of an infinite, universal idea, of a good, transcendent of all particular determinations which can influence it, is the absolutely

Our nature also has the infinite tendency to appropriate and to make its own everything that a value represents. We know it won't be satisfied by any finite value. Instead it pierces through everything and seeks the infinite; it vaguely feels it. This thirst also comes from our hollowness, of the insufficiency of trying to fulfill it with the values which exist outside us. But the dynamism of this thirst has something positive in it, which can't be explained only by our minus; this positive force can't be sustained in us except by the radiation and the attraction of the infinite value— we find ourselves tied to it by a delicate thread. But we know that the value most worthy of love seems to be the human person, because it represents the richest, most complex concentration of values. Each object only gives us a single, or a greatly reduced number, of values. And objects lack the value of consciousness; they lack the value of understanding to heal our loneliness. It follows that on the unseen level too, the supreme value, the value which can fulfill all our longings, can only be personal. This value must gather within itself everything that is worthy of value and of love, and carry it in the focus of a consciousness, of an intelligence; thus we are not connected to God only by an unbroken thread— that is by our mind and by the ontological longing of our nature. Instead, their dynamism shows us the possibility and need for this relationship to grow, and become closer and closer.

The nature of divine revelation— and our ability to receive it and to distinguish it from any earthly communication— also contributes to the reality of true communication between God and man. It builds a bridge between these two poles and therefore creates the possibility of this direct relationship.

We have seen that Protestant theologians[24] consider the word as the only means of divine revelation; they see in it something that is opposed to any real communication, to any contact between man and God. For this very reason He has revealed His will to us by the word, so that He won't reveal Himself, due to His separation from us. Protestant theologians from the dialectical school distinguish, of course, the revelational word from the independent, detached idea. They separate it from the personal thought which I think or say out loud to myself, or from the word of another person, equal to me. It is always the word of a divine

---

necessary condition for every consciousness to be the cause of every action proper to an agent still imperfect, of every truly initiating force. We can't insist too much on this capital truth in the universe, where there are secondary causes, truly productive of actions, except that the idea of an infinite, of a primary cause, of a transcendent order is communicated to the spirits which receive—with these notions and through them—something of the power which these notions carry with them."

[24] Especially those of the dialectical school. *See* for example Emil Brunner, *Wort und Mystik* (Tübingen, 1928).

Person to the human. The presence and will of the supreme Person, a divine Person who has something in common with me, is revealed in word. "The word isn't less, but more than the idea, because the idea means a spirit alone; the word, however, is a community of spirit. That which the Greeks call logos is the word from within me; that which the Bible calls word is the word to me."[25] The word is the relationship of a living person with me. Three elements are involved in a word: the person who speaks to me, I, the one who is spoken to, and the word by which I am spoken to. When I hear a word, I realize that a person distinct from me is speaking to me.

Protestant theologians accentuate the word as an exclusive means of divine revelation, not only to exclude the possibility of a direct revelation of God but also to avoid its confusion with a self-revelation of some substratum of our nature, in the sense of pantheistic-idealistic philosophy. The word is the sign of a person distinct from me, therefore of a total otherness of the divine Person.

They assert that the word is the exclusive means of divine revelation; here we will only show that it indicates a mystical communication between God and man. Up to this point we agree totally with the explanation which Protestant theologians of the dialectical school give to the word, as means of divine revelation.

But the above mentioned theologians contradict what they have said up to now. They try to keep the divinity in an absolute transcendence even when it reveals itself; they don't want to open the door to pantheistic idealistic philosophy by admitting our communication with God. If they have already attributed to this word certain virtues to make known the Person who is communicating it, they now denude it of any task distinct from the pure sense which a word usually has. Thus for example, they say that the word spoken by Jesus Christ bears nothing in it of His divinity: it has a purely intellectual meaning. So the revelation in Jesus Christ is no longer the piercing of a world new in time; it is the communication of a truth addressed to man's knowledge. It doesn't contain any sign that it is from God, no power which shows its divine origin. These theologians don't only exclude every psychism[26] that pertains to the soul from the content of this word and from the process of its reception; for them it has no task of a spiritual nature, which would show it to be a word coming from God. The clinching of man to revelation takes place by an exclusive act of knowledge. This is what faith is.

---

[25] *Ibid.*, pp. 197-8.
[26] Probably the author means here the exclusion of any force unexplainable by science. For a full discussion of the word see the *Oxford English Dictionary*. trs

"It has nothing to do with exercises or religious living; faith belongs to the dominion of the spirit" [in the sense of abstract, intellectualistic knowledge].[27]

From what has already been said we have seen the first contradiction in Protestant dialectical theology. On the one hand this theology tends to distinguish the "word" of Revelation from the "idea." The motive is that the former shows its necessary source from the Person who is directing His attention to me, while the latter is a meaning in itself, which tells me nothing of its source from another person. But on the other hand it confuses the word of revelation with an idea in a pure sense.

But how has every believer known and how does he know now the revealed word as the word of a person and namely of a divine Person, if as dialectical theology sustains, it contains only its intellectual meaning? Or how could the disciples of Jesus know that He who was speaking to them was not a human person, but a divine one? How could they know that this person had a significance which completely distinguished Him from all other people? How did the listeners to the prophets have the certainty that they spoke the words of God? For dialectical theology, the answers to these questions are very hard; it doesn't admit that together with the words of Jesus or of the prophets something from the divine power must have been poured out in the listeners' souls which convinced them of the divine origin of these words.

But an answer must be given; otherwise dialectical theologians couldn't say where the listeners' faith comes from, that Jesus isn't just a simple man, but God, that when the prophets are prophesying, they aren't speaking their own human words. To give an answer, they resort to the Holy Spirit: "Therefore it is through Him alone that the place within the created world where God speaks is distinguished from the remaining content of the word.... It is through Him that a place in the temporal world receives the accent of eternity." But this accent of the Holy Spirit must be perceived by those who listen. This is the second function of the Holy Spirit, carried out by the one and the same act by which He delimits in the real world the place where God speaks. The dividing line that is produced by God's choice is made visible to those with whom God wishes to enter into contact. "No one can perceive the eternal accent on this one place in time but in the Holy Spirit. He whose eyes the Spirit does not open cannot see anything at this place that does not fit in the framework of the whole."[28]

---

[27] W. Schmidt, *Zeit und Ewigkeit* (1927), p. 79. (Note: The bibliographic data provided by Fr Staniloae in his manuscript was sometimes incomplete, and not all citations could be traced by the translators. Hence the incompleteness of some entries. *trs*)
[28] Heim, *Jesus the Lord*, pp. 159-60.

THE POSSIBILITY OF UNION WITH GOD

This recognition is enough for us. By it the theory that the function of the revelational word is to exclude the entrance of God into a relationship with man, is totally refuted. Certainly somehow God extends Himself by His power, to the point where prophetic organs proclaim His revelational word. But for the listener to gain the certainty of the divine character of this word, the divine power must take one more step, namely into his soul, as radiation from the word itself. It is therefore distinguished in his eyes from just any human word; it is recognized as a power which makes him able to understand that which others, who have not received this power or don't want to, cannot understand. In any case, the power of the same divinity which speaks by its revelational organ also reaches the souls of the listeners.

If the revealed word of God, taken by itself, can't be only communication, but also the bearer of a dynamic interest of God in man, it must bring an extension of divine power to us. The phenomenon of faith is awakened in us by this word; we are made able to receive it. This is likewise the sign of a direct relationship which it establishes with us. In the phenomenon of faith, God's care for us really goes hand in hand with the attention He has awakened in us. But the encounter of two people by their mutual attention is an encounter of something proper to each of them. Even the fact that somebody's word obliges me to give an answer, shows my relationship to him. But this unconditional need to address someone and to answer him, shows that, by all words and answers, I have a relationship to God too.

The Fathers of the Church, when they speak of the "feeling of the mind," assert a direct contact of the mind with the spiritual reality of God, not a simple knowledge of Him from a distance. It's something like the "understanding" of a person with whom you are in contact.[29] Even words show us that we have from the beginning a relationship with God, ontologically, by a power of His and by the nature we have been given. Spirituality makes us conscious of this relationship.

But on the other hand, our creatureliness implies the sovereignty of God. It makes our transformation into a divine substance impossible, no matter how close we can get to Him. Our approach to God, our uplifting to an understanding of Him, can only be realized if God Himself clothes us with the things proper to Him; but even if we are penetrated by His power, we can't shed our created nature. Our nature can't become uncreated: We become gods by grace, not by nature.

We exclude then, as two impossible extremes: clear cut separation from God and identification with Him; it follows that our ties with Him

---

[29] *See* St. Simeon the New Theologian, *Ethical Discourses* 5, *RoFil* 6, p. 185.

must be developed on the basis of a real relationship; it must start with an encounter caused by the spiritual energy of attention and arrive at a "face to face" vision.

Identification is excluded not only by the quality of Creator, which God has and by man's earthly indebtedness as a creature, but also by God's personal character. Furthermore, God can only be a person, if the mode of free and conscious existence of a person is infinitely superior to the mode of the inert existence of objects. He can only be free and even sovereign; but precisely because He is a person and namely, the absolute sovereign Person, He couldn't bring the world into existence by emanation or the involuntary development of His being; neither could He do it by the utilization, from weakness, of an eternal material, but only by creation from nothing. Even by making an abstraction of this and by viewing the Person of God as a fact in itself, it makes the pantheist identification of man with God impossible. Instead it opens the way for an infinite progress of the communion of man with Him. Namely, man cannot know God as a person by an offensive on his part, just as it's impossible to enter into the intimacy of communion with Him against His will.

You can't know your neighbor in a personal way only on your own initiative, or by an aggressive expedition. In order to know him he must reveal himself, on his own initiative; he does this in proportion to the lack of your aggression to know him. How much more so with God, the Supreme Person and one who isn't clothed in a visible body; man can't know Him, unless He reveals himself.[30] So the first thesis of Christian spirituality is confirmed: The vision of God can't be reached without a special grace from Him. But this also excludes the possibility that our nature, with the thirst to conquer God by knowledge and appropriation, can reach the point of being absorbed into the divine nature itself, that it can be identified with God. Moreover, an identification of man with God would mean the disappearance of human nature as a distinct nature, and of the world too, as a distinct reality. It would mean that God would have to give up the existence of creation. But then why did God make the world? By taking away its existence by absorbing it into Himself, after He has run it through an ephemeral existence, in a round about way? If this form of created existence doesn't have a value as such, or the possibility of enjoying divine values, and remains in itself just a creature, wouldn't it have been more logical for it not to have been created in the first place?

---

[30] Max Scheler, *On the eternal in man,* transl.by Bernard Noble (New York, 1960), p. 333 ff.

On the other hand, if man also were created as a person, the intention of God was for him as well to exist as an irreducible "I"; he would be capable of guarding, in the relationship of communion, the intimate hearth of His being. Relations between created persons show us how close communion between them can be, and also the irreducibility of the "I's," even when there is the most permanent union between them. These relations are also an icon of the relationship of man with God. They help us to understand the relationship which can't be expressed by words, except in a contradictory way.[31] On the one hand it is "union," on the other, this union isn't an identification. God overwhelms our nature with His gifts and with His powers, but these gifts and powers don't become the natural gifts and powers of our nature. Our nature isn't made into the divine nature, because our created "I" doesn't become the divine "I"; so in this arrangement our "I" is always conscious that it enjoys all these blessings which it is tasting not by its own powers, but by God.

The spiritual Christian adopts this affirmation of supreme humility, but likewise of supreme daring: "I am man, but I live as God, by what God has given me; I am man, but I am on God's level by the grace with which He has been pleased to cloth me...." This reflects the expression of the Apostle Paul: "I live; yet not I, but Christ lives in me" (Galatians 2:20). In other words, my personality hasn't ceased to exist because I am conscious of it at the same time as I affirm it; my personality now lives the life of Christ. I am still a man by nature, but I have become Christ by the powers by which I my self now live. This is the experience of the Christian on the highest peaks of his spiritual life.

---

[31] Nicholas Cabasilas, *The Life in Christ* 1.3, (Crestwood, NY: St. Vladimir's Seminary Press, 1974), pp. 45-6. "As God's loving-kindness is ineffable ... likewise it follows that His union with those whom He loves surpasses every union of which one might conceive, and cannot be compared with any model. Therefore even Scripture needed many illustrations to be able to express that connection, since one would not suffice.... None of these figures is adequate for that union, for it is impossible from these to attain to the exact truth.... It would appear that marriage and concord between head and members especially indicate connection and unity, yet they fall far short of it and are far from manifesting the reality."

3. Orthodox Spirituality and our Neighbor

The word has gotten around that Orthodox spirituality calls for an indifference to life, for a withdrawal from its affairs, for a premature eschatology.

This idea is totally erroneous. St. Maximus the Confessor, especially, has demonstrated the movement of God's creation and the need for every person to participate in it, if he wants to reach the perfection represented by the mystical union with God: This movement is intended in general to elevate a person to the level of the highest good and to perfection.

Maximus formulates in his own way the idea of a dynamism of creation. Abbot Thalassios asked what Christ meant when He said His Father works (John 5:17), when in the six days of creation He finished bringing into existence all the categories of being which make up the world. The saint answered:

> God did finish the creation of the primary *logoi* [32] of [His] acts and the general essences of beings, as He knows. Nevertheless He is still working today, not only sustaining them in existence, but also bringing them out, developing and constituting particular models already given potentially in essence, furthermore by providence making the (single) particular models exactly like the universal essences, until uniting the voluntary impulses to the naturally more general logos of the rational essence, by the movement of the particular models toward bliss, He will make them move harmoniously and identically among themselves and with the whole. The particular will no longer have a will distinct from the general, but one and the same logos will be contemplated in all, unseparated from the ways of the things to which it is attributed. So the grace which deifies all things will be shown in complete action.[33]

We would like to point out here that St. Maximus admits a) "a more general logos of rational being," from which it follows that there are also more particular *logoi*, and b) "a distinct will of the particular," from which it follows that a more general will also exists. We find this idea

---

[32] In Romanian, Fr. Staniloae has translated the Greek *logos* as reason. One definition of "reason" is a ground or cause of, or for, something, or purpose. Further on in this chapter Fr. Staniloae calls these reasons, (*logoi* in Greek), "sleeping possibilities," or "the wise principles placed by God in all things." See chapter 24 for a complete discussion. Lossky tells us that the Word, "the Logos is the divine hearth whence fly the creative rays, the *'logoi'* peculiar to creatures, these causative words of God.... Every being therefore has its 'idea,' its 'reason' in God." *Orthodox Theology* (New York, 1978), p. 56. *trs*
[33] *Questions to Thalassios* 2, *PG* 90.272.

developed again by Blondel in his work *L'Action*. According to him every tendency in us has its logos, thus its apparent justification. This particular logos attracts the will to its side, and the latter becomes the will of a part of us instead of being the will of the whole of us. Thus the normal thing isn't to suppress the variant tendencies in us, but to subordinate them to the whole or to harmonize them. The more general logos is like the top of a pyramid compared to particular *logoi*. In the measure in which we raise ourselves toward the ever more general (universal) *logoi* in our knowledge and activity, we become more virtuous and we approach the most general supreme Logos. The more general logos of our nature tries to subordinate itself to a higher general logos which embraces many beings and things, and the most general Logos is the divine Logos. But working in conformity with the more general logos in our nature, at the same time we satisfy its true interests as aspirations for the happiness of all our parts. For satisfying anarchistic tendencies, we rend the whole structurally and we cast it into a torturous existence.[34]

In fact the world presents itself to us in a process of continuous "eschatological birthgiving," as Maurice Blondel puts it, in which each part is determined by the whole universe, determining in turn the whole: "... the relative fixation of beings has a development of which the multiple phases can't be isolated one from the other, without grave risks."[35] The holy Fathers say its purpose is to bring to light the deified spirit. Therefore this joint development isn't produced only within the enclosed system of the physical order, but it also influences the spiritual existence of human beings, just as their actions, generated by ideas and feelings, influence the physical development of the universe, and just as these persons influence each other. The spiritual and physical order of the created world develop together, by a mutual influence which holds for the whole universe.[36] Thus, each person is responsible for the development of the whole of the physical and spiritual universe. Our smallest gesture makes the world vibrate and changes its state. At the same time, the existence of every person as well as of everything is continually dependent on the convergence of the factors produced by the unfolding of

---

[34] This whole paragraph has been inserted here by the translators, because it is a commentary on the preceding passage by St. Maximus. It is taken from Fr. Staniloae's translation of *Questions to Thalassios*, RoFil 3, pp. 23-4; endnote 17, p. 465.
[35] Blondel, *L'Action* vol. 1, pp. 316-7.
[36] "We have seen in effect how the whole of creation is initially, in a primitive way, passivity; but also how it rises up, by the hand of God desirous of being raised gradually and by pure goodness of being to the dignity of cases, natural agents, living, conscious, according to a hierarchy of forms, comprising a solidarity in which the inferior prepare, sustain the superior which, in turn, take into consideration and carry upward the natural conditions of their own actions." *Ibid.*, p. 414. The world is thus found in a "dynamic hierarchy" and in a "progressive genesis." Everything in the world is totally connected. *Ibid.*, p. 372.

the whole.³⁷ "Everybody's action, slight as it may be, creates resistance or reaction, undergoes universal pressure, in order to fade into the universe, and it suppresses and dominates this weight of the universe. Thus our action is never carried out in an absolutely closed circle."³⁸

So this development doesn't happen by chance and isn't without purpose. We can't do just anything we want to the exterior world. Only by taking into consideration the natural possibilities and laws of nature, can man use it profitably. The shaping of nature for human purposes is prefigured in it. Blondel makes this comment:

> Not only a direct brutality can subjugate the forces of nature: Discoveries presuppose an inventive or even a deifying tact. Not only has man changed the face of the earth, but the work of man too has adapted itself to the secret of natural powers in order to also adapt them better. This kind of conquering action can't be explained except by a kind of connubium [marriage] between personal aspirations and the resources infused in the universe in which we are submerged as a point. ³⁹

St. Maximus the Confessor formulated this truth long ago, in terms even more fitting. He said that in the created universe there are hidden divine *logoi*; our mission is, by our action directed by the logos [40] in us, to make these *logoi* and the harmony between them come fully to light. This subordinates them to the one great logos. Technical civilization gradually discovers the energies of nature and the laws of their utilization. It uncovers more and more of these *logoi* and the ever greater harmony and for the esthetic of various civilizations shapes nature as man's environment and makes these *logoi* spread over the face of things as a light. We can't know how far nature will let such development go on. Both the work of the human spirit which seeks and finds and the physical movement in the world are the willed prolongation on a created level of the uninterrupted and eternal act of the divine Logos (Blondel). So we can say that the development of the world along the lines of dis-

---

[37] Louis Lavelle, *De l'Acte,* "The smallest of our gestures shakes the world; it is one with all the movements which fill it" (p. 89). "All the gestures which we make shape in their turn all the forms of reality, they multiply them, transform them and take their share of the responsibility for the very act which created them" (p. 91). "Our responsibility in regard to the Total Being is a proof in favor of its unity: No being exists which doesn't feel compatible with the whole universe; it feels that it must take upon itself the very burden of creation" (p. 90). "On the other hand, its whole existence is a series of encounters; but each encounter is transformed by it into such an occasion that the world gains for it a spiritual and personal signification which the system itself will in no way succeed in expressing" (p. 47).
[38] Blondel, *L'Action* vol. 1, p. 20.
[39] *Ibid.,* vol. 2. p. 186.
[40] Fr. Staniloae consistently translates *logos* and *logoi* as reason and reasons.

covering the *logoi* in it will go on as long as God wants to keep it in existence and only within the harmonious framework in which these *logoi* are found in the divine Logos. Because the divine Logos is reflected in the *logoi* of things, the road which we must travel until we discover and understand, that by these *logoi*, the Divine Reason, can't be defined, because we can't state precisely an end to the development of the work with all its possibilities. But if the purpose of this development is for man to see in the best possible way the harmonious rays of Divine *Logoi* spread over the face of the world and springing forth from the womb of things, it is obvious that man must not produce, among these *logoi*, an impossibility of coexistence (by pollution, by the exhaustion of energy, etc.)

Everyone is obligated to take part in this work, directed by divine providence but carried out by conscious created beings. Christian spirituality, far from excusing someone from this collaboration, imposes it on him as an indispensable condition of attaining perfection. From Evagrius Ponticus, or even from Origen, up to St. Maximus the Confessor and beyond, the believer who wants to gain perfection, before he becomes a *gnostikos* (a knower) must be a *praktikos* (a doer). Someone can't see the *logoi* in things and by them God the Word, the Logos, if he hasn't first dedicated himself to a "working philosophy" or to a "doing of the commandments."

Of course the "fulfilling of the commandments" doesn't consist only in an activity directed toward nature, but in one which also has in view our neighbor and ourselves. We don't have the mission just to develop the sleeping possibilities found in the physical world, but also those which are much more valuable and spiritual in each of us. By the attention, the counsel, the teaching, the example which we give to the other person, by cooperating with him we help to realize the spiritual potentials found in him and in us. And we work on ourselves by the disciplining of our conduct, by an unceasing attention to everything we do and think, by the good which we do for others. Not only do we meet Christ in ourselves, but also in the being of our neighbors. St. Isaac the Syrian insists that prayer be accompanied by the charity and the help given to others. He says: "Nothing can bring my heart so close to God as a good deed." Or: "If you have more than enough for the needs of the day, give it to the poor and then come and offer your prayers with boldness."[41] Or: "Support with the word the grieving and the right hand that bears all things will support you."[42] And St. Simeon the New Theo-

---

[41] St. Isaac the Syrian, *The Ascetical Homilies* 23 [in Greek] (Athens, 1961), p. 86.
[42] *Ibid.*, 30. Not found by *trs.*

logian points out: "He has condescended to assume the features of each poor man and make himself like all the poor, that each one should look on his brother and his neighbor as his very God and consider himself the least of all. We must therefore welcome [our brother]. We should honor him and put all our resources at his disposal, just as Christ and God empties out his own blood for our salvation."[43] And once again St. Isaac comments:

> He who directs his thoughts to God honors everyone; he finds help from everyone by the hidden will of God. And he who defends the oppressed has God as an ally; he who gives his hand to help his neighbor receives God's hand in return.[44]

The activity by which we help our neighbors and ourselves to grow, crystallizes in the virtues which culminate in love. And properly speaking these are the necessary stages through which we must bring our nature before reaching illumination and the mystical union with God. But a clear cut separation can't be made between the virtues and the activity directed toward nature. We must also prove our love for our neighbor by our work, not only in word. You can't give him a gift or do him a good deed, you can't help him, without a productive activity in nature. And likewise, we can't develop ourselves completely and harmoniously if we haven't in some way taken part in a physical activity directed toward nature; and by this we gain certain virtues of patience, of discipline, of self-denial.

Blondel makes a distinction between three types of activity: *poiein* (to create), the elementary type of human action, which means to do something with a material; *prattein* (to do), the action by which we "make the man"; we express in our profoundest nature our essentially human aspirations, modeling our members, our aptitudes, forming our character; and *theorein* (to view, to consider), contemplation, in which every kind of passive material, every interest, every useful purpose is gone. For that very reason it has the greatest efficiency in perfecting our spiritual energies.

But a clear-cut separation between these activities never takes place. By his work on nature, man also exercises himself in certain virtues; he moulds his character and indirectly does a favor for his neighbors. So spiritual endeavors have never overlooked manual labor as a means for the purification and the guidance of the faithful towards perfection. And we believe that today, when technical civilization has created a great

---

[43] Simeon the New Theologian, *The Practical and Theological Chapters and the Three Theological Discourses* 3.96, (Kalamazoo, MI, 1982), p. 101.
[44] *Op. cit.*, 23. Not found. trs

ORTHODOX SPIRITUALITY AND OUR NEIGHBOR

variety of new activities in connection with nature, nothing should hinder the believer from pursuing his perfection even if he works with a machine.

The road to Christian perfection doesn't exclude work, but it does require that it contribute to the winning of the virtues. No one should imagine that the work he does is an end in itself; it has the role of beautifying his nature, with the virtues of patience, of self-control, of love for his neighbor, of faith in God, and in turn of opening his eyes to the wise principles placed by God in all things. Therefore he doesn't let himself be carried along in time by a chance current of life. Instead he strives to guide his development toward its true goals. The ultimate purpose of work and the taking part in the life of this world isn't so much the development of nature as it is the normal development of the dormant possibilities in man and in his neighbors. Even in the enduring of troubles, which is one of the most important means of Christian striving, we don't have a running away from the life of the world, but a persistence in it. The care for one's own formation and that of our neighbors, by beautifying ourselves with virtues, doesn't mean a non-participation in the life of the world. It is the very fullest collaboration, if man is a part of humanity, and his formation is the ultimate goal of creation.

The one who has reached the peaks of spiritual living is no longer preoccupied with external activity, but with contemplation. Even so, he exerts an influence on the development of the world, by an attraction and a power which touch his neighbors, that they might become as he is, by the same fulfillment of the commandments, by the same virtuous work. He imitates God who, although unchangeable, doesn't stop the dynamism of creation by that unchangeability; but by an unceasing impulse and attraction exerted on it, He sustains it, giving it as an ideal goal His supreme perfection, which for that very reason is unchangeable. The person who has reached the peak of perfection exerts an influence and an attraction on his neighbors, which makes them strive to reach the ideal goal. Because the very highest of the virtues which the spiritual man struggles for is love. In love there is knowledge too. Now the love of God can't be separated from the love of people.

The one who believes that he is carried along without freedom by an indefinite flux of the world, without any direction, isn't the one who is putting true manliness and true initiative into his soul; rather it is the one who knows the direction and the goal of the perfecting of his life and of the world. It is the one who knows that by freedom he can contribute to the normal guidance of his development, which is moving toward love, and that he is therefore responsible for the spiritual form with which he imprints his life.

4. The Holy Trinity — the Basis of Christian Spirituality

Orthodox spirituality has as its goal the deification of man and his union with God, without being merged with Him. It has as a basic conviction the existence of a personal God, who is the supreme source of radiating love. He prizes man and doesn't want to confuse him with Himself, but maintains and raises him to an eternal dialogue of love.

Such a spirituality has no place where an evolutionary progress of man, connected to a divinity conceived as an impersonal essence, is affirmed. This progress can have no result other than man's disappearance in the impersonal divinity.

But the personal God, and thus the supreme source of love, can't be conceived of as a single person, but as a community of persons in a perfect unity. You see then why the Christian teaching of a Trinity of Persons in a unity of essence is the only one which can constitute the basis of a perfect spirituality for man, understood as a full communion with God in love, without his being lost in it.

A Roman Catholic theologian, Georg Koepgen has best described the Trinitarian basis of Christian spirituality.[45] At the same time he says that this spirituality has been most faithfully preserved in the Eastern Church, because she alone has kept in the most unchanged way the biblical teaching about the Holy Trinity and its central place in Christian piety. He establishes that, in religions which unilaterally accentuate monotheism, such a spirituality has no place; and in those with a pantheistic tendency, even if the divinity is manifested in a plurality of gods as expressions of the forces of nature, we find a false spirituality, or an illusory perfection, in other words, one which leads basically to man's meltdown in the so-called divinity.

On the other hand, man's personal spiritual perfection, by eternal unconfused union with God can't take place except where an eternal eschatology of man, in blessed union with God, is believed in. But such an eschatology is the result of the Trinitarian God.

Man's union with God for eternity, however, is guaranteed and mediated only where one of the divine persons takes flesh as a man for eternity, thus showing the eternal love of God for man as man. Koepgen considers that Orthodoxy has maintained the spirituality proper to the Christianity revealed in Christ; it has kept the mystery of the Trinitarian community of persons in God, unweakened by a rationalistic

---

[45] All the references in this chapter to Georg Koepgen are taken from the Introduction to his book, *Die Gnosis des Christentums*, 1st ed. (Salzburg, 1939).

philosophy which, accentuating the unity of God, has emphasized His essence. We can add that precisely because of this rational stress on the one essence of God, which tries to avoid its paradoxical combination with the Trinity of Persons, the doctrine of the "Filioque" resulted. According to this teaching the Spirit proceeds from what the Father and the Son have in common, that is from the divine essence; and so the essence is considered to be the cause of the persons, which actually leads to an impersonal god, to a pantheist one.

But let's give the floor to Koepgen:

> Mysticism always has a single goal: man's deification and union with God, without man's fusion with Him. And this can't be understood except by the Trinitarian idea of God. In Christianity the whole is oriented of necessity toward future perfection.... The Church is blamed because it recognizes mysticism, and is also condemned without mercy when it crosses the border into pantheism. But how can mysticism be recognized, if pantheism is rejected? Note our answer: Christian mysticism isn't based on man's predisposition, which pushes him into a fusion with the divinity, into a pantheist life of union with it, but it is the actualization of the incarnation of God in the believer. Between the Christian concept of God and the non-Christian, there is a fundamental distinction: Christianity is based on the Trinitarian God [therefore irreducible and eternally personal, or a personal community], not on a philosophical concept of an absolute spirit [and as such so impersonal]. It's noteworthy that Catholic theology too works almost exclusively with the philosophical concept of God, by which it avoids referring directly to the Trinity [of persons].

The God of the New Testament and of the holy Eastern Fathers is living and irreducibly three in one. The God of scholastic philosophy is impregnated with Aristotelianism or confused with a generally pantheistic one. We would say that the failure of scholastic theologians to make this distinction has led them to use the same name of mysticism to express the union of the Christian with God, a term also employed by pantheist philosophy. So Protestant theologians heap reproach on the notion of mysticism.

Orthodoxy has preferred, especially in the period of the holy Fathers and in the writings of the great saints who experienced union with God, to use the terms "life in Christ," "life in the Spirit," "the spiritual life," and "the life in God," to describe the life of the Christian in union with God, regardless of the level of this life. Orthodoxy has followed the example of St. Paul the Apostle (Galatians 3:28; 3:20; 2 Corinthians 4:11; 1 Corinthians 7:8; 6:19; 3:16; 2:12; Romans 8:15; 8:9-10; Ephesians 3:16-17; Colossians 3:3; John 14: 23; 1 John 3:24, etc.)

But Koepgen continues:

> God and divinity aren't the same thing. When the mystic [the spiritual person] speaks of God, he doesn't mean a metaphysical divinity *(ens a se)*, but he thinks of God in trinity, who has united in a completely incomprehensible way with men and has saved them. [If Christianity has as its basis faith in the Holy Trinity, spirituality is a part of its very being.] Mysticism [the life in relationship with God, the life which has God in itself, in different degrees, we would say], isn't an appendix annexed later by Christianity, which is offered as a new possibility to some specially endowed souls; it belongs to the very act of faith" [which is an act of entering into a relationship with God, but which can be developed by the purification from the passions, we would say.]

Due to its rational philosophic conception of God, which introduces a distance between God and man, "the connection of Catholic theology with mysticism [with spirituality, we would say] is very unclear."

Orthodox teaching, however, remains faithful to the New Testament: It doesn't rationalize the mystery of God in Trinity. It bases itself on the experience of God who communicates Himself to us through love, in the Spirit, by uncreated energies. It neither holds God at a distance from us as in the rationalist monotheistic religions (Judaism and Islam) nor does it bring us into fusion with Him, as in the pantheist and philosophic religions which recognize as the one reality an essence of one kind or another.

As an example of a false or seductive spirituality, or a mysticism proper to pantheist philosophy, which doesn't promise human nature anything but fusion with an impersonal divinity, Koepgen gives the following quotation from Plotinus:

> He [the mystic] doesn't see two, and the seer [contemplative] doesn't distinguish two, nor represent two to himself, but he becomes another and is no longer himself; and arriving there he no longer belongs to himself, but he belongs to the one there, and is one with him. The central point is united to the central point."[46] [And Koepgen commenting on this passage says:] Plotinus shows us here the essence of neo-Platonic mysticism, the basis of which is incontestable, because the essence of God is conceived as pure idea and is put on the same level with the categories of the human spirit and in relationship with him.

---

[46] Plotinus, *Enneads*. trans. by Micahel Atkinson (Oxford, 1983), The Sixth Ennead, 9-10 *ff*.

THE BASIS: THE HOLY TRINITY 49

Further on Koepgen cites St. Simeon the New Theologian, who keeps the spiritual person distinct in the act of seeing (contemplating) the Holy Trinity:

> What lips could describe what has happened to me and what happens everyday? Even at night and in the midst of darkness I see, trembling, Christ opening heaven for me and I behold how He himself beholds me from there and He sees me here below together with the Father and with the Spirit in the thrice holy light. Because this is one and nevertheless it is found to be in three. And the light is one and the same nevertheless in three images, although it is only one. And it illuminates my soul brighter than the sun and floods my spirit covered with gloom.... And this miracle was even the more astonishing because it opened my eyes and helped me to see, and that which I saw is He himself. Because this light helped those who behold to know themselves in light and those who see in light see Him again. For they see the light of the Spirit and in as much as they see Him, they see the Son. Now he who has been made worthy to see the Son, sees the Father too.

In opposition to St. Simeon, Koepgen shows how the turn-about of the Western Christian to the rationalist concept of God— weakening the accent put on the Holy Trinity, thus on the personalistic-communitarian character of God— brought him to the renewal of false mysticism, the fusion of the contemplative with the impersonal divinity. "In St. Simeon," according to Koepgen, "we have the case of a mysticism [or spirituality, we would say] explicitly Trinitarian. On the contrary, Western mysticism, under the influence of neo-Platonism has given Trinitarian mysticism [spirituality] a secondary place, at least in expression. Simeon is a Trinitarian mystic [a spiritual person] because he stands in the tradition of the Eastern Church."

Western mystical theology, to its detriment, has almost entirely overlooked its ties with this tradition and has seen in Eckhart or in Spanish mysticism the culminating point of mystical thought in general. Here the thought of the Holy Trinity is put in the background. When Eckhart says, "If I want to know God without mediation, I must become Him and He must become me," the influence of Plotinus is incontestable.[47]

Koepgen asks once again:

> What is the difference between Eckhart's mysticism and that of Simeon's? For Eckhart, the Trinity exists as a unity of Persons; he sees just one thing: divinity. On the contrary, Simeon sees the Persons in their differentiation. He sees the Father, first of all as Father,

---

[47] Eckhart, *Sermons* [in German] (Jena, 1934), p. 39.

and the Son, as Son. Here is the great difference between Eastern mysticism [spiritual life] and the Western. Western mysticism is under the influence of Plotinus, and is monotheistic in the strict sense of the word; it sees the Trinity as a matter of fact, but only as a unity of persons in divinity. Even our modern Catholic mysticism preoccupied with Christ speaks, as we know, almost entirely of the 'Divine Savior,' which means that it sees in Christ only God in His divinity. The Church from the beginning—and Simeon with her—on the contrary, saw something much greater in Christ: They saw in Him the Son.... We have closed our minds to a fact that was decisive for the Church from the beginning, and by which it was distinguishable from Judaic monotheism: We have lost the feeling for the Trinitarian life of God, for the reciprocal interpenetration and for the reference of the divine persons one for the other. For the Old Testament, God was in any case at least Jehovah the Lord of Hosts, the Almighty Master. For us, on the other hand, God has become also a spiritual concept empty of content.... He who wants to enclose the divine problem in a rigid plan of a doctrine of categories ends up after all in pantheism....

This is so because it makes God into an essence, and the essence, in submission to laws known by us, is no longer distinguishable from the general essence of a unique reality. Koepgen continues:

> The dogma of the Trinity, however, is found outside the categorical forms of thought. It is surpassed in the attitude and knowledge of faith, [which opens itself to the mystery of reality, beyond any simplifying logic]. Thus the Trinitarian mystic [the spiritual person who believes in the Holy Trinity and who is found in a living, personal relationship with It] is also beyond the danger of falling into pantheism. The dogma of the Trinity itself elevates the thinker into another spiritual order, which from the beginning protects him from this pantheist conception. The dogma of the Trinity raises the believer into a living relationship with the tri-personal divine community; even by this it also keeps him as a person unconfused in the divinity, but strengthened and preserved forever, by love, by its character of person.

But there also exists another alternative for Western mysticism, devoid of a living relationship with the persons of the Holy Trinity. It bases itself on mostly rational arguments—Koepgen says in the same pages—and therefore on considerations from a distance that God must be a God of love and that He must in turn be loved; so it becomes an experience shut up in subjectivism, a sentimentalism unanchored in the direct experience of God. This leads to the absence, in Western theology, of the doctrine of uncreated energies which come into us, an absence which is connected to the concept of God more as essence than as a loving communion of Persons.

THE BASIS: THE HOLY TRINITY 51

Georg Koepgen doesn't shrink from finding the fully systematized beginning of this philosophical, unbiblical, essentialist and impersonal or non-Trinitarian understanding of God even at the door of Thomas Aquinas, who according to the affirmations of the author:

> ... suffered a severe breakdown at the end of his life, due to the fact that everything he had written previously now seemed unsatisfactory. Maybe the day will come— and we would like to see it as soon as possible— when theology will take this event in the life of Aquinas just as seriously as anything else in it. In any case this would contribute in an essential way to bringing this frightful thing into the scientific-theological realm, which is connected with the very best tradition of a Paul, Augustine, Pascal or Newman.

For this change, Koepgen considers necessary the return to a knowledge of God based not on the laws of deductive reason, but on a real experience of Him, or of His power working in us. This is Christian "gnosis" distinct from pagan "gnosticism," which in fact is pantheism and doesn't know God the transcendent One, who comes to us by the grace of His love, by experience. Koepgen says:

> Our thought today is so used to identifying 'logic' with 'reason,' that it judges the correctness of any thought by the measure in which it corresponds to the laws of 'logic.' In reality, however, logic presupposes Plato's doctrine of ideas, or Aristotle's unity of concept. However, there is no place for this doctrine of ideas in the Bible, because here every thought is preoccupied not with idea but with person: It is existential.

But the person is infinitely more than ideas; his character is indefinable, alive, passionate, always new and thirsting for a living and loving relationship with other persons. Only a person truly warms me. Ideas are but some partial products of the person, incomplete means of communication between persons. And the thirst of the person for unending relationships with other persons implicates both the eternity of persons and the source of this eternity of theirs in a supreme community of persons.

We can systematize, complete and deepen what Koepgen has said as follows:

1. Only a perfect community of supreme persons can nourish, with its unending and perfect love, our thirst for love in relation to it and between ourselves. This nourishing can't only be theory, but it must be lived too. This is so because love isn't satisfied with only being theory, but wants to give itself, to welcome and be welcomed. A

monotheistic god in a strict sense must be considered as enclosed and self-satisfied, a fact which would correspond with a perfection, which we, however, can't understand, once it is lacking in love. A pantheist essence is poured out, or evolves into more and more forms, in an involuntary way; more precisely, it isn't poured out and it doesn't evolve, strictly speaking, because it can't go out of itself, or from the essential, monotone and involuntary forms which belong to it. In the pantheist conception, persons, if they too appear, don't have a supreme and permanent value, thus neither love between them.

[Pantheist] essence in itself lacks love, while love means conscious and voluntary self-sacrifice among persons, or the sacrifice of one person for another; [so pantheist] essence couldn't somehow produce love later, thus neither persons. Love, without beginning, eternal, presupposes that God is a perfect unity of the Divine Being, but at the same time it is a Trinity of Persons, from the same eternity. And as perfect love, the Divine Trinity can also give itself to other persons; however, only if they want it. It isn't forced to change itself into fleeting and passing alterations, which would have no purpose, lacking in real and permanent value. But for its free overflowing it creates other persons, not infinite in essence, because this would mean its infinite overflow in the form of these persons; but in another way, it can gradually share with them from the infinity of its life and love, deifying them. Now the only way it can do this is by really uniting them with itself by love, enabling them to experience in a real way its love. Only so are freedom and love manifested in existence, without which everything would seem without any purpose whatsoever. Love from the supreme community thus produces a new form of its manifestation. So, on the one hand, it isn't totally one in existence, but neither are [the persons] unsurpassably separated in it.

Created and thus finite persons can enjoy the infinity of divine love and life, or the one and supreme source of life and love— in other words the infinity of this source— in their infinite progress in deification; without it their unending existence and longing would have no purpose. They become partakers of that infinite life and love, gradually, because the infinity of divine love and life is communicated to them. At the same time the freedom of both sides is respected. This means that the finite beings can make their contribution too, to a personal effort for their growth, that this growth might be real.

2. So the Trinity, radiated by the love which is proper to it, can't be lived and conceived without its uncreated energies in ever increasing levels. Love is characterized by this paradox: On the one hand it unites subjects who love each other, on the other, it doesn't confuse their iden-

THE BASIS: THE HOLY TRINITY 53

tity. Love brings one subject to another, without merging their identities, because in this case love would cease. It would kill the persons who love each other; it wouldn't assure them of a permanent existence. This paradox can be explained by the radiation of love, as energy which is communicated from one person to another without them being depleted in this communication. Uncreated and unending love of the uncreated source of love, can't be communicated except as uncreated energy. But in the eternal and perfect community of love, subjects communicate their own being to each other, without they themselves blending together. This proves that the subjects are, on the highest level, just as valuable and as indestructible as their natures. Only in this way is their love truly perfect. An eternal nature, which would give birth later to other persons, would reduce the value of the persons and would give them a passing existence, and this would make of love itself something secondary, something obedient to certain laws of evolution to which it would be superior. On the other hand some persons existing eternally, with a unity of nature, would again be subject to an evolutionary love, so it would be second rate, which would leave these persons without a supreme purpose.

On the highest, divine level, the difference between nature and energy is surpassed in a way incomprehensible to us. The divine nature itself is energy, without ceasing to be an undepletable nature; the nature itself is communicating energy. But it is so because it is of the Supreme Persons. The Persons communicate their nature as an energy. Everything is an energy which is communicated from one person to another. Their love is perfect; they radiate their whole nature from one to the other. We can't live the whole divine nature in the energy given to us from God. It is undepletable, from an infinite source, and from a plane transcendent to us. We are beings brought into existence in time, and therefore finite, by a creative act of God.

3. But the Trinitarian community of Divine Persons, a dynamic structure of unending love, isn't a uniform love of the three Persons between themselves, but a love of Father, of Son and of a hypostasized communication between them, in the person of the Holy Spirit. The love isn't uniform. If I didn't have somebody else than me, if I weren't given a love other than mine, it wouldn't interest me very much. Without these distinct qualities, divine love, and thus infinite, would have something monotonous in it. The affection of a perfect Father for a perfect Son is something other than an affection, pure and simple, between just any two persons. Monotone and uniform affection doesn't exist, because people themselves aren't uniform. The Father loves the Son with an infinite parental sense *(simtire)*, comforting Him with the

unending sensitivity *(sensibilitatea)* of a perfect Father, and the Son responds to this parental love with the filial sense *(simtire)* of one who feels *(simte)* comforted by a perfect Father. We don't know if two uniform loves would still be love. However, the sensitivity *(sensibilitatea)* of the Father for the Son assumes the hypostatical and comforting image of the Holy Spirit. The Father rejoices together with the Spirit for the Son. But this hypostatic comforting of the Father, directed toward the Son also makes the Son respond with an intensified sense *(simtire)* of the Father's love for Him, without the comforting sensitivity *(sensibilitatea)* of the Father for the Son becoming proper to the Son, because in this case He too would be conscious of *(simti)* a paternal love for the Father, becoming fused with Him. He responds with His filial sensitivity *(sensibilitatea),* stimulated also by the Holy Spirit, but without His filial sensitiveness *(sensibilitatea)* being confused with the paternal sensitivity *(sensibilitatea),* or of taking the form of a fourth hypostasis, since this would open up a series of infinite multiplications of the divine hypostasis.

4. God wants to gradually extend the gift of His infinite love to another order of conscious subjects and namely to created ones. He wants to extend this love in its paternal form, as toward other sons, united with His Son. So after the creation of man, He wanted His Son to become man so that His love for His Son, made man, would be a love which is directed toward any human face, like that of His Son. In the Son made flesh we are all adopted by the Father. Strictly speaking, even by creation God made man as an image of His Son or so that His Son could become man too. The Father loves all of us in His Son, because the Son was made our brother. God the Son, too, thus shows us His love as a supreme brother. It is a new form of the love of God for us. But the Son's love for us isn't separated from the Father's love for us, but in His love as a brother He makes the Father's love, and also His love for the Father, engulf us. In us the Father welcomes other loving and loved sons because His Son was made our beloved brother.

However, along with the love of the Father for us and with our love for the Father in Christ the paternal love is poured out on us in the form of the Holy Spirit flooding His Son. We respond to this love of the Father, stimulated by the same comforting sensitivity of the Spirit, along with the Son.

If the Son would not have become man, the Father's love would not have been poured out on us; in Christ as man it reaches us too. By the incarnate Son the Holy Spirit radiates within humanity and the world, as the love of God for us and of ours for God.

The Spirit brings into creation inter-Trinitarian life and love. He raises creation to the level of inter-Trinitarian love and deification. The epiclesis, the calling down of the Holy Spirit in the Eucharist, says Koepgen, hasn't only the purpose of changing exteriorly the bread and the wine into the Body and Blood of Christ, but of bringing divine life into creation:

> The Eastern Church doesn't see the concept, but the process itself, the religious reality. What is the Eucharist for her? The change of the bread and wine into the Body and Blood of Christ? Certainly it is that too, but on the level right there, for her, not the change but the deification of the creature is present. In the depths of the Spirit the union between God and man is carried out. The sacrament is the point where the other world penetrates ours. And this is the work of the Holy Spirit (p. 241).

This is why the Church, in all her sanctifying services, invokes the Holy Spirit. By the Holy Spirit we are raised up to the divine world, or the divine world penetrates us. This changes us, with this our deification starts. This is what Orthodox spirituality, or our spiritual life, consists of.

5. The Christological, Pneumatological, and Ecclesiastical Character of Orthodox Spirituality [48]

The main difference between Christian spirituality and any other, besides the fact that it doesn't advocate man's identification with the divinity or with a total essence, is its Christological character. In other words, the ascent of Christians to God has Jesus Christ not only as a norm, but also as the way, according to His own words: "I am the way…." [49] No one can reach the mystical union with God, if he takes another way than Christ (He is the only Way), and no one in this union can go beyond Christ. In addition, our relationship with Him is realized and strengthened by His Holy Spirit.

Christianity teaches that any other union with the divinity, thus that which isn't realized through Christ and in Christ, is an illusion, because Christ is the only "Mediator" which God has given to man as a ladder to Him. "For in Him all the fullness of God was pleased to dwell, and through him to reconcile to Himself all things, whether on earth or in heaven, making peace by the Blood of His Cross." [50] "For through Him we both have access in one Spirit to the Father." [51]

Jesus Christ is the bridge stretching from God to the realm of our humanity, by His one hypostasis, which unites both the divine and human natures.

Even if we make an abstraction of the Incarnation, the Son of God is the one in whom "all things hold together," because "all things were created through Him."[52] He isn't only the one in whom the Father sees His own radiant light, but also the one in whom creation can behold the glory of the Father. The Son has an eternal revelational purpose: The Son was chosen that also in relationship with the world, He would be the revelation of the Trinity. When God undertook to bring the world out of nothingness into existence, the Son was given the role of being in the closest contact with it. The depth of the absolute transcendence of the divinity, of which the world couldn't have the knowledge that it exists, was made in some way knowable by the Son. By His Son, God is for the world in general a voice which is heard in our nature, a convincing sign of His existence, "the Word"; by the Son, too, God is somehow "Reason" (Logos) to the world, in other words reality to a certain degree

---

[48] A character marked by Christ, the Spirit, and the Church.
[49] John 14:6.
[50] Colossians 1:19-20.
[51] Ephesians 2:18.
[52] Colossians 1:17, 16.

intelligible, or the cause by which the world functions and is explained, and everything else too. Therefore the world was also made capable, by the Son, of being in a relationship with the Son. He is the reflex of the light of the Father in the world, by the *"logoi"* or by the meanings and purposes which are found in all things, without which the world would be sunk in the most discouraging darkness and nonsense. Even the futile, one-sided and imperfect ascent to God, by our reason affected by the disease of sin, is still just an ascent by the Son and in the Son as the supreme Logos of all things and as the ultimate which we can somehow grasp from God.

But God, by the Incarnation of this "Word," this Logos of His, also took another step forward in His exit from transcendence and in His approach to us. In Jesus Christ He became for us "a voice" of love, ringing out with all the affection of a human being, so familiar to us. But this means that man himself was made capable of becoming the medium by which the Son of God is communicated to us. Now He is as close to us as possible and in an ontological relationship with us, which means that no matter how we ascend to God we aren't alone, but with Him and in Him. But this objective fact is corroborated with a subjective one, made known in a consciousness awakened by the Holy Spirit: We don't make this ascent by our individual powers, like an expedition where we must conquer divinity, which lies before us, passive and impersonal. As Christians, starting on the lowest step of our spiritual state, we have our consciousness sensitized by the Holy Spirit. We know that in this weary and prolonged undertaking we have a continuous relationship with Jesus Christ, Who is standing beside us, sustaining our steps; but we also know that He is ahead of us, as an example, calling us to Him, to a fuller communion with Him. He is like a good friend, better than you are in every way, who is also beside you as you journey toward moral perfection, a friend who is also ahead of you, always prompting you to go on. Where Jesus Christ is absent, where the divinity is considered an absolute transcendence, it can have no personal face in the eyes of its adherents. It is conceived according to the hidden powers of nature. An approach to the divinity is attempted by way of the occult, but this way is totally human; these forces don't have a personal initiative and the capacity to give living help, by entering into personal communion.

We said that Jesus Christ is from the beginning "the Way" for the ascent to God, even in the phase of ascetical endeavors, when it seems to us that we are predominantly occupied with ourselves.

This truth is sustained in the spiritual writings of the Eastern Orthodox Church by the affirmation that the Lord first gives Himself to us by commands.⁵³ "The Lord is hidden in His commands and they that see Him find Him in the measure in which they carry them out," says St. Mark the Ascetic.⁵⁴ Origen first had this idea, and Maximus the Confessor developed it later. It means that he who wants to start out toward God must first take hold of the rope of the commandments which Jesus Christ offers us. If the person of Jesus Christ, as a model of perfection, is presented to us as a synthesis of the divine commandments fulfilled, if we too obey them we will also reach the likeness and the union with Him. Of course the presence of Jesus in the commandments doesn't have the attraction which He has in His personal, revealed form, as a synthesis realized in the commandments, or as when we see Him after we have gone through the phase of fulfilling them. Origen writes:

> He doesn't appear to the multitude in the same way as He does to those who can follow Him to the mountain peak. For those who are still below, the Word has neither image, nor beauty.... But for those who have received the power to also follow Him to the mountain peak He has a more divine form.⁵⁵

And St. Maximus presents the same idea in this way:

> The Lord doesn't appear to all in the same way. To beginners He appears in the form of a servant; to those who can climb the Mount of the Transfiguration, He has the image 'which He had before the world was.'⁵⁶

The first appearance hides His true glory. It is only the "symbol" of the other.

The first is for beginners, the second for the perfect. The first is according to the likeness of the first coming, in letter and in fact, the

---

[53] When the author uses the word commandment or command, he isn't referring only to certain ancient, revealed precepts, but also to the moment by moment guidance of the Lord, through our enlightened conscience and day to day happenings. Further on in this chapter he says: "The Lord hasn't only given us commandments once and forever, but He gives them every moment." And in his *Dogmatics* he writes: "Each believer knows God by the providential action which leads him in the particular circumstances of his life; sometimes God grants him blessings, other times he is deprived of them as a matter of discipline" 1 [in Romanian] Bucharest, 1978, p. 140. *trs*
[54] *On the Spiritual Law* 190, *PG* 65.905-30. See also *Phi* 1, p. 123.
[55] *Against Celsius* 4, p. 16. Quoted by Hans Urs von Balthasar in *Die gnostischen Centurien des Maximus the Confessor,* Freiburger Theologische Studien 61 (Freiburger im Breisgau, 1941), p. 43. Fr. Staniloae is paraphrasing and condensing here. The reader will find the passage in the ANF 4, p. 503. *trs*
[56] von Balthasar, p. 42.

second is the representation of the second coming, in spirit and knowledge.[57]

But as we have said, the Lord is hidden in His commands and in the effort to gain the virtues, not only as a norm, as a model divided into principles of right behavior,[58] but also as a personal power which is working in them, because only a superior person can command. Commands, somehow, also have an attraction and he who takes them to heart feels His helping attention constantly directed to him, because the Lord hasn't given us commands once and forever, but He gives them every moment. So in the effort of the person to obey them, he finds His help:

> The one who is perfected in virtue and in the patience of trials has in himself the working or the effective force of the first coming of Christ; while the one who has reached the angelic state of knowledge has the dispassion of the second coming working in him.[59]

St. Maximus even goes so far that he remarks: "The nature of virtues in each person is the unique Word of God, because the nature of all virtues is our Lord Jesus Christ Himself."[60] In the commandments that He gives He speaks personally to our conscience.

The Lord offers Himself to us through commandments, outside of us we might say, hidden but present in these analytical traits of His image; in the virtues which show the strong effect on us of the commandments and the progress in this living synthesis between us and them, the Lord is also manifested with us. In the commandments, taken by themselves, the Lord is hidden as an attracting, personal power, in the effort to carry them out through the virtues as a personal, active, power. From Baptism the Lord is concealed in the innermost sanctuary of our being, stimulating us to carry out the commandments, by imprinting the traits of the Lord on our spiritual face. So they gradually become clearer under the impetus of His commanding force, which works from the inside out, which is nothing else than Jesus Christ, the one dwelling deeply within us, unnoticed at the beginning in a perceptible way. By our virtues the presence of Christ is thus made even more

---

[57] *Ibid.,* p 41.
[58] Probably Fr. Staniloae is referring here to a moral theology which views the virtues "as certain unrelated states." See the first paragraph of the Introduction. *trs*
[59] von Balthasar, p. 41.
[60] *Ambigua liber, a discussion of disputed texts in the works of St. Gregory of Nazianzus*, [in Greek], *PG* 91.1081. The idea that by action, in discovering the reasons of things, the *logoi,* we discover God Himself, is developed in the following way by Blondel: "God, as we might say, himself visits his work, penetrates the place where the workers are toiling at the same time for themselves and for Him." Blondel, *L'Action* vol. 1, pp. 201-4.

obvious within us, manifesting itself even brighter in our exterior conduct. Notice how St. Mark the Ascetic describes it:

> This temple, that is the holy dwelling of the body and soul, also has a place on the inside of the altar screen. Jesus entered there as a forerunner, living there from the time of our baptism.[61] Therefore, O man, who was baptized in Christ, work as much as you are able and prepare yourself to receive the appearance of the One who lives within you.[62]

At the beginning Christ is, so to speak, buried in the commandments and in us, in the measure in which we are committed to them, by His power which is in us. By this collaboration we gain the virtues as living traits; they reflect the image of the Lord, and Christ is raised even brighter from under these veils. So Origen and St. Maximus consider the way of the pious Christian, from the carrying out of the commandments to knowledge, as a mystical way of the Lord in us, from the descent to earth in the humble form of a servant, to the ascent on Mt. Tabor, where deification was shown in all its glory. We make the ascent by ascetical efforts to the mystical contemplation of Christ, through Christ, toward Christ. Not for a moment do we travel it alone, turning off from this "Way" and going toward another destination. The earthly life of Christ thus has a permanent up-to-dateness, being repeated with each of us, just as a teacher covers, with each of the children which he nurtures, all the phases of his teaching. Each of us is a contemporary of Christ all of his life, or better said, He makes himself a contemporary with each of us and more than a contemporary, an intimate participant in the whole trajectory of our life, imprinting Himself spiritually in each of us.

We have said that it is really Christ who becomes a contemporary with us, because the life of each of us has its uniqueness, which it doesn't lose. Jesus takes part in all our sufferings, making them easier. He helps us with our struggle against temptations and sin; He strives with us in our quest for virtues: He uncovers our true nature from under the leaves of sin. St. Maximus comments:

> Until the end of the world He always suffers with us, secretly, because of His goodness according to [and in proportion to] the suffering found in each one.[63]

We know that an inter-communication exists from person to person; it's a fact that according to the extent that they bear them, the burdens,

---

[61] *On Baptism* 1, *PG* 65.996C.
[62] *Ibid.*, 5, *PG* 65.1005B.
[63] *Mystagogy* 24, *PG* 91.713. Compare the same passage in *Maximus Confessor, Selected writings,* Classics of Western Spirituality (Mahwah, NJ, 1985), p. 212.

pains and joys of others pass from one to another in a mystical way. It's a fact that one can feel all the moods of others, receiving them into himself, or penetrating them. A person, by the sensitivity of love, is able to know and to understand his neighbor, and can be burdened with the living of all his experiences. How much more can Jesus do this, the loftiest man, the man perfect in love, for His neighbor. He is one who has a perfect freedom from sin, therefore from egotism and indifference. This gives Him a unique sensitivity. He is close to everyone; He comprehends with supreme subtlety what is in everyone, and also takes part generously and without sin in the beating of every heart. He shares everyone's fondest hopes and his struggles against evil and He strengthens him.

St. Maximus the Confessor remarks that He looks after "all who want to be saved, everyday, that He might win them."[64]

Christ penetrates us by the holy mysteries, by the washing of Baptism, by the anointing with holy Chrism and by the partaking of Him from the Holy Table. By the medium of these holy mysteries, "Christ comes to us and dwells in us; He is united to us and grows into one with us. He stifles sin in us and infuses into us His own life and merit...."[65]

Certainly, we must work together with Christ who dwells in us through the holy mysteries; otherwise we aren't saved. But the basis for the possibility of our cooperation is arranged on high; it is the grace of Christ. "The one is entirely His work, the other involves striving on our part."[66] Or "... the baptismal washing is the beginning of life, its foundation and presupposition."[67] In Baptism our first "union" with Christ takes place but it is a "union" which must prepare us for the full union in the Eucharist, because the bride (the soul) is purified and washed for the nuptial union with the Groom, in the Eucharist.[68]

Christ dwells in us from Baptism. So He guides with power not only our striving for adorning ourselves with the virtues, not only the positive work of fortifying by the will the new man in Christ. He also guides the negative work of the slaying of sin, of the weakening, also by the will, of the old man: The new man in Christ doesn't grow and expand in

---

[64] The author has given a reference here (*PG* 90.77), which contains some general information about Maximus, but not the quotation. *trs*
[65] Nicholas Cabasilas, *The Life in Christ* 1.11, p. 60.
[66] *Ibid.*, 1.5, p. 48.
[67] *Ibid.*, 2.2, p. 67. Or "The bath of baptism does nothing else than awaken these feelings and powers in those who are washed." [The *trs* were unable to locate this last passage.]
[68] Jean Daniélou, "Le Symbolisme des rites baptismaux", *Dieu vivant* 1:31. "The mystery of the incorporation into Christ, the mystery of the return to Paradise, baptism is also the mystery of the marriage of the soul and of its divine Bridegroom, the mystery of union. It is necessary that the soul be purified and washed before being able to unite with its divine Bridegroom."

us except in the measure in which the old man gives way and shrinks in us. The meaning of Baptism, as participation in the death and Resurrection of the Lord by the one who is baptized, is manifested in the nourishing with the power of this spiritual process. The mystery of Baptism isn't only a momentary realization of a mystical death and resurrection by the one who is baptized; it is also the inauguration of a process in which this death and resurrection continue until perfection. This death is again the negative aspect of asceticism. It is the struggle against the old man of sin; the resurrection is the positive aspect. It is the raising of the new man of the virtues. Death is joined with suffering. We stifle and cut away from us a kind of life which has become our own. But then we realize that the Lord too died suffering and by our suffering we too take part in what He suffered. In this sense asceticism is our participation in the death and Resurrection of the Lord, in the continuation and actualization of Baptism, by our personal efforts. Christ as the source of the power which sustains the effort of asceticism, is the force, the "nature," both of the virtues, as the positive side of asceticism, as well as of the struggle against the old man, of sin.

Christ directs the work of the slaying of the old man of sin in us, not only by the power which He gives us, from the inside out, to fight willingly against sinful habits, but also by troubles and afflictions of every kind which He permits to come to us. If we accept these troubles, they gradually purify us; if we revolt, they sink us deeper in sin. Christ is the one who gives us the power to endure them, to suffer afflictions. In this sense, He participates with us in our sufferings, and in this sense too He is humbled with us, burying Himself in a kenosis, an emptying, in a death which He repeats in each of our lives. It is the death which, at the same time, is an exaltation.

Orthodox spirituality has a Christocentric character and this Christocentrism is accentuated by the role of the mysteries as the means whereby Christ dwells in man. So it is the source of indispensable divine power for ascetical efforts and for the living of the mystical life with Christ. It follows that Orthodox spirituality also has a pneumatological-ecclesiastical[69] character. Because where Christ is through the mysteries, there is the Church full of the Spirit in Him, or only the Church imparts Christ, as His Body, by means of the mysteries. Someone can't become or remain a limb, a member of Christ, unless he is integrated into and becomes a part of His mystical Body, as a well arranged assembly of many members. Faith, as the power of spiritual growth, comes into man from Christ, but through the Church, or through His Body, full of the

---

[69] A character marked by the Spirit and the Church. *trs*

Spirit of communion. A man's faith grows from that of the church community, in which Christ is the worker by His Spirit. By Baptism, man enters into a relationship with Christ, but also in the atmosphere of faith which, as a divine power, inspires the church community. Not stimulated and inspired continually by the faith of the church community, no one can be in a condition to stay in the faith, to grow in it and share its fruits. If someone progresses in the virtues which grow from faith and culminate in love, it means that he shows his working love to his neighbors and that he strives for the growth of the same faith in them; it means that he grows in communion with everyone, in Christ, by the Spirit. But this is the same as working for the strengthening of the Church, by taking a responsibility for it.

This is the responsibility which the Savior also had in mind, when He gave the hierarchical character to His Church. Dionysius the Areopagite tied the spiritual progress of the members of the Church to the hierarchy and he also saw their purpose in the sustaining of this progress. Of course, this responsibility would have no place if there didn't exist a gradation in the very arrangement of things. A hierarchy of spiritual blessings exists first and foremost, and only because some reach the upper steps before others, are they responsible to also help those on the lower steps to climb higher. "As our venerable tradition shows us, the hierarchy is made up of everything contemplated and spoken everywhere about holy things," states George Pachymeris, commenting on a passage from Dionysius the Areopagite.[70]

Those on the highest step of spiritual blessings didn't get there just by themselves, because then anybody could reach it, on principle, by themselves. There would no longer be necessary a hierarchy between people either, but only between material things. So hierarchy also means a relationship between the steps by the help which [those on] the higher ones must give to the lower and by the dependence of the lower on the higher. It follows that those on the highest step in the Church have gotten there with help from the angels, subjects higher than we are. This puts the purpose of angels in a new light; they have therefore a responsibility for people, their neighbors in creation. Angels too are arranged on the nine steps. The Cherubim are on the highest step; they are in the most intimate nearness to God. They receive the light direct from Him and can no longer advance to a higher one. This limitation of the highest step implicates a limitation of all the angelic steps in the sense that the passing from a lower to a higher no longer takes place, but all progress

---

[70] Dionysius the Areopagite, *The Ecclesiastical Hierarchy* 1.3. The commentary by George Pachymeris 1.3, *PG* 3.386.

eternally in knowledge. In regard to the angels there is no longer a question of some falling, nor of some getting ahead of others, because there is no longer sin. They are all consolidated in good.

Nevertheless, each step receives deifying light through the higher and in this sense needs the higher steps.[71] Otherwise they are fixed forever on their steps. This is perhaps their "rest," although this rest doesn't mean that they cease to eternally enjoy the reception of divine light and the continual contemplation of the infinite depths of God. They are stabilized in good, but they also progress in it. This means that they are in an "ever ennobling rest" of their spirit, or in a circular movement exclusively around the divine being, which our spirit too will attain in the future life. The faithful, in contrast to the angels, also go up from one step to another and because they have fallen into sin, the ascent means the gradual annulment of the effects of sin as well as the perfection of their nature by the fullest participation possible in God.

In the service of this spiritual progress stands the hierarchy of subjects, because only they are capable of helping each other through love. Thus the hierarchy is essential to the Church. (The heavenly hierarchy also belongs to the Church in a certain way and sustains the ascending movement of the Church hierarchy.) Man's ascent is realized with its help, and within its framework, in the Church. The ultimate goal of the entire hierarchy is the deification of those who are saved:

> Now deification is likeness to, and union with God, in so far as possible, [or] the unbounded love of God, worked in all in a unitary and divine way, and before this, the total and unregrettable forsaking of all that is contrary; it is the knowledge of created things as creatures, the seeing and the knowledge of the holy truth, the deified, perfect, and unitary participation in the Very One, in as much as possible, the taste of the vision which spiritually nourishes and deifies completely the one who seeks it.[72]

The work of the ecclesiastical hierarchy is singular but it is realized in degrees: It is "the cleansing of the imperfect, the illumination of the

---

[71] Dionysius doesn't speak only of an illumination and a perfection even of the lower angelic ranks by the higher, but also of their purification, even of a purification, illumination and perfection of the first rank above, by Christ. The purification is a cleansing from a certain ignorance *(nestiinta)*; the illumination is the participation in a higher knowledge, while perfection is the higher transformation by means of this knowledge. *The Celestial Hierarchy* 7. *The Celestial and Ecclesiastical Hierarchy of Dionysius the Areopagite,* trans. by John Parker (London, 1894), p. 30.
[72] *The Ecclesiastical Hierarchy* 1, *op. cit.*, p. 52.

cleansed and the perfecting of those initiated in the science of their initiation."[73]

The work of the hierarchy for [the salvation of] the faithful is essentially exercised through the holy mysteries, especially through Baptism, Chrismation and the Eucharist. While the angels as "pure mind" receive the divine things in an open way, we receive them in "perceptible images"[74] or in "symbols" by which we mean perceptible words, gestures and materials, which not only signify but also contain in a nonunderstandable way certain spiritual realities. These veils more or less cover the *logoi* of the mysteries. The perceptible forms of the mysteries don't hinder the perfect from contemplating and feeling their spiritual content, while for the imperfect, they are wisely adapted to their condition.

The vision of Dionysius the Areopagite propounded by him in the teaching of the hierarchies, is a liturgical vision. It demonstrates the need for a hierarchical church structure for the spiritual progress of the faithful.

But the hierarchy of the three grades,[75] to whom the guidance of the faithful has been entrusted, is completed by a kind of hierarchy of another, unofficial order. In as much as some believers are found on a higher step of participation in the divine blessings, the responsibility for others makes them help [those on the lower steps] to go up. It is the hierarchy of holiness, which doesn't slight nor hinder the work of the hierarchy based on the performance of the mysteries and prescribed by the visible organization of the Church.

The Christians found on the higher steps of holiness continue to draw their spiritual power from the holy mysteries. So they stand in dutiful dependence on the hierarchy entrusted with the celebration of the mysteries. Those who use the power of grace for their cleansing from passions and for the gaining of virtues, also gain various graces, as the lives of the saints and of the spiritual faithful show us. Thus the three steps of lay people (catechumens, faithful, and monastics) is completed with a much more supple variety of spiritual states of its members. Catechumens don't exist today,[76] and penitents no longer constitute a separate class; so deacons no longer reserve a category for them, that is for those who are being purified. Neither can the faithful be considered

---

[73] *Ibid.,* 5.1, p. 79.
[74] *Ibid.,* 1, p. 51.
[75] Bishops, priests, and deacons.
[76] Not in an official way but they still do in small numbers. There are always some who come and want to be members of the Orthodox Church. They go through a period of instruction and are thus catechumens, or listeners, for a time, before being admitted to the Church. *trs*

as all being exclusively on the step of illumination, neither monastics on that of perfection. Many of the faithful are still in the phase of purification and so too many monastics are still on the two lower steps. On the other hand, neither does purification, illumination and perfection in the radical sense of the word excuse those on these steps from the need for partaking of the holy mysteries.

So in the Church there is a more supple hierarchy, of an inner and unofficial order, a hierarchy based exclusively on holiness. But it too needs the mysteries and is dependent on the visible hierarchy, entrusted with the serving of the mysteries. No matter which step of holiness a believer is on, during the course of his earthly life he continues to be dependent on the official hierarchical order of the Church and needs to partake of the holy mysteries. Of course for him who is on a higher step of holiness, the mysteries are more revealed. He sees more of their content. He profits more from them. The material covering has become so to speak non-existent for him; but he continues to receive them, because the spiritual content of the mysteries is fed from the infinite content of divine life, and as such, is a necessary source of spiritual life for anyone.

The angelic liturgy seen in Church painting tells us that the Eucharist, even unseen, is still the Eucharist, as communion, "truer," fuller of the Body and Blood of Him who sacrificed Himself for the world. The divine graces imparted through the holy mysteries aren't, however, mixed together and therefore, even when the coverings of the mysteries are more transparent for some, these people nevertheless need special graces, according to their level, which constitute the essence of some specific mysteries. There is a hierarchy of graces, starting with the grace of Baptism and continuing to the graces partaken of by the Cherubim and the Seraphim. Even the Christian who moves on to heaven stays in the Church, in the heavenly part of the Church, somewhere, on a step of unending graces.

As long as he is on earth he must be in the Church if he wants to progress in the living of the union with God; and not only because he must stay in the hierarchical-sacramental structure of the Church on earth. He must also progress in the direction of the heavenly hierarchy of the angels, toward the Church of the saints in heaven. They haven't lost contact with the Church on earth, but maintain a necessary relationship with it. Because, in any case, a person doesn't reach the level of the pure contemplation of God if he hasn't been purified by the mystery of Baptism, for example. He must bring with him the results, the signs of the visible mystery of Baptism from the Church on earth.

The spiritual ascent, even if it carries someone close to God in Heaven, is an ascent within the Church, on the spiritual steps of the

CHRIST, SPIRIT, CHURCH   67

Church on earth, and on those of the Church in Heaven. There is no other ladder to God, except the one in the Church: All along this ladder, the grace of Christ, full of attraction, is extended. Here is "the Way," the power of Christ. And this is because at the top of this ladder and only there, as the peak of the entire hierarchy, Christ is found.[77]

In this way the "churchly" character of the spiritual life is identified with its Christocentric character. Even those who have risen to the state of "a pure mind" and of "contemplation" without symbols haven't left the hierarchical framework of the Church in a broad sense and haven't surpassed Christ, because He is the all-divine mind and beyond being. He stands at the peak of any hierarchy as an attracting force for anyone who is ascending its steps.

At first glance it would seems that the multitude of ecclesiastical, angelic, and hierarchical steps which Dionysius the Areopagite presents as the means of the divine light, would make the believer's direct communication with Christ impossible. If we look closer, however, we see that the power which works on all the hierarchical steps is the divine grace of Jesus Christ; or it is He Himself penetrating by His hierarchical organs and performing through them the mysteries served by them.[78] If created persons can be "within one another" how much more can Christ be in all.

The hierarchical steps don't replace Him; at the beginning we aren't able to see Him, and to understand Him openly, without the intermediary of symbols and without the explanations which the hierarchical steps give us. He takes into account this weakness of ours and communicates Himself to us through them. But according to the measure in which we progress with the help of the church hierarchy and of the angels, we too see God and feel Him with greater certainty; we come closer and closer to the light revealed by Him: We are deified:

> Jesus Himself— the supremely Divine and super-essential Mind, the Head and Being, and most supremely Divine Power of every Hierarchy and Sanctification and Divine operation— illuminates the blessed Beings who are superior to us, in a manner more clear, and at the same time more fresh, and assimilates them to His own Light in proportion to their ability to receive. As for ourselves, by the love of things beautiful, elevated to Himself, and elevating us, He folds together our many diversities, and by making them into an unified and Divine life, suitable to a sacred vocation both as to habit and action, He Himself bequeaths the power of the Divine Priesthood,

---

[77] "Now the power of the Hierarchical order permeates the whole sacred body and through every one of the sacred Orders performs the mysteries." *Ibid.*, 5.1, p. 80.
[78] "We see all the hierarchy terminating in Jesus." *Ibid.*

from which, by approaching the holy exercise of the priestly office, we become nearer to the Beings above us, by assimilation, according to our power, to the stability and unchangeableness of their steadfastness in holy things. Hence, by looking upwards to the blessed and supremely Divine Glory of Jesus, and reverently gazing upon whatever we are permitted to see, and being illuminated with the knowledge of the visions, we shall be able to become, as regards the science of Divine mysteries, both purified and purifying-images of Light, and workers with God, perfected and perfecting.[79]

---

[79] *Ibid.*, 1.1, p. 50.

6. The Major Steps of the Spiritual Life

To divide the spiritual life in a specific way, we must orient ourselves according to the holy Fathers and spiritual writers of the East.

The simplest way is to separate it into the active or practical phase and the contemplative phase. The practical phase, that of doing things, is intended to raise the believer's nature from the state subject to the passions and to elevate it to and by, the steps of the virtues, until it reaches love.[80] The contemplative phase represents its reintegration, unity, and simplicity, and its exclusive focus on God, the One and Infinite. The man in the practical phase is called *praktikos* (worker, doer), the one in the contemplative, *theoretikos* (seer). Many times instead of "contemplation" or "contemplative," the Fathers use the terms "knowledge" and "knower" *(gnosis, gnostic)*.

The purpose of the active phase is the liberation of man from the passions *(apatheia)*. For the monk this is an accessible goal, not a utopian ideal. This state of dispassion is considered equal with, or better said, the doorstep to, the love of God. This spiritual love is the passing from the active phase into the contemplative.[81]

Only he who has cleansed his mind through dispassion can go on to knowledge *(gnosa)*, or contemplation. The uncleansed too can get book learning, but only the cleansed have contemplation.[82] And purity or dispassion we gain only by carrying out the commands,[83] which is the preoccupation of the active phase. Only a clean soul is a shiny mirror, unspotted by passionate attachment to the things of the world, capable of receiving divine knowledge. This mind is empty *(gymnos nous)*. It alone is in the state of contemplation, of essential knowledge.[84] Once the soul has reached this state of dispassion, or cleansing, or quiet, or peace, or tranquility,[85] it is raised to the step of contemplation or of *gnosis*. But the holy Fathers strictly distinguish this *gnosis* or contemplation, from the spiritual knowledge of the world aided by divine grace, which itself is distinguished from profane knowledge.

---

[80] Evagrius Ponticus, *The Praktikos* 81: "Apatheia is the flowering of doing." See also The *Praktikos, Chapters on Prayer* (Kalamazoo, MI, 1978), p. 36, and W. Frankenberg, *Evagrios Pontikos*, (Berlin, 1912). For a more general treatment see W. Bousset, "Evagrios-Studien," in *Apophtegmata Patrum* (Tübingen, 1923), pp. 281-341.
[81] *The Praktikos*: "Love goes before the practical.... Dispassion leads to love, and love to knowledge." [The reference wasn't located by the translators.]
[82] Evagrius, *Kephalaia Gnostica* [*Chapters on Knowledge*] 4.90, in Frankenberg, p. 317.
[83] *Ibid.*, 34, p. 285.
[84] *Ibid.*, 3.70, p. 237.
[85] *Ibid.*, 7.3, p. 427.

Thus the twofold division of the spiritual life becomes threefold: 1) the active phase or that of doing; 2) the phase of the contemplation of nature,[86] and 3) the theological phase or the mystical contemplation of God.

It's important that in this scheme—which describes the progress of perfection—the knowledge of nature, of creation in its fullness, be absorbed. The acceptance of the pure contemplation of nature as an act of spirituality, is specific to the Eastern Fathers.

> Because the fall of the creature means a descent from unity with God and from the bliss of contemplating Him... the human spirit has the mission to gradually ascend, from the lower spheres, to the knowledge of the Monad[87] and of the Trinity, from ignorance, to knowledge. Then the contemplation of nature, with eternity in mind, enters into the process of the salvation of the pious.[88]

The pure contemplation of nature is a step which remakes and which proves the remaking of the human soul's perceptive powers.

This scheme has even more ramifications. Within the contemplation of nature "the contemplation of bodies" and of the "bodiless beings," or of the angels, is distinguished. So we have three steps of knowledge: of the corporeal world, of the incorporeal world, and of the Holy Trinity.[89]

St. Maximus the Confessor makes this order of the spiritual ascent very clear. He too first divides the ascent into two steps. The spiritual person is raised from virtue to knowledge,[90] (or from doing to contemplation,[91] or from active philosophy to contemplative theology,[92] or to contemplative mystagogy.)[93] Later he makes a division into three steps: doing, followed by the contemplation of the *logoi* in creation, then of God.

In this threefold division the steps are called: 1) doing, 2) natural contemplation or moral philosophy[94] and 3) mystical theology.[95]

---

[86] By natural contemplation we don't understand contemplation by the exclusively natural powers of the soul. The term "natural" is taken not from the state of the soul of the knower, but from the object of knowledge, from created nature; it means the contemplation of nature.
[87] *To en* (the one) or *monas* (a unit), Unity itself, that is, God.
[88] Bousset, p. 310.
[89] Evagrius, *Kephalaia Gnostica* 1.14, (Frankenberg,) See also 2.4; 3.61.
[90] *Ambigua*, PG 91.1144C; *Questions to Thalassios* 50, PG 90.469C.
[91] *Chapters on Knowledge. Two Hundred Chapters on Theology and the Economy in the Flesh of the Son of God* 2.51. In *Maximus Confessor, Selected writings*, p. 158.
[92] *Questions to Thalassios* 10, PG 90.288CD.
[93] *Ibid.*, 25, PG 90.332A.
[94] *Ibid.*, 329AC; *Ambigua*, PG 91.1413C.
[95] *Ambigua*, PG 91.1197C; *Questions to Thalassios* 55, PG 90.556A.

THE MAJOR STEPS OF THE SPIRITUAL LIFE

These three steps are also called: doing, natural contemplation, and theological mystagogy,[96] (or the active phase, the contemplative phase, and theological grace,[97] or virtue, spiritual contemplation, and pure prayer.)[98]

Because the contemplation of creation can refer either to the visible world or to the invisible, St. Maximus sometimes uses a division of four steps.[99]

Of the three steps, the first is that of beginners, who must strive to become proficient in the virtues. The virtues are seven in number. At the beginning stands faith; at the end love, immediately preceded by dispassion.[100] Love concentrates all the virtues in it[101] and carries man to knowledge or contemplation.[102]

The aim of the virtues or of the strivings of the first step is liberation from the passions or dispassion.[103] The virtues combat the passions and thus indirectly serve the spirit; they are a step toward the final goal which is knowledge.[104]

The third step is called contemplation, although St. Maximus, as we have seen, doesn't use this word in only one way, but gives it several meanings, according to the object it refers to. In general, however, this object is almost always a creature. Only rarely, and namely when he divides the spiritual ascent into two steps and not three, does St. Maximus also mean by it mystical contemplation, which is directed to God in a non-mediated way. When, however, he divides this ascent into three steps, and contemplation constitutes the second step, it almost always means contemplation oriented toward created things or phenomena (*fapturi*). In this sense, contemplation has as its object "the *logoi*" in phenomena.[105] By it, man gains a spiritual look at the *logoi* of created things; by it nature is a teacher, a guide to God.

---

[96] *Chapters on Knowledge* 2.95, *Maximus Confessor, Selected writings*, pp. 168-9.
[97] *Chapters on Love* 2.26, *Phi* 2, p. 69.
[98] *Ibid.*, 3.44, p. 90.
[99] *Ibid.*, 1.94, p. 64.
[100] *Ibid.*, 1.1-2, p. 53.
[101] *Questions to Thalassios* 40, *PG* 90.397B; 54, *PG* 90.516A.
[102] *Chapters on Love* 1.1, *Phi* 2, p.53.
[103] *Ibid.*, 2.16, p. 67; *Questions to Thalassios* 55, *PG* 90.541B; *Chapters on Love* 2.34, *Phi* 2, p. 71; *Chapters on Knowledge* 1.32, *Maximus Confessor, Selected writings*, p. 134.
[104] For this exposition I consulted Joseph Lossen, *Logos und Pneuma im begnadeten Menschen bei Maximus Confessor* (Münster, 1941), p. 8 *ff.*
[105] *Questions to Thalassios*, the Introduction, *PG* 90.252AB: *"Tous gegonoton logous, tous ton onton logous"* [the logoi of things, the logoi of beings]; *Questions to Thalassios* 25, *PG* 90.333B.

The third step, mystical knowledge, no longer is concerned with the reasons of things (inner qualities, or *logoi*), but with God Himself.[106] The object is all holy and all blessed deification, supra-ineffable, supra-unknowable, and above all infinity.[107] This knowledge of God is an ecstasy of love, which persists unmoved in a concentration on God.[108] It is reached in the state of the deification of man, or of his union with God.[109]

In content these three steps correspond with the phases of purification, illumination and perfection, which as we have seen, Dionysius the Areopagite used to describe the spiritual ascent of man: On the one hand, the active phase seeks the cleansing from the passions, while on the other the phase of perfection according to Dionysius is also the same as the phase of deification or mystical knowledge. We will also use this division in our exposition.

The step of purification belongs, category wise, to ascetical striving, while that of perfection or of contemplation, or of deification and union, represents the goal of these strivings. The step of illumination is hard to place between these two.

Nevertheless, instead of dividing this study into two parts, that is into purification and the mystical knowledge of God, we will divide it into three, according to the three steps: First, the step of illumination belongs to knowledge; by it the soul has reached the knowledge of God, other than the natural. This is a knowledge by the divine *logoi* of things, but no less one clearly and firmly connected to God. Next, this step is no longer a struggle with the passions, but something positive, which crowns the ascetical striving. It also resembles in this respect the culminating phase of the spiritual life. Secondly, however, the step of illumination also belongs to the way to the final goal; the knowledge on this step also is one directed toward creation and as such must be surpassed, in order to reach the final goal of the direct knowledge of God. True, it is a positive result, obtained with the liberation from everything that is evil, but neither is it definitive, because although good, it isn't the absolute good, sought by ascetical efforts, but a good which itself must be surpassed. We could say then, that the step of illumination also belongs to the ascetical ascent and its aim; or that on this step mystical knowledge meets asceticism, or that understanding encounters the effort

---

[106] *Chapters on Love* 2.26-7, *Phi* 2, p. 69.
[107] *Ambigua, PG* 91.1168A.
[108] *Chapters on Love* 1.39, *Phi* 2, p. 56.
[109] *Chapters on Knowledge* 1.54, *Maximus Confessor, Selected writings*, pp. 137-8; *Ambigua, PG* 91.1241C; *Questions to Thalassios* 63, *PG* 90.673CD; 40, *PG* 90.400CD.

THE MAJOR STEPS OF THE SPIRITUAL LIFE 73

to surpass it. It's the morning star along with the first light of day; the latter by its eventual brightness will replace the former.

But now let's follow in detail the ramifications of the three steps. In as much as the first step has as its preoccupation the liberation from the passions and their replacement with the virtues, it's necessary to first know the nature of the passions— how they are born and grow. Next we much research the way in which they are gradually overcome by the practice of the seven virtues in the order developed by St. Maximus the Confessor: faith, the fear of God, self-restraint, patience, hope, dispassion, and love which are connected with fasting, vigil, prayer, pious reading, and the endurance of troubles, as the means of gaining them.

In the second part, which is concerned with the knowledge of God through creatures, as the fruit of dispassion and love, we will analyze the nature of this knowledge, its connection with dispassion and with love, and with rational and mystical knowledge.

And in part three, we will present the direct knowledge of God by union with Him, which has the effect of deifying the human nature of the faithful.

PART ONE
PURIFICATION

PART ONE

PURIFICATION

A. The Passions

7. The Essence of the Passions

The passions represent the lowest level to which human nature can fall. Both their Greek name, *pathi,* as well as the Latin, *passiones,* show that man is brought by them to a state of passivity, of slavery. In fact, they overcome the will, so that the man of the passions is no longer a man of will; we say that he is a man ruled, enslaved, carried along by the passions.

Another characteristic of the passions is that in them an unquenchable thirst is manifested, which seeks to be quenched and can't be. Blondel says that they represent man's thirst for the infinite, turned in a direction in which they can't find their satisfaction.[1] Dostoevsky has a similar idea.[2]

Neilos the Ascetic writes that the stomach, by gluttony, becomes a sea impossible to fill—a good description of any passion.[3] This always

---

[1] "Hence human needs and appetites, as analogous as they are to those of the brute, differ from them profoundly. The animal has no passion; what is animal in man, on the contrary, lays claim to all that reason and will require, an infinite satisfaction. Human sensuality is insatiable and unreasonable only because it is shot through with a force alien to and higher than the senses; and this reason immanent to passion itself acquires such ascendancy that it can take the place of reasonable reason (*la raison raisonable*), that it confiscates its infinite aspirations and that it usurps the inexhaustible resources of thought." Maurice Blondel, *Action* (Notre Dame, IN: University Press), 1984, p. 193. (Note: This quote was taken by the translators from the English translation based on Blondel's original work entitled *L'Action*, published in 1893. Blondel later published, in 1936, a second work also titled *L'Action*. This two-volume work was written in 'the context of a systematic trilogy on thought, being and action' and is substantially different from the 1893 publication. Fr Stanlioae took all of his quotations from the 1936 work. *trs*)

[2] "All evil," says S. L. Frank, "which in Dostoevsky always has a spiritual origin: arrogance, vainglory, vindictiveness, cruelty, hatred, pleasure itself, for him comes from the aspiration of the soul to fight against suffocated and humbled holiness, or of imposing and of affirming its rights, even in an insane and perverse way." *Die Krise des Humanismus, eine Betrachtrung aus der sicht Dostoevschys,* Hochland, 28 Jahrgang, Heft 10, p. 295; cited by L. Binswanger, *Grundformen und Erkenntnis menschlichen Daseins* (Zurich, 1942), p. 580, note 12. In the same place Binswanger also gives the following quotation from S. L. Frank: "Faith persists in the fallen, degenerated, perverted person, too, yes, even in his fallen condition one can still see the features of his likeness with God; see the unique and nevertheless corresponding trait of the nature of Christianity, of Dostoevsky's conception of man."

[3] The nature which has become the slave of passion "...sends to the stomach through the deep canal dug by gluttony food prepared for it, as into a sea which can't be filled." Neilos applies the words of Solomon to the stomach: "Into the sea all the rivers go, and yet the sea is never filled" (Ecclesiastes 1:7), "for the stomach and the sea are alike: They absorb the rivers that pour

unsatisfied infinity is due both to the passion in itself, as well as to the object with which it seeks satisfaction. The objects which the passions look for can't satisfy them because objects are finite and as such don't correspond to the unlimited thirst of the passions. Or as St. Maximus puts it, the passionate person finds himself in a continuous preoccupation with nothing; he tries to appease his infinite thirst with the nothingness of his passions, and the objects which he is gobbling up become nothing, by their very nature. In fact, a passion by its very nature searches for objects, and it seeks them only because they can be completely under the control of the ego, and at its mercy. But objects by nature are finite, both as sources of satisfaction and in regard to duration; they pass easily into nonexistence, by consumption. Even when the passion also needs the human person in order to be satisfied, it likewise reduces him or her to an object, or sees and uses only the objective side; the unfathomable depths hidden in the subjective side escape him.

Now the infinite thirst of the passions in themselves is explained in this way: The human being has a spiritual basis and therefore a tendency toward the infinite which also is manifested in the passions; but in these passions the tendency is turned from the authentic infinite which is of a spiritual order, toward the world, which only gives an illusion of the infinite.[4] Man, without being himself infinite, not only is fit, but is also thirsty for the infinite and precisely for this reason is also capable of, and longs for, God, the true and only infinite (*homo capax divini*— man capable of the divine). He has a capacity and is thirsty for the infinite not in the sense that he is in a state to win it, to absorb it in his nature— because then human nature itself would become infinite— but in the sense that he can and must be nourished spiritually from the infinite, and infinitely. He seeks and is able to live in a continual communication with it, in a sharing with it. But man didn't want to be satisfied with this sharing in the infinite; he wanted to become himself the center of the infinite, or he believed that he is such a center; he let himself be tricked by his nature's thirst for the infinite.

The human being then, didn't understand that the infinite thirst of his nature isn't an indication of the infinity of that nature, because the true infinite can't be thirst. It's only a sign of its capacity to communi-

---

into them without being filled; the one consumes by digestion, the other by saltiness, the things that empty into them; they are never full and never shut their mouths." *Peristeria* 4, *PG* 79.821.

[4] "Evil is the irrational movement of the spiritual faculties toward something else than toward their final goal, because of a mistaken judgment. Now the final goal I call the Cause of things, toward which all things move in a natural way, even if evil, covering its envy under the image of goodness, by cunning persuades man to turn his longing toward something else than the Cause of all things, creating in him the ignorance of the Cause." St. Maximus, *Questions to Thalassios*, The Introduction, *PG* 90.253.

cate with the infinite, which isn't a property of his nature. So the human being, instead of being satisfied to remain in communication with the true infinite, and to progress in it, wanted to become himself the infinite. He tried to absorb in himself or to subordinate to himself everything that lent itself to this relation of subordination: dead objects, finite things. Instead of quenching his thirst for the infinite, he sought to gather everything around himself, as around a center. But because man isn't a true center in himself, this nature of his took revenge; it made him in reality run after things, even enslaving him to them. So passion, as a tireless chase after the world, instead of being an expression of the central sovereignty of our nature, is rather a force which carries us along against our will; it's a sign of the fall of our nature into an accentuated state of passivity. Our nature, whether it wants to or not, still has to express its tendency for a center outside of itself. By the passions, this center was moved from God to the world. Thus the passions are the product of a tortuous impulse of our nature, or of a nature which has lost its simplicity and tendency to move straight ahead. In it two tendencies meet; or there is a tendency which can't fulfill its purpose, but is turned against nature. Passion is a knot of contradictions. It's the expression of an egotism which wants to make all things gravitate around it; it's the transformation of the world exclusively into a center of preoccupation as well. Passion is a product of the will of egocentric sovereignty; it's also a force which pushes man down to the state of an object carried here and there against his will. Sometimes it seeks the infinite; other times it chooses nothingness.[5]

The spirit [of man] has no exact limits and is capable of being filled with the infinite and thirsts to receive it; yet instead of looking for the relationship with the infinite Spirit, it seeks to fill itself with finite and passing objects. So it is left with nothing and its thirst is never quenched.

Passion is something irrational. Everything in the world is rational according to St. Maximus the Confessor, with its basis in divine *logoi*; only passion is irrational. Note its supreme irrationality: The passionate man realizes more and more that finite things can't satisfy his aspiration for the infinite, and this bores and discourages him. Even so the next moment he lets himself be carried away by his egocentric passion, as if by it he is going to absorb the infinite. He doesn't realize that the true infinite is a free Spirit which can't be absorbed without His will, because

---

[5] "That which is sensible and affective in us, isn't, as in animals, good because of the instinct for the satisfaction of finite and passing necessities. Our spontaneous energies are themselves effected by the desire for infinitude; from it can come the paradoxical risk of the insatiable passions and of the irrational reason of infinitely wanting the finite." Blondel, *L'Action* vol. 2, p. 192.

He is a subject which one must freely enter into communion with. For example, the glutton knows that no kind of food is ever going to satisfy his gluttony. Likewise he who hates his neighbor, feels that this animosity can't put out the fire of hatred even if the neighbor is totally consumed by it. The logic should be that neither the glutton nor the hater should let himself be tortured by these passions. But neither one does anything about it, and continues with his irrational tortures.[6]

By their irrationality, by their deceptive character, by turning man away from his true goal, the passions keep man in the darkness of ignorance. By the struggle against the passions the human being escapes ignorance; he returns to the true infinity of God, as a goal of his life and as a liberation of his spirit from the slavery of the world and from the tyranny which the passions represent. This is the meaning of dispassion.

In early Christian spiritual literature, the passions are considered to be eight in number; when vainglory is joined with pride, seven. They are gluttony, unchastity, avarice, anger, dejection, listlessness, self-esteem and pride.[7] Basically, they coincide with the seven capital sins: gluttony, debauchery, avarice, anger, envy, sloth, and pride, if we identify envy and listlessness.

Some of the passions are of the soul, others of the spirit. But the close unity of the body and soul cause the bodily passions to be interwoven with those of the soul, or to have an inter-influence. The ascetical writers tell us that among the young, gluttony produces all the others, because it leads to unchastity— both of them need money to satisfy them, while he who finds himself lacking objects to satisfy these three passions, that is gluttony, unchastity and avarice, becomes dejected; and if someone wants to take things away from him or put their hand on them before he does, he becomes angry.[8] For older people,

---

[6] Blondel presents the contradiction of passions in this way: "On the contrary he who falls under the influence of egotism and the vainglory of rebellion doesn't in this way suppress the power of the infinite and of eternity, which constitutes his spiritual nature. If his desire to be everything and have everything for himself fails, this isn't and can't be the total loss which is talked about all the time; he's got what he wanted; and in realizing against himself this joy of self and of passing things, he didn't do anything but consecrate his isolation." *L'Action,* vol. 1, p. 245. In the same place he also writes: "In opposition to this, the ascetic puts much more energy into his action: A truly personal act of meritorious energy is necessary then to prefer the invisible reality of the eternal good to the attraction of the curiosities of immediate desire, of ambition, of independence. In this asceticism an action is used, which, negative in appearance, has within itself the maximum of power and of faith, because this confidence in that which has no perceptible charm at all, and as the psychologists would say, no dynamageny [no production of increased nervous activity], means a victory over the whole universe and over all the concupiscence of nature."

[7] John Cassian, *On the Eight Vices, Phi* 1, pp. 73-93.

[8] Evagrius, *Texts on Discrimination in Respect of Passions and Thoughts* 1: "Because it's impossible for someone to fall into the hands of the spirit of unchastity, if he hasn't been first

however, the main passion is pride. So vainglory and pride could also be an effect of gluttony and of accumulated wealth. But just the opposite could happen too: By love of glory and by pride man could seek wealth to live in luxury, which would bring him the praise of men and cause him to look down on others; or he would be dejected or angry when he isn't honored enough.

Precisely this interaction of the bodily passions, prompted by the gluttony of the stomach, and those of the soul, instigated by pride, make these same spiritual writers declare gluttony as the first passion and then later "pride as the first chick of the devil." [9]

Someone can be proud without being stuffed with food, just as there are plenty of ascetics who are proud of their asceticism. It could be said then that there is a double circuit which leads from gluttony to all the passions— including those of the soul— and again from pride, to almost all of the passions, including some of the bodily ones. Gluttony and pride represent one and the same egocentric thirst of man, under the double aspect of his psycho-physical nature. There is a close interconnection between the biological and the spiritual; one realm influences the other both in the decline and in the restoration of man. Here a vast field of research is possible on the details of the interdependence between the biological and the spiritual.

Both gluttony and pride have their root in *philautia,* egotistic love of self as an autonomous and independent absolute. "It's clear" says Maximus the Confessor, "that he who is egotistic has all the passions."[10] But egotism represents a rupture with God, as a center distinct from me, from my existence; and since man can't exist by himself, no matter how much he tries to create that illusion, egotism represents a gravitation toward the world.

Thus, since the forgetting of God is the ultimate cause of the passions, their healing must begin with faith: by a return to the most frequent remembrance of Him possible. By it, the first brake will be put on egotism. The former will be manifested in a practical way by restraint in a general way: the restraint of fleshly appetites and the restraint of pride, by humility.

The passions subordinate our spirit to the baser tendencies, but don't succeed in completely quieting it; they produce a tearing and a disorder in it and consequently, its weakening. But they don't have this effect

---

brought down by the stomach's gluttony, just as anger can't trouble the one who isn't fighting for food, possessions or glory. And it's impossible for a person to escape the spirit of dejection if he hasn't given all these things up." *GrPh* 1, p. 44; *cf. Phi* 1, p. 38.
[9] *Ibid.*
[10] *Chapters on Love* 3.8., *GrPh* 2, p. 29; *cf. Phi* 2, p. 84.

only on their subject, on one person. They also create disorder in the relations of that person with his neighbor. Many times passion extends from one individual to the life of another. One person's greed provokes that of another, as a defense mechanism. Almost any passion tries to reduce the people around it to the inferior level of objects. They try to defend themselves, and this gives birth to a struggle, which many times doesn't stop at a simple defense but goes so far as to treat the first subject of the passions as an object. The egotism and narrowness of the subject of the passions awakens, in defense and revolt, the egotism, narrowness and poverty of others. The passionate person doesn't only hurt himself, but others too. The passions have as victims their own subjects, and their neighbors as well.

Passion doesn't show its effect of weakening, of destroying and of havoc only in the passionate, but in others too. It hits them and most of the time they react in the same way. The dissolute uses other persons as objects for his pleasure; but in so doing he makes them dissolute too and they in turn try to use other persons as objects.

The proud person awakens, by imitation or by reaction, pride in others; and the relations of pride which are thus created between people are contrary to normal harmonious ones; the human community is fragmented. Its members devour each other as reptiles, as St. Maximus puts it.[11] All the passions are opposed to true love, which alone can reestablish normal harmony between men.

Thus the passions produce and maintain chaos between people. So Christ, founding the Church, seeks by it the reestablishment of human unity and conciliarity. But this isn't possible without the weakening of the passions.

One method for cleansing the passions is twofold: First, the one who is habitually their prime subject in relation to others, bridles them; secondly the latter restrain themselves from responding through their passions. They put up with and persist in loving him who is acting in a passionate way. This protects them not only from being infected by the passions, but also has a healing effect on him who wants to make them the victims of their passions. It also stops a more accentuated deterioration of the relations between the members of the human community. This is why Jesus told us not to answer evil with evil, but to love our enemies too. St. Isaac the Syrian says:

> Don't distinguish the worthy from the unworthy, but let all be equally good for you, for in this way you can also attract the unwor-

---

[11] *Second Letter to John the Valet, PG* 91.396.

THE ESSENCE OF THE PASSIONS

thy to the good.[12] [Or] force yourself, when you meet your neighbor, to honor him more than he deserves. Kiss his hands and feet and put his hands over your eyes, and praise him too for the things he doesn't have.... Love sinners and don't despise them for their sins.... By this and similar things you will bring them to the good.[13]

Just as love binds people together, so the passions destroy the ties between them. They are the fermentation of inner and interpersonal disorder. They are the thick wall put between us and God, the fog covering our nature made transparent for God.

---

[12] St. Isaac the Syrian, *Ascetical Homilies* 23, [in Greek] (Athens, 1961), pp. 86-7.
[13] *Homily* 6. This reference wasn't found in the place cited. *trs*

8. The Natural and Unnatural Passions

The birth of the passions is made possible by the existence of the natural passions: "Condemnable and unnatural passions, which depend on us," writes St. Maximus the Confessor, "don't have their source in us otherwise, except in the movement of the natural passions."[14]

What are these natural passions and how have they arisen in our nature? They are likewise called passions by St. Maximus, because they too represent a trait of passivity in our nature. Indeed they represent even a fuller passivity than the unnatural passions, because in the birth and growth of the latter, our will also contributes to some extent, even if later they completely dominate us. In this sense, they depend on us for birth and growth, and somehow it depends on us to free ourselves from them. The natural passions, however, don't depend on us in the slightest way. This is why we said that they manifest in an even more accentuated way the aspect of the passivity of our nature. And also because of this, they depend totally on nature and in no way on will; so they aren't condemnable. Such natural passions are: the appetite for food, the enjoyment of food, fear, and sadness. Moreover, they are necessary for our nature, and help to preserve it.

Nevertheless, they aren't a part of the original constitution of our nature; they weren't created at the same time. They sprung up in it after man's fall from the state of perfection. They penetrated into the less rational part of it; they accentuated its irrational traits, once the fall weakened the reason, the spirit.

In other words they represent the animal (irrational) aspect of our nature, accentuated after the fall from the spiritual, paradisiacal life, united with God. In this animal trait of theirs stands not only their inferiority, but their innocence too. Because just as animals are innocent in the instinctual manifestations of their organism, so too is man, as long as these natural passions stay within their bounds, serving his biological existence. But because man is spirit too and so has an irreducible aspiration for the infinite, he can associate this aspiration of his with the natural, biological passions, transforming them into unnatural passions,

---

[14] *Questions to Thalassios* 55, PG 90.541. "St. Maximus says, '...*ouk echonton allin archin en emin plin tis kiniseos ton kata physin pathon.*'" ('Not having any other principle in us except the movement of the natural passions.') Fr. Staniloae has translated *ta pathi,* the natural passions of St. Maximus, such as hunger, fear, and sadness, as affections. It seems to us that the English word *affection* is inadequate for this purpose. In older English affection meant not only loving attachment, but was also applied to bodily states such as hunger and thirst. Now, however, because affection has a more restricted meaning, we will use the same word *passion*, as St. Maximus, to express both the natural and unnatural passions. Other translators have done the same thing. See *Early Fathers from the Philokalia*, p. 261. trs

in other words into exaggerated passions, pierced by an infinite thirst for satisfaction The animal traits become diabolic, by the spiritual element which colors them.

We have said that these natural passions aren't condemnable in themselves, according to an expression of St. Maximus the Confessor. The idea must be refined, however, in the sense that in man the natural passions are never found in a totally indifferent moral state, due to the spiritual reflex that covers them. This reflex either keeps them within the limits which make them useful to our nature, or instills them with infinite tendencies. Only if they are kept within these limits by will, are they innocent. But when they deviate to one side or another, they become evil, or good; by them man goes toward God, or is fastened exclusively to the world. So, in another place, St. Maximus, responding to the question if "the natural passions are evil in themselves," answers:

> The natural passions become good in those who struggle when, wisely unfastening them from the things of the flesh, use them to gain heavenly things. For example, they can change appetite into the movement of a spiritual longing for divine things; pleasure, into pure joy for the cooperation of the mind with divine gifts; fear, into care to evade future misfortune due to sin; and sadness, into corrective repentance for present evil.[15]

So in other words, just as natural passions can become unnatural, so too they can become good impulses, according to which man's thirst for the infinite as a spiritual being is oriented towards the world, or towards God. They become good too, when by thinking of God, they are kept to their necessary biological function, in other words within the limits necessary for the conservation of the body.

Of course, in this case, they aren't as good as when they're directed exclusively toward God.[16] Asceticism must not fight for their eradication, nor can it overlook them, because then they can easily become [unnatural] passions; thus they have to be watched all the time and kept under control. By this, man is strengthened spiritually, disciplining himself day by day: "God arranges it this way so that man will come to the consciousness of his glory as a rational being."[17] They are a poison in

---

[15] *Questions to Thalassios* 1, *PG* 90.269.
[16] "...because simple food, too, gives us natural pleasure, even if we don't want it to, for it satisfies a need. Likewise drink, since it relieves the displeasure of thirst, or sleep, when it renews the powers spent while awake. Likewise all the other functions of our nature, which are on the one hand necessary for sustenance, and on the other useful for those who are diligent to gain the virtues." *Questions to Thalassios* 55, *PG* 90.541.
[17] *Questions to Thalassios* 1, *PG* 90.269.

our nature, but a poison which for us can be the healing of the venomous bites of evil.[18]

Not entering by definition into our nature, these natural passions aren't destined to accompany it to the future life. There we will be pure minds, in the sense of subjects preoccupied only with spiritual love and understanding as the angels:

> ... because the natural passions which conserve life here can't be transported with us to the immortal and eternal life. We will be 'pure minds,' as we were created. The specific life of our being will be the good understanding and pure spiritual joy.[19]

The evidence that in essence we are pure understanding and spiritual love makes St. Maximus believe that bodily affectivity [emotionality] isn't a part of our nature; but on the other hand, the evidence of the impossibility of conserving our earthly life by smothering the natural passions, makes St. Maximus of necessity tie them to our nature, in its present earthly life. He finds the solution in the idea that they appeared after the fall, but aren't condemnable. In other words, bodily affectivity, linked to our present state, is something inferior in connection with our nature, but nevertheless something necessary to its present earthly existence.

This element of bodily affectivity or emotionality which grows from the biological side isn't condemnable, and we must not struggle against it, because it constitutes the basis of our growth in the spiritual life. St. Maximus, in agreement with the whole of Eastern asceticism, isn't an opponent of biological life. Asceticism means, in the spirit of Eastern thought, the restraint and discipline of the biological, not a battle for its extermination. On the contrary, asceticism means the sublimation of this element of bodily affectivity, not its abolition. Christianity doesn't save man from a certain part of his nature, but it saves him as a whole. The power manifested in these natural passions is also tapped to serve man in his ascent to God. Natural passions can assume a spiritual character and give an increased accent to our love for God. He begins to be seen and loved through them. They become transparent so that the mind that seeks God can see Him through them.

This is the sense of their transfiguration or spiritualization. By putting a bridle and a limit on the pleasure of material things, a transfer of this energy of our nature takes place, in favor of the spirit; pleasure in spiritual blessings grows. By limiting biological pleasure, it becomes in-

---

[18] *Ibid.*
[19] *Ibid.*, 55, *PG* 90.541.

nocent; and the great plus which was stopped from being manifested on the physiological plane is transfigured on the spiritual. So instead of saying that these natural passions cease to exist when we leave this life, maybe it's better to say that all their energy is transferred, in favor of the spirit. And maybe in this way we can explain their appearance in our nature after the fall into sin, as a transfer of spiritual energy to an inferior biological plane. Our nature's pleasure in a relationship with something else was turned then from God and from the souls of our neighbors, to the world; this made the fleshly pleasure, produced by this relationship, grow. It's hard to conceive that the force of the natural passions came from somewhere outside.

In this sense we can understand the explanation which St. Maximus gives to the two trees in Paradise, to the tree of life and to the tree of the knowledge of good and evil, and to Adam's clinging to the latter.

> So in as much as man came into existence composed of an intelligent soul and a body endowed with feelings, according to the first meaning, the tree of life is the mind of the soul, in which it has its throne of wisdom; the tree of the knowledge of good and evil is the feeling of the body, in which it is obvious that the irrational movement has its stimulus. Man received through experience the divine command not to be touched by this feeling; by tasting he disobeyed. Both trees, namely the mind and feeling, have, according to Scripture, the power to distinguish between certain things. Thus the mind has the power to distinguish between things spiritual and things subject to the senses, between the passing and the eternal. Better said, it is the soul's power of discernment; it suggests that the former be laid hold of with all diligence, and the latter disdained. And feeling has the power to tell the difference between pleasure and bodily pain. Otherwise stated, it is a power of bodies endowed with souls and senses: It convinces man to embrace the first (pleasure) and to reject the second (pain). When therefore man isn't preoccupied in making another distinction except that between the bodily sensation of pleasure and pain, he disobeys the divine command. He eats from the tree of the knowledge of good and evil. He has, in other words, the irrationality of feeling as the only norm of discernment in the service of conserving the body. And by it he is totally captured by pleasure, as that which is good, and avoids pain, as that which is evil.[20]

Man's inclination to direct himself toward perceptible things stirs up in him the desire for them. This happens to the detriment of his mental power, which is considerably reduced, together with the pleasure connected with it. Man directs all his energy toward things subject to the

---

[20] *Ibid.*, 43, *PG* 90.412-13.

senses. He gives the greatest intensity to their enjoyment. Once stirred up, the affection of feeling can no longer be completely removed from him in his earthly life. But it can be partly limited, partly held in orientation toward spiritual and eternal blessing. Even from a part of it, through pain, which always follows pleasure, man can learn to oppose pleasure. Unfortunately, he does the opposite: The pain which follows pleasure, instead of making him avoid pleasure, as its source, (what a unity there is in the tree of the knowledge of good and evil!) pushes him anew into pleasure as if to get rid of it, tangling him even more in this vicious chain.[21]

It would appear from the theory of the natural passions, as it is developed by St. Maximus the Confessor, that every evil passion which can grow from them is of a perceptible nature; therefore vainglory and pride remain unexplainable. So we must see if somehow a relationship doesn't also exist between pride and the passions which nail the body to this visible world.

In fact, if we look at things a little more closely, we see that pride, after all, even that which doesn't grow as a result of perceptible things, is caused nevertheless by a certain factor in connection with the world. It is possible because man is thinking about his neighbors; he thinks he is superior to them. If he had the consciousness of an absolute aloneness, or the consciousness that he is standing before God, pride in him would be impossible. In some way, pride is still a victory of the world over men, a victory of the senses, as a superficial perception of the world over the mind, which even through the world, beyond the world, sees God. Indeed it could be said that even in the fallen angels, even though they are lacking in bodies, pride was born because they looked at the created world of man, and felt superior. The energy required to enrich themselves from God was transformed into an energy by which they tried to advance by dominating others. And the anger which develops from a natural passion that glues man too much to the world likewise has its cause in the feeling uncontrolled by the mind.

---

[21] "When we try to escape the harsh experience of pain, we throw ourselves into the arms of pleasure...and when we do our best to relieve the uneasiness of pain with pleasure, we again find ourselves tortured by pain—we are incapable of experiencing pleasure apart from torture and toil." *Ibid.*, 61, *PG* 90.628B.

THE NATURAL AND UNNATURAL PASSIONS

Keeping in mind that "natural passion is an irrational movement of the soul, caused by the idea of good or of evil,"[22] thus in itself still undetermined, let's look a little closer at the causes which make a natural passion become unnatural, and makes it turn toward evil.

---

[22] St. John of Damascus, *Dogmatics* 2.22, translated into Romanian by D. Fecioru (Bucharest, 1938), p. 114.

9. The Basic Causes of the Passions and their Effects

In the interpretation which he gives to the two trees in Paradise, St. Maximus also points out to us the primordial and perpetual causes of the passions. Passion is by its nature a diversion of the infinite aspiration of man to another goal other than the natural; it attracts him to the world which shrinks him and makes him an egotist, and not to God, Who enlarges him and makes him good. The question is then: How is it possible to keep man in this mistaken orientation, which fills the natural passions beyond the necessary measure? If we say that the reason for man's fall was pride, we haven't given an answer to the question of the first cause of evil, because pride is already an evil, a passion.

St. Maximus tries to penetrate this last, mysterious realm in which the first sinful movement of human nature was conceived and where it has its permanent motive. He stops at the influence of a satanic spirit, which directed a breath of confusion into man's mind. Yielding to this temptation, man's intelligence was darkened briefly; he forgot what his true cause was and thus his goal, and so he turned his desire toward it, toward the world.[23] This brief trickery was made easier by the attraction which the beautiful forms and sweet promises of the world exercised on his senses. The world was here, in the immediate vicinity, with all its calls and promises; God too was here, but harder to comprehend and with the promises of joy more spiritualized and more remote. The first cause of the passions must be sought in the enticing influence of the evil spirit and in the sensitivity of man. The first weakening of the perceptive activity of the mind resulted immediately, on the other side of the balance, in an intensification of the work of the senses. Better said, this attracted to itself all the energy which man would have put into the activation of the mind, in the sense of the transposition that we're talking about. Or the mind itself was put in the service of the senses: "... it got mixed up in the senses." It too became occupied exclusively with the emphasis on all the voluptuous aspects of the visible world, and "... this led to a compound and transitory knowledge of perceptible things, which in turn produced the passions."[24]

The mind forgot it own purpose, of knowing the one related to it, Who also is a personal spirit in a state to fill the mind's infinite longing for knowledge with His infinity. It entered a service foreign and inferior to it, which couldn't satisfy its thirst for the infinite. St. Anthony also

---

[23] *Questions to Thalassios*, PG 90.260; *RoFil* 3, p. 13. "Ignorance of God deified creation."
[24] *Ibid*. Passage not found. trs

tells us that this is possible: "The common mind is worldly and changing... because nature changes it."[25] Further on he writes, "If the soul doesn't have a good mind and good conduct it is blind and doesn't know God the Creator and Benefactor of all,"[26] or "The soul (in other words the mind), if it descends into the body, immediately is darkened by sadness and pleasure and is lost."[27]

We said that the world has attracted and attracts [our] sense perception, and through it, the mind too, by its perceptible, sweet, promises. This because feeling in the meaning of the function of sense perception is always accompanied by a sensation of pleasure or of pain, more or less intense, in apprehending the things of the world. Moreover, the senses' work of perception is capable of understanding in anticipation the pleasures or pains which things can give. In addition, the very sight of things creates pleasure or pain, even before possessing them. Feeling then [sense perception] has a double content and a double meaning: one gnosiologic, of knowing, and the other affective or emotional. This, its quality to grasp, through the process of perception, the pleasure which things can give, or to experience in their perception a sensation of it, makes pleasure dangerous for man. Or by this quality it has, the world becomes dangerous, because it is obvious that if it is left free, without guidance from reason, feeling will always choose between pleasure and pain. And in pleasure stands feeling's power: It often makes reason, as a function of judgment, retreat, and the mind as a function of knowledge, its servant.[28]

So three factors, or three causes, produce passions in man: 1) the mind weakened in its autonomous and proper work; 2) the work of sense perception, which has become predominant and has left its subordination to the mind, indeed, it has made the mind subordinate to it, and 3) an exclusive and irrational running after pleasure, even that obtained by the praises of his neighbors, and at the same time, a frightened flight from pain. These three causes are so interwoven, that in each one the other two are implicated.

Thus the passions represent a quantitative and hierarchical predominance of the senses over man's spirit. If the natural passions represent a sensuality held back by the spirit then the passions are an overflowing of

---

[25] *On the Character of Men* 7, GrPh 1, p. 5; cf. Phi 1, p.330.
[26] *Ibid.*, 118, GrPh 1, p. 20; cf. Phi 1, p. 347.
[27] *Ibid.*, 95, GrPh 1, p. 17; cf. Phi 1, p. 344.
[28] St. Anthony: "The souls which aren't held in check by reason and aren't guided by the mind, so that their passions, that is sadness and pleasure, master and govern them, are lost as dumb beasts; their reason is dragged by the passions as a teamster is by his runaway horses." *Ibid.*, 96, GrPh 1, p. 17; cf. Phi 1, p. 344.

sensuality, beyond all measure. The natural passions are a minimum of passivity, and this necessary minimum is imposed by our nature and no longer depends on our will. The passions, however, are an increase of passivity beyond what is necessary, beyond what is imposed by the necessities of nature, in other words a non-obligatory concession of the will, which means a slavery created willingly.

The natural passions are passions in conformity with nature, because they serve to conserve nature. (Evil) passions are contrary to nature *(para physin)*, because they don't do it any good, indeed they represent a damaging orientation of nature and an overthrow of the hierarchy in man.

St. Anthony makes the following distinction between the natural passions and (evil) passions:

> Things that are done according to nature aren't sins, but those done by choice; it's not a sin to eat, so that the body will be properly maintained in life without any evil thought, but it is to eat without gratitude and improperly and without restraint; neither is it a sin to look with chastity, but it is a sin to look with envy, pride and desire; it is not a sin to listen quietly, but it is with anger. It's not a sin to let the tongue be unrestrained in thanksgiving and prayer, but it is to speak evil; to not let your hands do acts of mercy, but to commit murder and theft. So each of our members sins if it does evil instead of good, doing things its own way and not according to the will of God. [29]

In other words neither are the pleasures, joined with what serves each member as a matter of necessity, guilty. But pleasures sought by unnecessary actions are guilty. The excesses or the deviations of the senses in finding pleasure at any price are guilty. Precisely because of this the passions bring our nature to disorder, to the weakening and decomposition of our bodies, by weakening the spirit which keeps it in order. And the feeling of weakness takes man even further, with the impulse of regaining his power from a source incapable of strengthening him. Certainly that which brings man closer and closer to taking somersaults on the slope of the passions is a hidden fear of death.[30] The boredom which follows any pleasure whatsoever is a void heralding death. Even more, God has even tied pain to pleasure— always— that man, in experiencing the former, will no longer look for the latter. But he, finding himself in pain, carried by the fear of death, which is announced to him by it as a punishment for the pleasures which he is still going to seek, throws himself into new pleasures, carrying his nature toward death.

---

[29] *Ibid., 60, GrPh* 1, p. 12; *cf. Phi* 1, p. 338.
[30] *Questions to Thalassios* 61, *PG* 90.633D.

"For the whole nature of bodies is corrupt and easy to scatter; by the ways by which it tries to fortify itself, it increases its corruption."[31] The close connection between pleasure and pain can be explained by the fact that the tension in which the nerves are put in the state of pleasure, is followed by a weakening, an exhaustion. And a repetition of the states of voluptuousness hurries the death of the body. Seeking by the passions, wrongly so, a fortification of the nature of the body, man weakens it, bringing it even more quickly toward death.

But even worse is the spiritual death which the passionate marching back and forth produces in the vicious circle formed by perceptible pleasure and pain. And here too we encounter another contradiction of the passions: They are an alternating, if not a joining of the state of passion and the commonplace, of effervescence and boredom, of tension and aridity; they are the death which tortures, the living death, not the death which gives the rest of non-being. Man's life of dullness, of superficial banality, in which the spirit has succumbed, seems never ending in this life, but in the future life the fact is it won't be; it will give man the kind of infinity he wanted, but an infinity of dullness.

The passions, however, produce still another disorder in our nature; they tear it to pieces. We have recalled what St. Maximus said, that the mind, putting its activity in the service of the senses, gains a "compound and perditious knowledge of things perceptible." Sense perception isn't preoccupied in finding ties between the *logoi* of visible things, or even of viewing something in its unitary integrity, fully placed in its own logos; but it limits its interest to a partial aspect, drawn by the pleasure which this aspect promises it. It doesn't work with a broad horizon, but it always sees only one aspect and forgets all the rest. The result is obvious. In this way, by the feeling led by pleasure, the world is divided into numberless, unrelated aspects without a tie between them. Each one is tied, too much so, only by the feeling which has gotten hold of it at the moment. By this, feeling contributes to the disorganization of the world itself. The mind which serves feeling is itself bent toward various singular aspects, and isn't concerned with the relationships between them, instead of seeing the unitary system of the reason which penetrates the world, and by this system the one God; the mind too in a conscious way, always remains one and the same. Every moment it forgets what it already knew, being divided into unrelated acts of knowing, because every moment it has received the impression of something isolated from everything else. This is the so-called scattering of the mind which the

---

[31] *Ibid.*, The Introduction, *PG* 90.260.

guarding of the mind, recommended by Christian asceticism, must deliver it from.

But this exclusive and passionate focus at a given moment on an isolated aspect of the world, makes the whole of man's nature concentrate on it in the greed to taste it; then too man's whole nature goes from moment to moment through alternative passions: from anger to dejection; from disgust of people to an avid seeking of their company, unable to keep its various impulses in equilibrium and moderation. But this tears his nature to pieces; because instead of being kept continually in the equilibrium of its functions, it is abandoned successively, a prey to the extremes which are self-contradictory by their exaggerated exclusivity. Man is no longer a unitary being, the same at every moment of his life. The forgetting of God also has as a result the forgetting of self, as a permanent unity of his own person. But this breakdown also extends to the level of inter-human relations. We want pleasure and we want innumerable objects which are going to get it for us, or we want to raise our ego to the highest level, by the passion of pride; so we get into trouble with those around us, or we awaken their envy. St. Maximus describes this effect of the passions in this way:

> As a result the one nature was divided into innumerable particles and we, of the same nature, consume one another as furious serpents. Because following pleasure by reason of an egotistic love of self and forcing ourselves to avoid pain, by reason of this same egotism, we fabricate the birth of innumerable corruption producing passions.[32]

It's enough to recall that the one who says "I" too much, so as to emphasize that he has done certain things and nobody else, in fact succeeds in cutting his roots of communication with others. He has no love for others, neither will he be loved by others. Pride has cut his nature off from others, which although borne by many subjects is nevertheless one in its visible and invisible communication and only so is maintained and grows in its strength, continually being enriched. In fact, a complete cutoff of nature between individuals can't happen. This would be its total death. If it is still maintained, even in the most egotistic person, and so in a tortured form, it's because he still has some kind of relationship, be it distorted, with others. Because, in reality, there doesn't exist a thing which someone has made alone, even if in appearance nobody helped him. The idea for that action, the stimulus to do it, the competence for it and so many other conditions for it were given him by the environment in which it developed. Everyone should say in regard to everything he has been able to do: "We" did it, not to put himself in the plural, but

---

[32] *Ibid., PG* 90.256.

in order to acknowledge the contribution of others to any endeavor of his. "I" is an expression of pride and indicates a dangerous cutting of our nature. "We" is an expression of love, of humility, of the recognition of the unity of our nature, of the conciliarity of subjects, founded on this unity of nature. This is why St. Maximus says that only love removes the shredding of human nature.[33]

When we know the principle causes and effects of the passions, however, we know our adversary. But in order to state these causes more precisely, we must first show, in a more appropriate way, the relationships of the various passions with each faculty of the soul.

---

[33] *Second Letter of John the Valet, PG* 91.396.

10. The Passions and the Faculties of the Soul

The conception of the holy Fathers regarding the soul is borrowed for the most part from Aristotle, who doesn't differ much from Plato, except that he rejects the preexistence of the *nous,* of the mind, or of the spirit and thus its separation from the soul.

According to this conception, the soul, one in essence, has three main faculties; the mind *(nous),* as a power of all the acts of knowledge and of thought; desire *(epithymia),* as a power of all desires and appetites and *(thymos),* the incensive power, the impulse for acts of courage, for manliness or for good or evil anger. Reason would be a certain function of the mind. When it takes the place of the mind, the soul has the same powers: reason, desire, and impulsiveness.

It is worthy of note, however, that the holy Fathers, although they reject the Platonic idea of the separation between the mind and the soul, as a passional and desiring whole *(thymos kai epithymia),* which is the idea of the preexistence of the mind, nevertheless consider that the two latter powers are related and differ from the mind to such an extent that they start to speak, on the other hand, of two parts of the soul: the mental or spiritual part, and the rational and the irrational which also include, together with other vital functions, the faculties of anger and desire. So St. John of Damascus writes:

> It should be known that the rational by nature leads the irrational. The powers of the soul are divided into the rational and the irrational. The latter has two parts: One which doesn't listen to reason, that is it doesn't submit to reason, and another one which does. The disobedient part, unsubmissive to reason is divided into: the vital function which is also called pulse, and the seminal function, in other words that of birth, and the vegetative function, which is also called the nutritive. The function of growth, which gives form to bodies, also belongs to the latter. These faculties aren't controlled by reason, but by nature. The part which obeys and is sustained by reason is divided into anger and desire. The irrational part of the soul is especially called passional or appetitive. [34]

Indeed the holy Fathers somehow appropriate the Platonic thesis of the immortality of the *nous* and the mortality of the other two powers in the following way: According to them, as we have already shown with passages from St. Maximus, only the *nous* is destined for everlasting life; anger and desire as the seat of the natural passions will cease to be, at the end of earthly life.

---

[34] St. John of Damascus, *Dogmatics* 2.12, p. 103.

But the mind, far from being something distinct from the soul, is strictly speaking, the very soul itself.[35] Anger and desire are powers which accompany it during the earthly life and which are born from the association of the soul with the body. They are functions proper to the care of the body and related to the tie between mind and body. Certainly, they aren't exclusively of the body, because the body in itself is inert. They represent an energy of the soul, oriented toward the body and colored by living with it. The soul also has in itself the energy of desire and anger, and it will have them too after the end of this life. They will cease then, as we know them on earth in their bodily and irrational element. The energy from them, spiritualized, will be turned exclusively to God.

The mind *(nous)*, understood as the soul strictly speaking, or the soul itself, in relation to which desire and anger have a more exterior position, is also threefold. Callistus Cataphygiotis considers the soul as made up of *nous, logos* and *pneuma,* mind, reason and spirit, in comparison to the Holy Trinity. This threefold aspect doesn't touch in the slightest way its simplicity.[36]

Such a conception has a marked importance. It helps us to understand a multitude of things from the mystical life of the soul. According to Mark the Ascetic, at Baptism Christ comes to live at the altar of the heart, or in the innermost part of our being, without our realizing it at first; we just become conscious of it by our gradual change. Diadochos of Photiki says the same thing. He writes that, at the moment of Baptism, grace "is hidden in the depths of the mind; Satan is evicted and he influences us from now on by the bodily senses and by the sweetness of irrational appetites."[37] It follows that there exists a depth or an interior of our minds unknown to us. We become conscious of it gradually, if we strive to cleanse our lives. Mark the Ascetic calls it the heart.

This teaching gives us the possibility to build bridges between the Christian view of the soul and modern psychology, even though the Christian doctrine contains something which is an integration of this psychology. The latter, for the most part, admits the existence of a sub-

---

[35] St. Maximus has written somewhere: "Reason is the servant of the same family that serves the mind, while anger and desire, are servants of another."
[36] Callistus Cataphygiotis, *On Divine Union and the Contemplative Life* 34, GrPh 5, p. 19: "I call the soul tripartite not because it is rational, incensive, and desiring. The soul isn't strictly speaking tripartite because of this. Because the rational soul doesn't have anger and desire as its own. They are taken from the irrational for the present animal existence. By themselves they are off to the side, irrational, and shadowy. But the soul is rational and its nature is full of understanding light.... So they aren't really parts of it, but its lateral powers, with a vital and inferior purpose."
[37] Mark the Ascetic, *On Baptism*, PG 65.985-1028; *cf.* Diadochos of Photiki, *On Spiritual Knowledge and Discrimination* 76-80, *Phi* 1, pp. 279-82.

conscious to reserve a place to deposit memories and where ideas, inspirations, intuitions, and tendencies are hammered out.

As we see, Christianity too admits the existence of a region of the soul which doesn't fall under the light of the consciousness. However, the term subconscious isn't suitable to indicate this region, first because of the prefix *sub* which puts it in a subordinate zone, and secondly because it is still loaded down with the Freudian heredity of so many disgraceful tendencies and thoughts, which the consciousness keeps repressing, because it is ashamed to bring them to the surface. We can admit that there is a subconscious for the shadowy baggage which we carry with us; we consider it is proper, however, for the region where the potential human energies of the soul are included and by which the divine energies enter it, to use the word *trans-conscious* or *supra-conscious*. The subconscious would be the room to the left or the cellar of the conscience, where all our bad things have accumulated, giving birth to the supports of the passions; it would be the starting point of desire and anger. The trans-conscious or supra-conscious would be the room to the right, or the room upstairs, where the superior powers are stored and function, ready to flood the conscious life and even the subconscious, with their cleansing power, when we offer them the conditions.

Thus the "spirit" of the soul, or of the mind, would be the uppermost part, or the innermost, because in the spiritual order, the highest is the innermost, most intimate. We believe that the term "heart" also refers to this part.[38] For example, Diadochos of Photiki uses, for the most intimate part of the soul where the grace of Baptism is hidden, sometimes the expression "the depth of the mind," sometimes the word "heart,"[39] and sometimes the word "spirit."[40]

So we would have an explanation for the fact that some Eastern spiritual writers scarcely use the word heart at all when they speak of the central place of the soul, but only *nous,* as for example Evagrius, Cassian, Neilos the Ascetic, or *nous* and *pneuma*, as Maximus the Confessor. Others use this notion very frequently, for example Mark the Ascetic; we also find it in the Jesus Prayer.

Among the three aspects of the soul, the most open to us is reason *(logos);* it has maybe the role of revelation, as the divine Logos has in

---

[38] B. Visheslavtsev, "The meaning of the heart in religion," [in Romanian], *Revista Teologica,* (1934). He thinks that the heart as the central part, the innermost part of man, is that which encounters God.
[39] On Spiritual Knowledge 74, 80, *GrPh* 1, pp. 258-9; *cf. Phi* 1, pp. 278-81.
[40] *Ibid.,* 57, *GrPh* 1, p. 250. "He who lives continually in his heart is far from all the tempting things of life, for walking in the spirit, he can't know the lusts of the flesh."

connection with the Holy Trinity. The mind *(nous)* with its more direct possibilities of knowledge, and namely of the knowledge of the spiritual is less open to us. In the beginning the spirit or heart is for us almost completely covered, because the spirit lives in our depths, as the Holy Spirit lives in the divine depths (1 Corinthians 2:11). In the same way as the Holy Spirit, our spirit goes down into the conscious and subconscious regions of our life on the surface, of contact with the visible world, only after reason *(logos)* has prepared us for His reception. The heart is closed for us, as long as we live a life of hardness and sin. In regard to such a person, it is said that he is a "man without a heart" or has "a heart of stone," in other words it has stopped working. The life "in the spirit" is totally lacking in such a man. He preserves only a "logos" lacking in depth. "The heart" is opened to us, it is made bigger for us by hope in God, says St. Mark the Ascetic. Otherwise it's congested, locked up by worries.[41] And "life in the spirit," "the knowledge of Christ in the spirit," expressions used by St. Maximus the Confessor, mean the knowledge of Christ dwelling with us, in our most intimate depths. It is further said that "the spirit" or "spiritual life" means the union between our soul and the divine Spirit, leaving us with the impression that we don't have in any sense a region of the soul named "spirit" before the encounter with God. But we do have a "spirit" in us before the meeting with God, as a region where the Holy Spirit can reside; but until Christ or the Holy Spirit dwells there it is a simple potentiality for us, and even after this it is at first unknown to us—we become aware of it in the measure in which we grow in virtue, and by this, in the consciousness that we have Jesus in us. Only after this do we consciously grow in a spiritual life. This is at the same time a life of the heart, if the heart is the power of love; it is the soul open to God and to our neighbors; and the life in the spirit is a life of love for God and our neighbors, if the Holy Spirit is also in the Holy Trinity the power of love. By this opening, the soul realizes at the same time its tie with the infinite, its potential to communicate with the infinite, to receive the infinite in itself, to unite with the infinite. The Holy Spirit descends to us and cooperates in the winning of the virtues, as an opening to God and our neighbors. Our spirit catches fire in us. It wakes us up. Our heart is softened. The walls of our soul become transparent. God's love wakes up our love. God's penetration within us makes us open to God.

In the light of this conception, we can understand why the heart or the loving state of the soul also has in Orthodox Christianity a gnosiological, a knowing function. The true understanding of the mind is at

---

[41] *On Those Who Think They are made Righteous by Works* 114. (Hereafter abbreviated as *No Righteousness by Works*), Phi 1, p. 134.

the same time too, love for that which is understood. The "spirit" is one aspect and *nous*, the mind, the other of the same simple soul. The "spirit" or the "heart" contains in itself the "mind" or the "understanding" and the "reason" just as the Holy Spirit contains the Father and the Son. Likewise the "understanding" contains in itself the "heart" or "love" and "reason"; and "reason" includes "understanding" and "love."

This concept of the soul can also be easily reconciled with modern psychological concepts which differentiate the gnosiological function (the mind) from the affective (the appetitive and incensive) in the soul, as well as the conscious from the subconscious.

It could be said that the psychic energies of desire and anger are implicated in the energy found in the upper room of the soul, in the "spirit" or in its "heart" and to the degree that the life of the "heart" or of the spirit is diminished or to the extent that the heart and the spirit don't use their spiritual energy, to the same extent the energy of desire and fleshly anger grows.

But now let's see how the passions are distributed according to the mental faculties (by that we also mean the reason and the heart or the spirit), according to desire and anger, or how they are altered when God is ignored or even when the certitude of His existence is weakened, or when He is forgotten. We mention that this ignoring, or doubting, or forgetting is the product first of the trickery of the evil spirit, who because he is a spirit who spends his energy in self-preoccupation, also urges or influences our soul to be preoccupied with ourselves; secondly it's the result of laziness, or indifference, influenced too by physical sloth.

So the ignoring of God also has a moral character (better said immoral), to the extent that the moral causes and the intellectual are interwoven. This is why St. Mark the Ascetic considers ignorance, forgetfulness and laziness as the prime causes of any evil.[42] St Anthony has the following opinion: "The cause of all evils is deception, error, and ignorance of God,"[43] strengthening his thesis that the impious man, the passionate person is irrational, just as the pious one is rational.[44] The passions, then, are the effect, and in turn the cause of a mind stripped of true understanding, of an irrationality and of a stunting of the spirit, or of the mind, or of love.

---

[42] Letter of Nicolas the Solitary, *Phi* 1, p. 159.
[43] *On the character of men* 26, *GrPh* 1, p. 7; *cf. Phi* 1, p. 333.
[44] Chapters 1, 5, 13, 22, etc., *Phi* 1, p. 329 *ff*.

On the part of the mind, the passions indicate a minus of activity, her abdication from the role of director; on the part of desire and anger, they indicate an excess, an overflowing of the normal limits of nature. Even sloth is connected with pleasure. On the other hand, this minus of the mind and of its effort and the plus of desire and of anger mean a breaking of the laws of nature, not to mention their orientation toward mistaken, narrow objectives incapable of satisfying the mind's thirst for the infinite, incapable of getting and keeping the "spirit," the "heart" working.

In the last chapter we found that a second and a third cause of the passions are that the senses are too busy and preoccupied with pleasure, and try to avoid pain at the same time. But the spiritual power which pleasure wants is desire. Likewise anger is what is incensed when it doesn't have pleasure and when it is taken away from it, or when man is threatened and seized with pain. So desire and anger are those things which, attracted by the visible world and its promises, tip the balance between the work of the mind and the senses, in favor of the latter. By the senses the mind can follow its preoccupation with spiritual knowledge, but desire too can follow its aspirations. Sense perception understood as a pure perception of the senses is in itself innocent and can be used for the service of the mind. Only when the desire for pleasure works through it does it become feeling in the sinful sense. A minimum of pleasure can stay in it, as a natural passion. But this natural passion must be overwhelmed with the spiritual pleasure of a knowing mind. For example, when we eat, if we concentrate completely on the taste and the pleasure which the food gives us, this feeling is sinful, because desire is working through it. The mind has only the subordinate role of discovering all the possibilities of the pleasure of the food. But if when we eat we bridle the feeling of pleasure, by different reflections on the purpose of food— the blessing which God has given us through it, the duty which we also have of being merciful to others with the things necessary for sustenance— we have conquered the passion of bringing feeling into the spiritual subordination of the mind.

St. Maximus thus divides the passions between the two psychic faculties of desire and anger, after which he shows that they are strengthened parallel to the growth of ignorance or of the abdication of the mind from its natural purpose:

> So the more man lives by the senses, concerned only with the knowledge of the visible, the more he amasses around him the ignorance of God. And the more he amasses around him the ignorance of God, the more he is engrossed in the tasting by the senses of known materials; and the more he consumes them, the more the passionate love of self

102 PART ONE: A. PURIFICATION FROM THE PASSIONS

(philautia) is inflamed within him, started by this taste. And the more he cultivates the passionate love of himself, the more he invents other ways of pleasure, as the fruit and the goal of self-love. And because pleasure always has pain as its successor, he pounces with all his strength on pleasure because of the passionate love for himself.... And forcing himself to avoid pain for the same love, he causes the birth of innumerable ruin-producing passions. Thus, if he pampers the love of self *(philautia)* by pleasure, he gives birth to gluttony, pride, vainglory, conceit, love of money, stinginess, tyranny, arrogance, stubbornness, anger, an exaggerated view of himself, haughtiness, disdain, insult, mockery, derision, squander, insolence, walking in the clouds, soft living, biting remarks, talkativeness, talking dirty and all such things.[45]

St. Maximus derives all these things from pleasure seeking. They are an exaggeration and a deviation from desire. Even pride, too, with all its ramifications, belongs to desire, not to mention laziness. On the other hand, as they are also a result of ignorance, they represent a sickness of the mind too. In regard to pride, he says clearly elsewhere that it is, and produces, "... confused thought, consisting of two kinds of ignorance: that of divine help and that of its own helplessness."[46]

If we make an abstraction of the fact that they result also from a weakening of the mind, we see that six of the eight capital passions belong to the faculty of desire: gluttony, debauchery, love of money, laziness, vainglory and pride.

St. Maximus continues: "Now when egotism is bitten harder by pain it gives birth to a hot temper *(ton thymon),* envy, hate, enmity, remembrance of evil, slander, grumbling, intrigue, sadness, despair, distrust, defamation of providence, disgust, negligence, lack of courage, indisposition, faintheartedness, ill-timed lamentation, crying, melancholy, complete unrest, excessive zeal and all the other things which a state lacking in opportunities for pleasure produces." These are the products and the diseases of the incensive power— all of them are reduced to the passions of anger and dejection. But the incensive power is manifested when desire goes unsatisfied. So, indirectly, these passions too are connected to desire:

> Now from the mixing of pain with pleasure, produced by any other causes whatsoever, that is from a state of perversity— because this is what some call the composition resulting from the encounter of two contrary evils— the following are born: hypocrisy, irony, cunning,

---

[45] The reference is missing here. *trs*
[46] *Questions to Thalassios* 56, scholia 4, *PG* 90.560.

pretense, flattery, false behavior to please others and all the other inventions of this villainous mixture.[47]

These passions, then, are the product of the combination of desire and anger. But the role of the psychic faculties in connection with the passions is more complex than has been described so far. The passions don't mean a total abdication of all reason and an exclusive work of desire and anger. We have seen that St. Maximus makes the following distinction between the natural passions and the passions: The first don't depend on us, while the latter do, at least until they become very strong.

Modern psychology makes this same distinction between the natural passions, in which it includes emotions, and passions; emotion is a primary and brute state, an instinctive movement, an abrupt and immediate reaction, while passion is a secondary and complex formation. It is thought in the service of instinct and of tendencies; it is made in part by a cold, rational, systematic will. Beret tells us:

> While emotion is a primary and brute state, an instinctive movement, a sudden and unexpected reaction (for example, anger as a result of being hit by someone), while it is characterized by its shortness and violence ... passion is a secondary and complex formation. It is made up in part of reflection and calculation, of cold, rational, systematic volition; it is characterized by its stability and duration. It is a chronic state.... Where much emotion is, says Kant, there is in general little passion.[48]

An outburst of anger devoid of reason is short. But the passion of anger is prolonged by will and argumentation, beyond the limit of that moment, and so becomes a permanent habit, which a man can't be freed from easily and which can often break out and in excess. An outburst of

---

[47] *PG* 90.256CD.
[48] Beret continues: "Impulsive and explosive temperaments, subjected to sudden and violent emotions, Ribot agrees, '...are not the ones to become truly impassioned: They are the craftsmen's torch; the latter are the blast furnaces which burn all the time.... A long lasting passion is always often accompanied by an excess of emotion." Ribot, *Essai sur les passions* (Paris, 1907). "Emotion is a realized state characterized by interruption; satisfaction or passion is a privileged or separate tendency, which is detached from the others, organized, imposed. It becomes the center of attraction for all the sentiments and moves toward realization. One is centrifugal, the other centripetal; the one is dissipation, the other is a concentration of movements; the one seems involuntary, the other voluntary. Passion is an inclination borne by excess, become predominant, which subordinates all the others or which excludes them.... How do they come about? We can admit that to start with, in the normal person, all the tendencies exist and that all are on the same level of mediocrity, [they are neither good nor bad]. But this equilibrium doesn't last. In effect, passion understood as the rupture of the equilibrium of these tendencies, is from the predominance of one over the others ... it isn't inborn, fatal.... We can look at it, together with the Stoics, as a disease of the soul." L. Beret, *Les etats affectifs*, in G. Dumas; *Traite de Psychologies* 1 (Paris, 1923): 480 *ff.*

anger is an emotion which is quickly satisfied. In a passion, however, reflection and will direct this insatiable, infinite thirst, which they have turned from its proper spiritual goal, toward nothing.

So a passion is much worse than a natural passion. If the natural passion is animalic and imposed by the physical life of man, a passion is diabolic and no longer an instinctual manifestation of nature; it is a boiling pot continually willed for and thought about. Where can we find the explanation for the capacity of these emotions or rebel natural passions to attract the will, more or less without its permission, to its side? Blondel explains this:

> In them there is an energy analogous to that of the will and a so-called rational character.... In voluptuousness, in ambition, a complexity, an amplification, an apparent fullness exists ... this world of human passions is full, too, of certain seeds of reason, but precisely because of this, also of the possibilities of abuse.[49]

In fact, the will must not be understood as a force in us that is detached from the ensemble of all the tendencies which make up the dynamism of our nature; but it, as a general tension of our nature to be, must be with all our aspirations. It has to want all of them, it has to be in all of them. It's understood, however, that it must want each one; it must be in each one as a force of realization, in as much as each one is harmoniously fitted into the general purpose of our whole nature, since it works together for the good of the whole.

The will, as a function of our entire nature, is with each of its tendencies and gives all of them a justification. All are made legitimate, all contribute to it and all as a group have a share somehow of our nature's will to be. The reason and the will in them stand in their justification to be and in the power to be, which the belonging to the whole of our nature confers on them.

The will and the reason in these tendencies either can fool the general will with the reason of our nature into joining them, or they can cause them to weaken in their function of protecting and promoting the interest of the whole of our nature from the force with which a given singular tendency momentarily breaks out. So they remain alone on the spot; they assume the role of action directing reason and will. They are substituted for the general will and reason, or work as though they were. In the same place Blondel tells us:

---

[49] Blondel, *L'Action* vol. 2, p. 192. The participation in some way of reason and of will in passion, the factor which gives it its infinite impetus, is brought out by Blondel, as we saw in the chapter on the essence of the passions.

... this contrary will, which catalyzes all of the excluded powers into one system, frequently succeeds, it's a fact, in supplanting the will itself; but it doesn't succeed in this way in taking control of the action except in the measure to which it makes itself reason or will.

Nicodemus of the Holy Mountain has more or less the same idea regarding the birth of the partial will, which is substituted for the general will. However, instead of calling it partial in regard to the general, he calls it inferior or irrational, which certainly is just:

> Know that in this unseen warfare, two wills existing in us fight against one another: One belongs to the intelligent part of our soul and is therefore called the intelligent will, which is the higher; the other belongs to the sensory part and is therefore called the sensory will, which is the lower. The latter is more frequently called the dumb, carnal passionate will. The higher will is always desiring nothing but good, the lower— nothing but evil.[50]

We still feel the presence of the general reason and will, however, which tacitly disapprove of what is going on. Thus, we usually feel in us two wills and two reasons. Only in those who have completely fallen under the power of a passion can the whole reason be totally perverted, so as to justify without reserve the correction of the tendency in this passion to dominate the whole nature. And only in such people is the whole will put in the service of the passion. In most cases, making an abstraction, maybe during the passion's moments of fury, moments of total blindness, a reserve of reason and will remain which plead, it's true, without an effective power, for the rights of the nature as a whole and which see that the reason and will which have been put in the service of the passion are erring, that this will is an irrational will, a will which doesn't fully bear the characteristics of freedom, just as the reason which serves the passion is a "disregarded" reason.[51]

---

[50] But, in some way, this irrational will must conquer the rational in order to be realized, in other words to work with the permission and in the name of the rational, to assume this role in a sophistic way, to gain the prestige of the rational will before its own conscience and before others. The rational will, writes St. Nicodemus, stands between the will of the senses and the will of God; each one tries to win it. "Every time your free will is acted upon and pulled both by the dumb sensory will and the will of God, voiced through conscience, each of them seeking to conquer it, you must, if you are sincerely to strive for good, use suitable methods on your part to assist God's will in gaining victory. For this purpose, then, as soon as you feel impulses of the lower, sensory and passionate will, you must immediately use every effort to resist them and not allow your own will to incline towards them." *Unseen Warfare,* trans. by E Kadloubovsky and G.E.H. Palmer (Crestwood, NY, 1987), pp. 100, 103.
[51] So says St. Nicodemus. Probably from *Unseen Warfare,* pp. 100-109. trs

We see, then, a rupture into two of the will and reason, or a ramification of their functions, into a perverse function and a healthy one.[52] We work in this case, "with the will, against our will."[53]

So the natural passion has become a sin only by making a complete or partial common cause with reason and will.[54] But the role of reason and of will doesn't stop here. After the respective partial tendency has been satisfied by attracting the reason and the will to it, they are forced to justify the adhesion which they have given to it, maybe, somehow, unwillingly.[55] By this the mistake once made becomes a passion, by the continual contribution of the reason and the will.

Three steps mark the growing power of this adversary of the will: First those who have invaded are foreigners or enemies in disguise... finally they are the triumphant who are accepted and flattered.... At first, almost without our will, the action contrary to our will breaks out; then we agree in our conscience with it; finally, what we have done almost without doing so, we end up by wanting done.... This clearly shows that in man everything is marked by this rational character, because reason is found even in the madness of passions.[56]

Man looks for a rational justification retroactively because in reality the realization of the passion has brought him a satisfaction, a pleasure. Its memory is stamped with a certain sweetness. So too the recall of committing it. Here the gratification for having done it, its ratification by an ulterior will and its justification by reasons which are included even in the satisfaction with the rational justifications of the fact which caused them and with the ratification by will, push him to repeat the sinful act. In this way the passion is born and grows, by a continual contribution of reason and will. Note how even what is evil and passionate in man is also marked by a rational and voluntary character. Without the descent of reason into desire and anger, or in the feeling (sense perception) conducted by them, the passions can't be born and grow. Thus the passions are born by the contribution of all the psychic faculties, in a mistaken activity of theirs, which show that the whole man is sick.

They are a return of the whole man to the outside, to live according to the senses, the change of the whole man into "body," into carnal

---

[52] Blondel, *L'Action* vol. 2, p. 207.
[53] *Ibid.*, p. 195: "It's that the will isn't whole and that it remains divided in itself."
[54] *Ibid.*, p. 205: "And this action which comes out of us against our profound and indelible wishes as if it were voluntary, this unreasonable action from which we make a new reason, is properly speaking, from passion."
[55] *Ibid.*, p. 204: "Whatever we have in fact decided, we are determined to justify and to consider reasonable, even when it is contrary to a previous will or to an impartial judgment."
[56] *Ibid.*, p. 210: "It's here that we clearly see that in man all is marked by this rational character, because it's found in him even in the follies of passion."

feeling. The passions mean living by the senses penetrated by desire and anger which have also dragged reason into their exclusive service. They thus mean living on the uppermost part of our nature, on the epidermis, or as it could be said, they are an exit of our nature from the true ontological region, from the tie with the sources of existence. They mean living on the edge of the abyss of nothingness, from which nothing comes to us, when we wake up from the fire of the passions. They leave us with the sensation of emptiness, of the false, of the shallowness of our existence, of nullity dominating our daily life, as analyzed so earth-shakingly by a Heidegger, or a Sartre. So the moment of the passionate attraction, and the satisfaction of the passion is the product of a great delusion. The superficial draws us as though it were profound, consistent and durable.

By the passions, as Blondel says, "We desire nothing with an infinite will," or we run back and forth from the effervescence which follows nothingness without realizing it to its feeling, revealed in the force and disgust which come after this effervescence. This exhilaration, however, shows an insatiable thirst. By the passions we find nil, we are on fire for it, we burn out for it, we move around it, and end up with the absence of any positive source of existence whatsoever. By the passions we open our parched mouths for the water which is but illusion for a moment, or which after a brief deception seems to us as a drop which makes us even more thirsty. In the measure in which we experience, by prolonged passionate trial and error, the impossibility of our satisfying ourselves by them, or by the naught found in them, this nothingness becomes more obvious to us. This frustration overwhelms us more and more; with time it throws us into apathy, into a murderous spiritual sloth. This is what the holy Fathers called *accedie*. It is, according to Evagrius and St. Maximus, more overwhelming than everything else. If the other passions predominantly affect one or the other of the three psychic faculties, as St. Maximus says, this spiritual torpor paralyzes all the power of the soul: the incensive, the desiring, and the intelligent.[57] It often affects those advanced in the spiritual life as well. Here is how Hausherr describes it, following Evagrius; he sees it more in the form it takes when it comes over those who are trying to reach perfection:

> The demon of listlessness is the hardest of all to bear. He pours out drop by drop his bitterness in all our motives to live in a supernatural way. There is no longer any love whatsoever around you. God Himself no longer cares for you at all, because why would He leave you tempted so by demons? The demon of listlessness cuts off all

---

[57] For Evagrius, see *Texts on Discrimination in respect of passions and thoughts, Phi* 1, pp. 38-52; for Maximus the Confessor see *Chapters on Love* 1.67, *Phi* 2, p. 60.

hope... (12, 14). And whether you know it, or whether you don't, if this thought persists, in the time of prayer, it shuts off the holy light from the soul (16). You no longer dare to seek the mercy of God with all your prayers (18). You want to cry, but a horrible thought suppresses the tears: They don't help at all (19). And this lasts for days on end and you can only foresee a life which must be endured with this torture (24). Certainly, there isn't anybody up there who sees my misery (32, 34). When this weight of listlessness falls on you, you want to scream about your discouragement and boredom (37). This can make you sick, because the intensity of your torpor eats up all your strength. You have run out of patience. You feel that you are almost crazy. You moan and groan and cry like a baby, but nothing from nowhere helps.[58]

Those who are on the ascending way of spiritual perfection, however, pass through these crises, because they know that their methods and their will are strong enough. The faith by which they have kept themselves in shape spiritually doesn't let them reach the irreversible verdict that everything is useless and in vain. They believe and know that only created things are relative. God is in the beyond. Those who have reached listlessness, however, before they have been strengthened on the way to perfection, after they have vainly tried to quench their thirst for the absolute in various passions, find no way out, if a miracle doesn't awaken in them a strong faith in God. Such people easily reach even the point of suicide, after going through insanity.

---

[58] Hausherr, I. "Do the Easterners [the Orthodox] know the 'nights' of Saint John of the Cross?," [in French], *Orientalia Cristiana* 12 (1946), pp. 1-2. The citations from Evagrius are from *Texts on Discrimination*.

11. How the Passions are Aroused — According to Traditional Orthodox Teaching

It's important for us to dwell a little on the way in which the passions are stirred up. This will also show us how to keep them quiet. We should point out that the path of arousal is in essence the same as the conception of the passion. This only to the extent that the birth is harder than the arousal. It doesn't yet exist in us as a sleeping beast which has only to be awakened. But a flammable material is in us even before any passion, made up of the natural passions; these help in some way in the conception of the passions, just as the already existing passion helps in its arousal.

Who hasn't had the experience, that a passion is stirred up sometimes after we have made a good decision, or when we are carrying it out, or after we have finished doing it.[59] Other times we find ourselves in a state of meditation or of spiritual rest in which the problem hasn't been presented to us of making a decision, and yet the passion is awakened. In all cases it is aroused as a resistance to, and a revolt against, disregarded tendencies. In such situations and in others, the passions have their antecedents in us.[60]

We can ask the question then: "How is the passion aroused in these cases?"

In all the Orthodox spiritual writings we find the following sequence as the way in which the passions are aroused in every circumstance: Satan puts a sinful thought into our mind, the so-called attack *(prosboli)*, which we think that we can also translate by the word *bait*. It is the first appearance of the simple thought that we can commit this or that sinful deed. It appears in the mind as a simple possibility. It isn't yet a sin, because we haven't yet taken a position in regard to it. It seems to be outside of us; we didn't create it, and it still has only a theoretical character, a not very serious possibility, which doesn't seem to concern us much. We are preoccupied with our whole being with something else. We don't know where it came from; it seems as though someone were playing and threw it on the side of the road. But we continue to think about it. So it has all the characteristics of a thought discarded by somebody else and therefore the holy Fathers attribute it to Satan. It is the

---

[59] Mark the Ascetic, *No Righteousness by Works* 88: "When the Devil sees that the mind has prayed from the heart, then he brings great and wicked temptations." *GrPh* 1, p. 115; cf. *Phi* 1, p. 132.
[60] Mark the Ascetic, *On the Spiritual Law* 179: "When you see that the appetites which lie within you are moving powerfully and calling the peaceful mind to some passion, know that the mind was occupied before hand with them and has stirred them up and put them in the heart." *GrPh* 1, p. 107; cf. *Phi* 1, p. 122.

110 PART ONE: A. PURIFICATION FROM THE PASSIONS

simple thought of a possible sinful deed, but no concrete image of this act and of the circumstances in which it could be carried out have yet taken shape in our minds.[61] There are cases, however, when a passion is stirred up all at once and inflames us immediately.

When a passion is aroused, though, as an ignited thought, from this attack until the sinful deed, we find numerous steps. St. Hesychios of Sinai numbers four: the provocation, the coupling *(synduasmos)*, the assent *(synkatathesis)*, the concrete action.[62] St. John of Damascus numbers seven: the attack, the coupling, the struggle, the passion, the agreement, the actualization, and the enslavement.[63] The decisive moment is when our thought takes a position. If we have rejected the thought at the first moment, we have escaped. If, however, we start to think about it, to relish the sin in our mind the "coupling" or the mingling of our thoughts with those of the wicked demons has already happened.[64] Now we have joined ourselves with the evil thought; it has become part of us. It is no longer something foreign in us. By it we have entered the area of the sin and we can hardly stop the full development of this process once it is set in motion. The assent to the fact follows next, or the plan composed by our thoughts and the thoughts of Satan for the realization of the fact.[65] Only now does the simple thought materialize in images.[66] According to St. John of Damascus, by the coupling of our thoughts with this thought, the inner passion is produced, as a second phase.

The bait, the provocation, isn't yet a sin,[67] because it doesn't yet depend on us to produce it,[68] and absolutely no man is spared from it.

---

[61] Mark the Ascetic defines the bait thrown out by Satan as "…the appearance of a persistent thought of evil." *On Baptism*, PG 65.1016A, or "A provocation is an image-free stimulation in the heart." *On the Spiritual Law* 140, *Phi* 1, p. 119. St. John of Damascus characterizes it this way: "A [provocation is a] simple suggestion by Satan, of a certain thing, for example: 'do this,' or 'that,' as he did with the Lord: 'Command that these stones become bread' (Matthew 4:3). See also *On the Virtues and the Vices* 146, *Phi* 2, p. 338.
[62] St. Hesychios, *On Watchfulness and Holiness* 46, *Phi* 1, p. 170.
[63] *On the Virtues and the Vices*, GrPh 2, p. 235; cf. *Phi* 2, pp. 337-8.
[64] St. Hesychios, *op. cit.*
[65] *Ibid.*, "Third comes our assent to the provocation, with both sets of intermingling thoughts contriving how to commit the sin in practice."
[66] Mark the Ascetic writes, "Once our thoughts are accompanied by images we have already given them our assent; for a provocation does not involve us in guilt so long as it is not accompanied by images." *On the Spiritual Law* 141, *Phi* 1, pp. 119.122.
[67] Mark the Ascetic, *On Baptism* 152, PG 65.1020A: "The bait is neither sin, nor righteousness, but the proof of our free will. Therefore the bait is permitted to be thrown to us, that on the one hand those that tend toward the fulfilling of the commandments be shown to be faithful, and on the other hand those who are immersed in pleasure, be shown to be unbelievers."
[68] *On the Virtues and Vices*, 146, *Phi* 2, pp. 337-8.

But let's look a little closer. What is this simple thought of sin, which appears without images, in our mind or in our heart? First of all, how does this thought come from the Devil? Does it come directly or by something in us too? St. Mark the Ascetic, says, in his treatise *On Baptism,* that it is thrown into us by Satan; in another place, *On the Spiritual Law,* in text 140 he writes, that "... the attack is an imageless movement of the heart," and again in text 179, that "the desires call the mind to some passion...."[69]

On the other hand Diadochos of Photiki states that from the time of Baptism Satan is no longer in the depths of the soul, in other words in the mind, but "... in the bodily senses... working via the easily influenced body on those who are still babes in soul."[70] "... now he rides on the juices [humors] of the flesh, as one who is nesting in the body, so he can make the mind turn somersaults on the slipperiness of the passions,"[71] "... enveloping the mind by the bodily juices as by smoke in the sweetness of irrational appetites."[72] Or, as St. John of the Ladder points out: "... many times a devil lurks in the stomach and keeps man from getting full, even if he were to swallow all of Egypt or drink the whole Nile."[73]

From this it follows that Satan sends the bait to us by means of the bodily appetites; he stirs up some appetite which is sleeping in the subconscious.[74] Diadochos comments: "... our mind, having a very fine sense, appropriates somehow through the body the work of the thoughts suggested to it by evil spirits."[75]

The bait is, then, the first appearance in our consciousness of an evil desire. At first it isn't vehement, and takes the form of a simple thought. Better said our consciousness takes notice of it already from the first stirring and this, its first activity in the consciousness, takes place in the form of a thought. Only if it isn't suffocated by our determined reaction, does this movement gain intensity. So we can resist it only with great difficulty.

---

[69] *On the Spiritual Law* 141, 179, *RoFil* 1, pp. 243, 246; *cf. Phi* 1, pp. 119, 122.
[70] On Spiritual Knowledge and Discrimination 79, *GrPh* 1, p. 259; *cf. Phi* 1., pp. 280-1.
[71] Chapter 82, *GrPh* 1, p. 262; *cf. Phi* 1, p. 283.
[72] Chapter 76, *GrPh* 1, p. 258; *cf. Phi* 1, p. 279.
[73] *The Ladder of Divine Ascent* 14.17, *PG* 88.868C; *cf. The Ladder* 14.27 (Willits, CA, 1973), p. 143.
[74] Vladimir Lossky, *The Mystical Theology of the Eastern Church* (Crestwood, NY, 1976), p. 130. "*Logismoi* are thoughts or images which rise out of the lower regions of the soul, the 'subconscious.'" Lossky refers us to a book which we wish we had: V. Zarin, *The Foundations of Orthodox Asceticism,* [in Russian] St. Petersburg, 1902.
[75] *On Spiritual Knowledge and Discrimination* 83, *RoFil* 1, p. 380; *cf. Phi* 1, p. 284.

Usually this first awakening of a desire—the first appearance of the bait in the conscience—is caused by the sight of some external thing.[76] This being the case, the idea might arise that Satan is nesting in the appearance of something and sends a thought of sin directly into our thought, without using the awakening of a subconscious appetite, as a means. Even so it isn't excluded that in this case too the appetite in us has been awakened before the sight of the external object. The desire already there, however, wants to put the blame on the object. The coming of the bait in most cases by this route has made the Fathers recommend the closing of the senses during the onslaught of temptation.

Sometimes, however, the bait appears in us without any exterior object. The remembrance of a repeated sin comes into play.[77] Nevertheless, however it may be, both in the first case, as well as in the second, it's very reasonable to admit that the ultimate driving force of the bait is a spirit distinct from us, because otherwise why is the memory of a certain passion aroused exactly in such and such cases and why is it aroused only at certain moments of looking at external things?

This is the Orthodox view in regard to the arousal of the passions. So we see that in essence there is no distinction whatever between it and that of Blondel. They are identical in detail too. If the bait or the attack is the first sign which the "mutinous rebel" sends to our consciousness, the coupling is the phase in which the mind finds the "reason" and the "justification." So it creates arguments in the bait's favor. It is convinced to go over to its side, completely or with some reserve. It is the phase of clothing the awakened appetite with rational principles, or better said with false ones, so that later, in the phase of assent, the will, too, might give its support to the movement which has won its respectability from reason. So this movement is also helped by the passage of every moment from its awakening in the consciousness, in other words from the time when the reason lingers over it. And so it grows more and more in

---

[76] Evagrius asks: "Does the idea stir up the passions, or the passions, the idea? Some think it's the first way, and some the second. But the passions are stirred up by the senses. When, however, love and restraint are present, the passion doesn't move, but when it isn't present, it moves.... Love is the restraint of anger." See also *The Praktikos* [37-8] and *Chapters on Prayer, 37-8* (Kalamazoo, MI), p. 26.

[77] St. Maximus, *Chapters on Love* 1.84: "First the memory brings a simple thought into the mind. Lingering there, it moves the passion. If it isn't removed, it bends the mind to consent. When this happens, it proceeds to bring the sin to realization." *GrPh* 2, p. 12; *cf. Phi* 2, p. 62. And here we have four steps: the simple thought (the bait), the stirred up passion, the assent, the deed. It seems that the simple thought (the bait, the attack), is nothing else than the arousal of the passion in the subconscious; it doesn't come from anywhere else. In reality the thought transmitted by the aroused passion hasn't yet penetrated the consciousness with vehemence. Therefore it isn't yet a passion for our consciousness.

intensity. Thus only because of the lack of the firmness of reason, does the movement of an appetite become sin. The reason could be firm enough to immediately reject the movement which appears in the consciousness; it could say "no" to pseudo-rationality. It could ignore the movement of the appetite and then it wouldn't become a passion. This is why the holy Fathers first of all ask for a strengthening of the mind in its position.[78] Of course this is also a matter of willpower, but willpower connected with the mind and which is also facilitated by man's determination to be enlightened in regard to his purposes and duties. For us, voluntary action is closely interwoven with the intellectual in the work of man's restoration, just as in his fall into sin moral and intellectual causes were equally interwoven.

So the work of man's reestablishment must begin with faith, which first is a question of will, and secondly is related to the mind; this gives faith an intellectual attitude, or a conception which gives it arguments against sin. Therefore the duty imposed on the one who wants to go ahead in his life toward perfection is to watch continually the thoughts which appear in the field of the conscience. He must eliminate the thought of any passion at its first appearance. The guarding of the mind, attention, and steadfast, alert resistance to thoughts *(phylaki noos, nipsis, karteria, prosochi)* are continuous recommendations of the spiritual masters for the one who doesn't want to fall victim to the passions. It would seem that this means that we are held during the course of our life to a difficult, narrow road, which would make any enrichment of it impossible. In fact, it means keeping the mind submerged, full of love, in the divine infinite, which enriches it with ever new and pure meanings.

The things continually discarded in asceticism aren't new enthusiasm and new inspiration of a spiritual order, but exaggerated tendencies of sensual appetites. Far from creating an enrichment of the spirit, they constrict it. They tie the infinite to finite things, and hinder it in the inclinations of the growth of its understanding. Things discarded often are boulders thrown in the stream which is surging ahead, and their removal makes it bigger. The body is allowed the satisfaction of strictly necessary

---

[78] Evagrius asks for a fixation of the mind so that it doesn't wander anymore. Wandering makes it easy for it to slide, easy for it to be enticed by any argument. "The mind that is flittering here and there is stabilized by reading, vigil, and prayer; the aroused appetite is withered by hunger, work and withdrawal; and anger is demolished by psalmody, longsuffering and mercy. *Praktikos* 15. See also *The Praktikos* and *Chapters on Prayer*, (Kalamazoo, MI), p. 20.

needs. But no truly rational motive whatsoever can plead for the removal of every dam in the path of the appetites which are directed impetuously down narrow, flooded streets.

12. The Passionate State and Care

The nerve of all the passions is the passionate state,[79] the longing which connects us to the visible appearances of things which promise us much and give us nothing or very little.

The passionate state, or enslavement to the passions attracts all of our psychic powers toward the exterior. It is the adhesive which glues us to the surface of the exterior world. The problem of asceticism is how can this enslavement to the passions *(prospatheia),* the substance of the passions, be slain, not how to slay our authentic nature and the world we live in. The challenge is, how can we live in this world as free beings, admiring it and understanding it as a transparent creation of God, without this admiration enslaving us to its purely perceptible and opaque surface, and thus hinder our development as beings oriented toward the infinite spiritual order. How can we use the world, the road toward our goal, without falling and succumbing on it?

But that which still ties us to things is care.[80] It is the bitter fruit of the passions or of being impassioned with the things of the world. Passion reaches its high point in the taste of pleasure and in the revolt against pain (dejection, anger). The passionate man alternates his existence between the voluptuousness of pleasure and the torture of pain. Many times these two extremes aren't easy to separate. The moments occupied by pleasure and by pain strictly speaking are perhaps rare but both keep our nature in tension long before they are actually experienced. Man spends most of his life waiting for and seeking pleasure and in the fear of present and future pain. This is the fruit of the passions, an unceasing manifestation of the passions in us. These periods of waiting and of fear produce care in us. But even in the moments when we no longer have the actual consciousness that we are waiting for pleasure, or expecting pain, we work for the certainty of pleasure and for the avoidance of some unspecified future pain. The driving force which compels us in this process is care. It represents the passionate state in the more conspicuous times of everyday life and steadfastly substitutes for it in the moments of its retreat to deeper levels. When this "Madam Impassioned One" is sleeping, her servant, Mrs. Care *(Frau Sorge)* is alert and watching, "with ruffled hair and with eyes almost always red from lack of sleep."

---

[79] We find no convenient word in English for the Romanian *impatimire*. We can call it "passionateness," or "impassionedness." The author gives the Greek in the next paragraph, *prospatheia.* In the patristic sense this means the attachment, the fastening of the soul to the body and its passions. *trs*

[80] In the sense of anxiety, worry. *trs*

116   PART ONE: A. PURIFICATION FROM THE PASSIONS

According to Heidegger, care is a structure which includes the whole of man's constitution. By it, man is forever "ahead of himself" *(Sichvorwegsein)*. It's an uneasy structure of his dynamics, an existential structure, not an unchanging trait. In this general characteristic of man "... of always being ahead of himself" the phenomenon of "fear" *(Angst)*[81] surfaces; it's another existential structure of man, fed because he is an existence belonging to the world,[82] an existence which is uncertain of the possibilities which the world offers him. Secondly he is nourished by the feeling that he is at the mercy of his responsibilities.[83] He has to forever launch out toward his future possibilities, in other words, toward his more appropriate opportunity.[84]

The motive for care is fear. By it man tries to continually assure the realization of his future possibilities in connection with the world to which he finds himself nailed. To be part of the world means essentially to be anxious.[85] Anxiety doesn't let him loose from its chains for a moment: *Cura tenet, quamdiu vixerit*, [he will have care, as long as he lives] says a legend from mythology, which divides man up between Jupiter (the soul), Tellus (the earth) and anxiety (earthly existence).[86]

Heidegger confesses that this interpretation of man as care, as well as this phenomenological analysis of it, came to him when he was trying to do an interpretation of Augustinian anthropology, in other words of the Hellenic-Christian.[87]

This author characterizes care as: 1) the fruit of fear, 2) the intertwining of man with the world (the fear of the world), 3) the cause of man's forever getting ahead of himself, 4) because of the consciousness that he has betrayed himself, 5) for the fulfillment of his more fitting possibilities. But by care man doesn't in fact look for or find the realization of his most fitting possibilities, because he has never really gotten to intimately know himself; so the proper purpose of his existence has

---

[81] Fr. Staniloae has rendered the German *Angst* as "fear." In English we would prefer to call it "anxiety" or "dread." See the glossary in *Being and Time*, mentioned below. trs

[82] "The 'what' of anxiety is the condition of having been thrown into the world. The 'why' of anxiety is the condition of being in the world." *Sein und Zei*, (Halle a.d. S., 1935), p. 191. *cf.* Martin Heidegger, *Being and Time* (New York, 1962), para. 41, p. 235.

[83] "The abandonment of existence [Dasein] to itself shows itself first concretely in fear." *Sein und Zeit*, p. 192. *cf. Being and Time*, p. 236.

[84] "Existence [*Dasein*] is being that revolves in its being around itself.... However: Being to the very own ability-to-be means ontologically that existence is beforehand itself in its being." *Sein und Zeit*, p. 191; *cf. Being and Time*, p. 236.

[85] See *Sein und Zeit*, pp. 191-200; *cf. Being and Time*, para. 41-2, pp. 235-244.

[86] "Being-in-the-world is essentially care." *Sein und Zeit* p. 193; *cf. Being and Time*, para. 41, p. 237.

[87] *Sein und Zeit*, note 4, p. 199; *cf. Being and Time*, Division One, Chapter Six, note iv, p. 492.

remained hidden by care. All of this corresponds to the Christian anthropological conception.[88]

But Heidegger's analysis of care isn't complete, first of all because the care which he has in mind has several more characteristics, and secondly because Christianity recognizes another care too, besides the worldly one. From his analysis of worldly care, in other words, three elements are lacking: the passionate state, pleasure, and pain; they are the existential spikes which fasten man to the world, by which he feels *In-der-Welt-sein* (Being-in-the-World), and which also explain man's fear of the world. The passionate state which looks for pleasure ties man to the world. Joined by pain, it makes him continually rush ahead of himself to assure his pleasure and to avoid pain; but worldly fear is one precisely determined: the fear of lacking pleasure in the future and of having a part in pain. Moreover, this makes man, instead of discovering his intimate self *(das Selbst)* to also look for the realization of his own possibilities, and to remain, because of care, fallen in the state of common self *(das Man)*; he realizes the possibilities improper to himself, or the unfulfillment which Heidegger doesn't explain, because he has overlooked the elements needed to explain it.

The things that Heidegger has emphasized of the effects of this anxiety are the total or exaggerated captivity of man by the world and his descent to an existence in ashes, inadequate, monotonous, enslaved and superficial.

Heidegger sees the final explanation of care in the feeling of man that he must realize "his most fitting possibilities," the goal unfulfilled by the care analyzed by him. Even the man who has regained his own intimacy continually rushes on ahead of himself in the realization of his most fitting possibilities. This shows us that another kind of care has nevertheless sparkled in Heidegger's mind; he was really too shy to call it by the same name. This is man's care for his eternal destiny, the care for salvation.

This care is opposed to the other one. It is no longer care for his existence in the world; it no longer comes from the passionate state for the pleasure of the world and so neither from the fear of its pains. On the contrary, it arises where we "lay aside all earthly care," because it means the care to please God, not to please the world and to take part in its pleasures and to be exempt from its pain. This care grows from the responsibility which man has for his true self, satisfying this command of

---

[88] "The because-of-why remains ungrasped.... To-be-beforehand in oneself means therefore the 'oneself,' the at-any-time, the Self in the sense of Oneself. Also in figurativeness the Being remains real beforehand itself." *Sein und Zeit,* p. 193; *cf. Being and Time,* para. 41, pp. 237-8.

responsibility; it is at the same time a continual launching out of man beyond himself, toward the source of his eternal life; but it is a launching out towards a height beyond the world, not towards one below. Thus it is a true overcoming. It too includes a fear, but it is man's fear that death ends all, and that this fear alone will succeed in delivering him from what he fears. However, in the definition of this fear the passionate state of the world no longer counts as man's absolute and total belonging to the world *(In-der-Welt-Sein)*. Man is still in the world, but above the world; he is, in a necessary way, in the world because of the fleshly side of his nature. But he is above the world; in the world as a free and spiritual being, but in a different way than things and animals. The world can dispose of him, but not of his whole nature. Rather he disposes of the world.

Man must escape from the first care, in order to become available to God. Then he is free from the passionate state; he has gained dispassion. He has gained freedom from the passions and the world. Purification aims at liberation from this care, not at liberation from care for God. By it, or by the fulfilling of the will of God, our authentic nature is realized.

PART ONE (cont.)

PURIFICATION

B. Purification by the Virtues

13. The Order of Purification and Patristic Spiritual Methods

The purification of the passions can't be attained by realizing a neutral state of the soul, but by replacing the passions with opposing virtues.

In Eastern ascetical literature, writings dedicated in a special way to the method of the gradual purification from the passions by opposing virtues, are well known. One is *The Ladder of Divine Ascent* by St. John Climacus;[89] another is *Directions to Hesychasts* by Callistus and Ignatius Xanthopoulos;[90] another *The Ascetical Homilies* of St. Isaac the Syrian, although the latter is less systematic.[91]

The first, which dates from the 7th century, is a complete treatise on the spiritual life. It describes the thirty steps which a monk must climb from the moment he renounces the world until he reaches perfection, in other words, love. He writes only for monks. Just in passing does he address a word to common Christians, in order to show them how they can also bring their lives closer to that of monks, which without doubt is the perfect one. St. John Climacus, also called St. John of the Ladder, wants to emphasize in his *Ladder* the ascent from a less perfect step in life to a more perfect one, thus to the laws by which life can be perfected.[92] Following these rules and writings for monks, the author establishes the renunciation of the world, an external renunciation, as the first step. On the second step, he places the mortification of the passionate state of the world, that is, of the impulses which tie us to it, as an internal renunciation.[93] In the third step, on exile, he perfects these

---

[89] *PG* 88.631-1210; cf. the translation by Archimandrite Lazarus Moore (Willits, CA, 1973). Note differences in the text and in the numbering of the paragraphs.
[90] *GrPh* 4, pp. 197-295; cf. *Directions to Hesychasts,* in *PhilPH*, pp. 162-270.
[91] [in Greek] (Athens, 1961).
[92] "The most hallowed virtues are like Jacob's ladder and unholy sins are like the spear which fell from Peter the chief Apostle. So the former connected the one to the other bear up to heaven the one who chooses them while the latter constrain one another." Chapter 9.1, *PG* 88.841; cf. Moore, p. 129.
[93] Step 2.1: "The man who truly loves the Lord will no longer love the world ... he will no longer be concerned with possessions, or with parents, or with the glory of life, or with friends —with nothing worldly." This chapter speaks of detachment. *PG* 88.653; cf. Moore, p. 56.

two renunciations. They have in view various fleshly passions (gluttony, love of money, unchastity, and then bitterness and anger which grow from them); obedience follows them as step four, by which pride and vainglory are cut off.[94] Here he shows the need for having a virtue opposed to pride. He follows with repentance for the life to come (step six) and mourning which causes joy (step seven). From tears come meekness and freedom from anger. So they are put on step eight. For "... as water slowly poured on fire, puts it out completely, likewise the tears of genuine sorrow truly put out all the flames of anger and fury."[95] Anger gives birth to the keeping in mind of the evil of others. So after he has shown how to get rid of it, the time has come to discuss the virtue which opposes this sin, that is, the forgetfulness of the evil of others (step nine). A result of hatred and of remembering the evil of others is slander, so it is combated on the next step (step ten).

The "door to slander" is talkativeness. Its control by silence takes up step 11. Step 12 deals with lying, the child of talkativeness, while number 13 discusses laziness, the nephew of gossip. On the other steps he follows with a description of each passion and the ways to combat them, starting with gluttony and ending with pride (steps 14-23), so that on the next step he describes simplicity or guilelessness as an opposing virtue (step 25); the discernment of thoughts is next (step 26), then tranquility of body and soul (step 27). Prayer, the mother of all the virtues follows (step 28), and then dispassion, as heaven on earth, as the perfection and resurrection of the soul before the common resurrection (step 29), and at the top of the ladder, the chain of the three virtues: faith, hope, and love (step 30).

The method of Callistus and Ignatius, called *Directions to Hesychasts* in the English *Philokalia*, and written in the 14th century, is also known as *The Century*, because it is divided into 100 chapters. At first sight it creates the impression that it is a long string of quotations without any definite plan, which led K. Krumbacher to the following opinion:

> This attempt to establish an ascetical doctrinal system wasn't successful; unrelated chapters are placed one after the other in a purely external way and the progress in exposition is obtained by clumsy periods of transition.[96]

---

[94] Step 4.5: "For obedience means to no longer trust in yourself for the rest of your life, no matter what good you do." *PG* 88.680; cf. Moore, p. 67.
[95] Step 8.1, *PG* 88.828; cf. Moore, p. 124.
[96] Krumbacher, K. *The Vision of God in the Hesychasm of Palamas, A Handbook of Late Byzantine Mysticism* [in German] (Würzburg, 1938), p. 15. Amman gives us a translation of the treatise with an introductory study. In 1397, Callistus was patriarch of Constantinople until his repose seven months later.

ORDER AND METHODS OF PURIFICATION 121

A completely different view is given in the introduction of volume five of the Russian *Philokalia*, which includes this work:

> The book of Callistus and Ignatius contains a sure systematic exposition of the whole spiritual way of life with everything that has to be done; no one had undertaken such a work up until that time, nor we might add, since.[97]

The truth can be seen in a presentation of the order in which the work describes the ascetical efforts in regard to perfection: Chapter one discusses the grace of the Holy Spirit, found in the hearts of the faithful since Baptism; chapters two to four give the purpose of the book, the beginning and the final end of the spiritual life— the beginning means to live according to the Savior's commands, while the final end means coming back to the grace given to us at Baptism.[98] Chapters five to seven emphasize the grace given to us at Baptism, the passions which have covered it and how to find it again by obeying the commands. The beginning of the work of the commands consists of the calling on the name of Jesus Christ, from whom comes peace and love (chapters 8-13). Chapters 14-15 deal with the renunciation of the world and submission.

So far we have seen the principle introduction; next follows practical teaching. So chapter 16 (divided into 10 parts) takes up once again the theme of faith, good works and the need for a peaceful soul, undistracted and quiet. After chapters 17 and 18 have treated the fears of beginners, the following (19-24), discuss the method of the Jesus Prayer. Next it is shown how the various parts of the day, the different days of the week, and the holy fasts are to be spent (25-27); then various virtues, such as humility, the gift of discrimination, and repentance are described (38-47), so as to take up once again the theme of pure prayer (48-54). Next the warmth produced in the heart by this prayer and the love of God contained in it are considered (55-57). The following chapters talk about tears (58), divine action (61), divine light (60, 63), good and bad imagination (64-69, 73), the mind and its dispassion (70, 72), divine and false comfort (74-76), meekness and quiet (77-78), again repentance (79-81), attention (82), the calling on Jesus from within the heart (83), ecstatic love (84), being left by God to learn (85), dispassion (86-7), the difference between dispassion and impassionedness (88-9). Chapters 90-2 are an exposition of the three theological virtues and of the Eucharist, while chapters 94-100 close with two summaries, recommending this way of spiritual life as the best, although there are also other saving ones.

---

[97] *Ibid.*, p. 110.
[98] Callistus and Ignatius, *Directions to Hesychasts* 5, *GrPh* 4, p. 199; *cf. PhiPH*, p. 166.

In Callistus and Ignatius' *Method* we don't find a detailed treatment of the passions and how to deal with each one, as in St. John Climacus, but the former presents instead the positive side of the spiritual ascent; it gives much attention to the Jesus Prayer, divine activity in the soul, enlightenment and dispassion, which shows the recent influence of the Hesychast movement on it. This is why the method of *The Century* integrates well with the method of *The Ladder*.

Although it does contain many repetitions, they can be explained by the fact that on the various steps of the spiritual life, the virtues already gained must be taken up continually in higher form. In the chapters of *The Century* we can distinguish three phases of the spiritual ascent.[99] After recommendations for a general spiritual attitude (chapters 16-24), beginning with chapter 24 and ending with chapter 39, we find numerous precepts regarding the external discipline of the spiritual life; from chapters 40-60, there are teachings referring to the inner life, for a life realized more by human powers, and up until chapter 89 the authors continue with precepts from the life lived by power from on high, all of which culminate in dispassion.

The homilies of St. Isaac the Syrian contain about the same material as *The Ladder*, but the former work isn't so systematic. On the other hand, the analysis of the different passions and virtues are much more thorough. A strong accent is put on the importance of the bearing of trouble for purification.[100]

It's not within the scope of this work to describe a practical, detailed method of purification, because it is a reflection on all the ascetical efforts and rules and of their culmination in union with God.

Therefore, in this exposition we will keep in mind all the methods, take what is characteristic of each and integrate them. We appreciate, along with John Climacus, the gravity of the passions, but we haven't put their analysis within the framework of the method of fighting against them; rather we have dealt with them already, separately, because their analysis and their way of being born and aroused, give rise to precious indications for the order of the means of combating them and avoiding them. And in fact, from the way the passions are born and aroused, we have seen that the decisive moment, when a natural passion becomes a passion is that in which reason is shaken loose and slides over to the side of the aroused appetite.

It follows that the first care which we must have is to stabilize reason in a firm position. This is done by faith. By putting the beginning of the

---

[99] *cf.* Amman, p. 15.
[100] See his *Ascetical Homilies*.

ORDER AND METHODS OF PURIFICATION 123

spiritual life in the grace of God dwelling in us by Baptism, we find ourselves again with *The Century* of Callistus and Ignatius.

In general the simplest scheme and the one that corresponds best with the development of the spiritual life seems to us to be that of St. Maximus the Confessor in seven steps:[101] faith, fear of God, self-control or restraint, patience and longsuffering, hope, dispassion and love. So we will follow this scheme and other writings too, especially *The Ladder*.

---

[101] *Chapters on Love* 1.1-2; *cf.* Phi 2, p. 53.

14. Faith, the Basic State for Purification

Faith is the first step in the spiritual life. "Faith is by nature the beginning of virtues." Moreover, "Good is the end of the virtues and is concentrated in faith." Faith is concentrated good, and good is faith realized.[102]

We can't take any systematic action against the passions and we can't get any virtue started if faith isn't present as an impetus. Self-control, as a steady effort, has a lack of legitimacy without faith, and the fear of God presupposes faith in God. It's true that self-control and in an overall way a virtuous life in turn strengthens faith, but the primary driving force of them is nevertheless faith. Before any virtue whatsoever, before any human effort, we must somehow get faith inside us. And in as much as we have faith by divine grace, it is necessary that grace come before any good which we try to do. So the beginning of good is put in us by God through Baptism. All our virtuous life is nothing but an unfolding of this good put there by God. Of course it's not a question of an automatic development, beyond our control, but a development willed and helped by us, by all our effort.

So before any virtue whatsoever we must have the faith won or strengthened at Baptism. But its efficiency depends on our cooperation, so that we can advance on the way of the virtues toward perfection. Faith, therefore, is a virtue too, a good, but it shows itself as a good by our cooperation. At the beginning this is only the simple will to believe and not to do something. So inevitably the first effort of our will in view of the good, can have only this object: to believe. As far as we are concerned, we can't begin anywhere else, by some change for the good in our life, except to believe. And the one who wants to believe, arrives at the point where he can. There isn't anyone, who really wants to believe, who doesn't get the power to believe. But the fact that someone wanting to believe is able to, is due to a previous grace in us. Because by his simple will, man would never get to the point of believing. By trial and error he tends to imagine that everything depends only on his will, in order to accentuate the necessity of his contribution. Beyond experience, however, grace is present as a help. Even the fact that he is able to want to believe is a gift of faith, which however, doesn't force him to want to believe immediately. But from the moment somebody wants to believe, he has started in fact to believe, and the grace hidden in him from Baptism, or faith as a virtuality, has been awakened to actuality, by the fact that man has made his contribution.

---

[102] *Questions to Thalassios* 55, PG 90.564.

FAITH: THE BASIC STATE FOR PURIFICATION

So before starting out on the way of purification, it is necessary for man to strengthen his faith received at Baptism, by will,[103] but since faith is a relationship of mine to God, it can't be strengthened except by my beginning to think more often of Him, not in a theoretical way, as of a philosophical subject for study, but of Him on whom I depend for everything and Who can help me in my insufficiencies. But the thought of God is made real, or maintained by a short and frequent remembrance of Him, made with piety, with the feeling that we depend on Him. Such a thought concentrates our thoughts on God or on Jesus Christ, on what He has done for us, as the basis for the trust that He will help us now too. You see then why we think that Callistus and Ignatius in *The Centuries*, were completely justified in placing faith as a gift of grace, and the remembrance of the name of Jesus Christ at the beginning of their entire spiritual ascent:

> The beginning of every action pleasing to God is calling with faith on the life-saving name of our Lord Jesus Christ, as He Himself said: 'Without me ye can do nothing' (John 15:5). This is why all the great teachers of asceticism taught that before any work and respectable occupation whatsoever, all, and especially those who want to enter the state of divine quietness and to consecrate themselves to God, must pray to God and ask for His mercy, without doubting; they should invoke His holy and most sweet name, bearing it always in the mind and on the lips. They should force themselves in every possible way to live, breathe, sleep, wake up, eat and drink with Him and in Him.[104]

Certainly such a continual remembrance of God and especially of the name of Jesus isn't reached all at once. Neither is it good to reach it too quickly, because then the remembrance would be automatic. But it is good that the frequency of the commemoration of Jesus be increased gradually according to the soul's habit of concentrating on God with its growth in faith and in its love of God. Yet it is good that even at the beginning the believer remember God as often as possible with one name or another ("Lord," "Jesus,") or even by just concentrating on such a name, during a moment of trouble, or of rest, on the road, or at work.

Faith as the first step of the spiritual ascent, however, is also made necessary because of the way in which the passions are aroused. We have seen that the decisive moment in their arousal is when the reason slips from its natural position, and is drawn by the appearance of an ap-

---

[103] *Directions to Hesychasts* 7, *GrPh* 4, p. 202; *cf. PhiPH*, p. 169.
[104] *Directions to Hesychasts* 13, *GrPh* 4, p. 205. The Romanian text, which we followed, differs here somewhat from the English. *cf. PhiPH*, p. 173. *trs*

petite aroused in the consciousness. In that moment the appetite or this innocent natural passion gains power and becomes condemnable. Sin always begins by a fall of reason, by a fall from truth, by its going into a skid on a wrong road,[105] and by forgetting its purpose.[106] So here the first reinforcement must be given; the enemy has established a foothold. In other words reason must be strengthened in order to resist. This is done with faith. It stabilizes reason in an intellectual attitude,[107] in a [balanced] conception of life. Of course faith isn't, at least at the beginning, intellectual evidence which convinces reason by an urgency exclusively gnosiologic. It is also assimilated to a large degree by the will and as such is a virtue. It has a double aspect: intellectual and voluntary.

It is a concept, a point of view, but also an act of will. It is an intellectual-voluntary synthesis. But neither is the slipping of reason a purely intellectual act, but a voluntary one too. Neither has reason gone over to the side of appetite because it was convinced on purely intellectual grounds of the truth represented by it, but it did this by a weakening of will, mostly pretending that it was convinced in an intellectual way, rather than being really convinced. It follows that in the bringing back of reason to its original firmness a purely intellectual act isn't necessary, or at least it's not enough. Such an act would simply convince it of its error of judgment. Moral help is also needed. Just as reason has fallen, because it wanted to, so it is now stabilized by faith, because it wants to be. The fall is an intellectual-voluntary act; its remedy must be made by a similar act.

Certainly, by accentuating the will in the act of faith, we don't want to say that faith doesn't contain some evidence. It isn't an intellectual attitude which functions apart from the will. A Roman Catholic theologian says: "In the light of faith the same divine names which the philosophers pronounce receive an unquestionable dimension; they are deepened in content. Their meaning becomes analogous to new powers." [108] Concepts referring to God, which natural reason has, gain by

---

[105] Diadochos, *On Spiritual Knowledge* 5, *Phi* 1, p. 254.
[106] Certainly, there are also cases when someone resorts to certain condemnable acts, assuring everyone that he does them against his will, by force, because his life is at stake, etc. But in these cases too reason must produce its arguments that it is necessary to take this attitude, even "against its convictions," that it commits them against the truth. Here reason plays the most perverse roles; it argues the "rationality" of certain contrary acts in a way conscious of reason.
[107] In *Directions to Hesychasts* 16, of Callistus and Ignatius we read that when faith "begins to shine in the soul from the light of Grace, by the witness of thought, it strengthens the heart wholly in the certainty of hope...." *GrPh* 4, p. 214; *cf. PhiPH*, p.184. And Diadochos says this about the faith which hasn't reached fear and love: "He that only believes and isn't in love [with God], doesn't have the faith which he thinks he has. For he believes with a certain lightness of mind, and doesn't work under the fullness of the glory of love." *On Spiritual Knowledge* 21, *GrPh* 1, p. 240; *cf. Phi* 1, p. 258.
[108] Ch. Journet, *Connaissance et inconnaissance de Dieu* (Fribourg, 1943), p. 96.

faith a new brilliance, unknown to metaphysics and the natural man; they are like pearls brought out into the sunlight.[109] Thus faith sheds new evidence on certain rational truths referring to God. It is an evidence which grows gradually, so that with time, faith becomes a vision. But even from the beginning it brings a plus of evidence to certain truths which reason also has, and this means at the same time the stabilization of reason on various certainties.[110] Catholicism considers that faith has the certitude of various divine truths even before faith. Orthodoxy is less optimistic in this regard; she recognizes that natural reason can decipher various truths about God from the contemplation of the world, but she considers that an absolute assurance in them is lacking. In any case, the plus of evidence offered by faith must also mean for Catholics a plus of certitude, a plus of strength in the decision of standing beside these truths.

Where does this plus come from? Even if it means an increase of rational evidence, it doesn't come from it, but from above. Orthodoxy applies here her doctrine of the uncreated energies of God. An uncreated energy of God penetrates the mind as a light. This is why we said that faith doesn't depend only on the will, but it is also facilitated by the internal evidence and by the power from on high which brings this evidence, or it touches the powers of our spirit so that it can grasp the reality of God. But if it must be grasped by our powers they must also make an effort even if it is helped by divine influence. Therefore will is necessary too— not to create this evidence, but to bring it out into the open. By the voluntary laziness of reason, it was darkened; by the voluntary efforts of reason, helped by divine grace to overcome laziness, it is illuminated again. On the one hand in faith there is an element of the strengthening of will and reason, of their stimulation; on the other hand, the will contributes to the emphasis on the evidence from faith produced by grace. One grows on the other in a mutual way. Hiding Himself before man, God stimulates him, by a certain pressure to seek Him; and sought He partly reveals Himself in order to stimulate man

---

[109] *Ibid.*, p. 92. "The light—we could call it the charm of faith—in drawing into the field of its influence conceptual statements such as 'God is,' or 'God is the one who rewards,' confers on them a value of the truth so high that all at once it reaches the ultimate level of the mystery of divine existence (the Trinity) and of divine Providence (the redeeming Incarnation)." *See also* pp. 97-8.
[110] St. Gregory Palamas: "Faith always frees our people from every kind of error and establishes us in the truth and the truth in us and absolutely no one is going to move us from it, even if he considers us crazy, we who go out in ecstasy above understanding, by the true faith, and witnessing with word and deed, that we are not 'carried about with every wind of doctrine,' but maintain the one and true knowledge of Christians. Faith, exceeding inborn ideas from the contemplation of creatures, has united us with reason placed above all things." *The Defense* 2.3.42, p. 491. "Faith is not insanity, but knowledge which exceeds all rationality." *Ibid.*, 2.3.43, p. 493.

more. He sets our will in motion, but without this will He doesn't reveal Himself to us.

In time faith grows to a very brilliant evidence. But it grows in the measure in which we obey the commands and gain the virtues, because through them we show that we feel God and we also open ourselves more to Him. This means that it is present at the beginning, but it grows by means of all the virtues which we gain later. Moreover, each virtue once gained is no longer lost if we stay on the ascending road of the Christian spiritual life. It also remains after other virtues are born from it. It grows and receives superior qualitative modifications, under the influence of new virtues, in order to be coordinated with them.

Faith is the virtue for starting our journey. It is the stream which is joined by those of the other virtues, which becomes a mighty river, of a totally virtuous life, all encompassing and irreversible. In love all the virtues are gathered.[111] Meanwhile faith, has become a contemplation of God, just as love is contemplation.[112] But faith can't be knowledge from the beginning. From the liberation of mind darkened by passions, to that of the contemplation of God, there is a long road. Meanwhile we

---

[111] *Questions to Thalassios* 54, *PG* 90.525: "By the woman he understood the virtues of which love is the final crown."

[112] Mark the Ascetic, *On Baptism, PG* 65.1005: "Therefore O man, baptized in Christ, do only the work for which you received power and prepare yourself to receive the showing of Him who dwells in you...." In the *Directions to Hesychasts* of Callistus and Ignatius, 16b, we read: "Faith is double: One is for all Christians in general," [but we're not talking about that] "...but about that which rises up from the light of grace hidden in the soul and has the witness of the mind which strengthens the heart so that it will be steadfast in the certainty of hope which delivers man from any thought of himself; this isn't shown by obeying with our ears [faith by hearing] but by seeing with our spiritual eyes the mysteries hidden in the soul and the concealed divine riches, hidden to the eyes of the sons of the flesh and revealed in spirit to those who are called to the table of Christ." GrPh 4, pp. 213-14; *cf.* *PhiPH*, pp. 183-4. St. Gregory Palamas has this to say: "Because on the one hand this faith is a vision beyond the mind, and on the other hand the enjoyment of the things believed is a vision above that vision beyond the mind." *The Defense* 2.3.41, p. 489.

partake of a bit of that light, and only in the measure in which we get the layer of the mud of the passions off ourselves, will the glimmer of faith becomes a blinding light. The escape from ignorance at the beginning causes self-control to grow by fear.

15. The Fear of God and the Thought of Judgment

With progress, faith becomes the fear of God.[113] On the one hand, faith isn't born from the fear of God, but fear from faith, because to be afraid of Him, you must believe in Him. On the other hand, faith can't develop without going through fear, or maybe, even helped from the beginning by fear (Acts 2:37). So even at the beginning faith isn't purely theoretical, but has, by the fear which goes with it, an existential character. Faith which hasn't reached fear or isn't accompanied from the beginning by fear hasn't gained a high enough degree of efficiency to lead to action.

The fear of God is the opposite of the fear of the world. Its purpose is to overwhelm the fear of the world. The fear of the pain and of the hardships of the world makes us with all heedlessness chase after its pleasures and prosperous situations to protect ourselves from future troubles. Fear of the world ties us to the world; it makes us obey it and not be obedient to a high calling from God, which comes to us by faith. So the world's force of attraction, manifested not only by the passionate attachment to the pleasures of the world, but also by the fear of the world, must be counteracted by a greater fear: the fear of God. At the beginning we aren't in a state to feel the joys of which God will make us a part; so we can't be torn from the world by them. Therefore we must be snatched from it by an act of power, of fright, by a great fear, by that of God. This is why the spiritual writers make a distinction between the two kinds of fear of God: the fear of slaves, that is the fear of His punishment, and the fear from love, that is the fear of not having His blessings. The first belongs to beginners, the second to the advanced. But the beginning fear of God is not only a weakness, but also a great power to confront the fear of the world, which is only weakness and slavery, totally lacking in freedom. We endure the fear of the world; it dominates us by the weakening of our will, which makes us active agents, instead of passive puppets. Even in it there is a power from God.

Heidegger distinguishes between 1) the fear "of something in the world" *(Furcht)* and 2) the fear of the emptiness of the world *(Angst)*,[114] that is of existence in the world; the latter is felt as threatening at every moment, with its dullness and nothingness, the personalness of living, which makes its intimacy transparent to everyone.

---

[113] "The divine fathers have put fear after faith." *Directions to Hesychasts* 17, GrPh 4, p. 219; cf. *PhiPH*, p. 190.
[114] In English we would call this anxiety. *trs*

FEAR OF GOD AND THOUGHT OF JUDGMENT   131

But the man fallen into the ash-like form of existence no longer knows the fear of the commonplace *(Angst)*. Once in a while it suddenly appears in his consciousness, as a brief revelation of the intimacy which is drowned and wants to be saved. Man has so weaned himself from the awareness of the presence of his intimacy and of his own existence—the common cliché that he is frightened by such revelations to the contrary—and throws himself even harder into the commonplace. This is the fear *(Furcht)* of something in the world, or it is the fear of losing something from the world. It is the fear of losing the opportunities for pleasure, which might bring him back to his intimacy, to independent living, without the comfortable support of the world.[115]

In this theory we find, in a more reserved form, three truths which basically agree with the Christian teaching of fear: 1) that the earthly life of man is inevitably accompanied by fear; 2) that by this fear the human being has been given a shield against being drowned in the world; and 3) that man has perverted this fear which must keep him from the world and bind him to God, the source of authentic existence, concentrated in the intimacy of the spirit. He has changed it into a fear of not being somehow deprived of the world, of existence in the ashy horizon of the world, into the fear of being detached from the world, to live as a spiritual being.

The fear of God, which is born from the faith in Him, could be then a resurrection of primordial fear, proper to the spiritual fear of man, a resurrection of *Angst*, in the terminology of Heidegger. However, in the primordial state man didn't have only this fear of being lost by separation from God, but also a fear joined with trust in Him.

Of course, Heidegger avoided saying that *Angst* is the fear of God. He considered it the fear of the world; not a fear of the world being lost, but rather a fear of being lost in the world; not an apprehension which would draw man to the world, as *Furcht*, but one that puts him on guard against its nothingness. We think, however, that human nature's fundamental and primordial fear, of falling into the automatism of sin, of the passions, of the world, can't be explained without the feeling that he is responsible for the preservation and development of his spiritual character. Now this feeling of responsibility, the consciousness that he will have to answer for this fall into the arms of the world, can't be explained

---

[115] "The 'of-what' of fear is inner worldly, approaching close by from a certain direction, derogative being that can stay away." pp. 185-6. "In distinction to *Furcht* [fear], the of-what of fear is not an inner worldly being.... The of-what of fear is totally vague...the threat therefore cannot approach from a certain direction close by; it is already there, and yet nowhere. In the of-what of fear the 'nothing is and nowhere evident'" pp. 186-9. *Sein und Zeit* (Halle a.d. S, 1935); cf. *Being and Time*, (New York, 1962), pp. 230-1.

without there existing a superior forum also of a spiritual character, on which it depends. If it would only be man with the assimilation with the world, man's fear of this perspective would be totally unexplainable. In the fear of being submerged in the world *(Angst)*, man's character of a spiritual being is revealed to him, a being made to have a relationship with God, Who can save him as a spiritual being.

The fear of sin by attachment to the world is basically the fear of God. If by faith we are given at the beginning an evidence of the presence of God, by fear the revelation of this evidence grows for us and we feel this growth as a force powerful enough to weaken and to break all the ties which chain us to the world: passionateness, fear, worldly care. God, who reveals His power to us by fear, makes us dread falling into the arms of sin, or of the world; He takes from us the fear of losing the opportunities of bliss in the world. The fear of God overwhelms the fear of the world, that of losing it. On the contrary, it promotes the fear of our being lost in the world, by attachment to it. It gives us the fear of the world in this second sense; it gives us the fear of the world as a danger for our true and eternal existence.

So in the fear of God is manifested the consciousness of our eternal destiny of not being assimilated by the world. The feeling of the nothingness with which the world threatens us is made known—the sense that the world runs contrary to our eternal destiny, assured by the living of our own intimacy.

Thus in the fear of God the consciousness of an authority is revealed to us, the sense of a reality superior to us, not inferior, as the world is, the consciousness of an authority which we can't disregard. We can't do just anything, we can't submerge ourselves in the world, because we feel the prohibition on the part of a forum to which we must give an account.

In fact, in the fear of sin, in the fear of falling into the embraces of the world, which is one with the fear of God, we don't have the consciousness of an immediate danger, but of a future one, and namely of an evil which will burden our existence to the infinite. Moreover, the deep fear itself, in man's nature, of being lost in the world *(Angst),* is a fear of an infinite evil. But infinity is right here, too. We don't fear that by our falling into the waves of the world we will completely disappear, but that our existence will become eternally unbearable. If there would be only the world, and the perspective of a total loss in it, this *Angst* which Heidegger talks about, wouldn't exist.

Hence the consciousness that the consequences of our fall won't be completely known until we pass over to life eternal. So the fear of God

FEAR OF GOD AND THOUGHT OF JUDGMENT 133

is a fear of His judgment which will seal our fate forever; it is the fear of the last judgment and of the tortures of an eternal, non-authentic, unfulfilled existence.

In this sense the fear of God is inseparable from the thought of the last judgment. Eastern asceticism advises us to meditate unceasingly on the last judgment, in order to increase in us the fear of God, by which we avoid sin.

Just as faith, growing by the virtues which spring from it, undergoes various transformations, so too fear persists on the highest steps of the spiritual life, but it is ennobled. St. Maximus harmonizing the verses in 1 John 4.13 and Psalm 34.10 says:

> Fear is of two kinds: One clean, the other not. Thus the fear which is born from waiting for the punishment for sin, having sin as its cause, because it isn't clean, will not remain forever, but will disappear with the sin. But pure fear which persists continually, even without the remembrance of sins, will never cease, because it is of our nature. It is somehow connected with the relationship between God and creature, as One who makes His glory known, who is above every kingdom and power.[116]

Some spiritual writers also recommend the thought of death as a means for the purification from the passions. But it is obvious that death in itself doesn't scare a true believer, but the judgment of God, which follows death. The perspective of a definite and total death doesn't maintain fear in man; but at the most a boredom for the lack of the meaning of existence. Only because death brings, after it or with it, the judgment and an eternal life, does it put a value on the thought of death.[117] The thought of death in itself is also of help, however, at least for beginners because it brings before the soul the nothingness of the world and of it promises. John Climacus dedicates a whole chapter, of the thirty in his *Ladder*, to this thought. Here are some quotations from it:

> As bread is the most necessary of all foods, so the thought of death is the most necessary of all things. It gives birth to pious labors and habits, and to the contempt of sins, better said to those who live in the midst of the world; while in those who have withdrawn from tumult and have cast off cares, prayer and the guarding of the mind continue.... The true sign of those who feel death in the heart, is

---

[116] *Questions to Thalassios* 10, *PG* 90.289; *cf. Directions to Hesychasts* 17, *PhiPH*, pp. 190-1.
[117] Evagrius, *Outline Teaching on Asceticism*, *Phi* 1, pp. 35-7. St. Anthony, *On the Character of Men* 49: "If a person keeps death in mind, it is immortality; if not, it is death; but we shouldn't be afraid of death, but of the loss of the soul, which is the ignorance of God." *GrPh* 1, p. 10; *cf. Phi* 1, p. 336.

dispassion, and freedom from all creation and the total forsaking of their own will. The thought of death is daily death; thought of the end is a sigh for every hour. Those who have this thought adding unceasingly fear by fear, don't rest until the very power of their bones is consumed. But we must be sure that this too is a gift of God; for otherwise, how is it that finding ourselves even by the grave some of us remain without tears and hardened?[118]

The thought of death and of the judgment makes our thought of God, where the strengthening of faith began, more frequent, thus increasing inner meditation. Or the fear and the thought of death are nothing but the thought of God, associated with the consciousness of personal sins and with the dread of judgment.

---

[118] Steps 6.4, 6, 7, 19, 20, *PG* 88.793-97; cf. Moore, pp. 110-13.

16. Repentance

The fear of God, sustained by the consciousness of a sinful life, leads both to repentance for past sins, and to the avoidance, by self-control, of future ones. "Repentance is a second grace" [after Baptism], says St. Isaac the Syrian, "and is born in the heart from faith and fear."[119] "Repentance is the renewal of Baptism," writes St. John Climacus, "... the cleansing of the conscience."[120]

The work of purification is realized by the powers which flow from the Mysteries of Baptism and Repentance, just as illumination is an actualization of the powers given by the mystery of Chrism, while union with God is an effect of the Eucharist. The grace of Baptism is the embryo of the new man. In the measure in which it grows, it weakens the traces of the old life, absorbing its powers and using them for itself. Baptism is the death of the old man, understood in two ways: first as a mortal blow which it gives to it, making the start for the new man, and secondly as a gradual mortification of the tremors which still last for a time. But it often happens that the remnants of the force which have remained in the old man thrown to the ground are resurrected by new sins. Then a new pouring out of grace by God is necessary, so that the new man will resume with more vigor the action of purifying the remains of the old man. Better said, when the powers which persist from the old man have grown too much, when the passions have obstructed the powers from Baptism so that he can no longer go forward, Repentance comes to set them aside, to make passage for the grace of Baptism. We have said that Repentance struggles more with its face turned toward the past, and Baptism, with its face toward the future. The former removes the garbage which has gathered in the soul with time, in order to open the highway of progress for the man born again at Baptism. If the grace of Baptism remakes the tendencies toward the good of our nature, the grace of Repentance strengthens the tendency of our nature to regret what it has done wrong.

In any case the powers which come to us by Repentance bring a new intensification to the work of the powers which are prolonged from the mystery of Baptism.

The holy Fathers recognize two kinds of repentance, however. They are Repentance as a mystery, that is, as a sacrament, and repentance as a permanent action in the soul. But the power of the latter comes from

---

[119] *Directions to Hesychasts* 80, GrPh 4, p. 275; cf. *PhiPH*, p. 248.
[120] Step 5.1. *PG* 88.764; cf. Moore, p. 98.

the former. Mark the Ascetic, John Climacus, and Isaac the Syrian insist on these two forms of repentance.

The idea of permanent repentance corresponds with the purpose of repentance in general. It is the shovel brought out to clean man from the sins accumulated after Baptism, so that the new man can keep on fighting, by the power of Baptism, with the temptations which confront him. So it is obvious that we who err almost every moment, in other words almost never gain a clear cut victory over a temptation, need a sorrow to constantly accompany us, which will permanently humble us, a voice to criticize all the time the imperfection of deeds committed; it will thus be an incentive for an even greater effort in our future actions.

St. Mark the Ascetic includes in this repentance, first of all, continual, uninterrupted prayer. (I think that it is the prayer which asks for forgiveness.) So we get rid of evil thoughts, an operation which should keep us busy most of the time; secondly this repentance includes the observation of thoughts, because sinful thoughts come to us all the time which we must be sorry for and get rid of, and thirdly the endurance of troubles. He considers that by the latter we are healed of past errors and imperfections.[121] Even when we do a good deed, we must repent, he says, because this shows us that we could have done it sooner, or perhaps, not at all—we are guilty. Today's good deeds must bring us to repentance for the lack of good deeds yesterday.[122]

John Climacus also includes in repentance not only sorrow for past sins, but also a practice of the virtues and patience in times of trouble. "Repentance is reconciliation with the Lord by the practice of the virtues in opposition to sins.... Repentance is the endurance of all troubles."[123]

The permanence of repentance is beautifully argued by Isaac the Syrian. We will dwell a little on the attributes which he ascribes to repentance.

Here is what St. Isaac says:

> If we are all sinners and no one is above temptations, not one of the virtues is above repentance. Its work can never end.... Because it is forever suitable for all sinners and righteous, if they wish to gain sal-

---

[121] *On Repentance, PG* 65 965-984. *cf. RoFil* 1, pp. 223-4.
[122] "Even if we overdo virtue today, it's the proof of past neglect; it doesn't merit reward." *No Righteousness by Works* 44, *GrPh* 1, p. 112; *cf. Phi* 1, p. 129. "If we are duty bound everyday to do all the good that we are able, what are we going to give to God in exchange for all that we didn't do in the past?" *Ibid.,* 43. *GrPh* 1, p. 112; *cf. Phi* 1, p. 129.
[123] Step 5.1. *PG* 88.764; *cf.* Moore, p. 98.

vation. And there is no end to their perfection, because the perfection even of the perfect is imperfection.[124]

We see that St. Isaac ascribes three attributes to repentance: 1) It is the highest of the virtues; 2) it doesn't end as long as we live and 3) it is a means of our continual perfection.

1. In regard to the first attribute, taken alone, without doubt the virtue of love is higher than repentance. But our earthly condition doesn't permit us to realize love in all its purity and fullness, and any other virtue either. We always know that love or another virtue of ours hasn't reached the maximum to fully satisfy us. After every virtuous deed and act of love we know that it was mixed with an impure element, or it could have been better. This creates a dissatisfaction with what we have done, which is the heart of repentance. Repentance is the hypostasis of the judgment of our conscience not only for our sins but also for our virtues, because we always realize them in an imperfect form. Nothing escapes it; it absolves nothing.[125] There is no virtue which isn't subject to the severe, determined examination of repentance. But couldn't it be said that repentance too can be incomplete and therefore it too can be subject to a judgment of the conscience, which in this case would be superior to repentance? Certainly. Incomplete and impure repentance is judged likewise by repentance, by a full repentance and not by another virtue.

Repentance is the critical act of the conscience; it is the self-criticism which man makes. As such, it is the act of the judgment of the conscience and we know that everything is subject to judgment.

But there is judgment and judgment: the judgment of another and the judgment which you make of yourself. In the judgment which you make of someone else the sentiment of pride can get mixed in; in self-judgment it is excluded by definition. It can at the most include some kind of leniency. But a lenient self-criticism or repentance leaves man unsatisfied, and it by itself looks for a more objective, more severe one.

In a word, any sin whatever, any incompleteness in virtue, is subject to self-criticism or repentance. Even the insufficiency of self-criticism or repentance, is likewise held responsible by self-criticism or repentance. In this sense no virtue stands above repentance; it can't elude the forum of the judgment of self-criticism. Thus repentance is the road to love; it serves love. It leads from an insufficient love to more love. So it's not a

---

[124] *Ascetical Homilies* 55, p. 193.
[125] The author is talking here about repentance as contrition and not as a sacrament. *trs*

contradiction to say that the greatest virtue is love and to consider repentance as the greatest too. Because the driving force of repentance is love.

    2. If so, it is obvious that repentance follows, or should follow, each act, state, word of ours. It follows our sins and our virtues, which are always incomplete. It tends to become a permanent current in our conscience, an uninterrupted presence, leading to more love. The rest of our dispositions and acts change with the circumstances; repentance is with all of them; it is the thread which ties them all together. Not only the simple consciousness that I am the bearer and the author of all my past dispositions and actions, not only the memory which I have of them makes them belong together, but also the repentance or vivid memory with the dissatisfaction for how I committed them. No man at all is indifferent to his past, or has only a theoretical knowledge. This would also rob the present moment of its vitality. Man embraces his past with a throbbing interest. But this interest full of passion for the past can be of two kinds: If it is the pride of satisfaction man not only wants credit for everything that has been done but also wants to squeeze out the recognition of others too; or it can be one of repentance, of dissatisfaction. In the latter case the praise of men makes him sick, because on the one hand he knows how little it corresponds with his inner evidence, by which he knows the reality of what concerns him, and on the other, because this praise tends to cover the true reality for him, to fool him, to weaken his own sincerity with himself, to darken his self-transparency, whether it be sincere or mere flattery.

But this repentance, which persists as a shadow in us shouldn't be confused with a discouraging dissatisfaction, which can paralyze all our enthusiasm. It must not be a doubt in our greater possibilities, but a recognition of the insufficiencies of our achievements up to now. If it is discouragement, it itself is a sin, one of the greatest. Our repentant conscience doesn't continually pronounce a critical judgment on our past actions because of the sentiment that nothing truly good can be accomplished. Instead it judges with the deep conviction that it can also do better, based on the experience of a mystical power much greater than its own nature, which can always be made stronger by the divine. It judges with the feeling that in what we have done and in the way in which we have behaved we have realized only in an insufficient measure and in a colorless way what we could have done. Repentance expresses the thought: "It can be better." Discouragement on the other hand says:

"This is all I can do. I can't do better." Strictly speaking discouragement is opposed to repentance, because where something better can't be expected, regret has no place. This is a fatalistic sentiment, a skeptical resignation. Repentance is borne by a faith in something better.

There are two characteristics which somehow make repentance a forum superior to man, always raising him above the moral and spiritual levels which he has reached. Repentance is a judgment which is always above our realizations and actualization. No matter how high we raise ourselves from a moral standpoint, it goes even higher. Is it a judgment in the name of an ideal? Yes, but it doesn't judge in the name of a simple ideal, considered subjectively. If this were the case, it wouldn't fill us with such uneasiness, with such unhealed and ceaseless pressure. Repentance is awakened and sustained by the intuition of an authority higher than us, to whom we feel responsible, but which also gives us power to do more, if we ask Him for it. Repentance is a window to God; it is the needle with which God unceasingly pricks our heart. It is His hand, which continually pulls us higher. Repentance is the relationship between us and someone above us. It shows itself to us as being in contact with that "Someone." If we weren't in this relationship, if we weren't positioned with our soul turned toward a forum of personal and supreme judgment, repentance would be inexplicable; the absolute judgments and claims of repentance would have no place to ring out in us.

But as we have said, repentance isn't only the judgment of the things of my past, but also a trust in greater possibilities in my powers continually strengthened by the power of the infinite God. So it is considered by Isaac the Syrian as the highest of the virtues. In this quality it also appears to us as standing in relation to a source of power beyond man. The nature of repentance, as well as that of humility, from which it is inseparable, is of a dialectical character; it contains in itself a joining of contradictory positions, which don't cancel one another, but which produce a very complex reality. On the one hand it is an unceasing dissatisfaction with whatever state we are in, on the other, it is a steady and unwavering trust in giant possibilities. "I am the greatest sinner," the man of repentance always says. "I am unworthy." With all of that he doesn't lose hope for a moment; the thought that he will be lost doesn't overcome him by any means. He doesn't let himself be submerged in discouragement or in the apathy of spiritual death. The fact that the man who repents trusts in God, as in a factor distinct from himself, is given as an explanation of this persistence in spiritual strength. But trust itself is an inner power. Thus on the one hand he experiences here his own weakness, and on the other a great power. Obviously it is the matter of a power which doesn't come from the resources of an isolated self, but from a communication with the vast and deep resources of the reservoir of the universal spiritual power of God. Repentance is a relationship with God, both by its character of absolute judgment, as well as by the undiscouraged virility with which it urges man toward the better.

Repentance is the highest of the virtues, because it isn't itself a virtue developed with the others— it always remains unsatisfied with what they accomplish; it always urges them to go higher. Without being a virtue developed by itself, it is the motor of all the virtues. If it wasn't for repentance, man wouldn't have the tendency to want to overcome. Repentance is a continual fire in man, which maintains the tension for the better. By it man surpasses himself and is judge in the name of the absolute claims of God. Thus he rises ever higher.

3. With this we have arrived at the third characteristic which St. Isaac the Syrian gives to repentance— he considers it as a means of man's continual perfection, a means which he himself constantly perfects.

St. Isaac compares this world to a sea, and repentance to a ship which takes us to the shore of the blessed life beyond, to the paradise whose nature is loved:

> Just as it isn't possible, [he writes,] for someone to cross the great sea without a ship, so someone can't reach love without fear. We can cross the tempestuous sea placed between us and the spiritual paradise only with the ship of repentance, borne by the oarsmen of fear. If these oarsmen of fear don't handle the ship of repentance well, by which we cross the sea of this world toward God, we will be drowned in it. Repentance is the ship, fear is the rudder, love the divine harbor. So fear puts us in the ship of repentance and we cross the tempestuous sea and it guides us to the divine harbor, which is love where all those who labor and have been enlightened by repentance arrive. And when we have reached love, we have reached God. And our journey has ended and we have reached the island which is beyond this world.[126]

We want the voyage on the sea of this life to lead to the heavenly realm, to the realm of love, which is Christ Himself. We don't want it to be without direction or anchorage, and finally a submersion in its darkness. We want it to be a passage toward perfection and life. So there is only one way to make the crossing— in the vessel of repentance for the incomplete love caused by our sins. The will for a greater love will keep us on board and help us to steer a straight course. It will keep our heads

---

[126] *Ascetical homilies* 72, *op. cit.*, p. 248.

above the giant waves of evil and the egotism which rises up within us. It will lead us straight ahead. Only in the vessel of repentance do we constantly pass over the sinful waves of egotism, which tend to rise up from deeply within us and beneath us. Only by it are we always above ourselves and moving onward from our present position, moving closer to full love, closer to the paradise where the tree of life is, in other words to Christ, the source of love which feeds our spirit.

Of course we share in a certain measure of love, which is ever growing, even before we arrive at the dominion of the full love of paradise. The air of this realm reaches us first with its ever richer perfume which gets stronger the closer we get. Our love and in general all the virtues are ever purer, ever more complete the closer we get to the kingdom of love.

From this we see that repentance must not be separated from the love of God and of our neighbors. We repent only because we have love. We repent because we haven't obeyed the commands of love, or because we realize that we don't have enough love. We shouldn't wonder that the tumult of egotistic appetites and of passions as evil in general, is like an ocean. There is a vast empire of evil, just as there is one of good; so the road of overcoming more and more the egotism of our sins is a long one. Man doesn't conceive of and want evil in isolation. The impulses to evil from within him don't have their roots in him, their point of origin, just as the inspiration and impulses toward good don't draw their nature and power only from him. We have visible relationships, but even more so invisible ones, with deep and innumerable forces of evil, which come from personal beings more powerful than we are, forces which combine continually among themselves and with our impulses, just as we are also helped by lofty winds or stimuli toward the good received in the sails of our nature, coming from the lofty, vast, and glorious kingdom of the angelic and divine world. There is an ocean of good and also one of evil, both trying to win us. But the ocean of evil is dark, tumultuous, spirit-killing, enslaving, the thief of purity and tranquility; it is dark, subterranean, suffocating, while the ocean of good, of love, is like an infinite atmosphere which we can't live without, whose breezes we have to have to move ahead, a pure atmosphere, so we can breathe deep and free, which fills us with a renewed life and a continual and unspeakable joy; it is an atmosphere of love and pure communion, life-giving, which awakens all our spiritual powers and gives them power to grow.

What can we do now so that by repentance we can gradually get ourselves out of the ocean of evil, from its thousands of embraces and go toward the kingdom of full love? What makes repentance into a vehicle going to the world of love? Repentance is the fire which gradually burns up the egotism in us. All the passions which are whirling about in us, often originating in the shadowy depths beyond us, strengthen our egotism. Be they fleshly passions, or psychic, they are only the heads of the same dragon, whose name is egotism. Repentance unceasingly watches for any appearance of this beast, any attempt to feed himself, to grow in the expanses of the soul. It is on guard so that he doesn't fill our well-intentioned thoughts, deeds and words with his stench; so that he doesn't weaken our powers which enable us to be in contact with the atmosphere of love, so that he doesn't pull the soul under. Repentance cuts off with a two edge sword, one by one, his heads; it burns him with the flame of self-critical alertness; it throws him with the sweet smell of humility. What can better mortally wound our egotistic pride than the ever present thought that we are nothing, that everything we have done is evil, useless?

So the greatest and continuous obstacle in the way of our progress to love is egotism. Until egotism completely dies, you can't have true love for anyone. You must leave far behind you the billows of the ocean of egotism, so that you can bask in the air which comes to you from the kingdom of love. He who loves himself, who is full of self-admiration, who considers himself as the most important of all, can't love others. To love others means to forget yourself, to always go beyond yourself, to consider yourself as nothing. The love of others is consolidated in us by uninterrupted repentance and humility. Egotism sees itself inflated to the extent that all reality is hidden. It thinks that it should own everything. It weighs every person to see how to use him, or at least it tries to avoid the danger which might come from his supremacy. In all things, in all actions, the egotist projects his own person; he sees and serves nothing else; he worships it, to him it is a god, or better said an idol in place of God. His own authentic nature is drowned in egotism. His concern for others is only a tactic, in order to really serve his own interests. Thus in a false way he fills his whole horizon with his inauthentic ego. He walls himself off on all sides with his false self. It's clear then that he can't see others for themselves, in a disinterested way, with true love, just as he can't see his authentic self within the framework of the loving community of all. In any gesture to others he is hindered by his inauthentic self; every drop of generosity is poisoned by an egotistic preoccupation. Love is the exit from the magic and illusory circle of egotism, a circle which I extend to the infinite, as in a delusive dream. It is a breaking out into a true relationship, in communion with others. It is an exit from the shadowy prison of the ego and the entrance into the life of the community, of solidarity, into the kingdom of love, which includes everyone.

It's clear that no one can approach or enter this kingdom, this paradise, unless he leaves behind the ocean of numberless sirens of egotism which try to attract him as so many violent waves. Now this ocean can't be overcome all at once. No one, with a single beat of the wings, can fly from the empire of egotism to the kingdom of love. The way is won gradually; the infinite embraces which egotism uses to hold on to us, to draw us down, must be fought continuously. At every step we must struggle with all our might, to go on safe and sound and to arrive as another Odysseus in our true land. Rowing powerfully, our muscles are made stronger and our course continually easier. Repentance is the critical eye which isn't fooled by the false pleasures offered to it by our egotism. It stops us from saying yes to the calls from the depths of the darkness of the ocean of egotism. It makes us go forward, scorning the doubts within us and the murky sea under us. It doesn't let us stop for a moment. By repentance God doesn't let us be satisfied with what we already are, but always calls us to go on; yes even more, it doesn't leave us in the darkness of egotism, but it calls us to the expanses of solidarity in love.

Heidegger says that man is always getting ahead of himself because of care. He isn't shut in the present moment, but every moment he outruns himself because of care; he has the horizon of an open future. But Heidegger didn't show that there is care and care. There is an egotistic care by which man is preoccupied with the anticipation of the things necessary for his ego. It is a care which somersaults us further into egotism. It is a care which doesn't really carry us forward, but which moves us in the enclosed circle of our interests. It is a worldly care, an egotistic one, which in Christianity is considered a sin, because it takes all of our attention and we can no longer think of the infinite truth of the transcendental.

But there is also a care to escape our egotism, not one of maintenance in this closed life, by death, but of salvation on an eternal plane. There is a care in favor of egotism and another care to melt the egotism in us. This latter one looks not only ahead, but behind too. But it doesn't look back in order to forget the present and the future, to be petrified like Lot's wife, but to contribute to the melting of the remains of the egotism put in the past in our way, so that we can work better in the future, so that we can really make progress. The face of this care looking backward to remove the obstacles accumulated by egotism in the path of our future is repentance. Better said, repentance looks backward too, with sorrow for what it has done and how it has acted in an egotistical way, but also ahead, with a decision to no longer do the same things. By it we embrace the past, the present, and the future all at once, making the look backward into a force for the future. But the future develops for us more and more in the direction of the realm of the light of the kingdom of love, thus toward more and more love for God and for our neighbors. The care for myself, with which Heidegger is occupied, is transformed into a love, into a care, for God and others. See how repentance embraces not only the past, present, and future, but our neighbors too, with the embrace of an ever fuller attention, of an ever fuller love. Repentance progresses slowly, but with full effort, in the realms of love, according to St. Isaac the Syrian's image full of poetry and light. And if this is so, repentance doesn't mean an isolated life, but one which involves to the highest degree the common destiny of the community. It can contribute in great measure to the realization of a more brotherly world, if it gradually consumes egotism and increases the assets of love. It can contribute in an important way to the bringing about of a real, inner and lasting solidarity between the members of the human community.

Therefore repentance isn't an occupation exclusively for old people. It certainly is theirs too. But its creative dynamics for life, its continuous power of overcoming which it gives to anyone, shows that it has a very special purpose and is especially important for the young person. The old man repents in order to arrive free of sin before God, but the young person also repents for this authentic self-realization in life; and he can do this only by continually surpassing himself. Strictly speaking only in this way can he attain the true realization of all his possibilities. A youth who doesn't move toward the continuous surpassing of himself, a youth who leads a static existence, is an old man instead of a young one. Youth by definition tends to get ahead, to be continuously ascending. But this unceasing overcoming can't be realized without a dissatisfaction for the level which he has already reached. And a theoretical dissatisfaction isn't enough, but one joined with suffering. This, however, isn't repentance.

But it's time to ask the question of how this permanent repentance is related to repentance as a mystery, or as they say in the West, a sacrament. Usually the holy Fathers call the first repentance properly speaking a change of mind, *(metanoia)* and the second, confession *(exomologisis)*.

From this it follows that the first is a permanent preparation for the second and a prefiguration of the effects of the first. By permanent repentance we prepare ourselves for repentance as a mystery, just as the latter must stimulate us for the former. If God left us repentance as a mystery, it's clear that we can't go to it unprepared or only with a brief recollection of sins at the last minute, or even a few days ahead. How many of our words and deeds we usually forget. We run the risk of no longer being able to recall our sinful thoughts, words, and deeds if we haven't dwelt on them by repentance as soon as they happened and if we haven't often recalled them with regret. In repentance as a mystery we rid ourselves of the garbage which we have already broken up, but which is still in us, after we have gradually gotten it loose from our souls. The riddance of it before the father confessor is necessary for us to more acutely experience the account which we must give before God as the supreme subject for what is in us but shouldn't be. Confession is necessary for us to accept the most accentuated feeling of humility and to realize that our deliverance from sin depends on the support, the help which our fellow creature gives us, that we are warned by him, that this liberation is a work of communion, surpassing the individualism in which pride stands guard. By confession we put ourselves in the humble situation of disciples receiving a teaching. By it we give ourselves the opportunity to hear an objective, external judgment on our deeds, not too abrupt, neither too merciful nor too condemning, as almost always happens, when we are alone, in the depths of our souls.[127]

Even if we haven't reached a perfect inner detachment from our sinful thoughts, when we go to the confessor, bringing them out into the open frees us from them.[128]

The holy Fathers find a relationship between repentance and tears. In fact the gift of tears becomes richer on the higher steps of the spiritual life, but because repentance is permanent, and also intensifies on the higher steps, it isn't wrong to say that tears should be considered as standing in a special relationship to repentance. Then too neither should they be absent from beginning repentance, although there is a big difference between the tears of fear at the beginning and those of love on the higher steps.[129]

Tears are the proof that repentance has overcome the hardness of the soul, brought about by sinning for a long time. With it they carry away the softened mud which they have washed from the window of the

---

[127] For the importance of repentance as a holy mystery see our study, "Repentance and Spiritual Resurrection," [in Romanian], in *Revista Teologica* (Sibiu, 1945).
[128] St. John Cassian, *A Useful Word for Abbot Leontius*, from the first two *Conferences*, PG 49.477-558: "Truly, until someone has been made worthy of the gift of discrimination, by the very fact that he reveals his evil thoughts, he drives them up and makes them weaker. The snake, driven from his hiding place into the light, forces himself to flee and hide—in the same way evil thoughts, brought out into the open, by means of a complete confession, hurry to leave man." See also *RoFil* 1 (1ˢᵗ ed.), p. 135; cf. *Phi* 1, p. 103. Here is an idea which psychology has revived; sometimes, however, the results are unrecognizable.
[129] *Directions to Hesychasts* 25, *GrPh* 4, p. 224; *PhiPH*, pp. 195-6.

soul, opening to it once again the perspective of God and neighbor and taking it out from between the walls of sin and the hardness of egotism. They appear after repentance has succeeded in piercing the heart,[130] making it sensitive and overcoming it and making it soft again, after it has become hardened by imbibing the cement of the passions. Tears bring back its transparency, so that the human subject can be seen through it and so that the subject itself can see heaven through it. Tears wash the eyes and make them beautiful, because they wash the heart and make it transparent, beautiful and innocent.

John Climacus, in Step Seven of his work has given us the most subtle analysis of weeping and of all its variations. Here are some of the characteristics of tears according to him. His thesis is that "Just as fire destroys straw, so the pure tear destroys every visible and spiritual stain."[131] But according to him there are many kinds of tears:

> ... from nature, from God, from adversity; or from praise because of vainglory, because of fornication, from love, from the remembrance of death and from other multiple causes. Let us, shaken by everything by the fear of God win pure tears and innocence of thought for death, because in them there isn't deception or self-esteem but rather they bring purity and a step forward in the love of God, the cleansing of sins and liberation from the passions. It isn't surprising that weeping begins with good tears and ends with bad ones. But it is a thing worthy of praise to begin from the contrary or natural, and to arrive at the spiritual. So don't trust fountains of tears before perfect cleansing, as you put no confidence in fresh wine that has just been poured from the press into the barrel.... He who travels with unceasing tears for God doesn't cease to have a feastday everyday, just as he that feasts continually with the body will end up with eternal sorrow.
>
> [Tears get rid of laughter:] Be like a king in your heart, seated high in humility, and commanding laughter: Go, and it goes; and sweet weeping: Come and it comes; and our tyrant and slave, the body: Do this, and it does it. He who is clothed in blessed and grace-given mourning as in a wedding garment knows the spiritual laughter of the soul. [Weeping on the higher steps is no longer one of our fleshly eyes.] Remove sin, and the tear of sorrow is superfluous for

---

[130] John Climacus: "Mourning is a golden needle which loosens the soul from all adherence to and connection with the world." *The Ladder* 7.1. *PG* 88.801; *cf.* Moore, p. 113.
[131] *Ibid.*, 7.31. *PG* 88.808; *cf.* Moore, p. 117.

your eyes of sense.... Adam had no tears, just as there will be none after the resurrection when sin will be abolished.[132]

---

[132] *Ibid.*, 7.31-45. *PG* 88.808-9; *cf.* Moore, pp. 117-19.

17. Self-control

A Romanian philosopher had the idea[133] that human nature is equipped with a built-in bridle, so as not to go too high and topple the sovereignty of the Great Anonymous from the peak of existence. Christ's teaching also acknowledges the usefulness of a restraint. But our nature imposes this restraint freely; it isn't a force to which it is subject in a fatalistic way. And its purpose isn't to hinder our nature from ascending toward the absolute, but on the contrary to free it from the chains which keep it from getting off to a running start. In the Christian conception, God isn't afraid to raise man to communion with His own nature, even so far as deification. Because even if man becomes a god, by the very fact that he has a created nature he is only a god by grace, and as such never endangers the sovereignty of the divine nature.

Self-control freely exercised by a believer isn't a restraint from the ascent to God, but the departure from evil things. The purpose is to keep him from total submersion in the world. It's true that the world, as a creation of God, has its positive purpose. It is to help us in our ascent toward God. The divine *logoi* which radiate from the world fill it with light and with a transparency, which give an infinite perspective to our understanding. Anything, any object or happening, by its inexhaustible meaning, by its never fully explained purpose in the whole universe, must constantly set us to thinking and carry our reason beyond this object. Anything, by its infinite sense and by its roots in the infinite, by its relationship of never-ending complexity, with the meanings of all things, is a mystery. How much more, the personality of our neighbor, which can never fit into a closed rational formula, which can never be exhausted in communicating and in its thirst to know and to love. How much a neighbor helps us to raise ourselves to the infinity of mystery by the interminable means in him; how much he strengthens us in our spiritual ascent by the unspoken and unending powers of encouragement, of trust, which radiate from him!

The world of things and of persons is thus meant to be a ladder to God, the support in the ascent to Him. But by the passions man takes this brilliant depth, this transparence, which reaches the infinite, from the world. Instead of still being "the horizon of mystery" the world becomes a consumable material content, an impenetrable wall, unpierced by any light from above. In fact the fleshly passions— gluttony, the love

---

[133] Lucian Blaga, *Transcendental Censorship* [in Romanian]. (Note: No further information available. *trs*)

of money, licentiousness—no longer retain anything but the material from things and persons, only what can satisfy our bodily appetite; and anger, dejection, vainglory are explained as well by this reduction of things to the aspect of theirs of being useful to the body and limited. Things are no longer anything but to eat, or give other comforts and pleasures to the body; they make it move, they give it pleasant aromas and tastes, they present it with a shiny material aspect, they offer it an easy rest, so our neighbor's person is only a body, which can arouse pleasures in our body, or so much manpower, usable as a tool for the production of goods pleasant to the body. Things and persons no longer contain anything but what falls immediately under the senses and nothing beyond the senses. Things and persons have become opaque. The world has become one sided, poor without any dimensions except the perceptible. The sin against God, the creative Spirit, is also a sin against the world.

But this change of things into simple consumer goods and this reduction of persons to the aspect of objects,[134] instead of making man freer, more sovereign in the midst of the world, makes him its slave, because it makes him the slave of bodily passions grown beyond all limits. So the restraint which Christianity urges man to exercise is for man's spirit to claim its rights from the lower impulses which have overwhelmed him. By the self-control which limits the passions, man reestablishes the limits and freedom of the spirit in himself. But in so doing, he awakens within himself the factor which sees in the world something else besides objects to satisfy these passions. By self-control man removes from the world the wave of darkness and gives it once again the attribute of making it transparent for the infinite. So disrespect for the world isn't shown in self-control, but rather the will to discover the entire majesty of the world; self-control isn't a complete turning away from the world, to see God, but a turning away from a world narrow and exaggerated by the passions, to find a transparent world which itself becomes a mirror of God and a ladder to Him.

Strictly speaking between the true world and God there isn't a relationship of mutual exclusion. But as a preliminary method for finding the true world a turning away from it is useful—from a world fallen because of man under the spell of evil, from a world which waits and sighs for its liberation.

Right here is where the two roads of Orthodox Christians go separate ways according to the level of faith, of the fear of God and of

---

[134] Paul Tillich has unmasked this reduction of persons to objects in our time in his little book, *Die geistige Lage der Gegenwart.*

repentance which they have been traveling together. Now monks take one road, Christians in the world another.

Monks take the surest, the most radical, the shortest way. They know that the passions have become entrenched in human nature and so man must fight the battle of controlling himself. But they also know that their own will is weakened by these passions and the battle with them is made easier by taking away from them the opportunity of getting started and being stirred up, in other words by taking from the passions the material which allows them to develop and catch on fire. So they choose to leave the world. Thus from the beginning they cut off the starting and arousal power of the passions. For monks, from here on, the problem is to persist in this withdrawal, because an appetite deprived for a long time of material to satisfy it, or of the chance to be active, withers away, and no longer becomes a passion, or at least it is weakened.

The road that other Christians take is longer and less certain, but it isn't impossible for some of them too to reach the peak of holiness; or in any case even if they don't go that far, any Christian is obligated to force himself to make some spiritual progress.[135] And a certain amount of restraint is connected with this progress. Of course Christians in the world can't exercise such radical self-control as monks, but they too can practice a certain amount of moderation, which as it grows can in time equal monastic self-control. They go slower, but they can get just about as far. If they are lacking in the toils of their own choosing, God compensates for it by giving them more troubles to bear; the unchosen burdens and obligations of life. If they accept them with patience, they can be purified from their passions, almost the same as monks. If self-control is more a virtue of monks, patience is more that of lay people, although neither one should totally forget the virtue of the other.

The monk's break with the world is strengthened by the three vows of poverty, chastity, and obedience. By them they obligate themselves to persist for life in this renunciation of their passion for the world, that is in self-control. In them the promise of self-control is concentrated, not only from the eight passions, but also from anything that causes them. By the vow of poverty they obligate themselves to restrain themselves

---

[135] St. Anthony the Great: "It isn't right for those weaker by nature to lose self-confidence and to abandon living virtuously and pleasing to God and to look down on it as something unattainable. They should instead study the power that they have and develop it. Because even if they can't attain virtue and salvation by effort and desire, at least they improve or don't get worse, and this isn't a minor thing for the soul." *On the Character of Men* 41, GrPh 1, p. 9; cf. Phi 1, p. 335. Lossky says that "The way of union with God may be pursued outside the cloister, amid all the circumstances of human life.... Eastern hagiography, which is extremely rich, shows besides the holy monks many examples of spiritual perfection acquired by simple laymen and married people living in the world." *Mystical Theology*, ch. 1, p. 17.

not only from the love of possessions, but even from any possession which might lead to an appetite for possession. At the same time, by this vow, monks are protected from the external power of the gluttony of the belly, which is deprived of the means to satisfy it. By the vow of chastity they are obligated not only to refrain from unchastity, but also from the marriage bond which might awaken unchastity in them. And by the vow of obedience they are obligated not only to refrain from pride but also from the right to speak their mind when they think that justice is on their side, because this too might be an occasion to stir up pride. By cutting off their gluttony, and the passions of unchastity, of the love of money, of pride, they also implicitly cut off their passions of anger and dejection which are sustained by them.

So the monk by taking these vows and strictly observing them, must refrain in a radical way from each passion separately. And namely from the seven: the love of money, unchastity, anger, dejection, laziness, vainglory, and pride, and even from anything that might cause them. In regard to food, however, a radical renunciation isn't required of them, not even an exaggerated decrease, but only moderation.[136] The monk must only avoid stuffing himself, from what is beyond measure, yes even from getting full— he has to get up from the table a little before he is satisfied. But in regard to quantities and kinds of food a uniform rule hasn't been given,[137] because the more feeble have to eat better, and those fuller of vitality, less. The principle is that the food should sustain the body as a spiritual working tool, so that it doesn't become an impediment by causing debility or too much vigor in him.[138]

In general, for monks, all the Fathers recommend lenten foods and from time to time partial or total abstinence from food. Fasting foods also have the purpose of weakening the uncontrolled power of appetite, which makes man a slave, which takes away from him the ability of seeing anything else in what he eats except material to be consumed. By weakening the appetite, eating becomes an act for reflecting and think-

---

[136] Neilos the Ascetic, interpreting the texts from Leviticus 8:29 and 9:14, that the breast should be taken out whole, but the entrails should only be washed remarks: "The wise man can completely get rid of anger, but he can't get rid of his stomach. Nature forces even the ascetic to use some necessary food. He can't do away with his stomach." *On Asceticism* 56, GrPh 1, p. 223; cf. *Phi* 1, p. 239.
[137] Generally, Orthodox monastics are strict vegetarians during fast periods, but they will also eat dairy products, eggs, and fish on non-fasting days. trs
[138] John Cassian, *On the Eight Vices*. This tract is published as Epistle Two of St. Athanasius to Castor, PG 28.871-906. "Just let a small portion be enough for us, to keep us alive, that we don't become slaves of the passions of appetite. The taking of food with measure and with consideration gives the body health, and doesn't take holiness from it. The rule of restraint and the canon laid down by the Fathers is this: He who partakes of food let him stop while he is still hungry and not keep on until he is satiated." *On the Eight Vices*, GrPh 1, p. 35; cf. *On Control of the Stomach*, Phi 1, p. 74.

ing about God. Reason is no longer the servant of appetite, but regains the role of leadership. A spiritual light descends on the act of eating; it is no longer an irrational act, shrouded in darkness. But fasting also means an act for the glorification of God, because it is an act to restrain our egotism, inflated by spiritual and fleshly appetites, to such an extent that there isn't room for anybody else, not even for God, creating for us the illusion that only my person exists and that everything is for it. Man suffers from a monstrous swelling of the ego, because its egotistic extension isn't a true growth, but a sickly inflation, which wants to encompass everybody and everything. It is produced by the convergence of all the passions; it is the manifestation of the work of all the spiritual bacteria in our ego. Fasting is the antidote against this pathological extension of our appetites and of our egotism. It is the humble return of the ego to itself, but by its transparence it sees God and is filled with a life consistent with God. This is the growth of the spirit in man, from the divine spirit. Only in God and from God the Infinite can man grow spiritually and in harmony with everyone and with everything. But because man's egotism wants to grow without God, without loving relationships with his fellow creatures, it grows only in appearance and for a little while.

Fasting with the body is itself an act of spiritual growth. It takes real will power and is a reestablishment of the domination of the spirit over the body. In the Christian concept, especially in the Orthodox one, the soul and the body don't live with lives isolated, but in a normal situation the soul must spiritualize the body, which is to become the medium for the work of the spirit.

But the holy Fathers emphasize in a distinct way, as an effect of fasting, along with the weakening of the other appetites of the body, the preservation of chastity. Fasting is especially necessary for young people. Saint Mark the Ascetic says:

> The young person's body, fattened with all kinds of food and the drinking of wine is like a pig ready for slaughter. His soul is slaughtered by the kindling of bodily pleasures, while his mind is enslaved by the heat of evil appetites. He can't resist the pleasures of the body. For the enrichment of the blood causes the scattering of the spirit. A young person especially shouldn't drink wine, not even smell it, lest somehow by double fire, born from the working of the passions within and from the drinking of wine, he enflame his desire for the pleasure of the body and cast from him the spiritual pleasure of pain, born from the constraint of the heart, and thus bring to it darkness and petrification. Yes, from the love of spiritual pleasure, the young person shouldn't think about drinking even too much wa-

ter. For moderation in water helps very much in the growth in self-restraint.[139]

The Fathers recommend a continuous restraint from all the passions. Although self-control from gluttony is what makes restraint from the others possible, we mustn't neglect a single one of them, because the passions are somehow a whole, one beast; if we cut off one of its heads, it raises up another. The passion of vainglory is more subtle. It is often present even when we think we are free of the passions. It even grows in the place where the others were cut off; it feeds on their blood. It even comes up to the edge of humility and in general to the border of any virtue.

By fighting with the passions, we diminish them gradually. St. Maximus lists four steps for this progress: 1) the stopping of their appearance in sinful deeds—the obtaining of sinlessness in deed is the first dispassion; 2) freedom from passionate thoughts caused by appetites in our consciousness; victory over them brings us to a second dispassion, without such thoughts they can't become deeds; 3) the control over our natural appetite so that it doesn't move toward the passions—this is the third dispassion;[140] 4) the complete removal from the mind of perceptible images—this leads to a fourth dispassion. No longer having them in mind, they can no longer enter the subconscious to move an appetite to a passion.

Certainly, the last dispassion isn't our final ideal, but after it we must reach a state where we can receive images of things without creating any passion within us. This happens when through them their divine *logoi* become transparent. Only after this does the mind unite with God in a state higher than prayer.[141]

The scheme of this battle doesn't contradict what we have already said, that the decisive moment in the development of a passion is the approval which reason gives it and so here is where the battle starts, not later, when this thought is on the road to realization. At the beginning of our spiritual life we aren't successful all at once at this stage. But even if we have lost the battle here, we can stop the sin from becoming a deed,

---

[139] *Letter of Nicolas the Solitary, RoFil* 1, pp. 324-5; cf. *Phi* 1, p. 154.
[140] Evagrius, *On Discrimination* 13: "Among the thoughts, vainglory alone uses many means.... All the demons, after they have been defeated, combine to make this thought grow and through it they will receive once again an entrance into the soul to make the latter things worse than the former." Then, too, all the passions have their perversions, or make the mind invent perverse arguments when they are provoked, ruining it. *On Discrimination* 22: "All the unclean thoughts stirred up within us bring the mind to ruin and perdition." *GrPh* 1, pp. 51, 56; cf. *Phi* 1, pp. 46, 51.
[141] *Ascetical Homilies* 32, p. 122.

by different means, the most important of which is to take measures to deprive the temptation of its opportunity or the material for realization. Now the monk has taken these measures in a radical way by leaving the world. Even if he is steadfast only in this state, he has obtained the first goal. But he is still only a monk externally. To become one internally, spiritually, he must at the very least attain the cleansing from passionate thoughts, that is he must be in a state to stop his mind from giving its assent to the passion aroused in his consciousness. Once he has reached this, dispassion of the first step will maintain itself, not by external means and in an artificial way. It should be noted, however, that the struggle for this second dispassion isn't totally separate from the first, although it also has a phase proper to it, because the person who continues with diligence in sinlessness in deed also weakens the thought of sin. Whether he wants to or not, he also makes arguments for sinlessness in deed and these arguments weaken those arguments which maintain the thought of temptation in the conscience. The same thing also happens with the third dispassion—it is partly obtained by persistence in the first and second, because by a long term avoidance of sinning in deed and by weakening the thought of sin, the appetite for the passion withers.

But in a special chapter, we shall concern ourselves with the self-control of sinful thoughts. We will deal with the weakening of appetite and of anger in part of the chapter on the patient endurance of troubles, and in the same chapter, a little further on, with the efforts of monks. Here we shall briefly discuss various restraints from sin in deed.

Withdrawal from the world doesn't excuse the monk from continuing the effort to refrain from sinning in deed. Because although he has left the world, he hasn't been able to do so completely. To some extent the world comes along behind him; there is still there an *In-der-Welt-sein* (to be in the world), as Heidegger would say. For example, the monk brings with him the need to eat, and this continually imposes on him a restraint to not become a glutton. In addition he might be proud, that is conceited because of the successes won by his efforts of purification, or he might be lazy, even in the most complete seclusion. Besides this seclusion he must spend time in the monastic community—if not all the time, at least for a long time after his withdrawal from the world, in order to learn from others various restraints and to be exercised in obedience and humility. There he is exposed not only to the passions mentioned, but also to the occasion to get mad, to gossip, to chatter, to lie. Anger and gossip go along with hatred for our neighbors and idle talk with laziness. And lying, when it isn't the slander of someone else, is an excuse for personal laziness; or it is self-praise, as idle talk can also be.

Here we shall dwell a little on the refraining from gossip, idle talk, lying and sleeping too much, as external sinful deeds. There will be a discussion further on of anger and pride as more inner passionate movements. Let's listen to what St. John of the Ladder has to say:

> Slander is the cub of hate. It pretends to love. I heard some gossiping and I marveled, because these workers of evil said, in defense of their deed, that they do this from love and care for the slandered. But if you say that you love him, pray for him; forget and don't bury him. Because this is the way acceptable to the Lord. Judas was in the circle of the apostles, and the thief in the circle of murderers and in a moment they changed places. Don't pay any attention to him who slanders his neighbor; instead tell him: 'Stop, brother, I sin everyday, so how can I judge him?'.... Do not regard the feelings of a person who speaks to you about his neighbor disparagingly, but rather say to him: 'Stop, brother! I fall into grave sins everyday, so how can I judge him?.... Just as fire is foreign to water, so the thought of judging is foreign to him who wants to repent. Even if you see someone sinning at the hour of death, don't judge him. The judgment of God isn't revealed to men. Some have committed great sins openly, but they have done much greater good things secretly. You will be judged in the same way that you judge others. That is we will fall into the same things that we accuse our neighbor of. Shrewd and exact accountants of the sins of their neighbor fall into the same passion, because they haven't been concerned and kept in full and constant memory their own sins. Because if someone considers in detail his own sins, after tearing off the veil of self-love, he will no longer care about anything else in life. He will realize that he doesn't have time enough to cry for his own, even if he were to live a hundred years and even if he would see pouring from his eyes the whole Jordan transformed into tears. The demons either urge us to sin, or if we don't, to judge those who do, that by the second sin we will be as defiled as with the first. The murderers!... As self-esteem, even without any other passion, can destroy a man, so the judgment of others, in itself, even alone, can cause us to be lost.[142]

Just as all kinds of self-control, whether they are only of the manifestations of external sins, aren't only negative actions, but have positive and inner effects, so too the self-control of gossip makes the soul concentrate on itself in a meditation of personal humiliation and deflation.

Regarding talkativeness, St. John Climacus says that it is "the throne of vainglory, which is manifested by it." It is "the proof of ignorance,

---

[142] John Climacus, *The Ladder* 10.2-15. PG 88.845C-848D; cf. Moore, pp. 132-134.

156   PART ONE: B. PURIFICATION BY THE VIRTUES

the door of slander, the teacher of unseriousness, the servant of lying, the loss of humility, the cause of lying, the precursor of sleep." Silence has the opposite virtues. "He who has known his own sins controls his tongue, but the talker still hasn't known himself. The friend of silence approaches God and talking with Him secretly receives light from Him."[143] By the passions of the flesh man looks outward, toward the world and is stripped of the spirit; in the same way talkativeness is the fishing gear by which vainglory tries to catch the praise of men, so it is likewise an enslavement of man to the things without.

John of the Ladder also says:

> Lying is the daughter of hypocrisy. But as all passions differ in the damage that they cause, so too lying. For one is the judgment which a man brings on himself when he lies from fear of being lost and another on him who lies without being threatened by danger; another on him who lies because of voluptuousness; another, on him who lies to stir up the laughter of those present, and another, on him who lies to ensnare his neighbor, to harm him. A child doesn't know how to lie, neither the soul emptied of evil. He who is giddy with wine speaks the whole truth, while the man who is drunk from a broken heart will not be able to lie.[144]

Monks must also restrain themselves from too much sleep, forcing themselves to keep vigil. Sleep makes the spirit lazy, it weakens its powers of self-discipline, of concentration, of mastery over the body. And vigil is a sign of victory over the will. It keeps the attention of the mind fully alert to its thoughts and makes the most sublime understanding spring from the heart. St. Isaac the Syrian writes:

> Don't consider the monk who is faithful in vigil as still in the flesh. This thing truly belongs to the angelic realm. Because it is impossible, as many as have this work, not to be made worthy by God of great charismas for the attention and alertness of their hearts.... The soul that is struggling in the work of the vigil, and is beautified by it, gains the eyes of the cherubim, in order to always see the heavenly sights.[145]

The Fathers also require of monks, in addition to the many restraints from sinning in deed, a series of toils. Thus besides vigils and sacred reading, they recommend a state of prolonged watchfulness, sleeping on

---

[143] *Ibid.*, 11.2, 4-5. *PG* 88.852BC; *cf.* Moore, pp. 134-5.
[144] *Ibid.*, 12.6, 8, 9, 13, 14. *PG* 88.856B-D; *cf.* Moore, p. 137.
[145] *Ascetical Homilies*, p. 106.

the ground, various bodily works. By them desire is dried up.[146] These things along with the whole range of restraints constitute the efforts or voluntary hardships, undertaken on their own initiative.

Another external restraint which is recommended in ascetical literature is the closing of the senses to exterior things, especially at the beginning, until we are exercised in defeating the passionate movements in us and especially in the moments when we feel that such a movement is about to be started. If we don't draw the curtains then over the windows of our senses, it isn't possible to restrain such an appetite from becoming a deed.[147] Of course, after someone has been fully freed from the passions, he can look at things on the outside and is able to see the divine *logoi* in them. Only as long as he is inexperienced, as long as he is a spiritual infant, does he have to keep from looking at things.[148]

---

[146] Evagrius, *On Discrimination* 3: "The man who hasn't been concerned about desire and anger will not be able to get rid of passionate memories. He will get rid of the first with fasting and sleeping on the ground; and the other he will tame with longsuffering, with suffering wrong, with not mentioning wrong, and with acts of mercy." *GrPh* 1, p. 45; *cf. Phi* 1, p. 39.

[147] St. Maximus the Confessor gives this interpretation to the decision of King Hezekiah to stop up the springs of water outside the city when Jerusalem was under siege by Sennacherib, king of Assyria: "He who therefore in the time of the uprising of the passions bravely closes the senses ... has plugged up the springs of water which are outside the city and has stopped the river which runs through the city." *Questions to Thalassios* 49, *PG* 90.452B.

[148] Neilos the Ascetic says that Dinah, or childish thought, falls when it goes out too soon to see things outside. *On Asceticism, Phi* 1.231-2. And Diadochos adds that "Sight, taste and the other senses weaken the remembrance of the heart, when we use them beyond measure. Eve was the first one to tell us that. For until she saw with pleasure the forbidden apple, she carefully remembered the divine commandment. So let us, always looking into the depths of our heart with unceasing remembrance of God, pass through this deceitful life as people lacking in sight. For it is proper to spiritual wisdom to always keep clipped the wings of our desire to see everything." *On Spiritual Knowledge* 56, *GrPh* 1, p. 250; *cf. Phi* 1, pp. 269-70.

18. The Guarding of the Mind or of Thoughts

Watchfulness and the blockage of the senses helps the mind to concentrate, to meditate on itself. The primary purpose of this return to itself is to observe its thoughts, so that the bad ones can be rejected at their first appearance, and the good ones can be immediately associated with the thought of God, so that they don't go toward evil. By this cleansing of ourselves from passionate thoughts we raise ourselves, according to St. Maximus the Confessor, to the second step of dispassion.[149]

As we have seen, the holy Fathers teach that our passionate thoughts are put into our consciousness, most of the time by Satan, by arousing some passion which we have become accustomed to. Diadochos of Photiki, interpreting the word of the Lord that "... evil thoughts come out of the heart,"[150] shows that the heart, that is our mind, by its nature, doesn't conceive such thoughts, but if sometimes evil thoughts also come from it this is due likewise to a habit gained by the influence of the evil spirit. But most of the time evil thoughts are really stirred up by evil spirits by arousing a passion.[151] But it seems that the heart has two meanings. There is the heart as the hidden center of the mind, as its face turned toward God, which we have called the supraconscious or transconscious.[152] It stays closed to our consciousness as long as we live in a lower, routine life, enclosed in the visible horizon of the world. Thus St. Mark the Hermit says that it is on the altar side of the icon screen,[153] where Christ came to dwell at Baptism, and that it isn't opened except

---

[149] Evagrius writes: "Now I call dispassion not simply the cessation of sin in deed, because this is known as restraint, but that which cuts out passionate thoughts from the mind, which St. Paul also named spiritual circumcision of the hidden Jew (Romans 2.29). *On Discrimination, RoFil* 1, p. 69. Not located. *trs*

[150] Matthew 15:19.

[151] *On Spiritual Knowledge* 83: "It's true that the heart produces by itself thoughts good and bad (*cf.* Luke 6.45) but it doesn't bear evil thoughts by nature; it gains the remembrance of evil as a sort of habit caused by the fall. However, most of the worst thoughts are caused by the evil of the demons. But we feel all of them as coming out of the heart. Most people, however, don't know that our mind has a very fine sense and assumes the thoughts whispered to it by evil spirits, somehow through the body, because its unstable nature leads, by its human nature, to this state in a way that we don't know. Therefore, if he takes pleasure with the thoughts breathed to him by the wickedness of Satan and inscribes them in someway in the memory of his heart it is evident that from this time forward they will bear fruit in his thought." *GrPh* 1, p. 262; *cf. Phi* 1, p. 284.

[152] "The conscious, [in] *Psychoanalysis,* the part of the mind containing the psychic material of which the ego is aware." *The Random House Dictionary of the English Language* (New York, 1966). *trs*

[153] The image is of an Orthodox church, where the icon screen or iconostas separates the altar area from the nave, or the place where the faithful worship. Here the picture is applied to the heart. *trs*

by God and by perceptive hope.[154] From there, from "the hidden temple of the heart, the mind receives good and beautiful stimuli from Christ Who dwells there," and Who nurses them into a virtuous life.[155]

But there is another "heart." This is the subconscious of the passions. We could say that this is the memory of our passionate arousals and deeds, impressed on our nature, connected to its biological side, just as the supraconscious would be the memory of spiritualized acts and the potential of superior energies. Both are called "heart" because they are central, hidden regions of our nature, one of the spirit, the other of the psychic life related to our biological side; and that which stays for a long time in us, that is in them, becomes dear and personal to us. The heart is what is most hidden and affectionate in us.

The meaning of a superior heart floats on the surface of Diadochos' thought. It is distinct from the other heart, the true center of our being, if we are principally spirit. This is proven by his words to explain why it is said that evil things also come out of the heart. "Only because the flesh always loves seductive comfort, and without measure, it seems to us that the thoughts sown by the demons in the soul come from the heart."[156]

So we could say that both good thoughts, which originate in their own supraconscious, as well as passionate thoughts, appear in the mind or consciousness. The latter are aroused by passionate movements and retained by the subconscious memory of the soul connected with the biological. Only because at the beginning the good heart, that of God isn't known to us, do we believe that everything comes from a single heart just as current psychology believes that everything, good and evil, comes from the same subconscious. But in the measure in which we turn away from the life of the surface to our true depths, is the true heart opened to us. Then it becomes plain to us that the good comes from where God is in us, and the evil doesn't, but from a lower region, which only improperly is called heart. The conclusion is that we can't say both that the heart is bad, and nevertheless say that "he has a wicked heart"; this is when the good heart is closed, not working. In the measure in which the work of the passionate heart grows, the good heart is closed and vice versa.

All of our efforts for the cleansing of thoughts, which is an important step to dispassion, are made in connection with the good heart and with Christ who dwells in it. Only by directing good thoughts toward

---

[154] *On Baptism*, PG 65.996C.
[155] *Ibid.*, 1008B.
[156] *Op. cit.*, 83, GrPh 1, p. 263; *cf.* Phi 1, p. 284.

this heart, which after all also spring up from it, and only by referring the evil ones to it at the first moment, can we succeed in the work of cleansing our inner selves. By this we struggle for the predominance of the good heart, or of Christ who dwells in it. Because our conscience becomes the field of battle between Christ and the evil spirit, by the good and evil thoughts which they send via the two hearts. Each one tries to win the loyalty of our conscience. By referring everything to the good heart, we contribute to the victory of Christ in us, Who will also cleanse the passionate "heart."

God works through the good heart; the evil spirits through the evil one. Man constantly has the good angel to his right and the evil one to his left; sometimes one wins, sometimes the other. Both are called heart, because each is borne by an infinite aspiration. But the good heart looks toward the infinity of light, and is enlightened by it; the bad "heart," toward the infinity of darkness, and is darkened by it. Before each one there is an abyss: before the good one is an abyss of life, before the other, an abyss without light, negative, empty, boring, which also attracts us, but in a passionate way, deceiving us with the attraction of a false infinity: before the good, the abyss of unending happiness, before the evil, brief pleasures followed by monotonous, unending dissatisfaction. The fact that each of these two hearts feels drawn by an infinite abyss caused the German mystics to consider the very heart of man as such an abyss. Ontologically, however, man can't be infinite, but the infinite only stands before him, as a medium in which he can go forward, in which he can breathe. In this sense Christ, who dwells in our heart, is the infinity of life, inseparable from our depths, at present a potentiality. His work is the infinity of the emptiness which, by the will of God we live eternally, because God no longer fills the subjects created by Him with life.

Dispassion is then the complete predominance of the good heart, open to the infinity of life, because if the passionate heart is agitated and disordered, the good one is calm, peaceful, sweet, and radiates rest; it is nourished by the rest of the infinite divine rest.

Note how, according to Mark the Ascetic, we should look after our thoughts, or how we should refer all of them to Christ who dwells in our hearts. First of all, we must bring any good thought that arises within us— just as soon as it appears— to Christ as a sacrifice:

> The temple is the holy house of the soul and body, and is built by God. The altar is the table of hope put in this temple. The first-born thought of each happening is brought to the mind by it as a first-born animal brought as a sacrifice for the forgiveness of the one offering it, if he brings it undefiled. But this temple too has a place behind the icon screen. There Jesus entered for us as a Forerunner,

and dwells, from Baptism, in us. This is the innermost chamber, the most hidden and the most sincere part of the heart; we can't know, however, in a sure way the One who dwells in it and neither can we know if the sacrifices of our thoughts are received or not if it isn't opened by God and by rational and understanding hope. Because as in ancient times, in the time of Israel, fire consumed the sacrifices, the same thing happens now too. The faithful heart is opened by the hope mentioned above, and the heavenly Archpriest receives the first-born thoughts of the mind and consumes them in the divine fire.... Now the first-born thoughts are those which don't appear in a second thought of the heart, but are brought immediately to Christ, when they appear in the heart. Because those which are offered to Him from the confusion of thought, Scripture calls lame, blind, and crippled and therefore they aren't received as a tithe by the heavenly Archpriest and Master Christ.[157]

Therefore let us dedicate to Christ every innocent thought which appears in us, or let us relate it to the thought directed to Him, at the first moment, because every thought is watched by "the beasts in the bushes,"[158] that is by the evil spirits, or by our passionate thoughts which spring from their hiding place and attack it, mutilating its beauty or carrying it off.[159] The way in which an innocent thought that comes to our mind is immediately bitten and infected by an evil one was first described by Evagrius, with the following example: "I have the thought to offer hospitality and truly for the Lord; but the tempter comes—he cuts it off and puts in the soul the thought to do it for glory."[160] The innocent thought is, according to Evagrius, either human or angelic. Human thought brings to the mind the simple form of something, for example the form of gold. The angelic thought associates the simple form of something with a good, spiritual meaning—for example it thinks of the good purposes of gold; it looks at it with a good thought. The evil thought or the passionate thought awakens the appetite for gold; it bites this thought and contaminates it and it is no longer whole and perfect.[161]

---

[157] *On Baptism*, PG 65.996BC.
[158] Psalm 63:31. This reference is apparently wrong. *trs*
[159] *Ibid.*, This passage wasn't located. *trs*
[160] Evagrius, *On Discrimination* 6, GrPh 1, p. 47; *cf. Phi* 1, p. 42.
[161] *Ibid.*, 7, 20, *Phi* 1, p. 42, 49. Note that the beast of hate, sinking his fangs into the thought about our brother, also wounds, poisons, troubles, infects our soul, which is no longer a transparent window to reality, but deformed and dirty; it also projects its dirtiness to him. Instead of loving him and being glad because of him, it makes us hate him, dislike him, and to feel tortured by his presence. This same sickness can also spread to our neighbor's soul, when we talk about him.

PART ONE: B. PURIFICATION BY THE VIRTUES

We must guard the innocent thought which has appeared in us so that it won't be captured by an appetite or overpowered by a passionate thought. Evagrius tells us:

> The thoughts of this world, the Lord has given to a man like sheep, to a good shepherd.... So the anchorite must keep this flock day and night so that no lamb be seized by wild beasts, or by thieves.... Thus, if the thought about our brother is spun around in us and enveloped in hate, we should know that a beast has gotten a hold of it. Likewise the thought of women, if it returns to us mixed with appetite.[162]

In a previous chapter we saw that, according to Blondel, just as soon as we have made a decision, a contrary movement is awakened in us which often succeeds in getting its way.

The surest method to keep a simple thought unharmed, or the good thought which has appeared in us, by which we can stand firmly, is to associate it with the thought directed to Christ, to bring it to Him as a sacrifice. By this we have foiled its abduction and its being carried off to the slope of a passionate thought. By this we have given our thought and will support to be faithful to this first form of the thought which has appeared. Otherwise, passion leads the mind, without our wanting it, on who knows how many side roads, producing the phenomenon called scattering, until we completely lose hold of the reigns of the thoughts in hand, which also leads to an uncontrolled and passionate external life. The guarding of the thoughts is a shield which the mind itself produces. Of course the mind can't be stopped from working continually. Therefore we must supervise it continually. The purpose of this watchfulness is twofold: When the thought is received we should see that either it develops into a devout one and creates an association with pious ones, or that with the appearance of other thoughts as the beginning of still more, we should see from the first moment that they are directed to the safe channel. This is a narrow way, a way sustained by a continual effort, which at the beginning is very hard, but in time also becomes easier.[163]

So we continually bring our first innocent thoughts as sacrifices to Christ. At the beginning we have the hope that He will make His presence felt in our heart, because although we don't feel it now, we will in the end have that experience, because He will open our heart, where He dwells, to us. Because anyway this is the heart: sensitivity to the presence of Christ and steadfast sensitivity for the good. In a practical way we will

---

[162] *Ibid.*, 16, *Phi* 1, p. 48.
[163] Mark the Ascetic, *On Baptism*, PG 65.1017A: "Because he can't help but not toil from his heart, he who pays attention everyday to the scattering of thoughts and to the pleasures of the flesh, has to stay within certain limits, not only regarding the outside, but also the inside."

gain the experience that we have a heart when we feel the presence of Christ, when it has been opened so we see Him. Until we have seen Christ in us, we haven't gained the "feeling of the mind," "the feeling of the heart" for Christ, as Diadochos of Photiki says. Our heart hasn't been opened, so that Christ is revealed to us there and so that His goodness and understanding, united with ours, are poured over our spiritual and exterior life. Until this opening takes place, this awakening of the "feeling" of the presence of Christ, by the mind, we must knock at its door, with thoughts sacrificed to Christ, with the hope that we will gain the awareness of His presence and by this our heart will be opened to us.[164] It is the only means by which we can make the heart open up to us and for Christ to be revealed to us, in us; it is the only way by which we can find out that we have a heart and that Christ is in us, by which we can become "people of the heart" in an effective way. We must exercise ourselves in sensitive acts, to gain sensitivity, because the heart, with Christ in it, doesn't receive any passionate, hardened, dirty thought whatsoever, and so doesn't open to the knocking of this kind of thought. "These clean rooms which are in the innermost parts of the soul and Christ's house don't receive anything of the vain things of this age, whether they be rational or irrational, without the three named by the Apostle: faith, hope, and love."[165] But these cardinal virtues express the state of sensitivity for Christ, of Him Who with each first-born thought knocks at the door of His heart, become by Baptism the house of Christ.

The heart too has its inmost depths, just as the feeling of Christ dwelling in it has its intensities. We don't experience all the depths, or fully feel Christ from the first opening of the heart. There is a progress in this feeling. Therefore the mind or thought which always brings its first reflection to the door of the heart, must seek each time to penetrate ever deeper into the heart, once it has opened to it, thus being filled with an increasingly intense sense of the divine infinity of Christ.

We have seen that there is an innate guard of the heart. It has the purpose of keeping it from scattering, of keeping each thought from being attacked by passing or passionate associations. This guarding of the mind, which is one and the same as the guarding of thoughts, can't be successful in its efforts, unless it continually brings its thoughts to the

---

[164] *Ibid.*, 996BC: "The altar is the table of hope placed in this temple. On it the first-born thought...of every event is offered by the mind and sacrificed. When the faithful heart is opened by the hope mentioned above, the heavenly High Priest receives the first-born thoughts of the mind." Because "...until it is opened by God and by understanding hope, we can't know for sure Him who dwells in it and we can't know if the thoughts of our mind have been received or not."

[165] *Ibid.*, 1017A.

door of the heart; so this steadfast operation is also called a watching of the heart, not only in the sense of guarding the heart from something unclean, but also in the sense of always being at its door. It is there with the offer of good thoughts, trying to penetrate further and further into it. Standing watch at the door of the heart, the mind does nothing but keep itself from going astray, because the heart is after all nothing but the depths of the mind. Strictly speaking, the heart whose door is being knocked on by contaminated, hardened thoughts doesn't open. That person no longer has a heart; he is a man "without a heart." His heart is so closed that it has become a simple potentiality. In bringing good thoughts to the heart, not only is it actualized, but the respective thoughts are strengthened in good.

> The mind must keep vigil over the heart and guard it with all watchfulness, trying to penetrate into its innermost and undisturbed chamber, where there are no winds of evil thoughts... to be vigilant over the heart and go ever deeper into it and to approach God alone, without becoming disgusted with the toils of attention and persistence.[166]

So the heart is the dwelling of Christ in us; for someone to direct every first-born thought of his to the heart means to associate it with the commemoration of Christ, or vice versa. And the mind oriented to the heart has the power to keep every thought which appears to it, pure, unharmed by the attacks of passionate thoughts. Because the Holy Spirit, found in the heart, is as a "candle of the conscience" which is shining in us:

> And when He shines constantly in the chambers of the soul, not only does He make these small and shadowy attacks (baits) of the demons evident, but also weakens them, by this holy and glorious light.[167]

This is why it is good for the mind to always have its attention directed toward the heart, that is toward the One dwelling in it. "As soon as it leaves the heart, it allows the devil to attack and it gets to the place where it welcomes his evil whisper."[168] This happens when the mind, instead of being concentrated in its intimacy, or in its heart, where Christ is, completely spills out over exterior things, in the regions of the passionate moments in us or in the world of the senses. So it is necessary for the mind to watch the thoughts from outside, brought by the appetites; when it is concentrated in thought on Christ it does this as a supervisor who doesn't abandon his place, that is the superior, discipli-

---

[166] *Ibid.*, 1016D, 1017A.
[167] Diadochos, *On Spiritual Knowledge* 29, GrPh 1, p. 242; *cf. Phi* 1, p. 260.
[168] Mark the Ascetic, *On Baptism, PG* 65.1016B.

nary role; and so it doesn't become the slave submissive to these appetites.[169] Here is how these things usually happen: First a simple thought appears in the consciousness. Immediately, somewhere on the periphery an evil thought shows itself, with the tendency of monopolizing the simple thought. Somebody talks to me about gold, the simple idea of gold appears in my consciousness. But immediately in a corner of my consciousness the appetite to have gold raises its head, or the regret that I don't have it. The simple thought has aroused an appetite which is concentrated in another thought. I must at the first moment associate the innocent thought with the thought of God. Otherwise it is conquered by the thought of passion. It can't stay neutral for long. Associating it with the thought of God, I have defeated the attack. The attack appears involuntarily to almost any person, even if he is on the highest spiritual steps.[170] And sometimes, even in keeping the thought which he is following simple, the passionate thought persists. This happens when a person is strongly controlled by the habit of the sin which the bait is offering.[171]

But we can't always protect a simple first-born thought from the claws of the beast that is ready to pounce on it. This happens especially when we haven't sacrificed it immediately to Christ, when the mind isn't directed with it to the heart but looked back as Lot's wife did, toward the attack, to the appetite which has made its presence known in the consciousness. The mind forgets itself for a little and lets itself be touched by the gentle breeze which is coming from the aroused appetite; it finds that it was robbed of its simple first-born thought and was bitten by the passions. It can still fight back so that the lamb will escape with as small a wound as possible or in any case, so that it isn't totally devoured by the wolf. The battle is worse; yet it still must be fought.[172] But help can be found likewise in directing the thought to God and likewise in fleeing to the heart. God won't be long in coming to help us, if we call Him with all our power. If we see that the thought about our brother was covered with hate, we must not allow this association to

---

[169] Diadochos, *op. cit.*, 57, *GrPh* 1, p. 250; *cf. Phi* 1, p. 270: "He who dwells constantly in his heart is removed from all the tempting things of life. For walking in the Spirit he can't know the appetites of the flesh."
[170] Mark the Ascetic, *On Baptism*, *RoFil* 1, p. 295.
[171] Mark the Ascetic, *On Baptism*, *PG* 1016C: "If the attack (bait) continues even when it is hated, this is not due to any recent event, but as a result of the strengthening of some old habit."
[172] Evagrius, in a quotation already given from *On Discrimination* 16, *GrPh* 1, p. 53; *cf. Phi* 1, p. 48, asks that the monk not give up the struggle even after the wild beast has stolen a lamb: "The thoughts of this world, the Lord has given to a man like sheep to a good shepherd.... So the anchorite must keep this flock day and night so that some lamb might not be seized by wild beasts, or by thieves...and if something like this happens, he must immediately snatch it from the mouth of the lion or the bear."

develop any further, but we must snatch the image of our brother from the fangs of hate, even if it is late.

This is the second category of cases. In it we have the duty not to offer the first-born thought as a sacrifice to Christ, but to cleanse our thoughts.

There is still a third category of cases, and namely when the attack comes out of the blue, not as an echo contrary to the innocent thought which has already sprung up in our consciousness. In these cases even the first thought has the character of an attack. But sometimes it is so gentle, so masked, that we can hardly guess its true character. It must, however, be unmasked at the start, so that it doesn't grow from an ant into a lion,[173] from which we will scarcely be able to escape. For this a special spiritual sensitivity is called for, won by steady practice and by a long effort to be cleansed from the passions.

By this the Holy Spirit has become in us a present power, poured out by Christ, found in the heart which has been opened to us, so that He illuminates all the shadowy corners of our consciousness and at the first moment surprises all passionate movement, no matter how weak and camouflaged it is at the beginning.[174] But maybe we haven't attained the sensitivity of a prolonged time of sojourn in the heart, or according to the spirit; even so, under the influence and the light of Christ and of the Holy Spirit, we can help by receiving in the name of God any thought which appears in our consciousness. If it is totally innocent, it can be

---

[173] Neilos the Ascetic, *On Asceticism* 49, *GrPh* 1, p. 218; *cf. Phi* 1, p. 233. [And the great Job, (4:11)], "wishing to show the snares which a passion lays out, made a comparison with the very bold lion and the very tiny ant. In fact the attacks (the baits) of the passions begin with the most minute images sneaking in unnoticed, as ants, but at the end they inflate so much that it constitutes for him who has been caught in the snare, a danger no longer small but greater than a lion. So, the struggler must fight with the passions even from the time they come as ants, laying out the minuteness as a bait, for if they reach the power of a lion it will be difficult to conquer them and hard to drive them into a corner. No food must be given to them from the beginning."

[174] Diadochos, *On Spiritual Knowledge* 28, *GrPh* 1, p. 242; *cf. Phi* 1, p. 260.

kept as such; if it isn't completely free of passion, it will be cleansed—the simple image of the thing will be separated from passion; and if it is wholly passionate, it will be extinguished.[175]

From all of this we see that the guarding of thoughts, strictly speaking, consists of a continual recital of the name of God in the mind, in the seeking of the heart, or in concentrating within it. But this is nothing but a concentrated uninterrupted prayer; however, it still isn't pure prayer which will be discussed in its place.[176]

---

[175] St. Neilos the Ascetic, *On Asceticism:* Our effort is to turn back the first attack of pleasure, for when this is defeated, its thrust will be weakened." *cf. Phi* 1, p. 226.
[176] Evagrius (under the name of Neilos the Ascetic) says in *Chapters on Prayer* 126, *GrPh* 1, p. 187; *cf. Phi* 1, p. 69: "He prays who always brings his first thought as fruit to God."

19. Longsuffering.
The Patient Endurance of Troubles

Evagrius and St. Maximus the Confessor say that God leads man to the peaks of perfection in a positive and negative way. The first, called providence, draws man upward in a positive way, by the beauty of the good, by the *logoi* of things, by the inner stimulations of his conscience and in general by everything which God has done and is doing for us. The second, called judgment, includes various punishments which God gives us as a result of sins to attract us from evil things: various privations of happiness to urge us to seek perfection. Just as providence is a permanent activity of God, likewise His judgment is exercised everyday. By the one He calls us to the good showing us its beauty; by the other, He shakes us with contrary things, as a father guides his child on the right way both by positive stimulation, as well as by punishments.[177]

> He who loves things good and beautiful, [St. Maximus writes] willingly moves toward the grace of deification: he is guided by providence, by the *logoi* of wisdom. But he who isn't in love with this is attracted against his will and this causes him to be rightfully judged by various kinds of punishment. The first, that is the love of God, is deified by providence; the second, that is, the lover of the flesh and the world, is stopped by judgment from arriving at condemnation.[178]

The passage itself, cited from the work of St. Maximus, which the preceding commentary explains, says:

> The wings of the son of righteousness are providence and judgment. The word, flying by them, dwells in an unseen way in things which are, healing by the *logoi* of wisdom those who want to be healed and curing by means of affliction those who are hard to get going toward virtue.[179]

From this quotation we see that these two ways have one characteristic: The way of providence is a way followed by personal initiative, by toils assumed voluntarily; the way of judgment is one which is imposed by force on him who hasn't assumed his toil by himself. So, we say at the start that the first is especially the way of monastics, and the second in contrast the way of lay people.

---

[177] Mark the Ascetic says: "In involuntary suffering the mercy of God is hidden. He calls to repentance the one who endures them and delivers him from eternal punishment." *No righteousness by works* 139, GrPh 1, p. 118; cf. *Phi* 1, p. 136.
[178] *Questions to Thalassios* 54.10, PG 90.532.
[179] *Ibid.*, PG 90.517D.

Judgment is a method which alternates permanently with providence; it also shows its effectiveness at the beginning, to guide man on the way of a purer life. It makes him leave a life dominated by the passions and to choose one more restrained. But it should be pointed out that the method of judgment doesn't cease even after a certain progress in such a life, but it intensifies after a certain progress in the life of self-control, in order to perfect its work. And because the monk, too, does not achieve completely satisfactory results, after a certain spiritual progress, a period of laziness and temptation come over him likewise, to put him to the test and to increase in him the virtue of patience.

Here we will talk about the initial troubles or about the usual ones, which accompany people's lives, especially that of lay people, and notably those troubles that come as a result of a certain progress in the life of self-control, whether of monks or of the lay people.

Self-control and the supervision of thoughts, usually carried out in moments when we are alone, are aimed especially at the passions of appetite (gluttony, unchastity, love and wealth); patience in the face of dissatisfactions which people cause us and the bearing of various troubles which come to us are meant especially to weaken the passions of anger (dejection and irritation), although they contribute too to a fuller withering of the movements of appetite. So this virtue has its place after the virtue of self-control. There is still one more reason why it is listed after self-control.

Usually the successes which someone has reached by various restraints and by the virtue of several virtues, expose him to vainglory and pride.[180] This is why God has arranged for him to have disappointments from people and various troubles, to heal him from these passions; they have reappeared in a new form after they have no longer been able to become established on wealth and over vain superficialities. For this reason they are felt as a kind of forsaking by God, of the struggler, when before he had felt Him constantly near, helping him in his efforts. Because this abandonment has a positive role, however, the Fathers call it pedagogic, or one of guidance, and they distinguish it from abandonment in the sense of rejection. It includes not only external troubles, but also certain inner discouragements. It is that which John of the Cross calls passive purification. After the trees of the passions have disappeared, the struggler must dig out their roots too; during this time he

---

[180] *Ibid.,* 54.15, *PG* 90.589B: "The demons which fight against the soul in the absence of the virtues are those which teach it loose living and drunkenness, the love of money, envy and the like. But those that fight it because of the excess of virtue are those which teach it admiration, vainglory, pride and the like, which by the things of the right hand let pass in a hidden way the temptation on the left."

lives with the feeling of discouragement and of the boredom of a vacuum and of a frightening aridity.

Diadochos says of this forsaking:

> Abandonment for the purpose of teaching in no way deprives the soul of divine light, but as I have said many times, grace only hides itself, its presence from the face of the mind, to somehow prod the soul forward, by the evil of the demons, that it might seek with all fear and with much humility the aid of God, knowing a bit the evil of the enemy. A mother does the same thing. She pushes her babe a little from her breast, if he is breaking the rules of nursing, that, scared by some people with ugly faces who are standing around, or by some animals, he might return with much fear and tears to her breast. But abandonment in the sense of forsakenness delivers the soul which doesn't want God bound to the demons.... Instructive abandonment brings the soul much sadness, likewise a certain humility and a measured hopelessness.... This so that his vainglorious and fearful side might be brought to humility. But abandonment in the sense of desertion leaves the soul full of hopelessness, unbelief, pride and anger.[181]

From the above statement of St. Maximus the Confessor and from the character of passive purification, attributed to St. John of the Cross, of passive pedagogical forsaking, we find the following additional distinction between the methods of providence and judgment, in addition to that mentioned: Providence attracts man to the good by urging him to assume certain efforts on his own initiative, while the method of judgment takes him through various sufferings.

The method of providence especially makes us reject the temptations of pleasure, that is the passions of appetite, while the method of judgment makes us primarily support the trials of pain, by which we weaken the passions of anger and pride.

The Greek word *peirasmos* and the corresponding Slavonic word have a general connotation of the means by which someone is put to the test so as to reveal his hidden nature (so the Slavonic verb *ispytyvati*, to tempt, test, means also to more deeply try something to find out what it is: *to try the Scriptures*). This test, to really get a self-revealing reaction from the one being tested, must be either attractive or repulsive. In other words it must awaken an appetite for it, or cause it to draw back from it and refuse to accept it: It must be addressed either to appetite or anger. The test which awakens the attraction of appetite is in general a

---

[181] *On Spiritual Knowledge* 86-7, GrPh 1, pp. 264-5; *cf. Phi* 1, p. 286.

sense of pleasure; that which stirs up the repulsion of anger is pain in general.

The Romanian language, more nuanced here than the Greek or Slavonic, has reserved a separate word for these two kinds of testing. By the word temptation *(ispita)* it almost always indicates a testing by pleasure. For the test by pain it reserves the word trial *(incercare)*. Thus when we hear about temptation we think of something attractive, and when we hear about trial we think of something that is hard to bear.

But in Christianity a testing hasn't only a scientific aim of making man know himself. It isn't simply an objective experiment, but has mostly a pedagogic purpose. By it man must not only know himself, but especially correct himself, or by knowing correct himself. The testing doesn't have the object so much of revealing the intensity of the appetites or anger of man, but especially that of making him able to conquer them. Certainly, just as you can't say you defeated somebody if you tied him up when he was sleeping, so too you can't talk about victory over appetite, unless you defeat it at the moment when it has all the conditions to show its power in a real way. If you master a passion to the point where nothing awakens it from its sleep, it doesn't mean that you have weakened it, or extinguished it. You can say that you have extinguished its power only if you test it so that it can be stirred up, and it isn't; or if it reacts nevertheless you can calm it down. So testings have on the one hand the purpose of revealing what phase you have reached in your efforts to overcome your passions, or what their present intensity is, or on the other hand, the purpose of making you stronger in the battle against them.

Temptations in a restricted sense thus have the goal of helping us to conquer the passions of appetite or the attraction which the sight of pleasures exercise on it; trials have the aim of making us conquer the passions of anger, or the repulsion and the reaction which pain awakens in us.

Temptations by their rejection, in other words by self-control, help us to grow spiritually just as testings fulfill their purpose by strengthening us by accepting them. We see that self-control is easier, because we can assume its toils on our own initiative. Strictly speaking, we shouldn't always wait for the presentation of exterior temptation to make the effort of self-control; because every man carries in him appetite like an arc which is extended from time to time after pleasure, based on memories, on habit or on a natural appetite which looks for an exaggerated satisfaction. Maybe this is the principle motive why man can go on to a systematic life of self-control on his own initiative, by voluntary toil.

It isn't the same with dejection, anger, disgust. First, refraining from them is harder; secondly, they are only servants of the passions of pleasure. Thus the struggle with them must be followed in a more advanced state of the spiritual life, when the battle is made easier by the weakening of passions based on appetite. But besides that, they are almost always aroused by certain external factors. Disgust doesn't have its last resort in us; we aren't disgusted for the sake of disgust itself. It is always a reaction, not a primordial initiative, as in the movement of appetite. Therefore external circumstances must be awaited to do battle with the passions provoked by them. Then too, if the temptation draws us by pleasure, while testing is painful, it is easier to give up pleasure than to look for pain.

After all, neither are we asked to look for suffering, on our own initiative, as we are asked to take measures, by ourselves for the rejection and prevention of pleasure. The primordial and direct cause of man's decadence isn't an avoidance of pain but a seeking of pleasure. The avoidance of pain comes later, because it is caused by pleasure. So first we must do battle with pleasure, principally and directly. Pleasure is often sought by our previous initiative, while pain is almost always avoided, by a reaction which is produced when it arises; likewise, if we wish to escape the preliminary initiative which looks for pleasure, we must also do it with a previous, contrary initiative, and if we want to escape the reaction contrary to pain which is produced at the moment of the appearance of pain, we must wait for that moment to stop the reaction. It is true that I can prepare myself ahead of time to accept the pain that is coming. But I don't produce suffering in anticipation, nor do I hurry its appearance, but I wait for it to happen. On my own initiative, I often cause pleasure. Likewise on my own initiative, I must reach a state where I no longer have that kind of initiative to look for pleasure. I run for pleasure as a reaction to something I am waiting for. But I must wait for the moment of pain to stop the repulsive reaction to it.

The Savior too had to go through these two kinds of testing in the same order: first the tempting by pleasure in the wilderness, and secondly, the supreme trial by suffering during His passion and death on the Cross. Both in the reception of pleasures as well as in the rejection of pain, the weakness of human nature is shown. This is so because the passions which crave and receive pleasure and those that reject pain are only manifestations of the weakness of our nature. Jesus strengthened human nature, and by it human nature in general, both by the rejection of pleasure as well as by the reception of pain.[182]

---

[182] *Questions to Thalassios* 21, *PG* 90.313D-316A: "So after victory over the first temptation, of pleasure, the Lord had nullified the plan of the evil powers, principalities and rulers; then He

In fact in seeking pleasure and avoiding pain a weakness of nature is shown. On a psychic plane it is experienced in the first case as an impulse that can hardly be stopped and secondly as a fear hard to master; and this fear (for life in the body) nourishes anxiety. Sometimes the fear of pain is manifested so unexpectedly, that we can consider it as the supreme characteristic of passivity before the tyranny which comes into conflict with our natural freedom and self-control.[183]

Now our headlong rush for pleasure isn't only the result of its attraction, but also of the fear of pain. For the man afraid of pain, used to taking refuge in its opposite, in pleasure, not only the pain, but even the absence of pleasure is a pain or a condition which he runs away from in fright. And he who is a slave of fear, whose nature is thus weakened, is at the opposite pole of the person with a strong nature. The man with a cowardly or weakened nature is, against his will, swept along by every stimulus of the senses; he is no longer a person, but an object easily blown around by any wind. The man with a strong nature who has control of himself, is a free man, whose own nature and that around him is ruled by spirit. So the restraint from pleasure and the patient endurance of suffering, far from being something negative-passive and of a weak nature, instead strengthen it and this means a spiritualization, or the putting of the spirit in control. After all, both pleasure and pain affect the fleshly side of the body. And he who has ennobled the spirit to overpower the flesh has brought it to the point where it no longer vibrates with such sensitivity to pleasure and pain.

Certainly there are also spiritual sufferings hard to admit: the lack of honor, attention, and gratitude from others. But these too are sufferings which come from a weakness, which magnify an egotistic, superficial sensitivity, oriented toward the world of our nature which, when it is overwhelmed by spirit, in other words by our orientation toward the deeply spiritual domain, is no longer shaken so easily. An excessive influence from either pleasure or perceptible egotistic pain is a sign of the adaptation of our perceptible nature to its exterior side; it is living superficially, forgetting its spiritual side, and covering it up along with its horizon. Sensitivity to pain is the proof of a material thickening of our nature, a proof of its fall to the sensitivity of biological beings, governed by reflexes. Therefore the voluntary abstinence from pleasure and the voluntary bearing of pain means a victory of the will as a spiritual factor

---

allowed them to deploy a second bait (a second attack), in other words, to also use the test which they still had, the temptation by pain; in this way He completely neutralized in Himself the corrupting venom [pain] ... from which man willingly was fleeing because of cowardice, as one tyrannized by the fear of death, and persisting in the slavery of pleasure only, to live."

[183] This is why Holy Scripture says that neither will the cowardly inherit the Kingdom of Heaven, because it belongs to the strong in spirit (*cf.* Revelation 21:8).

over biological sensitivity and a complete overwhelming of the biological by the spiritual. Our nature becomes for itself and for others a window for the light of its own spirit and for the light of God and it flows out of this window to the light from outside. When pleasure is rejected its layer of mud no longer covers the window between our nature and the spirit. When it accepts pain, it cleans and absorbs the mud on our nature.

By refraining from pleasure we have taken a big step toward the spiritual force of dispassion; by the patient endurance of troubles, of pain and of sufferings we have taken another step, the decisive one. Because, as I have said, patience and self-control don't represent something negative and don't weaken our nature from the passive resignation to the almost impulsive tendency to pleasure, and to the totally impulsive reaction against pain. Dispassion which comes from self-control and patience, or the dispassionate state, although it is a negative term, represents, on the contrary, along with purity, a free state of passivity, thus a full freeing of the spirit and a complete self-mastery. Dispassion isn't a minus, a neutrality of nature, but it is a state woven out of all the virtues whose gradual winning is nothing but an approach to dispassion. And virtue (in the Latin *virtus*), means manliness, strength, goodness. Dispassion isn't a passivity, but a concentration of the spirit in the realm of the good and of the spiritual world. Of course this isn't done by impulsiveness. So this concentration is, in contrast to impulsive agitation, a rest, quietness. But we will say more about dispassion in its place.

St. Mark the Hermit and Isaac the Syrian have given us the most beautiful sentences about the role of sufferings;[184] they are a true theology of this subject. First of all, God attracts us by sufferings. Secondly, in many cases they are the result of sin, even if we have confessed them.[185] By them our backslidden nature is reestablished, is strengthened once again. There is a harmonious compensation between the sin willingly committed and involuntary suffering.[186] Thirdly sufferings are sent for a testing, for the strengthening of our nature and of the avoid-

---

[184] St. Mark the Ascetic, in his writings, *On the Spiritual Law*. and *No Righteousness by Works*, and so on; and St. Isaac the Syrian in the *Ascetical Homilies*.
[185] St. Mark the Ascetic, *No Righteousness by Works* 139, Phi 1, p. 136.
[186] "If you don't want to suffer wrong, don't have the intention of doing it either. Of necessity the first is followed by the second; for what a person sows, that will he reap (Galatians 6:8). By voluntarily sowing evil and reaping involuntarily, we must marvel at the justice of God. But because He ordained a certain time between sowing and reaping, we don't believe that we're going to have to pay for it." Mark the Ascetic, *On the Spiritual Law* 116-18, GrPh 1, p. 103; *cf*. Phi 1, p. 118. See also *No Righteousness by Works* 9, Phi 1, p. 126.

ance of future sins.[187] Fourth, they can come even if we haven't sinned: They come to us because of the sins of others.[188] Fifth, their patient endurance is a sign of power and wisdom and endows us with them.[189]

In general, sufferings in a necessary way enter into the economy of salvation; he who receives them is exempted from eternal sufferings.[190] Furthermore, there is a harmonious alternation between joys and sufferings in this world. You should realize that even the thing that has brought you joy will later bring you suffering and vice versa.[191]

A wise order governs the destiny of each one of us. Joy can make us a little less heedful of our duties. Thus it needs to be sprinkled with a cold shower of sufferings so we don't slacken in our efforts. But sufferings don't have to last long, that the doubt doesn't arise that we no longer have someone who cares for us. On the hills of joy—in the val-

---

[187] "Any affliction from God is a part of the nature of piety. For real love is tested by the contrary." *On the Spiritual Law* 65, *GrPh* 1, p. 100; *cf. Phi* 1, p. 114. "Don't say that you can gain virtue without affliction, for virtue untested by troubles isn't tempered." *Ibid.*, 66. "It's a great virtue to patiently endure whatever happens to us and to love those who hate us." *No righteousness by Works* 47, *GrPh* 1, p. 112; *cf. Phi* 1, p. 129. "If you don't want to be troubled by evil thoughts, accept spiritual humiliation and affliction of the flesh." *Ibid.*, 207, *GrPh* 1, p. 124; *cf. Phi* 1, p. 143.

[188] "Don't think that every trouble is due to sin. Because there are some good people who are nevertheless tempted. It's true what is written: 'The lawless and ungodly will be persecuted' (*cf.* Psalm 37:28). But likewise it is written that those who 'seek to live a holy life in Christ Jesus will suffer persecution' (2 Timothy 3:12)." *On the Spiritual Law* 174, *GrPh* 1, p. 106; *cf. Phi* 1, p. 122. "Don't say that the one delivered from passions can't have trouble. Because even if not for himself, he is indebted to have trouble for his neighbor." *No Righteousness by Works* 132, *GrPh* 1, p. 118; *cf. Phi* 1, p. 136.

[189] Wisdom isn't only the knowing of the truth from the natural course of events, but also the enduring of the meanness, as our own, of those who do us wrong." *No Righteousness by Works* 206, *GrPh* 1, p. 124; *cf. Phi* 1, p. 143. "He who accepts the troubles of the present time in hope of the blessings to come, has found the knowledge of the truth and will be quickly delivered from anger and sorrow." *Ibid.*, 168. *GrPh* 1, p. 21; *cf. Phi* 1, pp. 139-40.

[190] "If someone has sinned openly and not repented and neither received any punishment until death, be sure that his judgment will be without mercy there." *On the Spiritual law* 112, *GrPh* 1, p. 103; *cf. Phi* 1, p. 118. "If you are injured or insulted or persecuted by someone, don't think about the present, but wait for the future; and you will see that he was the cause of much good for you not only in the present age, but also in that to come." *Ibid.*, 114, *GrPh* 1, p. 103; *cf. Phi* 1, p. 118. "He who fights with people out of fear of being wronged or insulted will either suffer more trouble here or without mercy in the age to come." *No Righteousness by Works* 171, *GrPh* 1, p. 121; *cf. Phi* 1, p. 140. "He who wants to avoid future evils is obliged to bear with pleasure the ones of the present, for in this way he will avoid, through small pain, great punishments." *Ibid.*, 187, *GrPh* 1, p. 122; *cf. Phi* 1, p. 141.

[191] "Exalted by praise, expect shame." *On the Spiritual Law* 137, *GrPh* 1, p. 104; *cf. Phi* 1, p. 119. "Don't be glad when you do good for someone, but when you endure the enmity which follows, without animosity. For as nights follow days, so evils follow good works." *No Righteousness by Works* 137, *GrPh* 1, p. 118; *cf. Phi* 1, p. 136. "Compare the troubles of the present with future blessings, and discouragement will never infect your will." *On the Spiritual Law* 156, *GrPh* 1, p. 105; *cf. Phi* 1, p. 121. "When you suffer some disgrace from people, immediately think of the glory which will come from God, and the shame will leave you glad and peaceful." *No Righteousness by Works* 68, *GrPh* 1, p. 113; *cf. Phi* 1, p. 131.

leys of suffering—so goes the life of a spiritual man; but he chalks up real progress in this alternation. Joys that come from patience are purer, more spiritualized, less tainted by self-satisfaction; sufferings are also more firmly endured. Strictly speaking, joys are subdued by the certainty of sufferings on the way, while sufferings are endured with a mixture of tranquility, with an inner smile, as St. John Climacus says, because of the certainty of joys which will come in turn. So as changeable as the outer circumstances are in which the life of the spiritual man develops, on the inside it has reached a kind of equilibrium, which gives him a constant peace. It is the strength of the spirit in the face of the waves of the world.

In the pursuit of pleasure and in the flight from pain the instability of our nature is manifested, which is the result of sin and the sign of its defectiveness; likewise in the stability and steadfastness manifested in self-control and patience, the firmness and earnest of incorruptibility are shown, which it has regained by the example of the human nature of Jesus Christ and by His help.[192] Exercises in patience are thus necessary for our nature and so too the sufferings which occasion them, whether they are the result of some sin or not. And the world is so ordered, that not only will divine providence and the Giver of blessings be revealed to us, but also the Judge, Him who wants to strengthen us, by a stricter pedagogy from time to time. Our nature itself requires this strictness, so it won't be defiled; it requires it until it is fully strengthened in the future life. It doesn't need it all the time, because it would be too much to bear, but in alternation with signs of affection. God uses the world and time as grace and judgment for us. And both of these aspects are good for us.

---

[192] "Accept equally the weaving together of good and evil and God will level out the disproportion of things." St. Mark the Ascetic, *On the Spiritual Law* 159, GrPh 1, p. 105; cf. Phi 1, p. 121.

20. Hope

The patient endurance of trouble, or longsuffering, at the beginning can be mixed with the consciousness that it can't be otherwise. But in time hope grows out of it, which then accompanies it steadfastly and gives it strength, making it seem completely voluntary. When man sees how much he has to endure, he begins to see that it is impossible for him not to have comfort from God, if not in this world, at least, in the next. This hope becomes for him with time very sure. Thus we can define hope as a certitude of the future things which appears in the person who hopes. If faith is a certitude of various present unseen realities and if when it is powerful it gives even a communion of those realities to the one who believes, hope is the certitude which one has in certain future realities and of the participation which he will have in them. So hope is faith oriented to the future for the one who has it. Hope is faith in an advanced stage, a power which gives transparency to time, which penetrates through time, as faith penetrates space and visible nature. In hope there is a plus of evidence, a plus of knowledge. Where does it come from? Is it real, or only an illusion? Does it come from a will which habitually insists that it knows that the future will be such, under pressure from the present which doesn't meet his expectations? The answers to these questions will be found in the discussion which follows.

Hope is an advance, a leap over time. As by care[193] man is continually bent over toward the future, so is he also by hope, but in another way: By care he has a foreboding of an unpleasant future, which he takes measures to avert; by hope he senses a favorable future which he reaches with difficulty. Heidegger didn't see in man this opposite care, this "existential" which is just as much a part of human nature as care. So, just as a gnosiological[194] virtue is recognized in care in relationship to the future (Heidegger, Scheler), in the same way, it must also be recognized in hope.

But when we say that hope belongs just as much to human nature as care, we don't mean that they actually coexist at every moment in the soul. At least religious hope, the hope of blessedness in the future life is present in the soul in direct proportion to the absence of care, and vice versa. In regard to hope in an earthly future the same thing can't be said except to a lesser degree, but this only because such hope doesn't contain the same certitude as the religious. So it could be said that hope and

---

[193] Remember that the author uses *care* here in the sense of a state of anxiety or worry. *trs*
[194] As included in *gnosiology*, the science of cognition, "the act or process of knowing including both awareness and judgment." Fr. Staniloae uses this term throughout this book. In English *epistemology* is perhaps preferred. *trs*

care have a single root in human nature: preoccupation with the future. But when the fruit of hope grows from this root, in other words the certainty in the anticipated future, the fruit of care no longer does, or at least worldly care, but only the care to not compromise the winning of something sure. And the fruit of worldly care grows big where the fruit of hope doesn't.

If we closely compare hope and care we realize that the reason for the impossibility of their coexistence is the fact that in the same measure in which hope contains proof, care contains uncertainty. So the uncertainty of care is present where the proof and quiet of hope are lacking. Because the care which serves hope isn't the nourished uncertainty of worldly care, but it is just cautious not to lose something of sure hope.

The certainty of hope in the future blessings which God will give us and the uncertainty of worldly care are shown by the peace which the first gives and the continual fragmentation which is included in the second. Putting the contrast between them in other terms, St. Mark the Ascetic says: "Largeness of heart means hope in God; constriction means bodily care."[195]

You have the experience of the congestion of the heart when you are disturbed, and "ample room" when you are peaceful. But uneasiness, in regard to the future is the fruit of uncertainty, just as peace is the fruit of certainty. Care is the offspring of the fear of the future, thus of uncertainty, of the timidity that it won't be just the way we want it.

In the treatise *On Baptism* Mark the Ascetic repeats many times that the heart where Christ dwells from Baptism can't be opened but "by Christ Himself and by intelligent hope,"[196] in other words by the hope that sees the unseen, or the things in the other life. Then the heart is really opened, no longer being ruled by care itself. And only when hope gains control of us and by it the heart is opened, do we escape the thoughts of the world, or thoughts of care.

Thus the opening of the heart coincides with the victory of hope in us and with an escape from care and its thoughts. This opening of the heart is one of the proofs of things beyond the world. Hope is vision with the heart, with the deepest part of our spirit, thus it is an intimate mystical conviction, a state of the transparency of our nature to the things beyond this world.

Truly, if care is existential, if it pertains to life, and is structurally related to human nature after the fall, what a miracle it is that man can escape it, better said that it can be transformed into the "existential" of

---

[195] *No Righteousness by Works* 114, GrPh 1, p. 116; cf. Phi 1, p. 134.
[196] *PG* 65.996C.

hope. How could the foreboding of an unsure future be changed into the presentiment of a blessed, sure future, or uncertainty into certainty? The process of this transformation could only be explained by the intervention of a power distinct from the power of human nature, or by the coming into contact somehow of the depths of this being with the reality hoped for. Thus hope can't be only an illusion. In hope we experience a certainty, which doesn't depend only on our will, which doesn't have only the strength which we give it. The strength of hope has grown in us from somewhere else and it is imposed on our will, or as in addition to what we can will. We previously had no hope, we didn't feel it in us, although maybe we weren't in despair either. But after a while we noticed that hope in the things to come had grown stronger in us, as a certainty which filled us with more and more peace. Along with this, the poisoned sap of the weeds of care which had grown over our hearts, which were growing on the hard ground under which our heart was hidden, dried up; and it seems that as hard as we, too, want to take the cares of life as seriously as our neighbors around us, we can't do it any longer.

The problems which make people around us lose sleep have lost all their meaning in our eyes.

21. Meekness and Humility

Meekness and humility are the flowers that grow from the patient endurance of troubles and from hope. Meekness is born after the passions of anger have been eliminated from our nature through patience. It comes immediately after humility. "The dawn precedes the sun and meekness humility," writes St. John Climacus.[197] Meekness is a firm disposition of the mind, and is unaffected either by honors or insults. It means to be unaffected by the disappointments which your neighbor has caused you and to pray sincerely for him. It is the rock that rises above the sea of anger, and is unmoved by its waves.

Meekness is the support of patience, the door, or better said, the mother of love.... It is the aid of obedience, the guide of the brotherhood, the restraint of angry, the cause of joy, the imitation of Christ, the property of angels, the chaining of demons, the shield against bitterness. In the heart of the meek the Lord rests, while the soul of the agitated is the throne of the devil. The meek will inherit the earth, better said they will control it.... The gentle soul is the throne of simplicity. The quiet soul will make a place in it for the words of wisdom. Meek souls will be filled with knowledge, while the angry mind dwells with darkness and ignorance.... Simplicity is an invariable habit of the soul, not being able to be moved by perverse thoughts. [Or] wickedness is a science, better said a devilish ugliness, devoid of truth, trying to deceive the many.... Wickedness covers the multiple variety of the passions.... Simplicity, however, is the exalted cause of humility and meekness.... He who is simple and uncomposed wants the soul that approaches Him to be simple and innocent.[198]

By meekness we approach love, which stands at the very top of the virtues. If love is the opposite of egotism, manifested by the passions, by meekness we reach the doorstep of love. The meek person has removed from himself all the causes which maintain his separation from his neighbors. By mildness he has taken the decisive step toward the unification of his human nature, with the human nature of others. Mildness anticipates the gentle breeze of dispassion, in other words, the quietness which is at the same time the lack of egotistic passions. Those who think that mildness is a weakness should think of its force to heal hate and to attract all those who would otherwise tend to separate and distance themselves from each other. Truly, the meek person is the only one who gains the control of the earth.

---

[197] *The Ladder* 24.1, *PG* 88.980C; *cf.* Moore, p. 186.
[198] *Ibid.*, *PG* 88.980D-984B; *cf.* Moore, p. 186 *ff.*

By meekness the soul approaches simplicity, which is the ideal of spiritual nature. At the same time it helps us to understand the beauty and the positive richness found in simplicity. Simplicity is a profound and encompassing wisdom, which arises when the meek person puts himself into everyone else's situation. Exactly because of this encompassing wisdom, the meek soul isn't disturbed and doesn't go from a good to a bad mood; he judges every situation in a much broader light. He takes into account so many considerations, which the passionate soul doesn't know or even willingly overlooks, obsessed as it is by a one-sided passion. The very wise simplicity of the meek person is due exactly to the lack of passions in him. On the one hand he doesn't have passions which he wants to hide, on the other hand, nothing hinders him from judging objectively, nothing influences him to judge unfairly or to be one sided. The evil person is always in a state of duplicity, saying one thing and thinking something else, in order to cover up the ugliness of a passionate intention. He judges in a narrow minded or crooked way and so presents every situation as something hidden, according to how his interest of the moments dictates. He creates the impression that he is smart, but his smartness is the art of falsifying and of covering up the truth, of presenting the twisting of true realities as fact. It is the art of making the dark look like daylight. The wickedness of evil doesn't submit itself to any realities beyond the egotistical "I," while wisdom and simplicity of the meek person are watered by the fountains of the truth of the open sea.[199]

"Humility is an anonymous grace of the soul."[200] It is the opposite of pride, which is the most resistant of the passions. Pride seems to lift us up, while in reality it drags us down to the depths of hell, because it is the worse case of evil; so humility, which seems to lower us, carries us up to the highest steps, and takes its place as a virtue immediately before dispassion and love. If pride as egotism is the source of all passions, humility is the concentration of all virtues. If pride tears human nature into as many pieces as the individuals it exists in, humility brings it together again. If pride deforms judgment and darkens the right contemplation of reality, humility reestablishes the proper view of things. Each virtue is equal to a growth of the will. But this growth is based on knowledge, on a growth of the right view of things, as the holy Fathers say, because what darkens and distorts reality are the passions. The passionate person, if he has done something from a personal interest tries to justify his action by saying that it is in the interest of others. He changes his whole conception of a certain sector of life by continu-

---

[199] *Ibid.*, Step 25.69, *PG* 88.988 *ff*; *cf.* Moore, p. 201 *ff*.
[200] *Ibid.*, 25.3, *PG* 88.989A; *cf.* Moore, p. 191.

ing this sin, and tries to convince others too that this is the way to do things, even though until yesterday he was preaching something else. He doesn't admit that objective truth is something else, because he has sinned out of weakness in regard to that truth, but he distorts the truth and the norm of general orientation so that everybody will agree with him.

But if the passions twist the view of things by adapting their general objective order to an egotistical personal interest, each virtue, as an overcoming of a passion, and of egotism too, brings a growth in the proper view of things.

If this is the case, humility is— as the highest and most inclusive of the virtues, as opposed to egotism, the source of the passions— the fullest reestablishment of the true understanding of natural realities. It remains for love to understand things supernatural.

The struggle with pride however doesn't start only after the victory over the other passions, but even in the beginning, because from a certain point of view, even the battle with the other passions is also one with the egotism of pride, or must be accompanied by it; so humility has, according to St. John Climacus, multiple steps:

> One is the sight of this most blessed vine in the winter of the passions, another, in the autumn of fruit bearing and another, in the harvest of the virtues, although all its forms flow toward one and the same joy and fruit bearing.... When in other words this most blessed vine begins to sprout, we hate right away, not without pain, all human glory and praise, casting out from us all anger and fury. Then with spiritual age, as this queen of the virtues advances in the soul we no longer value, yes we consider it even a thing of abomination, any good whatsoever we might have done, and we believe rather that everyday we add something to the burden of our sins, by some unknown dissipation. And the riches of the spiritual gifts (charisms) that we partake of we consider as an addition of even greater shame, of which we are not worthy.[201]

He distinguishes especially three phases of humility, in the following way:[202]

> Pure repentance, weeping which cleanses us of every stain, and most blessed humility of the perfect are as far apart and as distinct from one another, as are bread, yeast and flour. By repentance, the soul is effectively broken into pieces, by the water of tears it is united, if we might put it that way, and mixed with God. Next, blessed humility ignited by

---

[201] Step 25.4, *PG* 88.989AB; *cf.* Moore, p. 191.
[202] Step 25.6, *PG* 88.989D; *cf.* Moore, p. 192.

the fire of the Lord, makes the soul solid bread, lacking any fermentation and spoiling conceit. [203]

In another place St. John of the Ladder writes:

> Understand, beloved, that the valleys are full of grain and spiritual fruit. A valley is the humble soul in the midst of the mountains, that is of pains and virtues, remaining always humble and unmoved.... Repentance rises up, mourning knocks at the door of heaven, and most holy humility opens them.... In the absence of light everything is dark, in the want of humility everything is empty and withered.... It is one thing to exalt yourself, another to not exalt yourself, and another to humble yourself. The first means to judge everyday; the second to not judge, but not to judge yourself either; the third to condemn yourself in everything, without being worthy of condemnation.... Humility is a divine shelter to keep us from seeing our own accomplishments. Humility is an abyss of modesty which can't be taken by a thief. Humility is a strong tower in the face of the enemy.[204]

Humility is the supreme consciousness and living both of the divine infinity and our own littleness. It is at the same time the consciousness that the divine infinity pierces everything and everybody around us. This is why we said that it is a giant growth of knowledge. The humble person gives in to his fellow as he would before God. If pride blinds our eyes to the infinite reality of God, humility makes them see it. So, whatever we do, as long as we lack humility, as long as there is a trace of pride in us, we lack the thrill of contact with God; we lack the profound consciousness of a deeper relationship with God, and neither do we make others feel it. Where humility is lacking, there is superficiality, the commonplace, a closed horizon, the kind of conceit that provokes a smile of pity. Only the humble lives in the immeasurable depths, full of mystery, in God. Only his deeds and attitudes are seasoned with salt (understood as seriousness and deification). You have to make yourself little, and then some, so little that you must consider yourself nothing, to see the majesty of God and to make yourself feel humble by His action. Humility is all encompassing wisdom. The humble person, far from becoming poor, embraces the infinite more than anybody else and offers it to others. The proud person is mostly smoke. Humility is the valley of

---

[203] Diadochos distinguishes the two phases of humility: One, which appears at the middle of the struggles for perfection, another, at its final head. The first is humility provoked by the weakness of the flesh and by different enemies without foundation, the second provoked by the abundance of divine goodness. The first is joined to sadness, when it is deprived of earthly blessings, the second is entirely spiritual and blessed. *On Spiritual Knowledge* 95, *GrPh* 1, p. 270; *cf. Phi* 1, p. 292.
[204] Step 25.14-16, *PG* 88.993AD; *cf.* Moore, p. 193.

the lush field of corn which draws its vitality from the vigor of the infinite. Pride is the barren rock battered by the icy north wind of nothingness, which draws out life. Humility is the supreme transparency of our nature, won after getting rid of the host of passions; it penetrates all the faculties of the soul. By the passions, secretly driven by pride, man is continually thinking of himself; he doesn't see the reality and work of God—he gets in the way so he can't see them. He is his own darkness and smoke. The passions are growths, sick ones, of the ego, blotting out his reality. And they don't only obstruct the view of reality distinct from himself, but also his true sight. The inflation of the ego, or the smoke that comes from it, gets between his view and the true ego, so he takes himself for somebody who isn't real. And I wonder if when the mind transcends itself, that is, reaches ecstasy, in order to see God,[205] doesn't it mean precisely this humble forgetting of self in the face of His overwhelming reality? To know something you have to forget yourself, because you are nothing but an instrument for seeing, or receiving the infinite realities, not even an instrument that exists by itself. You are a worker only because of the good will of the owner.

Humility looks like self-reduction to nothing; in reality it is a return of our nature to the place where it is a window of the infinite and empty room intended to be filled with divine light. In fact, the window does exist for itself—the room which God sends light to is dark without it. So it is with man—if he only accepts this role of being nothing but a reflector and a receiver of divine light, he has a tremendous destiny: that of living with the infinite. If he is ashamed of this role and is filled with his own smoke, he can no longer see anything even in himself.

---

[205] Maximus the Confessor, *Chapters on Knowledge* 1.81; cf. *Maximus Confessor, Selected writings*, p. 143.

22. Dispassion or Freedom from Passion

Dispassion is the peak towards which all the efforts of personal endeavors, all the steps of all the virtues, lead to, if the whole of asceticism has as its aim the direct purification of the body and of the soul from the passions.

Dispassion isn't a negative state, because the absence of evil can't be considered as such. Dispassion "is a peaceful condition of the soul."[206] He who has reached it no longer sins easily either in word or deed, and neither does anger or appetite any longer easily move him to sin. He has almost totally extinguished the passions in the faculties of the soul—those of anger and appetite— and they no longer can be easily stirred up either by things, or thoughts or the remembrance of sinful deeds.[207] We can say that the passions have become for him an ontological impossibility, that is, that his being is incapable of harboring the passions, as the case is with God. But they are for him almost a moral impossibility, as for example, it is impossible to imagine that a man who has kept himself from stealing for decades now doing such a thing. St. Isaac the Syrian says:

> Dispassion doesn't mean to no longer feel the passions, but to no longer accept them. For by the multiple and varied virtues, evident and hidden, which he who has reached it, has gained, the passions have been weakened and can no longer easily rise up in against the soul. The mind therefore no longer needs to be constantly concerned with them because all the time it is filled with [good] thoughts....[208]

And Diadochos of Photiki adds:

> Dispassion doesn't mean to be no longer attacked by demons, because then we would have to leave this world, according to the Apostle (1 Corinthians 5:10), but being attacked by them, to remain unconquered. Because iron clad warriors are also the targets of the arrows of the enemies and hear and see the arrows shot, but they aren't wounded, because of the strength of the attire of war. By being covered by iron while they fight, they remain unconquered.[209]

So dispassion would be that state of the soul in which it defeats every temptation. The moment it has received the temptation whether from

---

[206] St. Maximus, *Chapters on Love* 1.36, GrPh 2, p. 6; cf. Phi 2, p .56.
[207] Evagrius says: "The soul which has *apatheia* [dispassion] is not simply the one which is not disturbed by changing events but the one which remains unmoved at the memory of them as well." *Praktikos* 67 (Kalamazoo, MI, 1978): 34.
[208] *Directions to Hesychasts*,86, GrPh 4, p. 280; PhiPH, pp. 253-4.
[209] *On Spiritual Knowledge* 98, GrPh 1, p. 271; cf. Phi 1, p. 294.

within or from without, it has fallen from the state of dispassion. Certainly this state, although it has become a habit, hasn't become an inalienable attribute of the soul, as it has with the angels, or will be with us in the future life; although it also is helped a great deal by habit which has penetrated our nature, it nevertheless needs to be sustained by our will. So it can be also at anytime, although this has become very unlikely, almost a moral impossibility. Usually we don't consolidate ourselves all at once in a state of dispassion but we reach it repeatedly, and even if there is some minor backsliding, we stay in it most of the time. This is why John Climacus, when he calls dispassion "the heaven in the heart of the mind, which considers the cunning of the demons as just toys,"[210] is talking about several grades of dispassion. According to him "One can be dispassionate, and another more so; the first strongly hates evil, and the other enriches himself continually with innumerable virtues."[211]

But the state of dispassion implies a positive strength, if it is capable of conquering every passion. This strength is nothing else than that of the virtues. "That soul has dispassion which is as imbued with virtues as the impassioned are by the passions."[212] It is nothing but the robe of the total cleansing of the soul, woven out of all the virtues.

If the definition of gluttony is to force oneself to eat even without hunger, the definition of restraint is to hold nature in check when it hungers without blame.... If the sea of wrath consists of losing your temper even when no one is around, the ocean of longsuffering is to remain peaceful when your slanderer is present.... If the sign of complete dispassion is to give way to all the suggestions of the demons, I think that the sign of holy dispassion is to be able to say clearly, 'When the evil one left me, I didn't know it,'[213] neither when he came, nor why, nor how he left, but I am totally insensitive to this, because I am now and will be in the future united with God.... A king's crown isn't made of a single stone and dispassion isn't perfected as long as we leave a single virtue, no matter how common, undeveloped.[214]

Thus the state of dispassion expressed negatively means freedom from all the passions, and positively, the possession of all the virtues. But dispassion also has other important positive aspects.

First of all it is a state of peace and quiet, of spiritual rest. As much as the soul ruled by passions is agitated, off balance, troubled, sometimes excited, sometimes calmed down, so the soul freed from passions

---

[210] Step 29.2, *PG* 88.1148B; *cf.* Moore, p. 258.
[211] Step 29.6, *PG* 88.1148D; *cf.* Moore, p. 259.
[212] Step 29.9, *PG* 88.1149A; *cf.* Moore, p. 259.
[213] The author gives a reference to Psalm 51:4, which is wrong. *trs*
[214] Step 29.10, 13, *PG* 88.1149; *cf.* Moore, pp. 260-1.

DISPASSION OR FREEDOM FROM PASSION

has self-control, is calm and quiet. This is the quietness of monks, which isn't only a lack of exterior noise, or a *dolce farniente*, a sweet peace, but a state won and maintained by a concentrated effort of will. It is a gathering of the mind and all the psychic powers in God, a mastery of the movements of the body. Man is no longer the prey of innumerable movements and centrifugal tendencies of the mind, of the appetite and of the senses.[215] The mind and will have gained their full firmness of no longer being easily attracted toward something other than God.

And still neither by this characterization has all that is positive in the state of the dispassionate quiet of the soul been mentioned. Because this quiet and concentration is due to the fact that mind, appetite and will now have a higher object for preoccupation. So precisely because of this the cleansing from the passions or dispassion is pursued, so that the mind freed from the domination of the passions, will be able to direct its course in quietness toward the higher meanings inherent in its nature. Mark the Hermit says:

> When by the Grace of God the mind does the works of the virtues and comes near to knowledge, it feels little from the evil and non-understanding of the soul. Its knowledge catches him up to the heights and frees him from all the things of the world; and by the purity in them [the saints] and the fineness and the lightness and sharpness of their minds, and again by their asceticism, their mind is cleansed and becomes transparent, by the withering of their flesh in the school of quietness and by staying a long time in it. This because the contemplation in them easily and speedily grasps everything and to their amazement leads them.[216]

To the extent that the mind has been freed from passions for longer periods of time, in other words, to the extent that it has wilted them, so will it make progress in contemplation and in the tasting of the divine blessing, and to the extent that it progresses in this contemplation, so the passions will be wilted more and more. This is the perfection which

---

[215] Isaiah the Solitary comments: "As long as the war lasts, a person lives in fear and trembling, wondering if he will win or be defeated today, or if he will win or be beaten tomorrow. For the battle constricts the heart. But dispassion is without war. The dispassionate has received his reward and is no longer concerned about the separation of the three, because peace has been made between them through God. And the three are: soul, body, and spirit. Thus since the three have been made one by the work of the Holy Spirit, they can no longer be separated. So don't think that you have died to sin, as long as you are under pressure by your enemies, either in time of vigil, or in time of sleep.... When the mind is strengthened and readies itself to follow the love which extinguishes all the passions of the body and which, with its power doesn't allow anything contrary to nature to dominate the heart, the mind stands up against what is natural until it separates it from the unnatural." *On Guarding the Intellect* 18-19, *GrPh* 1, p. 33; *cf. Phi* 1, p. 26.

[216] *Directions to Hesychasts* 86, *GrPh* 4, p .280; *PhilPH*, p. 254. He is following Evagrius.

188 PART ONE: B: PURIFICATION BY THE VIRTUES

has no end. Ephraim the Syrian says that those who have been cleansed of the passions:

> ... the dispassionate, reaching out without satiety toward the highest place, make perfection imperfect, because the eternal blessings are unending. On the one hand, it is perfect compared to human power, but on the other imperfect, surpassing itself by daily additions and lifted up continually in the ascent toward God.[217]

Thus we understand how dispassion is the preliminary condition for contemplation, which is the indirect purpose of the whole of the ascetical purification. Of course, the simple absence of the passions still doesn't mean the contemplation of God. For this, a distinct revelation of God is necessary. But this revelation can't take place as long as man's spiritual eyes are troubled and his time is preoccupied by the attraction of the passions. The absence of passions, however, gives him the capacity to see and to remember things in their simple meaning, without associating them with a passionate interest. Evagrius says: "He who has reached dispassion, still might not pray properly, because he can follow certain simple thoughts and be caught up by them and be far from God."[218]

In fact, the state of dispassion doesn't mean a permanent state of the contemplation of God. It's true that without the permanent thought of God, without the commemoration of His name, it can't be attained or maintained. But this remembrance of God, doesn't totally eliminate the other ideas from man's mind; it doesn't absorb them. It doesn't make them disappear. Yes, they aren't even permanently a transparency by which he can contemplate God.

Therefore the peacefulness of this state must not be understood, except for certain moments, as a total disinterest in the world. However it does exclude an egotistical interest. In this sense it is disinterest. But it doesn't exclude a general disinterest, the interest of love. On the contrary, love in all its amplifications appears after the winning of dispassion. Therefore, as dispassion isn't an end in itself, but is pursued for contemplation— and once the zone of dispassion has been entered, contemplation begins to appear too— likewise dispassion is pursued for love. We cleanse ourselves of the passions of egotism in order to gain the altruism of love; and pure love appears at the same time as dispassion, and love grows in the measure in which we progress in dispassion. This is the great and radical difference between Christian dispassion and

---

[217] *Ibid.*, 87, *GrPh* 4, p. 281; *PhilPH*, p. 255.
[218] Evagrius, *On Prayer* 56, *GrPh* 1, p. 181, under the name of Neilos the Ascetic. *cf. Phi* 1, p. 56.

DISPASSION OR FREEDOM FROM PASSION 189

Buddhist apathy.[219] There, he who has reached apathy has no concern whatsoever for people, because of trepidation not to disturb his egotistic tranquility. So no matter how complete this disinterest seems, it hasn't eliminated the worst thing: egotism. Christian dispassion, on the contrary, is a generous disinterest. When we talk about the passions which the Christian has succeeded in extinguishing one thing is clear: They are the twisted manifestation of egotism, that has become all powerful. This is the very thing that the spiritual Christian doesn't want to trouble him. The dispassion which he seeks is precisely the condition for the appearance, activation and unhindered growth of disinterested love. The endeavor for dispassion is one of pulling up the weeds which hinder the growth of the grainfield of love; it is a breaking down of the wall of the egotism of the soul, to let the soul be of real use to others, not a more complete enclosure within the walls of total indifference.

For this reason Evagrius and Maximus the Confessor consider dispassion as having two aspects. First, it is the state of the soul which permits it to receive and to conceive things in their "simple" meaning, in other words not interwoven with a passion. Secondly, it is a state which doesn't exclude but implies love.[220] These two requirements are integrated in the following sense: The absence of passion when either seeing or thinking of things is the absence of egotism. The dispassionate person no longer sees and thinks of things through the prism of passion which wants to be satisfied by them; in reference to himself, things no longer seem to be gravitating around him, but they appear as having their own purpose independent of his egotism. Other people appear to him as human beings who are purposes in themselves, who need help from him. Of course, he doesn't stop here. He will see God through the *logoi* of persons and things, he will see them as gifts and as his solicitation or words. But at first it has been necessary for him to realize that he isn't the center of all things, to be free from the illusion that things gravitate to him, in order to realize later that they gravitate toward God. And when he sees God later, he views them as eternal and in God, and as he loves God, so he loves them too, as gifts of divine love and wisdom.[221] But this view of the world in its "simple" meanings *[logoi]*, with disinterested love, and implicitly with an interest for his salvation and that of his neighbors, doesn't produce a turbulence analogous with the

---

[219] Fr. Staniloae is using *apathy* here, not as indifference, but in its original Greek sense of lack of passion, insensibility. In English, in regard to Buddhism, we say *nirvana*. trs
[220] Dispassion doesn't exclude love, but produces it. *cf. Chapters on Love* 1.2, Phi 2, p. 53; "God, by nature good and dispassionate, loves everybody equally, as His creatures...likewise, too, the good and dispassionate man willingly loves all men equally." *Ibid.*, 1.25, GrPh 2, pp. 5-6; *cf. Phi* 2, p. 55.
[221] St. Maximus, *Chapters on Knowledge* 2.4; *cf. Maximus Confessor, Selected writings*, p. 148.

190 PART ONE: B: PURIFICATION BY THE VIRTUES

passions and egotism. The dispassionate person knows that he influences his neighbors more by his quietness, as a sign of his deep certitude, as an example of the strength given by trust in God and by cleansing from passions. He works for the salvation of others, with the unwavering confidence in the plan which God has for every soul.

Agitation belongs to the passionate person, because egotism gives him the continuous feeling that he is alone, confined only to his own powers. But he who knows that God is watching over everything, is no longer subject to agitation and care. Dispassion, far from being opposed to love, is dispassion precisely because it is anchored in love.[222] In fact, the greatest unrest which comes to us from the suspicions or news that somebody else is doing something evil to us, undermines us. That same suppressed consciousness is hidden here— our own aloneness. But he who has a deep trust in God no longer fears other people and so no longer has any motive not to love them. Dispassion is tranquility because above it the gentle breeze of love is blowing and in the measure in which he progresses in this zone it is consolidated. It is tranquility because it is full, as love is too, of divine power. The tranquility of the dispassionate grows from the consciousness and from the experience of the penetration of divine love into all that he is and has. The strength to remain pure in all things, to live in the fullness of the virtues and not to be upset by anything, he has from Christ, Who lives in him, "... guiding him in every word, deed and thought"[223] The dispassionate, if it is necessary to say more, no longer lives, but Christ lives in him (Galatians 2:20). "... Dispassion is the palace of the heavenly King, which has many mansions.... Let's break down, friends, the middle wall of the barrier, which we have sinfully raised by disobedience."[224] Dispassion leads us into the innermost part of the mind, to the heart, where Christ is found and the winds of the passions aren't whistling and blowing, but where the peaceful and conquering breezes of love are stirring.

The exit of our nature from the convulsions of the passions is a sign of strengthening and has it as a result; it is the beginning of the experience of that incorruptibility which Jesus Christ brought to human nature as a pledge of the resurrection.[225]

Dispassion can reach dizzying heights; by the victory over the passions, as exaggerated movements contrary to the nature of the natural

---

[222] St. Maximus, *Chapters on Love* 1.42: "He who loves God, lives the angelic life on earth, fasting and keeping vigil, singing psalms and praying, and always thinking good of every man." *GrPh* 2, p. 7; cf. *Phi* 2, p. 57.
[223] *The Ladder*, Step 29.11, *PG* 88.1149C; cf. Moore, p. 260.
[224] *Ibid.*, 12, 14, *PG* 88.1149D, 1152A; cf. Moore, p. 261.
[225] *Ibid.*, 3-4, Moore, p. 259.

passions, a person can ascend even above the natural passions and needs, at least intermittently. He thus anticipates the post-resurrection state, when the body will no longer need anything, when there will be no longer sadness or pain.[226] It is the life of the saints, who can go for a long time even without the absolute minimum of food, who are not hurt even by the bites of vipers.[227]

---

[226] St. Maximus says: "He who has conquered the irrational movements of the unnatural passions, by faith and by love of God, goes beyond the law of nature, and his rationality is moved to the land of the intelligible, delivering from foreign bondage all those of the same nation by nature, together with the things that they have." *Questions to Thalassios* 55, Scholia 5, *PG* 90.560.

[227] Evagrius, *Chapters on Prayer* 109, *Phi* 1, p. 68.

PART TWO
ILLUMINATION

PART TWO

ILLUMINATION

23. The Gifts of the Holy Spirit

Until we have been cleansed from the passions, the gifts of the Holy Spirit received during the Mystery of Holy Chrism aren't fully manifested, although they too work in a covered way through each virtue. But once the passions which cover them are removed, the gifts of the Holy Spirit blaze up in our consciousness, from the hidden part of the heart, in all their brilliance.[1] Strictly speaking, in distinction to the grace of Baptism which directs the work of mortifying the old man and of the general growth of the new, they are intended to remake and intensify the powers of the knowledge of the soul and of courageous perseverance in God, after he has known Him. They are first of all the gifts for enlightening the mind, and precisely because of this, gifts for its fortification in its orientation toward God. Therefore they show their full efficiency only when our intellectual powers, which work with them, have been sufficiently developed.[2] They are the fruits of a Mystery which imparts to us the gifts of the Holy Spirit; they are meant to open the spirit in us and to make rich the life "in the Spirit," but this can't be realized before purification from the passions.

Only after the termination of the work of purification, driven especially by the powers of Baptism and of repentance, does the work of the gifts of the Holy Spirit appear first and foremost.

Of course this doesn't mean that the soul is left only with these gifts, but the beginning of the activation of the gifts of the Holy Spirit also means an activation of His direct influence. Where grace is, there is the Spirit; this is why the words *grace* and *Spirit* are used alternately. By the Mystery of Holy Chrism, the Holy Spirit built Himself a dwelling in the hidden interior of our nature. Since then He has been in constant contact with us.

---

[1] Nicholas Cabasilas, *The Life in Christ* 3.6, p. 110: "Of the various rites each has its own effect; participation of the Spirit and of His gifts depends on the most holy chrism. Therefore, while one may not be able to demonstrate the spiritual gift at the very time that the sacred rite takes place, but only much later, we should not be ignorant of the cause and origin of the power."
[2] *Ibid.*, 3.5, p. 109: "On all, then, who have been initiated the Mystery produces its proper effects. Not all, however, have perception of the gifts or eagerness to make use of the riches which they have been given. Some are unable to grasp the gifts because of their immature age, others are not eager because they are not prepared...." Or when they receive the Mystery they don't demonstrate all the preparation and love necessary to receive it.

From there, the grace of Baptism sets in motion the gifts of the Holy Spirit; their work is to pierce the heavy layers of the passions, so that finally the light of these gifts, in other words, of the Holy Spirit, might flood through the opening into the deepest region of our nature. But already before flooding in freely at the end of the total cleansing of the passions, this light becomes stronger. By each virtue, won at the removal of every passionate layer in us, it becomes more transparent. But first we feel the power which works in us during this cleansing. That is, the Holy Spirit at the beginning shows more of His power, and later more light, until illumination breaks out fully in our consciousness. In this way we must understand that of the seven gifts of the Holy Spirit— the spirit of the fear of God, the spirit of strength, the spirit of counsel, the spirit of understanding, the spirit of knowledge, the spirit of comprehension, the spirit of wisdom,[3] the first two almost exclusively indicate the power of action: The spirit of the fear of God keeps us from evil, the spirit of strength urges us to good. From this initial phase, knowledge is lacking. It only comes later and is represented by the other five gifts.

After we have made some progress in the winning of the virtues, the horizon of our consciousness begins to redden with the first glow of illumination so that on the peak of dispassion the whole sun of the Holy Spirit might rise.

This is how St. Maximus the Confessor interprets the gifts of the Holy Spirit: After the cessation of sin by the fear of God and after the action of the virtues by strength, we win by the spirit of counsel the skill of discernment. This helps us to carry out with the best judgment the divine commands and to best size up the circumstances of every situation. At the beginning we act mostly from the fear of God, carrying out the commands for the simple reason that God has given them. Later, however, we begin to realize by our own judgment that what God commands us to do is good, but what stops us is evil. At the same time, we begin to understand what is most suitable to fulfill from the commands in each circumstance.

From this first flickering of light, we progress to a brighter one by *the gift of understanding*, which teaches us how to realize in a practical way the blessings which have been revealed to us by the commands, in such a way as to gain the virtues. Because it can happen that someone can realize what blessings are contained in the commands and nevertheless not know how to execute them in the most satisfactory way,

---

[3] This is the order in which St. Maximus the Confessor gives them in *Questions to Thalassios* 54, *PG* 90.521.

because he works without judgment. The gift of understanding then is what teaches us how to do a good thing with judgment.

Next follows *the gift of knowledge,* which in distinction to the gift of counsel, no longer discerns only in a general way the blessings in one command from the evil in another, but it reveals the very reason or deeper motivation of each command and virtue. Now I no longer just know in general that it is better to be humble than arrogant, but I realize that by humility I reach the point where I can see the glory of God; I realize that arrogance blinds me— it lets me see only myself.

From this gift we are raised to that of *comprehension* which changes the most theoretical penetration of the *logoi* of the virtues into a personal, affective identification with them, which "produces a fusion of our natural powers with the ways and the logoi of the commands," or "it changes our natural powers into the known logoi of the virtues."[4]

From this gift we advance to the last, which is *the gift of wisdom.* This makes us:

> ... ascend to the cause of the spiritual logoi in the commands and to union with it. By this we know, as far as is humanly possible, in an unknown way, the simple logoi of things found in God; we take out the truth from everything, as from a gushing spring of the heart, and we also share it in different ways with others.[5]

In other words, this gift brings us to the simple and exact contemplation of the truth in all things. "Going on from here we shall bring to light many and varying *logoi* of the truth by the wise contemplation of perceptible things and of intelligent beings."[6] In everything that we do or understand, we now have a vision of the whole, of the relationship of our deed or thing with the universal order.

We have reached wisdom after we have gained all the virtues, in other words after we have gained the state of dispassion. It is full sunlight, after it was anticipated by stronger and stronger rays. With this full sunlight, illumination, in the strict sense of the word, begins. In all the partial virtues which preceded dispassion a ray of wisdom appeared in each one; we saw a little of it.[7] Each one was a gift from the illuminat-

---

[4] *Ibid., PG* 90.524.
[5] *Ibid.*
[6] *Ibid.,* "Thus following with these eyes of faith [the virtues], or by these illuminations, we gather ourselves into the divine unity of wisdom, concentrating the gifts which have been imparted for us, by our gradual elevation on the ladder of the virtues."
[7] *Ibid.,* 55, *PG* 90.541D: "Or perhaps Scripture understands by the four myriads the four steps forward in the fulfillment of the divine commandments, to which an increase along the line of contemplation and knowledge correspond." But these illuminations are due to the works or gifts of the Holy Spirit, or these gifts are manifested in the effort for the virtues, which are the means

ing gifts of the Holy Spirit. Now the whole of wisdom appears, concentrated and simple at the same time.[8] It is always united with the fullness of the illuminating gifts of the Holy Spirit. The wise person understands in an all-encompassing way the truth in all things, that is, he sees them in an interdependence, each with its purpose and at the same time its cause, that is God.

Wisdom is the gift of seeing God simultaneously with all things or through them, as the Maker, Sustainer and effective Guide of all things. It helps us to understand at a glance our past life, its purpose, the path that we should follow, the interdependent meanings of the events of human life, of the things in nature, because the unique Power and Cause which stands at the base of all things and shows its action simultaneously in them also explains them.

On the basis of this concurrent overview and comprehension, we can then grasp the meaning of each thing and the norm of each act that must be carried out. If at the beginning we were raised gradually from the partially known to the universally unknown, now, from the peak of the view of the whole we sometimes lower our eyes to one detail, sometimes to another, immediately finding its place, immediately understanding its purpose and function in this landscape.

In another place St. Maximus the Confessor distinguishes between discernment and knowledge *(diakrisis, gnosis)*. The first is born from virtuous activity, the second, from faith; the first is of a practical nature, the second of a contemplative. By the first we distinguish good from evil, by the second we know the *logoi* of visible and invisible realities;[9] they have their foundation in God. We could identify the first with the gifts of council, understanding, knowledge, and comprehension, and the second with the gift of wisdom, because elsewhere St. Maximus doesn't consider that faith develops into knowledge along the distinct line of the virtues. But we could consider that practical discernment and contemplative knowledge or wisdom are two convergent peaks, which meet in love, and give birth to a higher, mystical knowledge of God, distinct

---

of the revelation of His light. "The illuminations of the Spirit are given to us by means of the virtues." *Ibid.,* 54.

[8] *Questions to Thalassios* 54, scholia 27, *PG* 90.533: "The unity of wisdom exists undivided in the various virtues which spring from it, and according to the measure by which we grow in the work of all the virtues, we concentrate it more and more, so that in the end it is discovered again as a simple unity by the return to it of all the virtues which come from it. This happens when we, for whom it is diffused from itself by the birth of each virtue, return again to it, going up by each virtue." An identification is obvious here in some way of wisdom with God the Word, Who is at the same time the whole of wisdom and the totality of the virtues borne hypostatically.

[9] *Chapters on Love* 2.26, *Phi* 2, p. 69.

THE GIFTS OF THE HOLY SPIRIT   199

from wisdom, or from the knowledge of him in the things of the world.[10]

The gifts of the Holy Spirit guide us and sustain us in the mediated knowledge of God. Distinct from it is the direct knowledge of God, which will constitute the third phase of the spiritual ascent, or the phase of the union of the soul with God, or of the vision of the divine light. In this second phase, or of illumination, we will concern ourselves with the knowledge of Him by means of nature and of human actions, individual and collective. It is a knowledge which follows immediately after the step of dispassion, which is a cleansing of the passions, but not yet of the simple images of things too. Only after the mind is cleansed not only from the passions but also from the simple images and representations of things, will the direct knowledge of God be produced, a theological knowledge, in phase three.[11]

But because the mediated knowledge of God is also a knowledge by the Holy Spirit, that is, by His gifts, already in this second phase man's knowledge has become a knowledge in the Spirit. But it is a knowledge by the Holy Spirit, that is by His gifts already in this second phase because it takes place after man by the virtues and by the Holy Spirit has unlocked or actualized the spirit in himself, as the central and intimate place of the mind; he has opened the eye destined for the vision of God. The illuminating gifts of the Holy Spirit become obvious to man only by this opening of this eye of his, of this room meant to be filled with divine light. The Holy Spirit makes Himself known to us only by the activation of our spirit.[12]

So the knowledge by the Holy Spirit is one of the mind returned to its spirit, from the disorder at the surface. The knowledge in the spirit is one in the intimate interior of man, in the midst of the divine light

---

[10] *Ibid.*, "When the mind progresses in practical activity, it reaches wisdom; and in the contemplative, knowledge. The first leads the one who struggles to the power to discern between virtue and vice, the second leads the one who takes part in it to the *logoi* of the corporeal and incorporeal. And if the grace of theology is partaken of then when he flies by the wings of love over everything mentioned already and reaches God, he sees by the Spirit the logos regarding Him, as far as it is possible for the human mind." [*ton peri autou logon.*] *GrPh* 2, p. 17; *cf. Phi* 2, p. 69.

[11] Here is how St. Maximus describes the steps of this ascent: "The one who rallies from the division caused by disobedience first separates himself from the passions, then from passionate thoughts, then from nature and the things of nature, then from concepts and knowledge derived from them, and finally getting away from the abundant variety of the logoi concerning Providence he reaches in a way which transcends knowledge the very Word of God himself. In him the mind considers its own stability and 'rejoices with unutterable joy,' as a peace comes from God which surpasses all understanding and which continually keeps secure the one who is worthy of it." *Chapters on Knowledge* 2.8, *Maximus Confessor, Selected writings*, p. 149.

[12] St. Maximus in many places speaks of a *pneuma* (spirit) of man and of a *psichi kai soma* (soul and body). *Questions and the Dubious*, PG 90.881D.

which fills this spirit. By this light all things become transparent before the one who knows in spirit. His vision, the surface of things and of human actions are no longer an opaque wall, but their meanings and relationships with God become crystal clear.[13] He is no longer stopped by the passions at this surface— he has penetrated beneath his own surface, and through the thick surface of things.

This vision into the depths of things and of human destinies is a great mystery. These depths can't be opened only by the sensory comprehension of things because then anybody could grasp them, as they grasp their perceptible structure by their *logoi*. They could be understood by the bundle of common attributes of the examples in the same species, by the so-called "notions" or "essences" of things. But if the depths become transparent only to the one who has attained knowledge "in the spirit" to the one who has been raised "in his spirit" from his thick shell, it means that this spirit is a power which penetrates the depths of things. Either the light from the spirit penetrates beyond the opaque layer of things, or it makes the light hidden in them transparent. Only in the measure in which someone becomes transparent to himself, are things also made transparent to him, because this power which works in him later reaches the exterior. The holy Fathers use this comparison: For our eyes to see the natural light and the things in it, they themselves must be filled with it already; so too, for the eyes of our soul to see the light of intelligible and divine realities, that is the depths of things, they must first be filled with the light which radiates from these depths. In him who sees must be found something of what is seen. Thus St. Maximus calls the depth of Scripture its "spirit," just as the depth in man he calls his "spirit." The one who looks into Scripture from his spirit, understands it. In other words, the depths of man and of things are illuminated by a common light, or a common light radiates from them. A common light unites the subject with things or with his neighbors. He who has received this light has penetrated into the zone of the depths distinct from himself. His self and these depths form by this light a dual unity; in a more reduced measure such a unity and a visible zone of the world is formed by the natural light which envelops it, or penetrates it, with the seeing power of the bodily senses.

---

[13] J. Lossen, interpreting this passage says: "This isn't a division into three parts (see *Questions to Thalassios* 43, *PG* 90.412C), but neither should uncreated Spirit be understood in these places. He is speaking of the parts of human nature, which are listed in a descending order.... Perhaps in this place there is a higher part of the soul. It's possible that here the supernatural is already included."*Logos und Pneuma,* pp. 89-90.

A Christian thinker says that this mystical knowledge "transcends the gnosiological distinction between subject and object and the absorption of reality into the world of either of them."

Spiritual experience, upon which realist symbolism rests, lies altogether beyond the antithesis between subject and object and the substantialist conception of them. Spiritual life is no more subjective than it is objective. The symbolism of it, that is, its embodiment in forms belonging to the natural world, may be understood as an objectification, but that is precisely why it is not objective in the rationalist sense of the word. The symbolic mode of thought includes both subject and object within itself, and that at an infinitely deeper level of consciousness. If objectification is nothing more than a process of symbolization, then for that very reason all objective rationalism and all naïve conceptions of an object-substance cease to possess justification. What are called objective realities are in fact only realities of a secondary order, for they are merely symbolic and possess no reality in their own right. But subjective realities, such as the reality of the affective life and that of the subject and its subjective world, are likewise merely secondary and symbolic in character.[14]

On this plane the separation between subject and object are surpassed, without the two becoming confused. The subject and object are distinct, but not separated. The separation of the subject from the object is surpassed and nevertheless both are preserved, because the subject in its depths experiences an "object" distinct from itself. But the "object" experienced within, as a spiritual reality or connected within with the subject, is in a continuity or intercommunion with the knowing subject and both, with the supreme Subject who is the base of all things. Of course this spiritual reality isn't uniform, but varies; it is a world full of reason, from which the structure proper to each thing in its visible aspect, in the structure proper to each person, to each distinct action is incorporated. But it isn't less true that they are woven into a whole, or that they are bathed in this same understanding and comprehending light. And when this light has filled us within, it doesn't appear to us to be limited to our nature alone, but it extends over everything with which we are united by purity and love.

We have said that by this light individual things and nature in totality become a transparency by which their higher *logoi* and their relationships with God become transparent. God Himself in some way is seen through things.

---

[14] Nicholas Berdyaev, *Freedom and the Spirit* (New York, 1935), pp. 55-6.

We will now proceed to describe this knowledge of God in creation, because it constitutes, according to Evagrius and St. Maximus the Confessor, the essence of phase two of the faithful's ascent to deification, the phase of illumination.

24. The Contemplation of God in Creation

The contemplation of God in nature is, for St. Maximus as well as for Evagrius, the preliminary step to the direct contemplation of Him. For both, but especially for Maximus, this step is absolutely necessary, just as necessary as the positive law decreed by God.[15]

Just as the Law is the teacher to bring us to Christ, so man, because he is a child with understanding, is guided by the reflections and puzzles of the created world to the knowledge of God.[16] The *logoi* in it take the place of visions which make possible a partial understanding *(merikin katanoisin)* of God's wisdom.[17]

But as much as St. Maximus sometimes emphasizes that creation has only a passing interest for the knowledge of God, at other times he gives it a permanent value— its *logoi* also persist after the revealed appearance of God in the future life.

Hans Urs von Balthasar, from whom we took the above quotation, continues: "Neither must it be forgotten that, along with the appearance of the divine archetype, creation will be manifested in its perfect, eternal form." For an example he cites text 15 of the Second Century on Knowledge by St. Maximus,[18] where he says that when the Son of God comes in the glory of the Father with His holy angels, Moses and Elijah will appear too, in other words "the more spiritual logoi of the Law and of the prophets," as Maximus calls them, or the "spiritual logoi of creation," as Hans Urs von Balthasar develops their meaning.

In this regard St. Maximus corrects Origen, according to whom Moses and Elijah are absorbed on Tabor by the Lord.[19] "Maximus, on the contrary, accentuates here and elsewhere, that precisely the manifestation of the glory of God gives the world the possibility to shine in its distinct originality."[20] We could compare the world with a room full of all kinds of things, and the divine glory with the light of the sun. The darker the room is, the harder it is to see what is in it. And the more the windows are flooded with light, the better the things in it can be seen more clearly and beautifully.

---

[15] von Balthasar, *Die gnostischen Centurien*, p. 117, where he notes chapter 1.70, *PG* 90.1109.
[16] *Chapters on Knowledge* 1.70; *cf. Maximus Confessor, Selected writings*, p. 140: "But when what is partial ceases with the appearance of what is perfect, all mirrors and hidden meanings pass away; once the truth arrives face to face, the one who is saved will be above all worlds, ages, and places in which he was once nurtured as a child, and will reach his end in God."
[17] *Ibid.*
[18] *Op. cit.*, p. 45. Chapters on Knowledge 2.15; *cf. Maximus Confessor, Selected writings*, p. 150.
[19] *Homilies on Leviticus* 6.2; *PG* 12.468; Matthew 12:43.
[20] *Ibid.*

The *logoi* of things in the world, far from becoming unnecessary after the revealed vision of God, will help us understand the fecundity of the divine Logos; it will even be an example of it, just as the rays of the sun are an example and a manifestation of His light. Of course, then we will look directly at the Sun of Righteousness, or at his light and only indirectly at the *logoi* of things; in the same way now we don't look at the direct light of the sun, but only see its blurred reflection from things. In other words, when we contemplate God directly we will contemplate the *logoi* of things in Him Himself, not in things, as now. Then we will see them so much better illuminated, more profoundly, more clearly.[21]

In the present life "from the things which are we know their Maker, as being strictly speaking the logoi of the things which have been made."[22] Because "the mind which cultivates in the spirit natural contemplation ... receives the proof of the creative Logos of all things from the beautiful order of visible things."[23] St. Maximus interprets the sheet covered with beasts in this sense: It appeared in a vision of the Apostle Peter, and came down from heaven. "By sheet and by the beasts on it God revealed to Peter as spiritual food the visible world, understood by the unseen on the basis of its logoi, or the unseen shown by the images of perceptible things." Looked at in this way, the world no longer contains anything unclean in it. "He who has been raised from the false view of things has sacrificed the visible forms as Peter did, and eating unseen logoi has gained natural contemplation, that gained in the spirit."[24] He "looks only toward the intelligible sights of things that are, mentally leaving the visible forms of things. As a result he receives in the most clear way possible the proofs of divine things which gives him a more divine form to his mind."[25] "He who doesn't limit the nature of things seen only on the horizon of the senses, but investigates with the mind in a wise way the logoi in each created thing, discovers God, finding in the visible majesty of things their very cause."[26] Another time, St. Maximus considers the *logoi* of visible things as being the Lord's

---

[21] Those who "because of much purification of the mind have received from God all the grace which men can receive, penetrating with the help of this grace the vastness of mystical visions, see only the *logoi* of written things, stripped of the cloak of figures." *Questions to Thalassios* 55, *PG* 90.536.

[22] St. Maximus comments on the coming of Jesus with His disciples to the master of the house in Jerusalem on the occasion of the celebration of the Passover: "The master of the house is the mind enlarged by the brilliance of the exercise in virtue, by the loftiness, the beauty and the immensity of knowledge. The Savior and His disciples come to this mind, in other words with the first spiritual *logoi* of nature and the body, and He imparts Himself." *Ibid.*, 3, *PG* 90.276A.

[23] *Ibid.*, 25, *PG* 90.332A.

[24] *Ibid.*, 27, *PG* 90.353BC; 356A.

[25] *Ibid.*, *PG* 90.357.

[26] *Ibid.*, 32, *PG* 90.372B.

THE CONTEMPLATION OF GOD IN CREATION 205

"body," which He gives as food to those who are worthy of Him, the blood being the "the *logoi*" of intelligible realities.²⁷

So it is a main idea of St. Maximus that things hide divine *logoi* in them, as so many rays of the supreme Logos. He who discovers them in things ascends on their thread to the knowledge of God and this knowledge must anticipate His direct knowledge.

This teaching attributes to creation and the thought referring to it a necessary role in the ascent of man to God. St. Maximus is a stranger to the idea of a vision which we might attain by bypassing the forms and laws of the cosmos. On the road of our approach to God stands the world— we must pass through the understanding of it. Every man has a mission connected with the world. Everyone must know it according to the power given to him, in as much as knowledge can't come until the gaining of the virtues; everyone must develop beforehand a moral activity in relationship to the world. A mainly negative attitude toward the world frustrates salvation itself. The world is imposed on everyone as a stone for sharpening his spiritual faculties.

By the world man grows to the height of the knowledge of God and to the capacity of being His partner. The world is a teacher to lead us to Christ. Of course it can also be the road to hell. It is the tree of the knowledge of good and evil, the tree of testing. If we look at its beauty in order to praise its Creator, we are saved; if we think that its fruit is pure and simply something to eat, we are lost. Salvation isn't obtained in isolation, but in a cosmic frame. This value of the world as a road to God is explained by the fact that man must have an object of giant proportions for strengthening his spiritual forces, but also from the intrinsic structure of the world as a symbol of transcendent divine realities. A symbol (from the Greek *symballein*, to throw together, to unite two things without confusing them), is a visible reality which doesn't only represent, but somehow makes an unseen reality visible. A symbol presupposes and shows two things simultaneously. It is "a bridge between two worlds" as somebody has said. A word, for example, is a symbol of the spirit, uniting and simultaneously presenting the materiality of the sound with the meaning of thought without confusing them; the human face likewise, makes the spirit in man transparent by its materiality, and if he is living in Him, God Himself.²⁸ A symbolic consciousness of the world:

---

²⁷ *Ibid.*, 35, *PG* 90.377.
²⁸ Olivier Clément, *Le Visage interieur* (Paris, 1978).

... sees everywhere in this world the signs and symbols of another world, and perceives the divine as the mysterious and infinite, beyond that which is finite and transitory.[29]

All flesh is a symbol of the spirit, the reflection, the image, and the sign of another far off, yet much more profound, reality.[30]

The alliance of these two worlds, the possibility of their interpenetration, the transfusion of energy from one world into the other, are all communicated to us by means of this symbolic sign. This symbol unveils for us the life of God and signifies for us the entrance of divine energy into the life of this natural world. But on the other hand it guards for all time the sense of infinite mystery and affirms the impossibility of reducing to a common denominator the life of the world and the life of the spirit. Symbolism does not admit the validity of that ossification and isolation of the flesh and the natural world which results from transforming them into entities incapable of permeation by the infinitude of God and the Spirit.[31]

As we turn aside from the life of this world our whole attention is fixed upon the unfathomable and the ineffable; everywhere we are in contact with the mysterious and we see the light of another world, in which nothing ever comes to an end, and which knows no subordination. The world is open to the light, it has no limits, it penetrates into other worlds, and they in turn penetrate into it. Here there is nothing hard or rigid which cannot be subdued.[32]

These observations throw light on and enlarge the meaning of the holy Fathers' concept of creation, as a symbol from which divine *logoi*, which have their origin in the divine Logos, can be extracted.

But the question arises: Is the extraction of these *logoi* from nature and their relationship with the divine Logos realized by the discursive method of forming notions and deductions from the things which are seen, and then discovering their first cause, or is it realized by a faster intuition? Thomistic scholasticism doesn't admit another way of knowing the *logoi* of things and of God in the world except the discursive-deductive, which according to it, is the only way of knowledge.

The holy Fathers and more recent Orthodox theologians sustain that the penetration into the spiritual depths beyond the natural world can't take place by the rational way. A symbolical knowledge of the world, distinct from the rational, corresponds with the symbolic structure of

---

[29] Berdyaev, *Freedom and the Spirit*, p. 59.
[30] *Ibid.*, p. 61.
[31] *Ibid.*
[32] *Ibid.*, pp. 81-2.

the world. The categories of reason define, that is set limits, and distinguish one thing from another. Thus they are applicable only to the limited realities which differ from one another. As the divinity is infinite, inexhaustible, it can't be the object of rational determinations. Reason fits only the natural world, not the spiritual.

Divinity is an object of knowledge both infinite and inexhaustible, eternally mysterious in the unfathomable depth of its being. Thus it is that the knowledge of the divine is a dynamic process which finds no completion....[33] A symbol by its very nature does not subject the infinite to the finite. On the other hand it renders the finite transparent and allows us to see the infinite through it. In the finite world our horizons are by no means completely restricted.[34]

But this sparkle isn't something given to just anyone, but it is revealed only by living spiritually, only to a look "in spirit" as St. Maximus the Confessor would say. But for this look "in the spirit" at the *logoi* of the world, distinct from their deductive, rational understanding, a previous purification of our nature, by long-term toil, is necessary.

But it is well to describe more fully this look "in the spirit," at the *logoi* of the world, by the mind of one purified from the passions. St. Maximus the Confessor doesn't give us, anywhere, the analysis itself of the act of the grasping of the *logoi* of things, which he calls "natural contemplation." The term "contemplation," which he uses for the knowledge of these *logoi* in nature, is an indication that it is a matter of intuition, if in fact contemplation is, on all the steps that act in which, as Blondel puts it, "the discursive powers no longer keep looking for answers, but have found their rest."[35] We find it necessary to draw the same conclusion because St. Maximus considers that this contemplation is a knowledge "in the spirit," thus under the influence of the grace of the Holy Spirit and a previous cleansing of man from the passions is necessary.

On the other hand St. Maximus maintains that from the *logoi* of things "we know that there is a Creator of visible things, but how He is we can't understand."[36] From this, as well as from the role which the saint attributes to "reason" in the knowledge of these aspects of things, which he likewise persistently calls *logoi*, it would follow that this contemplation has a rational character. Then St. Maximus unceasingly requires the man who strives for perfection to purify and reestablish all

---

[33] *Ibid.*, p. 65.
[34] *Ibid.*, p. 60.
[35] Blondel, *L'Action* vol. 1, pp. 91-2.
[36] *Questions to Thalassios* 51, scholia 5, *PG* 90.488.

his psychic faculties, including reason. Thus we have said that the soul's approach to God isn't realized in a leap without reason, but after a prolonged exercise of reason in the knowledge of the meanings of things. So the world has been set up for us as a road to God.

The existence of the world is seen as having the purpose, among others, of exercising all our spiritual powers in our ascent to God. If God had wanted to make Himself known directly, all at once, the world of things would lack one of its purposes. The existence of the world itself as a way to God is a proof that the supreme knowledge of God isn't an irrational act, but suprarational; that is, it isn't realized by a premature renunciation of reason, by a direct leap without reason, but by the surpassing of reason. The supreme knowledge of God attains a level which doesn't do away with reason, but involves it. It activates and uses all the resources of reason, to the fullest exercise of its powers. [37] We are raised to a suprarational, but not anti-rational, knowledge of God; after our reason itself is exercised to the maximum, we understand that the domain in which we have penetrated surpasses our limited rational powers, by a plus of light, not by a minus. On the peaks of the knowledge of God we know what is impossible; we grasp too many meanings and in an overly luminous form, but not too little for the pretensions of reason. This is a fact which stops us from pretending that this abundance has its source only in our reason. It also has its source in a super-reason which lifts up our reason beyond its powers, without annulling it. But to arrive at this excessive intelligibility, it must be enough for us to know the upper limits of our powers of understanding.

According to the holy Fathers, to discover the *logoi* in things, prolonged purification of the passions and prolonged exercise are required. This shows us that reason, in its common meaning, is not that which grasps the reasons, the *logoi* of things, and through them, God. Rather it is a reason which is also exercised by the choice of rational things required by divine commands and by the gradual rationalization of man,

---

[37] From this point of view, Blondel has given us as many suitable observations as possible. "Precisely because this contingent existence, with all its indefinite aspirations, springs forth from all parts and doesn't know at the beginning anything except by restrictive forms, *sub specie finiti,* it is inevitable and salutary that transcendental truths, the absolute Good, not appear in the beginning except in the mixture of immanent gifts, under the traits of the relative and particular. If idealism...would realize that which it pretends, we would be nothing more than those little insects, invincibly attracted in the middle of the night by the light in which they burn their fragile wings. Right here also stands the illusion of that theosophy which, scorning thought and discursive reason, is precipitated, or better said—for it excludes any pronoun or active verb whatsoever—is absorbed by the bottomless and formless pit of pure indetermination: extreme error and danger, because it resembles the poor butterflies, spirits disillusioned by the false clarity of risky mysticism, burning their wings destined for their flight in the darkness, to fall alive in the aberrations of which false mysticism and immanentism can never protect them." *L'Action* vol. 1, pp. 351-2.

gained by virtue. But this gradual exercise of reason by knowledge and doing has as a basis the act of intuitive knowledge, in which reason, exercised for a long time, is implicated.

We will try in the pages that follow to explain this teaching of the holy Fathers, which is more complicated than the one-sided solutions of simple rationalism or of intuitionism.

First we note that there is a truth or an objective sense in regard to everything. This is what is meant by the term *logos* used by St. Maximus and by other church Fathers. Truth or meaning is not a subjective product, varying substantially from one subject to another. Everything has in an objective way its own sense, as well as purpose—a cause, a finality, and a special relationship with everything else. Our judgment of this truth or sense can vary according to interest, preconceived ideas, our intellectual capacity and preparation. This, however, doesn't modify the truth or sense of this thing, which remains untouched in itself, waiting to be discovered. Thus every fact must have its "logos" and only then is it rationally objective when it conforms to it. If from various interests we don't make the fact conform to the reason which it is called to serve, in vain do we try to endow it with another "reason"; it remains irrational.

Everything that God has done and everything that happens and is carried out according to His will, in other words that follows the true line of the development of creation, in totality or of every fact in part, is rational, says St. Maximus. Only a passion is irrational, although it is given its rational justification. The rational character of this truth or meaning stands not only in the unchangeable objectivity, harmonically woven into all reality, but also in the power with which it compels recognition once we have attained the purification of passions. God sparkles then from everything, from the threshold of any fact whatsoever, from the first moment. In this sense a discursive thought is no longer necessary to extract it and to make it obvious. It is in a way its intuitive sparkle. But it sparkles as an overwhelming reason, as an objective logos understood by us, yet beyond our understanding. It imposes itself by its fully convincing and evident rationality and at the same time, by its supra-rationality as a reflex of a harmonious and immutable order of the existence of a thing or fact within the framework of the whole of reality.

We arrive, however, all at once at this state of contemplation of various objective truths, of the certain *logoi* of things, only after a long preparation of a pronounced moral character; this makes us more carefully look for the reason why such preparation is necessary for the grasping of a truth all at once. Therefore, we should look for the nature of this quick understanding.

Preparation is also necessary because our reason, in every condition of our life, doesn't remain invariable with the same capacity to objectively grasp the truth. According to the usual expression of the holy Fathers, it weakens, it doesn't firmly maintain its sovereign position as an objective judge. The passions drag it off its throne. They make it invent rational arguments for every sinful deed. Such deeds misuse things; they consider them only as objects for material satisfaction. Reason justifies irrational behavior, as rational. It also finds *logoi* in things which don't belong there, *logoi* which it presents in an altered light and are really false.

In the face of a logos which has fallen to the role of the servant of the passions, the vision of the world undergoes the following modifications:

1. The deeper, more spiritual *logoi* of things are covered; only their materialistic side and fleshly utility are still seen. For example, the beauty of an apple, the sweetness of a grape, are no longer seen as having the purpose of making us realize that the creative energies of beauty and of sweetness come from God; we should still have this knowledge even when there will no longer be apples and grapes; we see them pure and simple, for awakening and satisfying a bodily appetite. They say that the beauty of young girls is a tempting form produced by nature in the service of the multiplication of the species. The material attributes of things make a wall which prevents seeing anything beyond them. The world becomes exclusively material and utilitarian, or usable exclusively for the flesh. The tree of the knowledge of good and evil becomes, pure and simple, pleasant to look at and delicious to eat. Thus the horizon is narrowed.

2. The reason of the passionate person, or one with special interests, tries to justify its actions which he carries out for personal motives with the same old argument: "Everybody is doing it." And remarkably, the unstable character of reason succeeds in convincing itself with these arguments. This means a replacement of objective *logoi* with subjective ones. Of course these subjective *logoi* aren't strictly speaking *logoi;* they are passionate ones, while true *logoi* are objective: I discover them when I have the experience that my judgments submit to the *logoi* in things, and not the other way around. This is a new distortion, a new fall from truth.

THE CONTEMPLATION OF GOD IN CREATION   211

But only objective *logoi*, which this individual has replaced (or maybe didn't have them to begin with), are the ones which serve the general development; they are those which things in their healthy development move toward. He who replaces them with subjective *logoi* puts the general in the service of the particular, hindering the normal development of the whole. The general and objective truth is replaced by each person with a truth of his own. In so doing, the world no longer looks the same to all, but each one sees it differently, so that the true one is no longer recognized. This creates the doubt whether or not a truth really exists and whether the whole isn't an illusion. In fact all the opinions given in this way as truth are illusions. But objective truth does nevertheless exist; however, it is beyond the biased judgment of all.

The German theologian Karl Heim thinks that in a fatal way the world must appear different to each person and at each moment according to the center of perspective *(perspektivische Mitte)* from which he looks at it. But this center is usually one of special interests, a center of the passions. There could be innocent motives, which make possible the variety of perspectives from which the world is viewed: lack of experience, concentration on one area of the world, cultural influences. But whether these motives are also mixed with individual-passionate ingredients— for example the acquisitive culture might be influenced by a one-sided passionate point of view— or whether these innocent motives are also overtaken by the cleansing from the passions, which is gained by experience, these innocent motives are also surpassed, the fact is that finally these perspectives too, in appearance completely innocent, can be only partly surpassed. In any case a unique truth exists which is beyond subjective perspectives and truths. We can approach it, however, only gradually and maybe never have it completely in our lifetime. But neither in the life to come. Only God knows the whole, because He Himself is the whole Truth. And the angels are purified ceaselessly, says Dionysius the Areopagite; in other words they progress in an unending way in the knowledge of the Truth.[38] And the general idea of the holy Fathers is that to each one is given gifts, so too gifts of knowledge (of the truth), according to his power. But among those who have gained this partial knowledge of the truth, in other words from an individual perspective— determined by dispassionate motives (knowledge in part)— and those who willingly falsify the truth, there is a great difference. The first are on the way of truth, pilgrims to heaven, the second have turned their backs on the truth; they are travelers to hell, to the father of lies.

---

[38] Dionysius the Areopagite, *The Celestial Hierarchy* 7, *The Celestial and Ecclesiastical Hierarchy* (London, 1894), p. 30.

The appearance of "truth," of subjective opinions is explained by the fact that they are refractions of the one truth, in the distorted receptacles (various people) of the passions.

According to the Eastern Fathers, the truth isn't subjectivity, as Søren Kierkegaard said, but it is the most objective reality. On the contrary, to find it, subjectivity must be completely defeated. Certainly the truth isn't found in a purely theoretical way, in reason which is detached from the whole life of the specific individual. Such a detachment is impossible. Reason in itself, uniform among all people, can't in fact be found. The passions have made it unstable. But according to the measure of dispassion, it increases from person to person in the knowledge of objective truth. From this point of view, knowledge also depends on a "subjective" state of reason. But the truest subjectivity is the most conformable to the "objectivity" of truth. In the person who hasn't been purified from the passions reason is always in the service of the passions and of its distorted judgments of the truth. This sinful "subjectivity" must be overcome. But it isn't conquered only by disobeying it in moments of reflection. A person can't live split in two. Even if for the moment a part of him, and namely the emotions and the complex of interests seem to be asleep they influence the judgment of reason. A person must be unified. This subjectivity which falsifies the truth can't be overcome except by a battle in which all man's powers are engaged, not only reason, for the full victory over passionate subjectivity. The virtues must be put in the place of the passions.

Only reason which is modeled after a virtuous life, in other words after a life which has sacrificed, after prolonged exercise, egotism and the self-importance of personal opinion, can come to the truth. This too can be called subjectivity, but only with a precise meaning: as a struggle of the whole man against egotistic subjectivity, as a struggle to attain self-forgetfulness and the experience of it. Only the subjectivity which means the living of the surpassing of personal subjectivity can approach the truth. Therefore Kirkegaard is right when he says that the truth is the evidence for which he is ready to lay down his life, but this capacity of sacrifice means a forgetting of self.[39] He who has approached the

---

[39] This is also the meaning of the insistent recommendations of the holy Fathers, that before attaining, and to attain, the capacity to discern what is the right thing to do and what isn't, one must find an experienced guide, to perfectly obey. Thus John Cassian gives us the following dialog between his friend, Germanos, and Abba Moses: "It has been fully and completely shown both by recent instances and by the decisions of the ancients how discretion is in some sense the fountain head and the root of all virtues. We want then to learn how it ought to be gained...."
"Then Moses: 'True discretion, said he, is only secured by true humility. And of this humility the first proof is given by reserving everything (not only what you do but also what you think), for the scrutiny of the elders, so as not to trust at all in your own judgment but to acquiesce in their decisions in all points, and to acknowledge what ought to be considered good or bad by

truth has succeeded in this, because by prolonged exercise he has succeeded in forgetting himself, in going out of himself, and once found, he makes himself also forget himself more and more (*ekbasis eautou*). But this state is a whole way of life. Here is no longer only reason which has forgotten the emotional side of life, but the whole man has forgotten himself. This doesn't mean only something negative, but something positive too: The whole man is in love with truth, he is pulled toward the truth, he is happy for having conquered himself, and of living and dying for the truth. In this sense we too can speak of an existential finding and living of the truth. But reason isn't put out of order. However, it isn't a cold reason, but reason assisted by all the powers of the soul. It feels free because it has the evidence that it serves the truth, which conforms to it in a real way, not to a semblance of truth, foreign to it, not conformed to it. The truth holds it captive— as the whole man— and the truth has freed it. It and the whole man are found on a higher step, identified with truth, in other words, raised to a step higher than its nature.

This going out from oneself in objectivity in order to re-find the truth and to live it as something in conformity with the most personal subjectivity, means this whole identification of oneself with the objective logos; it also means a going out from isolation and an entrance into the universal, in relationship with the Person who encompasses everything. In the measure in which we know the truth more fully, we leave behind our own opinions, which knock heads with each other, and we think in the same way. We attain a unity in thought which has as a result union too in will and feeling. This is the restoration of the unity of human nature, shredded by sin. It is realized by the one truth, Who is the supreme Person, to whom it conforms: It is one with the truth known after liberation from the narrowness and isolation of the passions which divide us; this restoration comes at the same time as the gaining of love. It is realized in other words by God, because truth is God and we are made in conformity with God. Where God is known, Who is everything as a Person, there communion, the Church, is realized. The truth can't be known and confessed except "with one mind and with one heart."

So after we have seen the causes of the distortion of the truth and the covering up of the *logoi* of things, as well as the general remedy by which we can return to the way of truth, we should look at the steps of this healing, because it can't be realized all at once. This will enlighten us

---

their tradition. And this habit will not only teach a young man to walk in the right path through the true way of discretion, but will also keep him unhurt by all the crafts and deceits of the enemy. For a man cannot possibly be deceived, who lives not by his own judgment but according to the example of the elders, nor will our crafty foe be able to abuse [his] ignorance'" *Conferences* 2.9-10, NPNF 11.311-12; *cf. Phi* 1, pp. 102-3.

too in regard to the nature of this lightning flash of intuition of the truth in us and in everything which we have already considered, and in regard to the way we can gain the capacity for it.

The steps for the return to the way of truth and to its ever clearer light are the following:

1. An initial faith, as the will to explain all things by their *logoi*, which are rooted in God as a Person, or as a supreme loving communion of persons; and obedience in every circumstance to the command given by Him. We should obey even if we haven't yet any experiential and satisfactory evidence of the relationship of the *logoi* of things with God and, of the motives for which we must carry out His commands. It is for the moment a general faith regarding the presence of God as a Person in all things, Who only in a general way makes us conscious that we are in the truth and are traveling the road to an ever clearer understanding of Him.

2. A long term effort to direct our lives, and to explain things in the world, in the light of faith. These two things are closely related. Because the guidance of our lives according to the Lord's commands on the basis of faith means a purification from passions and the gaining of the virtues, in other words an exit from our narrowness and the conformity of our nature to God, by a relationship with Him. But this is nothing else than the giving up of the consideration of things as simple objects for egotistic satisfaction and of looking at them as the rays of the divine glory, love, and all powerfulness. All the time I am making, on the basis of faith, certain value judgments regarding things I have to do and explanatory judgments on the *logoi* or true purposes of things in relationship to God. This striving by deeds accustoms me with these judgments. For example I train myself so that when I see a delicious apple I no longer consider it as a material to stimulate my appetite, but much more as a sign of divine goodness and beauty. Or I always try to find the logos, the reason for any fact in a command of God, Who wants me to respond to His love and to conform to Him in my actions, just as any deed which doesn't conform to this command I should find irrational.

3. The experience of life gained by the effort mentioned, confirms the value judgments which I have become accustomed to make in regard to happenings. It also sanctions the explanation of the *logoi* of things as having their source in God. Experience shows me that in fact the beauty and sweetness on the surface of things

THE CONTEMPLATION OF GOD IN CREATION   215

is passing. It teaches me that a life directed only to fleshly and egotistic satisfactions, sought in this beauty and sweetness on the surface of things, is lost by the withering away of the body, which it puts all its hope in. So that what remains from beautiful objects is the revelation of a beauty independent of its material manifestation, just as a man after the weakening of the flesh is left with a nature that has reached purification. Thus, the judgments sustained at the beginning by faith, passing through the experience of a virtuous life, begin to be illuminated by an interior evidence. Faith, until it is prolonged by carrying out commands, "has in itself the logos of truth,"[40] but unenlightened, not made known. So faith guides us well.

However to reach the evidence of truth implicated in faith, to attain the evidence of the judgments which we make based on it, we must be well exercised in the virtuous life.[41] This clear evidence is called discrimination *(diakrisis)*. Discrimination is on the one hand closely related to the understanding *(gnosis)* of the *logoi* in things. It appears at the same time and develops in parallel with it. On the other hand it gives birth to this knowledge of the *logoi* and not the other way around. This justifies St. Maximus in placing discrimination sometimes on the same step, sometimes on a step lower than the knowledge of the *logoi* of things.

We realize that discernment is based on evidence larger than what we can include in our judgment or conception. Because we realize that the logos itself, for a command or for something, can't be grasped wholly and precisely in a judgment of ours— how much less the logos or meaning of a person. Thus with this evidence, we constantly are drawn towards more adequate concepts. Although the moment we arrive at a more comprehensive concept, at a more nuanced judgment, once again the evidence has become larger, deeper. Even during the phase of simple faith and of judgments made on its basis, without an explicit evidence, there existed at least the evidence that in things and commands there are *logoi* and divine directions which we don't see, that thus its indications are just. Even from that time, besides the judgments there

---

[40] St. Maximus the Confessor, *Questions to Thalassios* 54, *PG* 90.520B.
[41] *Ibid.*, 54.28, *PG* 90.533CD. "He who doesn't fulfill the divine commandments by faith has a blind faith. For if the commandments of the Lord are light, it is evident that he who doesn't fulfill the divine commandments is lacking light and bears an empty name, not the true one, of light.... Let's not neglect anything of what has been said, that somehow, neglecting them little by little, we make our faith blind and without eyes, lacking the illuminations of the Spirit, which are given through the virtues."

was an evidence which they couldn't contain.[42] In this infinite virtuality, potentiality, the presence in the world of the intentional divine energies[43] is manifested. The *logoi* in things are nothing but *logoi* from God, reflected in the mirror of things by the intentional divine energies. From the *logoi* mirrored in imperfect ways in things, perspectives of ascending by the thread of divine energies to the *logoi* from God are opened. But we can never restrict them to concepts. The evidence therefore can never be contained within the margins of concepts and of rational judgments, on the one hand, because it isn't yet clear enough, on the other hand, because it is potentially infinite and we at every moment feel its lack of borders.

Discrimination, as a grasping of the *logoi* in commands and in actions that must be carried out, becomes ever clearer, and the knowledge directed towards things penetrates their increasingly spiritual *logoi*. Deeds which in appearance are good, by discrimination or right judgment as the monks call it, are found lacking in this quality. *Logoi* which once seemed to be final, after steady progress in a life of virtue, I ascribe to ever deeper *logoi*. By exercise the power of observation is sharpened more and more, as well as the comprehension of the *logoi* of things, the intentions of God by them, and the consequences of our deeds for our neighbors and ourselves.

4. But this increased sharpness also has as an effect, an acceleration of the act of grasping the *logoi* from deeds and things, in such a measure, that after long practice, what is evil in an event, even good in appearance, or the deeper logos of a thing is discovered at first glance. By a long habit of discerning truly good happenings from those only apparently so, as soon as I am asked for advice about something, or as soon as a thought urges me to do it, I intercept its quality. By a long habit of observation I realize that the *logoi* of things don't consist simply of their fleshly utility, but in the revelation of a spiritual sense, of a divine intention. When I see something new, there beyond it, beyond the surface of its fleshly usefulness, I see its spiritual sense, the divine attribute to which it is directed; I catch on to the divine will and relationship or my spiritual enrichment or impoverishment, which want to be realized by it in me.

---

[42] Ch. Journet, p. 109: "Because obscure knowledge, as that of faith, is known as obscure, in other words as being surpassed by its object, and also it manifests it in some manner. And because it is known as obscure, it can be the knowledge sufficient to found a love which goes beyond it."
[43] Directed by the hand of God. *trs*

This is the quick as lightning "intuition" of the *logoi* of things and of the values of actions. As it can be seen, it doesn't appear as something out of the blue and isn't something irrational; it is the result of a long term exercise of reason guided by faith and sustained by striving in a virtuous life. We can reserve the name of contemplation for this sharpened vision and this rapid comprehension, as St. Maximus the Confessor did. Nevertheless we must not forget that it comes at the end of a prolonged effort to purify the passions, to gain the virtues. It comes when we can truly look at things in their simplicity and at the same time in their profoundness. In other words it means that we can perceive the divine *logoi* in things unaffected by our passions. We also see God through these *logoi* in the sense that the long habit of bringing everything to God helps us to do this operation now with the speed of lightning; we see at first glance the divine attributes which realized a certain quality; we understand the purpose for which it was given us, as a sign of His love in order to stimulate our love, in order to realize a dialogue of mutual commitment in love between us, God, and neighbor. But as we have already said, in this quick comprehension too there is a larger evidence than we can put into a concept. As quickly as we can associate the beauty of a thing with God by habit, just as quickly do we realize that the divine beauty is more than the beauty of the thing. Immediately the mystery of something sparkles.

This evidence, always bigger and different, always surpassing the limits of a concept, is the mysterious in the visible. That which is associated as a contemplative element with the rational can't be expressed. But this element proper to contemplation doesn't appear, doesn't develop unless it is accompanied by rational efforts; it stimulates them in turn. It always appears as a plus in addition to the rational sense, not as a minus. This plus is present on all the steps—we could say the rational is always accompanied by contemplation. But nevertheless it is good to reserve the name of contemplation for this step of the quick comprehension of the *logoi* of things and as a plus corresponding to this step.

This quick grasp of the spiritual sense of things and of the plus of meaning is distinct from phenomenological intuition *(Wesenchau)*, which knows nothing of a similar preparation. Even the act of the religious knowledge of God, which Scheler talks about,[44] wouldn't be capable in our opinion of such intuitions becoming permanent, without the previous steps listed, in other words without a long moral preparation.[45] They could take place at most in rare moments, while the contemplation

---

[44] Max Scheler, *On the Eternal in Man*, pp. 246 *ff.*
[45] Maybe this is why Protestantism looks at faith as being totally blind, as a simple, voluntary affirmation produced in us by God, lacking in any illumination whatsoever.

which the Fathers speak about, although quick as lightning, has a permanent sparkle. The man who has matured spiritually, immediately and continually refers everything to God—he contemplates God through everything. Of course he doesn't abandon discursive thought. But he performs this operation most of the time after he has contemplated in a moment, simultaneously, the thing and its relationship to God. This process in its components and this rational demonstration of a lightning-like vision he also carries, in turn, further, as he has previously prepared it. Discursive reasoning and lightning-like contemplation are not mutually exclusive, because the latter has grown from the former, or along with the former; it is again the starting point for it. Contemplation is a reasoning or a series of reasonings plus an element not included in them, but occasioned by them, and these reasons *(logoi)* are a contemplation developed to the point in which it has meanings possible to define.

Eastern ascetical writings say that this quick discrimination is also a gift from on high, and the capacity gained with time proper to the advanced. Thus the monk must seek their advice in everything. The fact that it is gained gradually and that it doesn't appear all at once, out of the blue, confirms what we said above about the gradual winning of the capacity to "see" all at once the *logoi* of things and of actions to be performed. But the fact that it is a gift shows on the one hand that the effort for its gradual attainment is guided and sustained by a grace of the Holy Spirit. He helps in the development of certain predispositions in man; and on the other, that besides the sustaining of this effort which develops the power of man's understanding, grace opens a plus of revelation, of evidence, which, however, doesn't exclude a preliminary rational development. Contemplation isn't a lightning strike of evidence, coming unexpectedly. But it comes, as St. Maximus says, after a long rational quest.[46] But then it isn't only what results from this quest, but

---

[46] St. Maximus the Confessor says: "The powers of searching for and investigating the divine things are planted in the nature of man, in its essence, by the Maker, by the very bringing of it into existence. And the power of the Holy Spirit imparts the revelations of divine things by grace.... The grace of the Holy Spirit has reestablished the power of those who have not persisted in error.... Because it's not right to say that only grace works by itself in the saints in the knowledge of the mysteries, without the powers which are capable by nature of knowledge. For then we consider that the holy Prophets didn't understand the illuminations given to them by the Creator.... On the other hand the power of nature alone wasn't utilized in the searching for and finding of the truth in things, without the grace of the Holy Spirit." *Questions to Thalassios* 59, *PG* 90.604. "Neither does divine grace produce the illuminations of knowledge if someone isn't in the state to receive the illumination by his natural faculty, nor does this capacity of his produce the illumination of knowledge, without the grace which grants it. He who seeks without passion receives the grace to be able to work by the deeds of the virtues; he who seeks without passion finds the truth from things by natural contemplation, while he who knocks in a dispas-

THE CONTEMPLATION OF GOD IN CREATION 219

also a gift or opening of the Self of the Holy Spirit, after which He too has stimulated us to search.

5. The capacity to rapidly and more precisely discern the *logoi* of things and of individual human acts means at the same time the capacity to grasp rational relationships of a thing or of an act, with the *logoi* of other things or acts.

By habit this capacity gains the power to see the sense of everything in its relationships with the whole world, as well as each act in relationship with the entire life of that person, or with the lives of others. He now sees in a unified way the truth or the sense which gives life to all things and binds them together; it radiates from everything, from each virtuous deed. This is wisdom.[47] It makes one-sided judgments, the need for later retraction, impossible. The wise man, every time, on the basis of an integrated vision of the truth in everything, gives a balanced judgment, in other words one which keeps a balance between all things. It doesn't lean to one side or the other.

Such a person has been raised by habit to exact, nuanced, and rapid discernment in regard to individual things and deeds, to wisdom, in other words, to the capacity to see one truth from the whole of the world. From then on, when he must make a judgment on individual things or deeds, he will start with this view of the whole and keep in mind the unitary truth seen in all things.[48]

Just as the comprehension of individual *logoi* dazzled the mind with a plus of evidence, which couldn't be conceptualized, even more so the truth or unitary sense of all things is an evidence which far exceeds the limits of any concept or reasoning. Because it is the image of the divine Logos reflected in the world. The deeper we get in the thought of this image, the more we advance on the thread of the divine energies to the heavenly model and the more we realize His infinity. But this progress means at the same time an understanding caught in concepts more and more nuanced, more and more comprehensive.

The divine Logos is for us the potential womb of all concepts and meanings. But He always remains more and something else than can be

---

sionate way on the door of knowledge will enter unimpeded into the hidden grace of the mystical knowledge of God." *Ibid.*, 617.

[47] St. Maximus sometimes links wisdom with the mind as a general organ of knowledge, and (partial) knowledge with reason. *Ibid.*, 617B.

[48] St. Maximus says that after we have ascended to "the simple and exact contemplation of the truth of all things going on from these things we will bring to light many and varied logoi of the truth from the wise contemplation of perceptible things and of intelligible beings." *Ibid.*, 54.524B.

included in concepts.[49] No concept whatsoever can adequately describe Him. This is why the holy Fathers consider the identification of God with the concept of Him as a worshipping of an idol, because the idol is the raising up of something created to the rank of the absolute. This doesn't need to stop us—even though we don't have the pretension to see the divine nature itself—in once again putting into concepts at least some of the *logoi* or energies of His. Such concepts or symbols help us to define what we know can be continually surpassed. Otherwise nothing more would be said of God, and the religious life of the majority would no longer be sustained and make progress. Furthermore the holy Fathers strongly affirm the development of faith in knowledge, in other words in a certain understanding, by means of the virtues. Considering that apophatic theology is justified with reference to the divine nature, we consider it an exaggeration that here this would mean the elimination of concepts under all circumstances.

Even V. Lossky, who accentuates apophaticism so much, recognizes to a certain extent the need for concepts. Below we give an opinion of his,[50] which admits the necessity of concepts on each step of knowledge, as a step of a ladder toward Him who is beyond all steps and beyond the ladder too.

This progress of the spirit, by faith, by virtues, to healthy reason and from this, to contemplation (in the strict sense), and wisdom, coincides in depth with the order of the gifts or illuminations of the Holy Spirit, already discussed. It explains why the holy Fathers use for the same knowledge both the term *logos* (reason) and *theoria* (contemplation). For them, the connection between reason and contemplation isn't one of mutual exclusion, but they fit together; they condition and nourish each other. God is beyond discursive reason, but He isn't devoid of reason—He is the Supreme Reason *(Logos)*, the Reason from which the reasons *(logoi)* of all things and the reason in our souls proceed, although He is more than the one and the other, more than we can ever

---

[49] In regard to this plus, whose perspective the concepts open for us, *see* Ch. Journet, p. 104: "The mind is lifted up by a certain affective experience.... Because it penetrates and knows that in the things of faith there are many more things hidden besides what it shows; and because of this plus which love proves is hidden there, the mind judges in a more lofty way divine things by virtue of a special instinct of the Holy Spirit."

[50] "At each step of this ascent as one comes upon loftier images or ideas, it is necessary to guard against making of them a concept, 'an idol of God.' Then one can contemplate the divine beauty itself.... Speculation gradually gives place to contemplation, knowledge to experience; for in casting off the concepts which shackle the spirit, the apophatic disposition reveals boundless horizons of contemplation at each step of positive theology." *Mystical Theology*, ch. 2, p. 40. He shows rather justly, though probably in too limited a way, the role of concepts: "These are not the rational notions which we formulate, the concepts with which our intellect constructs a positive science of the divine nature; they are rather images or ideas intended to guide us and to fit our faculties for the contemplation of that which transcends all understanding." *Ibid.*

put into rational concepts. If God is the supreme Reason why wouldn't reason be present in human contemplation too, or why wouldn't human reason be developed contemplation, and contemplation reason which has been gathered from this development: Human reasoning is a temporal way of the contemplation of God, while human contemplation is an anticipation of non-temporal life, an approach to God as a Person above every explanation.[51]

The *logoi* which we contemplate in the things of the world are, according to the holy Fathers, God's ideas. Better said, things send our mind to the ideas of God Who made them. These are the *logoi* of the divine Logos and as they form in Him one whole, so too things are such a whole. Wisdom, grasping the unitary truth from all things, grasps the whole of the divine ideas of the Logos. As St. Maximus says:

What man, once he has seen with wisdom the beings brought by God from non-existence into existence and has directed his psychic power of contemplation to the unending variety of things in nature and has looked with understanding at the *logoi* according to which they were created, wouldn't know the one Logos, as a multiplicity of *logoi*?.... Because He possessed the *logoi* of things from the ages; He created the visible and invisible world, according to them from nothing.[52]

As St. Maximus writes, just as the divine Logos is hidden in the letter of the Old Testament Law, so too He is hidden in the things of nature, in other words in the natural law; both these laws are teachers to bring us to Christ, to the acceptance of His appearance in a human body. Thus a three-fold incorporation of the Logos can be spoken of: in nature, in Scripture and in His individual human body.

The Logos materialized[53] and became flesh. This can be understood in the sense that He, Who according to His nature is simple and without a body and nourishes in heaven all the divine powers according to their order in a spiritual way, was pleased by His coming in the flesh to interpret in resounding words and in riddles the knowledge of secret things, which surpass the power of expression of all words... later, in the sense

---

[51] Volker also finds in Origen this gradual progress, from the knowledge of God by created things, to the direct knowledge of Him and this interweaving of the rational and contemplative element, with the progress of the predominance of the latter: "Thus the development of the gnostic adapts itself exactly to the ascent of the pious. In its beginning it is more knowledge of the world, in its culmination, the mystical vision of God. One can study the peculiar spiritual attitude of Origen as in a focus. If in his works a rational and a mystical element belong together, then one can observe a gradual disarrangement of the center of gravity, without the other factor being completely eliminated. Also on the lower level both are present even if in a different degree of intensity. *Das Volkommenheits-ideal bei Origennes* (Tübingen, 1931), p. 120.
[52] Maximus the Confessor, *Ambigua*, PG 91.1077C-1080A. This passage wasn't located. trs
[53] The Greek is *pachynesthai*. The verb in the active voice is *pachyno* which means to thicken, to fatten. trs

that He covered Himself for us and hid Himself, in a mystical way, in the nature of things and He lets Himself be shown in a similar way by every visible thing as well as by letters (as complete in His wholeness, untouched in anyway... as the uncommon One and eternally the same in distinct things; as the One simple and without parts, in things composed; as the One without beginning, in the things which had to have a beginning; as the One unseen in the things which are seen; as the One uncontainable in things palpable). Finally, in the sense that for us who are lazy minds, He became incarnate in letters too and was pleased to be expressed in syllables and sounds, that through all these things, He might bring us to Himself, having become one in spirit.[54]

For man to know the Logos from nature and Scripture, something necessary for him if he wants to reach perfection, he must understand both of them "in the spirit" going beyond their material covering.[55]

---

[54] *Ibid.*, 1285C-1288A.
[55] Maurice de Gandillac, reviewing the book of J. D. Danielou, *Platonism and Mystical Theology, an Essay on the Spiritual Doctrine of St. Gregory of Nyssa* [in French], Aubier, 1941, in *Dieu Vivant* 3 (Paris): 132-4, says that in the phase of illumination, which is centered in the Holy Spirit received in the Mystery of Holy Chrismation, "the one confirmed is raised above perceptible illusions. He discovers that the world is only an appearance, that consciousness never surpasses phenomena, but at the same time material itself can serve as a symbol of the spiritual ascent, that the spirit can discover the 'energies' of God everywhere in created 'miracles.' And at the end of them, the soul arrives at 'the vision of the tabernacle,' which is already surpassed on the symbolic plane.... At this level, the soul which contemplates the intelligible world moves freely among the angels, to the third heaven where Saint Paul was ravished. That which it [the soul] discovers is not the 'essence' of God, but the 'true' universe, that which God conceived in his first intention." Gandillac remarks, however, that Angelus Silesius and even Hans Urs von Balthasar in his study on Gregory of Nyssa, *Presence et pensée* (Paris, 1941), doesn't admit an intermediary between the soul and God, in the mystical ecstasy, neither angel, nor physical world. It appears that this is also often maintained by the holy Fathers. But these

THE CONTEMPLATION OF GOD IN CREATION

We have already spoken about the spiritual understanding of nature. Now we must speak about the spiritual understanding of Scripture, but we should mention that the sure understanding of the Logos in them has been made easier by His coming in a human body and soul.

---

two theses can be reconciled: The mind in the phase of union sees God without any go-between, but is at the same time among angels and sees in God the universe of all *logoi*. This would justify the effort of the mind to know in this world the *logoi* of things as preparation.

25. The Spiritual Understanding of Scripture

"Man," says St. Maximus, "has the absolute need for these two things, if he wants to keep the right way to God without error: the spiritual understanding of Scripture and the spiritual contemplation of God in nature."[56]

In his interpretation of the transfiguration of the Lord, Jesus' shining face means the law of grace, which the veil no longer hides, while the white and glowing vestments mean at the same time the letter of Scripture and nature, which both become transparent in the light of spiritual understanding full of grace.[57] From the human face of the Logos light flows over the old Law and nature.

The spiritual understanding of Scripture is a permanent tradition of Eastern spiritual writing. In this context, St. Maximus also has the sternest words for those who can't go beyond the literal meaning of Scripture. Ignorance, in other words, Hades, dominates those who understand Scripture in a fleshly (literal) way:

> He who doesn't enter into the divine beauty and glory found in the letter of the Law falls under the power of the passions and becomes the slave of the world, which is subject to corruption ... he has no integrity but what is subject to corruption.[58]

The exact understanding of the words of the Spirit, however, are revealed only to those worthy of the Spirit; in other words, only those who by prolonged cultivation of the virtues have cleansed their mind of the soot of the passions receive the knowledge of things divine; it makes an impression and penetrates them at first contact.[59]

So the spiritual understanding of Scripture or the entering into a relationship, by its words, with "the words" of the living meanings and with the deliberate energies of God, requires preparation as well as the knowledge of the *logoi* or of the living words and present workings of God by things. Those who are full of passions, to the extent that they are glued to the visible surface of things, are also glued to the letter of Scripture and its history; both nature and the letter of Scripture are for them the wall which blocks the road to God, rather than being transparent for them or a guide to Him.

---

[56] *Ambigua, PG* 91.1128C.
[57] *Ibid.,* 1128AB, 1160CD.
[58] *Questions to Thalassios* 65, *RoFil* 3, p. 442. (The same subject is discussed here, but the quotation wasn't found. *trs*)
[59] *Ibid.,* p. 420, *PG* 90.737A.

So Scripture and nature too must be considered as a symbol, in the sense already discussed, as a medium by which the infinite depths of the spiritual meanings communicated by God as a person, shine through. He who isn't submerged in them, he who doesn't have this capacity, but limits himself to the letter on the surface, such a person cuts the ties of Scripture to the depths of God. If it contains the divine thoughts and intentions addressed to us and if these thoughts and intentions are eternally valid, Scripture must have an unending depth and a permanent validity, valid for every age and person. To understand Scripture in this way means to leave the confines of the letter and of the moment in time when a divine word was spoken for the first time and to understand it as referring to me personally, and to my generation, to our time, to our future; it means that when I read the letter I hear God Himself speaking to me and to us today, or about me and us, and about our duties. To understand Scripture in the "spirit" means to see the constant relationship between God and us, and to live it in the way it affects me, at the present moment, because I am living the present moment.

It has to be further specified that both the words of Scripture and the actions of God in it, as the supernatural Revelation of God, have a clearer meaning and have a more direct claim on us than the meanings or words of God incorporated in things and in relationship with people. The whole life of Jesus interpreted by His Words, the fact of His crucifixion and resurrection for us offer us more direct, more profound meanings and require that we, too, live according to His image, that we too might reach the resurrection and union with God, as He wants.

This means that only those who have in them the Spirit of the Word non-incarnate and incarnate, those who read by this Spirit, will have a part in the understanding of the "spirit" of the Scripture. This doesn't mean that their subjective state borrows from Scripture meanings which objectively it doesn't contain. Such meanings would no longer be objective words of God the Word. Because by the same preparation which we have seen in the preceding chapter, they have made their minds capable of receiving the power of the Spirit of Christ, in order to grasp the depths and objective demands of Scripture. By becoming men and women who live in the Spirit they grasp the spirit of Scripture (its deep and permanent meaning), because this same Spirit which worked in its inspiration and is hidden in the text of Scripture has set their spirit in motion for them. Now by "spirit" is meant the depths in the inner life of man which correspond to the depths of God. In other words they live according to the objective norms of the spiritual life and from the objective source of the Spirit and so comprehend these norms or this source as well in the text of Scripture. The light of the Spirit in me is projected on Scripture and penetrates the wall of the text, which covers the light or the Spirit in it, or the light in it is made known to those who have eyes for it. So the light in me isn't subjective, but the objective light of the Holy Spirit which is won by purification from the passions and by the prolonged exercise of thinking of God and by prayer.

Two things anchor this understanding so it doesn't become subjective: a) The spiritual meanings of Scripture, or the Spirit of Christ working in it, correspond to my spiritual states and aspirations (but not to just any of them but only to those gained after I have conformed, with the help of the grace of Christ, to the objective norms of the spiritual life in the Church. Then my states are in conformity with the common model in the Church. I have modeled myself after those who have the Spirit in them and so have the same Spirit.) b) The frequent reading of patristic spiritual commentaries, as well as prolonged meditation on the texts of Scripture in the light of these commentaries will accustom me to immediately discover analogous meanings in any other of its texts.

The virtuous life, according to the living norms and models of the Church, and first of all according to Christ the model, and the reading of the holy Fathers sharpen discernment in relationship to the texts of Scripture. It becomes more and more nuanced, more and more profound and faster, as we have seen in the case of discernment referring to things in nature, to people and to human actions. This preparation is a growth in the love of Christ; it makes me feel Christ Himself more and more speaking through Scripture. With time the spiritual man gains a capacity for the understanding of the meanings of Scripture as a whole and sees them as radiating from the same Christ, Who reveals Himself in the interpretation of every text. This keeps the reader from error by an arbitrary interpretation, because the one wisdom of Christ, communicated by His Holy Spirit, which the spiritual man has gained too, is in Scripture. Scripture, just as our inner being, and nature too, but in a clearer, more direct way, has depths which lead to the divine infinite and make the Person of the divine Word felt. This wisdom makes way for an infinite progress in the deeper study of the Scripture and in the increasingly accentuated feeling of Christ. Every concept in which I might put newly discovered meanings and by which I might express the presence of Christ, are constantly surpassed by the evidence of a larger content, of a more vivid presence of Christ, although there can't be any contradiction whatsoever between what I have succeeded, on a certain step of understanding, in grasping in legitimate concepts and that which remains inexhaustible.

THE SPIRITUAL UNDERSTANDING OF SCRIPTURE   227

The progress in the deeper study of Scripture is in proportion to our progress in the life according to the Spirit, in proportion to our purification from the egotism of the passions. It is the love which we have by the virtues for Christ, a love developed by effort, but also by the gifts of the Holy Spirit which come to us by Christ, in other words by our encounter with the love of Christ.

If the spiritual understanding of Scripture also means its reference to our own lives and to this generation, then it makes Scripture up to date, and each person in it becomes a type for our souls, and each event in it, a real event or possibility for our spiritual lives. All are types for that which happens all the time with people: King Hezekiah in his different phases refers to the life of the human soul, so too to our souls in different phases; David is the mind purified of the passions, the mind which governs the watchful soul, as a Jerusalem which is a city of peace; Saul is the spirit with the fleshly understanding of the Law; the iron gates which open before the Apostle Peter so that he can leave the prison, are the hardened heart of anytime, and so of ours too; Babylon is the soul gripped by the confusion of the passions.[60]

In this way all things in Scripture not only become contemporary, but in some way a biography of our relationship with God. In this sense the events of salvation of the life of Jesus become present events which happen in the depths of my life, if I want to receive Him in me. At Baptism He hid in me, in a supreme kenosis. At the beginning His effectiveness in me is covered, later it becomes ever more visible in my effort to carry out His commands. He is resurrected in me when I reach the state of dispassion. He is transfigured for me when I become worthy of seeing the divine light. He penetrates into me in a hidden way at baptism. He is the effective force which guides and empowers my whole ascent along which He becomes increasingly more transparent in me, by my gradual deification, making me like Him by the dialogical communi-

---

[60] All this in St. Maximus the Confessor, *Questions to Thalassios* 55. Some Western Christians are also realizing today the need for this spiritual interpretation of Scripture by the resumption of the patristic tradition. See the periodical *Dieu Vivant* 1 (Paris, 1946): 8. Here we have Roman Catholics, Orthodox, and Protestants cooperating in an irenical spirit. In the Prolog we read: "The recent labors of exegetes have renewed the knowledge of the Bible; they have restored deformed and equivocal passages to their primitive state, for a better understanding of the texts, of the historical milieu where the drama and the first hours of Christianity are unfolded. It is impossible to ignore this fact. But doesn't contemporary criticism, even when it is the work of Christian scholars, sometimes lose sight that although it is made up of sacred writings, the principle author of the Scriptures is still the Holy Spirit? Severed from the symbolical and spiritual interpretations which a Bloy or a Claudel have brought back to their rightful places, by taking up again the tradition of an Origen or of an Augustine, the Bible usually doesn't appear to be any more than a treatise of dogmatics or moral theology, when it is something much more lofty, the image of the invisible world, and as Bloy has written, 'the very history of God'."

cation with Him. He reflects Himself in numerous human lives, as the sun does in numberless window panes.[61]

This actualization of Scripture and of the events in it, this understanding of it by each soul as referring to it in the concrete circumstances in which it finds itself, gives the present moment an auxiliary role in the understanding of Scripture, and as a matter of fact a role in the understanding of nature too.[62] Scripture is eternally the same and nevertheless eternally new for every moment of the unfolding of creation. The problems which our time confronts us with, the preoccupations which it imposes on us, the fears which it causes us and the resulting stress, do not introduce new meanings extraneous to Scripture. Instead they bring out, in continuation with the previous ones, new ones, formulated in new concepts, united with the old. Thus the Holy Spirit doesn't avoid time, but He pierces it, He transfigures it. Our spiritual fabric will retain forever something of the color of the time in which we lived.

But the development of creation can also be understood better and better in the light of the spiritual understanding of Scripture and, generally, of Christian teaching. This development isn't monovalent.[63] In it is manifested, at the same time, the *logoi* of divine Providence and judgment, the knowledge of which are won on a higher step of the spiritual life.[64] The *logoi* of Providence are the light side of the development of creation in time, and those of judgment, the dark side. This development brings out the positive forces, aspiration and values which are the expression of the dynamic *logoi*, of the main ideas of Providence. Frequently, good times and an effort for good are followed by periods of suffering which are on the one hand the effect of the irrational actions of certain passionate factors, and on the other the manifestation of the punishments of God, which have their reasons [*logoi*]; by them He diverts the world from evil. But Providence and judgment, in history, don't only alternate by epochs, but sometimes they are mixed too. New

---

[61] "For the Lord does not always appear in glory to those who are standing before him; rather, he comes in the form of a servant to beginners, and to those who are strong enough to follow him in climbing the lofty mountain of his transfiguration before the creation of the world. Thus it is possible for the Lord not to appear in the same form to all those who meet him but to some in one way and to others in another way, that is, by varying the contemplation according to the measure of faith in each one." *Chapters on Knowledge* 2.13 *ff*. *Maximus Confessor, Selected writings*, p. 150.

[62] St. Basil recommends "the spiritual reading of Scripture, especially of those texts that further the salvation of the soul, according to the state which he has reached." Quoted by St. Peter of Damascus, *GrPh* 4, p. 68; *cf*. *Phi* 3, pp. 154-5.

[63] Perhaps the author means here, in using this chemical term, that it isn't one-sided. *trs*

[64] St. Maximus the Confessor, *Chapters on Knowledge* 1.16, *Maximus Confessor, Selected writings*, p. 131; *Questions to Thalassios* 54.19, *PG* 90.532.

THE SPIRITUAL UNDERSTANDING OF SCRIPTURE 229

ideas and orders are sometimes introduced into the development of human life by stern means.

In the development of this life the energies of divine *logoi* are thus active, and we progress in the understanding of them according to the measure of our spiritualization. For the spiritual man this development is also an increasingly transparent and mobile symbol of God, as it appeared to the prophets in the Old Testament and to the author of the Apocalypse. Time, with the events in it, as well as space with its material things, are a medium in which God works.

For the spiritual man, in the depths of Scripture, of nature and of the unfolding of creation in time, the same Spirit is present and active with him; the Spirit sustains his efforts of purification and illuminates for him everything around that they might become transparent symbols of divinity. All things give him the consciousness that "in God we live and move, and have our being," as St. Paul said on Mars Hill in Athens (Acts 17:28).

26. The Negative and Apophatic Knowledge of God in General

The knowledge of God by means of the *logoi* of nature, of the development of human life, and of Scripture, represents the affirmative way of our knowledge of Him. But, as we have seen, in the progress of this knowledge, the consciousness that God surpasses that which can be understood about Him in concepts and words, becomes stronger and stronger; on the peak of this progress, it becomes predominant. So at the beginning the affirmative way is less dependent on the consciousness of the ineffable character of God; later it is more so. After a long ascent, it becomes almost totally dependent on the consciousness of the inability to comprehend and express God in concepts. So thought uses, along with affirmative concepts and expressions, negative ones, and after a long spiritual ascent almost only the negative.

But these negative concepts and expressions don't express the feeling of the soul that God can't be known by any means. In other words, negative theology isn't only a unilateral action, the simple consciousness of the intellectual impotence of knowing God, but in it a "feeling" of the incomprehensibility of God is also expressed, an experience of Him, which grows along with the spiritual ascent of man. This "experience" can also be expressed in certain positive terms, but equipped with corrections which show that their usual meaning isn't intended. For example this experience is called a "vision" of God, or a "vision of the divine light," higher than any feeling, etc. All the Eastern Fathers have spoken of such an "understandable feeling," of such a "vision" of God, of an "experience" of Him.

In order to distinguish between a simple negation of the knowability of God and this "experience" of Him, gained not by the powers of human nature, but by the Holy Spirit, we will use for the first expression *negative theology,* and for the second *apophatic theology;* sometimes, however, even in the use of the negative terms a mystical experience of God can be expressed.

We make this distinction, because usually in Roman Catholic theology, along with the affirmative, only negative theology is known in the sense of a simple intellectual renunciation of the affirmative terms. It is to V. Lossky's credit that in recent times he brought apophaticism to Orthodox theological consciousness as a dominant characteristic of Orthodox theology. And it is also to his credit that he has specified that the apophaticism of the Fathers is something else than the intellectual negative theology known in Roman Catholic theology.[65]

---

[65]*Mystical Theology.* See Chapter 2, "The Divine Darkness," pp. 23-43.

We will state Lossky's description of this apophaticism and then add some explanations, since it seems to us that he describes it mostly in negative terms, and furthermore he doesn't include that theme so essential to Orthodox apophaticism and namely the vision of the divine light.[66]

Lossky begins by pointing out the two ways of the knowledge of God, according to Dionysius the Areopagite:

> Dionysius distinguishes two possible theological ways. One—that of cataphatic or positive theology—proceeds by affirmations; the other—apophatic or negative theology—by negations. The first leads us to some knowledge of God, but in an imperfect way. The perfect way, the only way which is fitting in regard to God, who is of His very nature unknowable, is the second—which leads us finally to total ignorance. All knowledge has as its object that which is. Now God is beyond all that exists. In order to approach Him it is necessary to deny all that is inferior to Him, that is to say, all that which is.... It is by *unknowing (agnosia)* that one may know Him who is above every possible object of knowledge. Proceeding by negations one ascends from the inferior degrees of being to the highest, by progressively setting aside all that can be known, in order to draw near to the Unknown in the darkness of absolute ignorance. For even as light, and especially abundance of light, renders darkness invisible, even so the knowledge of created things, and excess of knowledge, destroys the ignorance which is the only way by which one can attain to God in Himself.[67]

After this general description, Lossky continues:

> If we transfer Dionysius' distinction between negative and affirmative theology to the plane of the dialectic, we are faced with an antinomy, which we then seek to resolve; in the attempt to make a synthesis of the two opposed ways we bring them together as a single method of knowing God. It is thus that St. Thomas Aquinas reduces the two ways of Dionysius to one, making negative theology a corrective to affirmative theology. In attributing to God the perfections which we find in created beings we must (according to St. Thomas) deny the mode according to which we understand these finite perfections, but we may affirm them in relation to God *modo sublimiori*.... We may indeed ask how far this very ingenious philosophical invention corresponds to the thought of Dionysius. If, for the author of the *Areopagitica*, there is an antinomy between the

---

[66] Lossky wrote a book on the subject, which Fr. Staniloae doesn't seem to be familiar with. See *The Vision of God* (Bedfordshire, England: The Faith Press, 1963). It was translated from the French by Ashleigh Moorhouse. *trs*
[67] *Mystical Theology*, p. 25.

two theologies which he distinguishes, does he admit this synthesis of the two ways?[68]

So Lossky proposes that Dionysius' *Mystical Theology* be analyzed, in order to concentrate on "the true nature of that apophaticism which constitutes the fundamental character of the whole theological tradition of the Eastern Church."[69] He then reproduces in continuation, almost word for word, chapter one, text 3, of the *Mystical Theology,* where it says that we have to give up rational activity, all perceptible or intelligible objects, everything that is and is not, in order to attain, in absolute ignorance, union with Him Who is above all existence and all knowing. "It is already evident that this is not simply a question of a process of a dialectic but of something else; a purification, a *catharsis* is necessary."[70] Because Dionysius, as quoted by Lossky, says:

> One must abandon all that is impure and even all that is pure. One must then scale the most sublime heights of sanctity leaving behind all the divine luminaries, all the heavenly sounds and words. It is only thus that one may penetrate to the darkness wherein He who is beyond all created things makes His dwelling.[71]

This ascent is compared by Dionysius with that of Moses on Sinai. Moses begins by purifying himself. Then Dionysius, again cited by Lossky, says:

> He hears the many notes of the trumpets, he sees the many lights which flash forth many pure rays; then he is separated from the many, and with the chosen priests he reaches the height of the divine ascents. Even here he does not associate with God; he does not contemplate God (for He is unseen), but the place where He is. I think this means that the highest and most divine of the things which are seen and understood are a kind of hypothetical account of what is subject to Him Who is over all,[72]

in other words certain hypothetical reasons *(logoi)* of the attributes of Him Who is totally transcendent, (Lossky),[73] or the symbolic language of things subordinate to Him Who Himself transcends them all, (Dionysius). "Through these things His incomprehensible presence is shown

---

[68] *Ibid.,* p. 26.
[69] *Ibid.*
[70] *Ibid.,* p. 27.
[71] Dionysius the Areopagite, *The Mystical Theology* 1.3, quoted by Lossky, *The Mystical Theology of the Eastern Church,* p. 27. Lossky is paraphrasing Dionysius. *cf. The Divine Names and Mystical Theology,* trans. C.E. Rolt (London, 1979), p. 193.
[72] Lossky, p. 27.
[73] *Ibid.,* p. 28.

walking upon those heights of His holy places which are perceived by the mind."⁷⁴ Only then is Moses freed from the seen and those who see and plunged into "the Darkness of Unknowing wherein he renounces all the apprehensions of his understanding and is enwrapped in that which is wholly intangible and invisible, belonging wholly to Him that is beyond all things and to none else (whether himself or another), and being through the passive stillness of all his reasoning powers united by his highest faculty to Him that is wholly Unknowable, of whom thus by a rejection of all knowledge he possesses a knowledge that exceeds his understanding."⁷⁵

On the basis of this text Lossky concludes:

> It is now clear, for Dionysius, that the apophatic way, or mystical theology— for such is the title of the treatise devoted to the way of negations— has for its object God, in so far as He is absolutely incomprehensible.⁷⁶

Lossky finds the foundation of divine incomprehensibility in the Dionysian system in the fact that, for the latter's Christian conception, God doesn't stand in continuity with the world, as Plotinus' "One." According to Plotinus, the mind must forsake all things in order to reach the One, because they represent fragments of the One, not because it is beyond all things and incomprehensible by nature. It is possible to reach the essence of the "One" after the mind has been simplified, because it is in continuity with the multiplicity of things. But it isn't possible to reach God even after we have surpassed all things, because between them and God there is a discontinuity of nature which can't be overcome by the mind. The discontinuity of nature is shown by the uncreated nature of God and by the created character of all things that are and of which we are a part.

This is a basis of the divine incomprehensibility affirmed by the apophaticism of Eastern theology. This apophatic content, says Lossky, was also defended by the great Cappadocians against Eunomius, who argued for the possibility of expressing the essentials of the Divinity⁷⁷ in rational concepts.

Lossky discovers apophaticism in most of the Fathers as a religious attitude in the face of the divine incomprehensibility. According to Clement of Alexandria, the very consciousness of the inaccessibility of

---

⁷⁴ Rolt, 194.
⁷⁵ Rolt, 194.
⁷⁶ *Op. cit.*, p. 28.
⁷⁷ In Romanian, "posibilitatea expremarii esentiale divine...." *trs*

God can only be gained by grace.[78] The theme of Moses approaching God in the darkness of Mount Sinai, first used by Philo of Alexandria, will be the figure preferred by the Fathers to express the experience of the inaccessibility of the divine nature. St. Gregory of Nyssa consecrates a special treatise to *The Life of Moses*, in which the ascent on Mt. Sinai toward the darkness of incomprehensibility is considered as the way of contemplation, preferable to Moses' first encounter with God, when He appeared to him in the burning bush. Moses knows God because he realizes that he can't know Him.[79]

"Then Moses saw God in light; now he enters the darkness, leaving behind him all that can be seen or known; there remains to him only the invisible and unknowable, but in this darkness is God.... Our spiritual ascent does not but reveal to us, ever more and more clearly, the absolute incomprehensibility of the divine nature. Filled with an ever-increasing desire the soul grows without ceasing, goes forth from itself, reaches out beyond itself, and, in so doing, is filled with yet greater longing. Thus the ascent becomes infinite, the desire insatiable."[80]

As can be seen, by apophaticism Lossky doesn't mean negative theology as an intellectual operation, because the experiencing of the divine incomprehensibility doesn't require only an intellectual purification, as the Platonic system does, but a renunciation of the whole created realm. It means an existential going beyond the self which engages the whole man; it is a supra-conceptual union with God, which has different grades.

"In Dionysius the mystical union is a new condition which implies a progress, a series of changes, a transition from the created to the uncreated, the acquiring of something which man did not hitherto possess by nature.... Here union means deification. At the same time, while intimately united with God he knows Him only as Unknowable, in other words as infinitely set apart by His nature, remaining even in union, inaccessible in that which He is in His essential being.... Apophaticism is not necessarily a theology of ecstasy. It is, above all, an attitude of mind which refuses to form concepts about God. Such an attitude utterly ex-

---

[78] *Carpets*, 5.17. See Lossky, *op. cit.*, p. 34.
[79] By *light* St. Gregory of Nyssa means piety, as a return from the darkness. "Scripture teaches by this that religious knowledge comes at first to those who receive it as light. Therefore what is perceived to be contrary to religion is darkness, and the escape from darkness comes about when one participates in light. But as the mind progresses and, through an ever greater and more perfect diligence, comes to apprehend reality, as it approaches more nearly to contemplation, it sees more clearly what of the divine nature is uncontemplated....This is the true knowledge of what is sought; this is the seeing that consists in not seeing...." *The Life of Moses* 162-3 (New York, 1978), pp. 94-5. See also Lossky, *Mystical Theology*, p. 33, note 2.
[80] Lossky, *op. cit.*, p. 35.

cludes all abstract and purely intellectual theology which would adapt the mysteries of the wisdom of God to human ways of thought. It is an existential attitude which involves the whole man: there is no theology apart from experience; it is necessary to change, to become a new man."[81]

"At each step of this ascent as one comes upon loftier images or ideas, it is necessary to guard against making of them a concept, "an idol of God." Then one can contemplate the divine beauty itself: God, in so far as He manifests Himself in creation. Speculation gradually gives place to contemplation, knowledge to experience; for in casting off the concepts which shackle the spirit, the apophatic disposition reveals boundless horizons of contemplation.... This contemplation of the hidden treasures of the divine Wisdom can be practiced in varying degrees, with greater or lesser intensity: whether it be a lifting up of the spirit towards God and away from creatures, which, allows His splendour to become visible; whether it be a meditation on the Holy Scriptures in which God hides Himself, as it were behind a screen, beneath the words which express the revelation (so Gregory of Nyssa); whether it be through the dogmas of the Church or through her liturgical life; whether, finally, it be through ecstasy that we penetrate to the divine mystery, this experience of God will always be the fruit of that apophatic attitude...."[82]

Summing up his view of apophaticism Lossky comments:

> Unknowability does not mean agnosticism or refusal to know God. Nevertheless, this knowledge will only be attained in the way which leads not to knowledge but to union—to deification. Thus theology will never be abstract, working through concepts, but contemplative: raising the mind to those realities which pass all understanding. This is why the dogmas of the Church often present themselves to the human reason as antinomies, the more difficult to resolve the more sublime the mystery which they express.[83]

We consider Lossky's presentation to be accurate, because he sees in apophaticism a general attitude of consciousness in facing the divine mystery and a union with the divine which transforms, or deifies man. But we would like to supplement this presentation with certain nuances and additions.

In reality unknowability in a mystical way is joined with knowledge; and in the measure in which we ascend toward the divine mystery, we

---

[81] *Ibid.*, p. 38.
[82] *Ibid.*, pp. 40-2.
[83] *Ibid.*, p. 43.

are filled with more and more knowledge, of course with another kind of knowledge, but also with the knowledge that the divine nature is above all knowledge.[84] Or, in the language of St. Gregory Palamas, the experience on the higher steps isn't called knowledge because of the absence of knowledge, but because of its superabundance. "It shouldn't be called knowledge, because it is much higher than all knowledge and the viewpoint from knowledge."[85]

So we would like to accentuate more the difference between the unknowability on the lower steps and that on the higher ones of the spiritual ascent. It isn't total on each step.

St. Gregory Palamas rejected the idea of Barlaam that after created nature there is nothing but the divine nature, which is totally inaccessible and unknowable. Although Lossky knows the difference between the divine nature and energies, he doesn't concern himself with the vision of the divine light, but speaks only in general of an unknowability of God lived somehow, which is also admitted by more recent Catholic theology.

---

[84] It is true that St. Gregory of Nyssa writes: "When, therefore, Moses grew in knowledge, he declared that he had seen God in the darkness, that is, that he had then come to know that what is divine is beyond all knowledge and comprehension, for the text says, 'Moses approached the dark cloud where God was'.... The divine word at the beginning forbids that the Divine be likened to any of the things known by men, since every concept which comes from some comprehensible image by an approximate understanding and by guessing at the divine nature constitutes an idol of God and does not proclaim God." *The Life of Moses* 164-5, pp. 95-6. But, a little further on, St. Gregory comments: "These things and others similar being taught by the vision of the tabernacle, the spiritual eye of Moses, borne up by similar visions, is again lifted toward the heights of other meaning." *PG* 44.386. This reference wasn't found. *trs*
[85] *The Defense* 2.3.17, "On the Holy Light," p. 447. *cf. The Triads*, pp. 61-2.

27. The Steps of Apophaticism

In this and subsequent chapters we will consider negative theology, apophaticism at the height of prayer, and the apophaticism of the vision of the divine light.

For Orthodox Christians, after the knowledge, by the intermediacy of nature, of the divine *logoi* and energies, the knowledge of the divine revealed energies follows. Of course, the knowledge of these energies is accompanied, especially in the second case, by apophaticism. Furthermore, the knowledge of the energies enveloped in nature is accompanied by the consciousness of the unknowability of the divinely revealed energies; and the knowledge of them goes together with the consciousness of the absolute incomprehensibility of the divine nature. Thus apophaticism is present at the same time as knowledge, or alternatively, on both steps, but is more accentuated on the second.

Between the knowledge of the divine *logoi* and energies through nature, however, which also has something apophatic in it, and the revealed vision of them there is a hiatus, a gap. This represents an apophaticism almost unmixed with any positive element of knowledge. It is an intermediate apophaticism in which we have left behind every mental operation, even that of negation, but we still haven't received the light. We accentuate, however, that all the time that we know by concepts the divine energies in nature, we have the consciousness that these concepts are inadequate for the energies which are manifested through nature. Then we realize that they are even more insufficient for the divine revealed energies, and completely inadequate for the nature of God. In this sense not only negative intellectual theology, but also a comprehension of these energies by feeling, always accompanies or alternates with affirmative theology.

Intellectual negative theology is the first form of apophaticism; but just as affirmative theology isn't without the negative, so both are accompanied by an apophaticism of an unexplainable feeling of these energies. But with an elevation above that which nature can give us, the consciousness of a hiatus or of the total insufficiency of the concepts taken from nature and the inadequacy of our mind and feeling to know the divinity through them reaches its highest point; in other words the apophaticism of negative theology and the unspeakable feeling of these energies becomes almost total. It is the supreme consciousness of our inability to know God by human spiritual activity. The moment we leave behind every consideration of concepts taken from nature and every preoccupation even to negate them when we therefore also raise ourselves beyond negation, as an intellectual operation, and beyond some apophatic feeling of them, we enter a state of silence produced by prayer. Now we have the second step of apophaticism. It is a much stronger feeling, but one in the darkness of the divine energies, which has surpassed intellectual negative theology and the apophatic feeling which goes with it.

But we don't think that this second step of apophaticism should be identified with the supreme step of the spiritual ascent either, as it seems to be in Lossky. Likewise we don't think that even the *Mystical Theology* of Dionysius the Areopagite has this in view. Because St. Gregory Palamas has shown, in his polemic with Barlaam, that the areopagitic texts refer to another darkness, that is to the supra-luminous darkness which doesn't mean either negative theology alone, nor just any feeling of God in the dark. Rather, it is something else than theology by negation and even than some apophatic feeling of Him in the darkness. It is a darkness not because there is no light in it, but because there is an over abundance of light.

It's true that not just anybody is raised to a vision of the divine light or that it is a permanent state. For those who haven't reached it, or for the moments when they aren't there, negative theology accompanied by some kind of feeling of the divine energies, produced by prayer, is the highest step. In the best case, they reach the apophaticism of silence or of a more intense feeling, but in the darkness of the divine energies. Namely they attain the apophaticism of the second step. St. Gregory Palamas distinguishes the vision of the divine light from negative theology as an inferior intellectual operation, as a work of the mind which thinks that these affirmative concepts of a certain intellectual content don't fit God, as a work accompanied by a certain apophatic feeling; he also distinguishes it from the apophaticism of the second step, in which there is no longer any intellectual operation whatsoever, but all thought ceases. There is the consciousness of a total inability to understand God with our minds, an exclusive feeling of Him, in darkness.

And now let's see how St. Gregory Palamas distinguishes negative theology, the apophatic feeling which accompanies it, and the stronger one which follows it as certain lower steps, from the divine light, which in spite of its incomprehensible character has nevertheless something positive compared to the other two steps. We mention that St. Gregory sees negative theology as unaccompanied by the feeling of the presence of God, but we think that he doesn't refer to it because it is extremely reduced in intensity. What then is this union which "... isn't anything that exists, because it surpasses them? Now isn't it theology by negation? But it is union and not subtraction. Then for theology by negation neither do we need a going out from ourselves *(ecstasy)* when even the angels need it for this union.... Furthermore the light of this theology is in some way knowledge and a rational discourse *(gnosis tis kai logos)*. But the light of this contemplation is seen as possessing objective reality *(enypostatos theoreitai)* working and speaking spiritually and in a mystical way in the deified one. In fact, the mind understands things contrary to God, theologizing by subtraction. Here it works discursively (by development). But is this union?"[86] So a vision of divine light isn't a negative theology.

Palamas knows— in addition to the negative theologizing which is an intellectual operation, because the mind thinks about the things that it is eliminating and is carried along at the same time by evidence that God is more than it— an additional apophatic state of the soul, before the holy light comes to it. It is a state born during prayer when the soul abandons all the thoughts of things and goes out of itself. But this exit, or ecstasy, isn't yet a vision of the light. It is thus a lived apophaticism, experienced in a much more intensive degree than that based on the mental operation which eliminates positive attributes from God. Palamas says:

> In prayer the mind gradually leaves relations with the things that exist, first those that bind it to the shame of things evil and perishable, then those things which tie it with things in the middle, between us and God.... For this reason the Fathers advise us not to accept thoughts which the enemy produces in the time of prayer so we won't be robbed of the better. So the mind, rejecting these things as well as relations with things superior to them, leaves completely all things that are, in the time of pure prayer. This ecstasy [going out] is incomparably higher than theology by negation, because it is proper only to those who have reached dispassion. But still he doesn't have the vision of the light until the Comforter illumines from above the one who is praying in the upper room of the physical extremities and waiting for the promise of the Father; and seizes him by His revelation to contemplate the light.[87]

In answer to Barlaam, who argued that the vision of the light is only negative theology, that therefore this represents the supreme step of the spiritual ascent, St. Gregory Palamas replies:

> This work, higher than the mind, is superior to that within the mind; they don't know God, not in the sense that they see nothing, as those do who conceive Him by negation, but by the vision itself they

---

[86] *The Defense* 2.3.35, pp. 475-7. *cf. The Triads*, p. 64.
[87] *Ibid.*

see that which is beyond seeing.[88] [Because] those who are worthy of this blessed vision, not by prayer, but by a vision in the spirit, know that which surpasses vision, by this deifying work.[89]

Barlaam interpreted, according to his concept, "the divine darkness" of Dionysius the Areopagite. Barlaam said that only he who has abandoned everything that can be seen and known is able to penetrate it. He argues, as quoted by St. Gregory Palamas:

> If someone enters this darkness, he does so by the negation of all that exists. Thus this darkness, which is the most perfect contemplation or vision, is nothing but theology by negation. Because nothing is beyond the knowing of nothing. So too this light, which you speak of, whatever it may be, you must abandon in order to elevate yourself to the theology and contemplation by negation.[90]

To this St. Gregory Palamas answers:

> The divine light which the mind sees in ecstasy is a pledge of the light which surrounds the saints in the future life. Now is this an absolute nothingness? Or is it inferior to this nothingness of negative theology? If this were so, we, raising ourselves to negative theology as to a higher step of contemplation, would find ourselves above the blessed state of the saints. So why such an ingenious endeavor to make us abandon the light which will surround us forever, so that we can enjoy the contemplation *(theoria)* which you consider all-perfect? And if we now can leave behind and surpass this light, but then not, the present age is higher than the one to come.[91]

Let's consider, says St. Gregory, the words of Dionysius which provoked these thoughts:

> The divine darkness is the inaccessible light, because of its overwhelming brightness and the exuberant flooding of the supernatural light. He who is worthy to know and to see God reaches this, even by the fact of no longer seeing or knowing; he is raised to that which is above sight and knowledge. He knows exactly what is beyond everything perceptible and intelligible.[92]

This is St. Gregory Palamas' answer:

> So here he says that the same thing is darkness and light, that it is seen and not seen, known and not known. How then is that light

---

[88] *Ibid.*, 2.3.26, pp. 459, 461.
[89] *Ibid.*
[90] *Ibid.*, 2.3.50, p. 505.
[91] *Ibid.*, p. 507.
[92] *PG* 3.1073. This passage wasn't located in the place cited. *trs*

darkness? 'Because of the overwhelming outpouring of light,' he says. Therefore strictly speaking it is light; it is darkness in the sense of overabundance *(kath'hyperochin)*, since it is invisible to those who try to approach it and to see it by the senses and the mind.

Only those like Moses are made worthy to see this light, while by negative theology, anyone who honors God, can.

So this light (strictly speaking) and this darkness (in the sense of overabundance) is something else than theology by negation and the former surpasses the latter in an incomparable way—let's say as much as Moses surpasses the multitude in the vision of God.[93]

They that practice only this theology by negation:

> ... don't see and don't know anything strictly speaking; rather they suffer from a lack of knowledge and sight. As a result, they have forgotten themselves; they say that this is true unknowing in the sense of deficiency, higher than all knowledge and taking pride that they know nothing in the sense of deficiency.

If the divine darkness of Dionysius were only this negative theology, [argues Palamas] it would also be nothingness, an absence. The divine darkness, however, can't be darkness in a negative sense, nothingness, and absence of any vision whatsoever. It is something positive, or suprapositive. If contemplation *(theoria)* by negation and the divine darkness are one and the same thing, and this contemplation brings about strictly speaking a lack of any vision, according to those who say that further on there is nothing, not even a divine vision, then this divine darkness too is strictly speaking a darkness by deficiency and it makes those who are in it foolish.[94]

Negative theology is only an icon which anticipates the vision of the divine light, but it isn't itself that vision:

We have examined negative theology in the previous treatises on light; we have shown that it is the icon of that vision, without image and one of fulfillment which the mind enjoys beyond itself in the Holy Spirit, but it isn't the light itself. So all those who have been found worthy of the Mystery (Baptism) by faith can praise God by negation, but they can't unite with Him and see Him by the light— unless they receive the supernatural power of vision by the carrying out of the commands.[95]

He distinguishes in a subtle way between the vision from outside the darkness where God is, beyond the human mind which works by its powers, and the penetration into the interior of this darkness by the

---

[93] *Ibid.*, 2.3.51-2, pp. 507-9.
[94] *Ibid.*, 2.3.53, pp. 509-11.
[95] *Ibid.*, 2.3.53, p. 513.

mind drawn there by God Himself. The first is negative theology. At the most it can tell us that the darkness in which God dwells is also beyond all images and concepts of things:

> If then the ascent of Moses would have been only to the vision of that place, it could be rightly dogmatized from this that there is no vision after the theology by negation. Moses went beyond the vision of that place and penetrated into the truly mystical darkness, by the cessation of every cognitive activity in the sense of eclipse. He was united on a higher step with the unknown one and saw Him and knew Him who is beyond mind. How then shall we enclose the vision in the divine darkness only within the margins of the theology and contemplation by negation? Because he saw it too before he entered the darkness higher than light *(hyperphoton gnophon),* by that place.

But is it possible that Moses detaching himself from all things and thoughts which are seen and which see:[96]

> ... and going beyond the vision of the place and penetrating the darkness, saw nothing? But he saw the immaterial ark, which he showed to those below by material imitation.... Thus the ark and the things which belong to it, the priesthood and the things which belong to it are perceptible symbols and veils of the visions of Moses in the divine darkness. However, these visions themselves weren't symbols.... Can someone also say then that in the divine darkness and according to theology by negation no higher vision whatsoever is shown?[97]

It has been demonstrated then that negative theology, as a lower step, is something else than the vision of the divine light. Likewise, that between it and the vision of the divine light there is also an intermediate apophaticism, experience in an existential way by our whole being, in a culminating state of prayer, as a feeling in the darkness of the presence of God and as a total quietness of the mind. The first two states effect man by his natural powers, aided, of course, by the grace received at Baptism and in the Mystery of holy Chrismation. By them the mind reaches the abyss which separates its knowledge from God, but it is still here, on the human side. But carried off by God, it goes over there, to the vision of the divine light. Certainly the vision of the divine light is also accompanied by an apophaticism, which we could call the third step. But it is no longer an apophaticism in the sense of a void, as the

---

[96] *Ibid.*, 2.3.55, p. 516. "*...panton apolytheis ton te oromenon kai ton oronton pragmaton te kai noimaton.*"
[97] *Ibid.*, 2.3.54-5, pp. 516-19.

two previous ones. First it consists of the consciousness of the one who sees it: that it can't be contained in concepts and expressed in words. Secondly, that beyond it is the divine being, which remains totally inaccessible and that this accessible light itself remains infinitely inexhaustible. But it has a positive content of knowledge higher than knowledge, of apophatic knowledge, a feeling higher than experience and of natural feeling.

As we have said, the vision of the light means that it has carried the mind across the abyss which separates us and God, so that it is no longer on this side of natural knowledge, but on the other. This is why we treat negative theology and apophaticism in the second part of this book, and the vision of the light in the third, along with the union of the soul with God.

Hausherr claimed that Hesychasm abandoned the Eastern tradition of joining the affirmative with the negative in expressing the mystical experience—that it kept only the affirmation of the vision of the divine light.[98] This isn't so. The first treatise of the first series, and the third of the last of St. Gregory Palamas' defense of Hesychasm never stop calling the vision of the divine light "knowledge above understanding" or "unknowing in the sense of surpassing." The divine light seen in an incomprehensible image also remains for Hesychasm a mystery; it doesn't exclude, but implicates apophaticism, without leaving it by itself. What distinguishes this apophaticism from the vision higher than the vision of light, is the fact that it isn't a void but an overwhelming divine presence; and it isn't an intellectual negation and a feeling in the darkness of the presence of God, but an overwhelming experience of this presence. Furthermore, the divine light isn't entirely known by just anyone, at the beginning, but its knowledge is an eternal progress, according to the theology of St. Gregory Palamas. The consciousness of this unending reserve of light—but strictly speaking it isn't an awareness, as neither is the incomprehensibility of the divine nature—is an unceasing experience

---

[98] I. Hausherr says: "The theology of the whole light cannot integrate the supra-luminous darkness. And this is why it hasn't conceived the idea of joining under the same symbol the dark and happy night, knowing and unknowing, light and obscurity, union and disintegration, joy and the suffering of contemplation.... To remark in passing, Palamism has nearly eliminated darkness from its theology. Due to the real distinction between essence and the energies of God, it has disassociated the Dionysian notion of a "total unknowing, which is the knowledge of Him Who is above everything which can be known" (Dionysius the Areopagite, *Epistle* 1, *PG* 3.1065). We have now, on the one hand, total unknowing of the essence and, on the other, a knowledge of the energies which is no longer darkness. To the extent that contemplation can become "complete light" in connection with the energies and remain total darkness in connection with the divine essence. But in such a way too the Dionysian idea is lost in depth, and we enter or remain in the Evagrian intellectualism or in the estheticism of Macarius." "*Do the Easterners* (the Orthodox) *know the 'nights' of St. John of the Cross?*", p. 45.

in the seer of the light. If, however, he becomes wholly light, this doesn't mean that he fully understands, but he becomes full of mystery, as a deified supernatural being, and he is continuously surprised by what has happened to him.

In the West the one who understood the "darkness" of Dionysius in this positive way was Cardinal Nicholas of Cusa. He explained this darkness not as an absence of light, nor as a real mixture of darkness and light, as Hausherr wanted to have it for Hesychasm, but as an abundance of light which by this very fact overwhelms the vision and can be called not only light but darkness too.[99]

But let's talk a little more about the apophatic steps beginning with the first.

---

[99] "He, however, who leaves behind the visible light enters in a necessary way into something which is no longer visible light and therefore for the eye it is darkness. And when he finds himself in this darkness, which is a darkening for the eye, and knows that he is in a darkness caused by the incapacity of his eyes, he also knows that which has penetrated before the sun. Because that darkness for the eye comes from the supra-luminosity of the sun." Nicholas of Cusa, *De Visione Dei*, German translation by E. Bohnenstadt, *Das Schauen Gottes* (Leipzig-Meiner, 1942), p. 70.

28. Negative and Positive Theology: A Dynamic Relationship

Negative theology is still a mental operation, the final one, mixed, however, as prayer is, with a feeling of the powerlessness to comprehend God. It is related to the comprehension of God through nature, history, Holy Scripture, art, dogma and in general through everything which is between us and God either as an external reality or as a system of concepts and symbolic images. Every reality, concept or symbolic image mirrors God as well as awakens in us the proof or unexplainable feeling that God is totally different, in comparison with them; so they compel us to negate all the positive attributes which, because of them, we ascribe to God. In other words all things in between open for us a perspective to God; at the same time they confront us with an infinite abyss of divine reality which we can't grasp with our minds, and which first of all doesn't show us anything that created realities, concepts and symbolic images do. But our mind, faced with this abyss still doesn't give up looking at things, concepts and symbolic images, but turns its gaze from this to that and finds that they don't give it the means to describe the abyss. It tries, we might say, to measure it with every measure in the world, in other words with every attribute or image, or with every concept based on created things. Finally, the mind realizes that not one is suitable. So it eliminates them one by one. Negative theology is therefore a mental operation because it investigates the content of various attributes and concepts and compares them with the divine abyss, which it lives somehow with feeling, and finds that they are insufficient.[100]

In a certain sense, negative theology is still a rational operation; it is still an exact weighing of each concept, whose limits only now appear to the mind in all their clarity. But the comprehension of the definite content of a concept is made at the same time as we cast our gaze over the divine abyss which reason can't encompass, but which the mind gains by intuition, by a look or feeling of another nature; so this operation, although on the one hand mental, isn't only rational, not only deductive, but has an intuitive element in it, the ascertaining of which is limitless and therefore can't be described. It is a rational operation by which the mind concludes, nevertheless, that reason is insufficient.[101]

---

[100] St. Gregory Palamas says: "But we too know that in negative theology the things which negate God, the mind understands." *The Defense*, 2.3.35, p. 477.
[101] Jacob Bohme makes a distinction between reason, which can't comprehend much, and understanding (*Vernunft, Verstand*) which, without eliminating or covering the mystery, penetrates it. A. Koyré, "Gotteslehre Iacob Böhmes," in *Jahrbuch für Philosophie und phenomenologische Forschung* (Niemeyer, 1929), p. 234. We attribute this capacity of understanding or at least of the discernment of the mystery, to the mind which is the largest faculty of knowledge—reason

It is an operation by which reason itself becomes conscious of its limits and of its inability to lay hold of the totally different and infinite One. With its gaze the mind doesn't abandon the solid shore of definite things, but aided by its own kind of feeling *(noera aisthisis)*, it goes from definite things to the divine abyss— it hesitates between the two. Negative theology doesn't discard or forget, as being totally useless, the positive concepts gathered from the created world. Because even if it sees that they don't correspond to God, nevertheless only in comparison with them does it find that God is something else. The mind considers these concepts one by one when it negates them in relationship to God. Therefore negative theology doesn't eliminate the enriching of our spirit with concepts ever higher and more enhanced. It also measures divinity with them and always finds it incomprehensible; so the feeling of the divinity's unsurpassable glory overwhelms us even more. "In this sense the knowledge of God is a dynamic process," as a Christian thinker describes it:

> The limits which are imposed by agnosticism do not exist. The gnosis which searches for truth further and further afield and ever more deeply is an effective possibility, for the process of knowing God is a movement of the spirit which has no end. But the mystery always remains and can never be exhausted.[102]

Negative theology needs positive terms to negate. And the loftier they are, the more subtle, the better they express the richness of the power and imagination of God who created the realities expressed by them— and by their negation they also make an icon (a negative one) of the divine glory which is also higher than they are. Negative theology doesn't justify a laziness of the spirit, an abdication of reason, but requires a continual raising of the scaffolding of reason; then on the higher steps, the limitless divine ocean can appear to us in a vision which will thrill us even more. Negative theology, far from forever insisting on the renunciation of rational concepts, longs for their growth. It is the supra-rational point of the untiring exertions of reason which must never stop its investigation of nature, of human life, of Scripture. Any progress whatsoever in the knowledge of physical, biological and psychological processes within the womb of creation means a new level on the scaffold from which negative theology, guided by a feeling of the mind, gains a deeper and broader view of the divine incomprehensibility, which at the same time itself makes possible the continuous building

---

is only a part of it, the discursive. Reason is often, in its function, accompanied by the mind which sees more than it does. So much so that many times reason stifles or scorns the mind's view. But in negative theology the mind imposes it's more decisive role.

[102] Berdyaev, *Freedom and the Spirit,* p. 65.

up of this scaffold. So we don't think that the disrespect with which some Orthodox theologians speak about positive theology is right. If the world and Scripture are the revelations of God, and they tell us something positive about Him, it is clear that positive theology has its rights. How would it be if we no longer said anything positive about God, not even that He is: Wouldn't religious life itself be endangered in the absence of any affirmation? What would happen if we wouldn't say that God is great and full of love? If God hasn't revealed Himself by creation and that we haven't known Him at all by supernatural revelation.[103] But once He has been pleased to reveal Himself by them, we must use them to say something positive about Him. It is true that positive theology is a theology of the finite, but far from excluding the infinite, it makes the ascent to Him possible. "Only if it is used without negative theology does it have but a limited character, being adapted to this world and to the natural man, so that [it possesses] only a pragmatic and juridical value."[104] The divine reality is infinite and inexhaustible and cannot fit into rational concepts.

Therefore we must say only that positive theology has the continuous need for the negative, just as the negative does for the positive. He who emphasizes negative theology, however, borrows the terms of positive theology, which he continually negates. More than that, he must first have tried, and continually be trying to approach the divinity with the terms of positive theology in order to know that they don't fit it and consequently to negate them. In other words, someone can't use negative theology except in alternation with the positive. The cause for this is found in the human spirit, but not only there; it is something deeper.

Strictly speaking, there are two deeper causes:
1. First, the ultimate creative principle which made existence and which can explain it can't be as the world itself. Otherwise it wouldn't be the ultimate principle and transcendent to the world; the uncreated being wouldn't differ from the created world. Second, this principle and this source must include everything which can explain existence and the content of the world. So the absolute and transcendent principle can't contain even one of the qualities which are found in the world or in any

---

[103] Koyré says, repeating the thought of Jacob Böhme: "On the other hand it's clear that it is precisely created nature which allows us to elevate ourselves toward God in his quality of its Creator and foundation. If the created world didn't exist, presupposing that we would still be present to ask such a question, we wouldn't know anything about God. If God wouldn't make Himself known through nature, if He wouldn't have created, but would have remained eternally in Himself without revealing Himself, we would know absolutely nothing about him." *op. cit.*, p. 232.
[104] Berdyaev, *Freedom and the Spirit*, p. 65.

of its parts. It can't be a part of the world, not even a basis of the world, of the same essence as it is, neither existence itself as we know it, because this existence requires its explanation in something superior to it, other than it. It can't be anything but the negation of existence, if we understand by this the imperfect form of the existence of the world, the only one which we know. It is the negation of any category of this existence; to sum it up, it is non-existence.[105] But because the absolute principle is the source of the power which has made everything, which has made possible the existence which we know and which explains the nature of all things, it must have a certain relationship with things and with the world; it must have a certain likeness with things of which it is the creative and fundamental principle. Existence, with all its variety, must have something in it which makes it possible, on the basis of certain *logoi* and energies, which correspond to different attributes of the world.

Thus, even in the relationship of this creative principle with the created world stands the cause which we must speak about in contradictory terms, those of positive and negative theology; in a way all the attributes of the world fit it, but at the same time, not one is adequate, not even existence. This creative principle is the same for all things and is shared by all things and at the same time is absolutely "other," totally unlike them. On the one hand it is inaccessible to understanding, because it completely transcends it; but on the other hand because something which can't be understood, can't in any way be a principle of the world; it must be understood to some extent, in order to explain all things by it.[106]

So both ways of approaching the absolute, the positive and the negative, are equally necessary and legitimate; they are both likewise insufficient. The first cause, as Dionysius the Areopagite puts it, is above affirmations and negations. Both are needed to properly direct the mind toward Him, but neither do the two together reach all the way to Him. If God were only finite in relationship with the world, and not different from it too, negative theology wouldn't be necessary. It would be enough to extend, with the imagination to the infinite, every attribute of the world by the so-called lofty way of analogy and we would have an attribute of God. But this would mean that God is in a continuity of nature with the world. So even if there were a difference between Him and it, this wouldn't be a dif-

---

[105] "God is *Nichts*, says Jacob Böhme" Koyré, *op. cit.*, p. 225 *ff*. This study is a fragment from Koyré's book, *La Philosophie de Iacob Böhme* (Paris, 1929).
[106] Koyré, *op. cit.*, p. 227.

ference of nature between God and the world. Yet God isn't only infinite, but also absolutely other than the world. So the lofty way *(via eminentiae)* isn't enough, or the method of analogy to correct the insufficiencies of positive theology. God is absolutely indeterminable, not just because every determination is complete within the finite, and He is infinite, but especially because no category whatsoever of existence which we know fits Him, while at the same time neither does the more general category, that of existence, fit Him. In fact His existence isn't incorporated so to speak in the larger kind of existence as such. But He is outside and above existence in general. Not even the words *is* or *exists*, with which we designate everything that is more general, which is common to all things and beings, are suitable for Him, because neither do they take us out of the created order. So just the amplification of the attributes of the world to the infinite isn't enough to characterize Him, not even their correction by an analogical attributive. After this, negative theology is still necessary. It considers that even the equivocal idea of analogy must be negated, no matter how many possibilities it leaves for keeping God very distinct from the world, even though, on the other hand, the things in the world must have a certain analogy with God.

2. Another justification for negative theology, but in alternation with the positive, is the fact that the nature of God is other than that which its manifestations and its works show. All the names which we give to God refer to these manifestations or works which show their effect in the things and attributes of the world. They do not show the divine nature. Therefore, on the one hand, we give God many names, on the other, He is the unnamed; by nature no name is suitable for Him.[107] When we think of the manifestations of God, we make positive manifestations about Him, but when we think about His nature, we negate all affirmation. The names which we give God refer to the divine energies which descend to us, according to St. Basil, not to His nature which remains inaccessible;[108] they refer to the powers which radiate as so many rays from God *(proodoi)*, creating and sustaining different aspects of the world. *Being* is the name which is given to the being-creating energy; *wisdom* to the energy which creates wisdom, says Dionysius the Areopagite. Above them, however, is the divine "hiddenness" to

---

[107] Dionysius the Areopagite, *The Divine Names* 1.5, in *The Divine Names and The Mystical Theology* (London, 1979), p. 59.
[108] *Against Eunomius* 1.6, PG 29.521-4; 2.4, PG 29.577-580; 2.32, PG 29.645-648.

which no name can be given and which enters into no relation *(aschetos)* and isn't imparted at all.

"For all Divine things, even those that are revealed to us, are only known by their Communications. Their ultimate nature, which they possess in their own original being, is beyond Mind and beyond all Being and Knowledge. For instance, if we call the Super-Essential Mystery *(hyperousion kryphiotita)* by the name of 'God,' or 'Life,' or 'Being,' or 'Light,' or 'Word,' we conceive of nothing else than the powers that stream therefrom to us bestowing Godhead, Being, Life or Wisdom....."[109]

But that hiddeness remains above *(hyperkeitai)* these powers; it is above being, above divinity *(hypertheos)*, above life, above every name and impartation.[110] Certainly our names, borrowed from the effects of the divine energies in the world, don't adequately touch even these energies. So the negation of names is justified if and when we think of them. But nevertheless we can attribute these names to them, adding to them the coefficient of a use by analogy.[111]

St. Gregory of Nyssa also develops at length the idea that the nature of God is higher than anything, that we comprehend all the names from what He does in relationship to our life and that therefore, these names refer to these multiple actions:

> For God is not an expression, neither hath He His essence in voice or utterance. But our God is of Himself what also He is believed to be, but He is names, by those who call upon Him, not what He is essentially (for the nature of Him Who alone is unspeakable), but He receives His appellations from what are believed to be His operations in regard to our life.[112]

"Whereas no name comprehends the divine nature, we use many names, making it as far as possible for each of us to understand something about Him from the wide variety of their meanings."[113] From works the human mind expresses as much as it can. "'For,' as saith the Wisdom of Solomon, 'by the greatness and beauty of creatures propor-

---

[109] *The Divine Names* 2.7, *op. cit.*, pp. 73-4. These are called "the beneficent Emanations of the Supreme Godhead." *Ibid.*, 2.11, pp. 78-9. *(agothoprepeis proodooi tis thearchias)*.
[110] *Ibid.*
[111] "For there is no exact similitude between the creatures and the Creative Originals; for the creatures possess only such images of the Creative Originals as are possible to them, while the Originals Themselves transcend and exceed the creatures by the very nature of Their own Originality." *Ibid.*, 2.8, p. 75.
[112] *Against Eunomius* [Answer to Eunomius' Second Book] 12, *PG* 45.960; NPNF, second series 5.265.
[113] *PG* 45.967. This quotation is not in the place cited. *trs*

tionably the Maker of them is seen.'"[114] But in applying such appellations to the Divine essence, "'which passeth all understanding,' we do not seek to glory in it by the names we employ, but to guide our own selves by the aid of such terms toward the comprehension of the things which are hidden."[115]

The holy Fathers, in order to show that the divine nature can't be known, that it is something else than its manifestations, give us an example of created things, whose nature also remains inaccessible:

> We pass our lives in ignorance of much, being ignorant first of all of ourselves, as men, and then of all things besides. For who is there who has arrived at a comprehension of his own soul? Who is acquainted with its very essence.... But how can he who is ignorant of himself take knowledge of anything that is above himself? And if a man is familiarized with such ignorance of himself, is he not plainly taught by the very fact not to be astonished at any of the mysteries that are without? Wherefore also, of the elements of the world, we know only so much by our senses as to enable us to receive what they severally supply for our living.[116]
>
> For as they who would indicate some person ... as of good parentage and descent ... or rich ... and in so speaking they do not set forth the nature of the person but give certain notes of recognition... thus to the expressions of Holy Scripture ... that He is without cause and without limit: they are from the things around Him *(ek ton peri ton auton)*.... But His very essence, as not to be conceived by the human intellect or expressed in words, this it has left untouched as a thing not to be made the subject of curious inquiry, ruling that it be revered in silence, in that it forbids the investigation of things too deep for us, while it enjoins the duty of being slow to utter any word before God.[117]

And St. Gregory Palamas, speaking of the relationship between the many energies of God and His simple nature says:

> God has all these, better said He is above all things, unitary and undivided, just as the soul has unitarily in it all the powers by which it cares for the body. Because just as the soul, even when the eyes are blind and the eyes deaf, has in it the powers to care for the soul, so even when there is no world, God has in Himself the providential powers of the world. And as the soul is one and simple and uncomposed, not multiplying and not being composed because of the

---

[114] Wisdom 13.5.
[115] St. Gregory of Nyssa, *op. cit., PG* 45.961, *NPNF* 5.265.
[116] *Ibid., PG* 45.945C, 949B; *NPNF* 5.261-2.
[117] *Ibid., PG* 45.945; *NPNF* 5.260-1.

powers which are in it and come out of it, the same with God, although He is not only multi-powerful, but all powerful, doesn't lose His simplicity and unity because of the powers which come from Him. In as much as God is a being above being, unspeakable and unthinkable, without outside relations and non-partakable; in as much as, however, He is the being of things and the life of the living and the wisdom of the wise, He is conceived of, named, and partaken of by the created.[118]

So, because of the fact that, by His hidden nature God is unknowable but by His works which come into the world and are mirrored in their created effect, He is knowable, stands the necessity of expressing God antinomically, in other words in positive terms, immediately replaced by the negative. Thus on the one hand we must say that God is life, according to His life-creating power which He manifested by working in the world; on the other hand we must say that He isn't life, because the hidden nature from which the life-giving power comes and acts in the world, isn't identified with this, but is greater than it. God is a nature, wisdom, power, goodness, according to the powers which come from Him, according to the manifestations in the world, but His nature, as an infinite source of innumerable powers, isn't any one of these, or all of them together; He is more than all of them and is totally indeterminable. They are all from God's nature, uncreated and inseparable from it, but nevertheless they are not identical with it.

The nature of God isn't any one of these, but not in the sense of the lack of them, but of the surpassing of them *(kath hyperochin)*, says Palamas. God, on the one hand is existence, on the other, He isn't, but not in the sense that He doesn't exist, but that He is above existence.

Our soul and its manifestations offer an analogy of this relationship between the nature and powers of God and thus an illustration of the necessity of alternating positive and negative terms in relationship to Him. For example, we can say that He is mind, will, feeling, movement, if we think of all His acts of thought, will, feeling, of movement. But immediately we must correct ourselves and say that He is neither thought nor will, feeling, movement, because as the source of all these actions, He is more than all of them and isn't depleted by them: He remains forever above, as a center distinct from them and indeterminable.[119]

---

[118] *The Defense* 3.2.22, p. 683.
[119] S.N. Bulgakov, *Tragedie der Philosophie* (Darmstadt, n.d.), pp. 139-42, makes a distinction between the "I" transcendent to our knowledge and determination, between the nameless "I," from that indicated by a substitute for a name (a pronoun), and between its physical, voluntary, and intellectual manifestations, as Palamas does between the absolute-transcendent nature of

NEGATIVE AND POSITIVE THEOLOGY   253

According to the view of the holy Fathers there is a mystery of things and of natures, but especially a mystery of the divine nature. In negative theology the consciousness of this mystery of the divinity is expressed; but as in the "I know that I know nothing" of Socrates, this same consciousness is expressed in relationship to the general mystery of things. The mystery, however, isn't put as an immovable wall of absolute darkness in front of our minds. So it would be if it had no manifestation whatsoever. But from it lights flow unceasingly, and they show its presence and contours. Mystery means an interminable reserve of truth which, revealing its aspects to the infinite, remains forever an inexhaustible reserve; it means the spiritual bread of the mind, imparted continually to all minds and never exhausted. Without a divine transcendent nature of knowledge, eternally inexhaustible in its manifestation of light and power, we would soon finish the work of knowing the truth. That would mean, however, that it is limited and that the thirst of our nature to know is finite. But we see that it can't be so. Our nature in this case would reach an insupportable boredom and our immortality itself would be without purpose. Reincarnations were invented as some kind of palliative for this boredom.

Without unceasing emanations of light, without creative and perfecting power, mystery would lack the purpose of fertility for the spirit; it would be as though it didn't exist, contributing nothing to the growth of the light. By the lights which it emits unceasingly from itself, we are given the power to formulate positive affirmations about the truth. But they don't express the whole truth, but only continuously new sparks

---

God and His works, which enter into a relationship with the world and are made known. Only by them do we know something about Him: They are His predicates. [They designate a property or relation.] The "I" is truly real, nevertheless it doesn't exist in the ranks of existences in the usual sense, just as the center of a circle isn't a usual point on the surface of a circle, as it is often asserted in geometry. It could be said that the "I" isn't existence (in the usual sense). So neither can it be expressed, for the concept is a symbol of existence, a taking hold of it; it fully belongs to the sphere of existence, of which the "I" doesn't. Even so, the word "I" is for everyone an intelligible, mystical sign which points to the depths of the inexpressible, to the depths of the darkness, from which the light frequently tears away a little piece, which becomes "light" because it defines something of itself. The "I" points to the depths of the unspeakable, of the totally indefinable, to the depths of the supraluminous shadows, to the ultimate supraexistential source, from which something continually spills over to the knowable surface. The "I" is the subject of the sentence for any predicate whatsoever, for anything that can be said about it. It is, however, above everything which can be said about it. "It is our physical subject, in other words that sea continually moved by states, experiences, excitement, passions of the noumenal 'I.'...And not only the physical subject, but also the gnosiological 'I,' in other words its step forward in existence.... In the ultimate analysis the 'I' must be determined antinomically, in the same way as negative theology: On the one hand the 'I' is a full and definite 'no,' because in the usual sense it 'isn't,' but nevertheless it doesn't become a zero, a vacuum, non-existence, because it has supraexistence; on the other hand, the 'I' is everything, because the whole can become its predicate. The tie between the 'I' and the predicate can't be severed even for a moment."

from it. But this doesn't discourage us. An eternally fertile nature does exist, so we have the possibility of an infinite progress in the knowledge of the truth. This eternally new mystery is the infinite Person and only a person can have a thirst for Him. The eternal dynamic of knowledge implicates not only the inexhaustible mystery and the apophaticism which belongs to it, but also the relation between the Supreme and the created person.

Affirmative theology expresses the grain which can be taken from the "nature" of the truth—negative theology, the consciousness or evidence that these grains aren't everything, that by them the knowledge of the truth isn't finished. It expresses the consciousness or evidence of the inexhaustible mystery, which as such is the inexhaustible source of the truths which will be known in the future. Positive theology strikes the balance of the truths already known. Negative theology gives the assurance for the knowledge of the future. Thus, far from being discouraging, negative theology is just that which invigorates our spirit with the unending perspectives which the mystery, as the never failing womb of truth, opens to our spirit.

29. Pure Prayer

As we have seen from a previous quotation, St. Gregory Palamas knows a step superior to negative theology: a fuller and more existential apophaticism, realized by pure prayer.[120] It is an ecstasy of interior quietness, a total cessation of thought in the face of the divine mystery, before the divine light descends to the mind thus stopped by astonishment.[121]

So before we concern ourselves with the higher steps of the knowledge of God by complete silence and by the vision of the divine light, we must consider pure prayer. Prayer itself has several steps, each one corresponding to one of the steps of man's spiritual ascent, because prayer must permanently accompany man on his ascent.

Making an abstraction of the prayer which seeks material good and which is inferior, we can judge the progress in praiseworthy prayer according to two criteria: by its object and by its more or less perfect concentration, and by the state of the quietness of the soul that is praying. In regard to the first criteria, Evagrius recommends that first of all you should pray "...to be cleansed of passions, secondly to be delivered from ignorance and forgetfulness; and thirdly from all temptation and abandonment."[122] In their generality these three kinds of prayer, distinguished by their content, correspond with the three phases of the spiritual ascent: purification, illumination and union. In regard to the second criteria, on any step, pure prayer must try to keep the mind unplundered by any thought or care.[123] In the measure in which it succeeds in more fully, and for a longer period of time, in expelling thoughts, it is a more perfect prayer.[124] The truly perfect prayer is a pure one, in other words the one that the mind makes when it has reached the capacity to easily expel, and for a long time, any thought while it prays. But man

---

[120] Also called noetic prayer or prayer of the mind. *trs*
[121] "Thus the mind slowly abandons all relation with these things, and even with those superior to them, in order to be totally separated from all beings through pure prayer. This ecstasy is incomparably higher than negative theology, for it belongs only to those who have attained impassability. But it is not yet union, unless the Paraclete illumines from on high the man who attains in prayer the stage which is superior to the highest natural possibilities, and who is awaiting the promise of the Father; and by His revelation ravishes him to the contemplation of the light." *The Defense* 2.3.35, p. 477; *cf. The Triads*, p. 65.
[122] *On Prayer* 38, *GrPh* 1, p. 180, under the name of Neilos the Ascetic. *cf. Phi* 1, p. 60.
[123] "Struggle to make your mind deaf and dumb during the time of prayer, and then you will be able to pray." *Ibid.*, 11. *GrPh* 1, p. 178; *cf. Phi* 1, p. 58.
[124] "Sometimes standing at prayer you will be able to pray well right away...and the mind finds itself at much rest praying purely at once. Other times with the usual war threatening us the mind struggles and can't quiet down, because formerly it was mixed with various passions. Even so, if it keeps on seeking, it will find." *Ibid.*, 29-30, *GrPh* 1, p. 179; *cf. Phi* 1, pp. 59-60.

attains this capacity only after he has gained freedom from the passions. Not even innocent thoughts should any longer trouble the mind when it prays, during pure prayer. So pure prayer is made only after the mind has been raised from the contemplation of visible nature and from the world of concepts, when the mind doesn't have any image or form or concept.[125] Therefore we think that pure prayer is also such when it no longer has any object. After it has passed over everything in the order of their ever-higher values, the mind only asks for the mercy of God, feeling Him as the Lord on whom mercy depends. Two more criteria could be added, however, with which the progress of prayer is measured: the decrease in words and the increase in tears.[126]

On its peaks, prayer is pure because it no longer has an object and it no longer uses any word whatsoever. The mind free from everything is conscious that it is face to face with God; so it is also called prayer of the mind.

Of course, not even on the highest peaks of the spiritual life, is the mind emptied of all content, all the time, even of the simple, nonpassionate ideas of things. If, nevertheless the one who is struggling for perfection is required to pray more and more without interruption; this is strictly speaking, a more and more unceasing remembrance of the name of God or of Jesus. However, this doesn't mean the exclusion of innocent ideas, but prayer in parallel with them, as a means of its maintenance in purity.[127] So "unceasing prayer" is something else than "pure or mental prayer," during which the mind no longer has any idea, or thought, besides the formless thought of God.

Certainly there is a close relationship between "unceasing prayer" and "pure prayer." The one and the other use the same few words. Then too, someone can't reach perfect prayer all at once, which is pure prayer. He must have gotten used to having God in mind all the time; it must have become a sweet thought of God. So pure prayer is but the flame which flares up more and more frequently from the fire of unceasing prayer.

In general Eastern spirituality recommends the following conditions for the mind to reach the state of pure prayer:

---

[125] "He who has reached dispassion still doesn't truly pray. Because maybe he is following some simple thoughts and is taken up with them and he can be far from God." Evagrius under the name of Neilos the Ascetic, *On Prayer* 56, *GrPh* 1, p. 181; *cf. Phil* 1, p. 62.
[126] "Tears during prayer are a sign of the mercy of God, which your soul has been made worthy of in its repentance." Isaac the Syrian, *The Ascetical Homilies*, p. 126: "Silence is a mystery of the age to come, while words are an organ of this world." *op. cit.,* Epistle 3, p. 319.
[127] Mark the Ascetic, *On Baptism, RoFil* 1, p. 304.

1. The mind must come back from things outside to within itself, to its "heart," forsaking every object. Certainly by the mind, the action of the mind is understood, as St. Gregory Palamas explains it.[128] And the heart, to which it must return, is nothing but its center, where it no longer looks outward towards things, but towards God. The mind, returning to the heart, returns home from loneliness, we read in *Watchfulness and Guarding the Heart* by Nicephorus the Monk.[129] Diadochos sometimes calls this the mind's "inner shrine," sometimes the "depths of the heart."[130] And when by "mind" its action is understood, its center is called heart; and when by the mind its nature is understood, then the center is called "the depths of the mind" or "the inner shrine" of the heart, etc.

2. It should maintain only a few words addressed to Jesus, in other words the insistent remembrance of Him. They help it to avoid scattering and guide it towards the one goal which it must reach. Even the most pure prayer must keep the thought of the presence of Jesus.

In Diadochos of Photiki these words are reduced to just two, that is, to what is strictly essential to keep Jesus in mind as our master: "Lord Jesus." Later several words were added to them. By them a partial petition isn't expressed, because that would give the mind an object, a definite form. So we use only a general petition for Christ's mercy, which expresses the feeling of the need for His mercy. Here is the usual content of this short prayer: "Lord Jesus Christ, Son of God, have mercy on me a sinner." These words contain, along with the consciousness of Jesus' presence, the thought of personal sinfulness and the need for His mercy. They express a relation of man's dependence not on an impersonal force but on the loving mercy of a supreme Person. This feeling doesn't need concepts to be lived but it creates and sustains a unitary, simple, existential state of humility before the merciful Jesus.

The first petition is tied in a necessary way to the second. If the mind can give up images and concepts it can't give up in general every kind of activity and feeling, except for a few moments of silence or of interior rapture, reached at the height of prayer. So if the mind's exits are closed and it is forced to return to its center, "to the heart," it must be given

---

[128] "There are, however, those who assert that the mind is not separate from the soul but is interior to it, and who therefore question how it can be recalled within. It would seem that such people are unaware that the essence of the mind is one thing, its energy another." *The Defense* 1.2.5, p. 129; *cf. The Triads*, p. 44.
[129] *GrPh* 4, pp. 16-28.
[130] Diadochos, *On Spiritual Knowledge* 59, *Phi* 1, p. 270.

another content; in other words that one content in which we want it to gather. Thus the statement by Diadochos:

> We shall escape this debilitating and torpor-making passion if we vigorously hold our thought within very narrow limits, seeking only the remembrance of God. Because only when the mind turns itself again to its warmth can it be delivered without pain from this unreasonable scattering. When we shut all the outlets of the mind with the remembrance of God, it seeks an occupation which will put its full worth to work. We must give it the *Lord Jesus*.[131]

When the mind, that is its activity, returns to the heart (to the depths of the mind), and is preoccupied with the continuous short prayer addressed to Jesus, several results are obtained:

1. The mind (its activity), no longer spends its time looking at external things, and isn't in danger of being robbed by passionate thoughts.[132] Thus the mind conquers its instability and scattering; it becomes unitary and concentrated or simplified.
2. By this concentration and by the name of Jesus it also guards its interior from sinful thoughts. Sometimes it is said that the heart must be kept so that passionate thoughts don't enter it, or that it must be cleansed of the thoughts which rule it.[133] But Diadochos of Photiki has explained that this heart in which passionate thoughts can enter isn't the heart strictly speaking but the regions around the heart, thus in general the interior of the soul. "The spirits from below" try to penetrate it, as St. Gregory Palamas says, from the passionate subconscious.[134] The guarding of the heart, in this sense, means to leave no part of the soul or any movement of the body, unsupervised. In another sense, the guarding of the heart really means the guarding of the mind, so it doesn't leave the heart.[135]

---

[131] *Ibid.*, 58-9, *GrPh* 1, pp. 250-1; *cf. Phi* 1, p. 270. See also St. Nicodemus of the Holy Mountain, *A Handbook of Spiritual Counsel* 10 (New York, 1989), p. 159, the paragraph, "When the mind Is in the Heart It Must Be praying."

[132] St. Mark the Ascetic says: "The mind, as soon as it leaves the heart and the searching for the Kingdom of God found within it, immediately makes a place for the bait (the attack) for the devil and leaves itself open to receive his evil suggestion." *On Baptism, PG* 65.1016B.

[133] In the method attributed to St. John Chrysostom we read: "The thought directed to our Lord Jesus Christ shakes all the work of the enemy in the heart; it conquers this work and gradually pulls it up by the roots. When the name of the Lord Jesus Christ descends into the depths of the heart, it conquers him who completely rules there, while it saves the soul." See D. Staniloae, *The Life and Teaching of St. Gregory Palamas,* [in Romanian], Sibiu, 1938, p. 45.

[134] *The Defense* 1.2.9, p. 137.

[135] The method of St. John Chrysostom says: "Keep the heart under full guard, so that somehow it doesn't lose the thought of God, but in a pure and uninterrupted remembrance let the thought for God be imprinted in your souls, as a seal." Staniloae, *op. cit.,* p. 45.

PURE PRAYER

3. But even if these thoughts themselves can't enter the heart, they bunch up around it, and keep it from being opened. They array themselves as a cloud around it and it loses the habit of looking openly toward heaven. Heaven has become a simple potentiality, which no longer makes its existence felt.

So at the beginning, the mind which wants to return to the heart hardly finds the way. It must struggle much with the thoughts around it, to make its way toward it and to open it. In other words, the mind with difficulty regains its habit of looking toward God, by means of the heart, of being preoccupied with Him, of reopening its eye whose function is to see the spiritual. Yet the working of the mind, accustomed to occupying itself with exterior things, can regain its habit of being busy with God. It can return completely to the interior, into the heart and open it. Then it meets God there, face to face, without seeing Him by any image, or without thinking of Him with any concept. Then it lives His presence directly, or feels itself in His presence.[136] Penetrating into the heart, it meets Jesus Christ Who has been there— in other words, in the transconscious, where the grace of Jesus Christ has been— since Baptism.[137] It begins to use the great treasures there and the capacity to grasp divine realities. Because it puts itself in a living communication with Christ Himself, the source of all the supernatural powers and meanings.

Pure (or mental or noetic) prayer doesn't contribute to the knowledge of God through creation but by the depths of its own soul, by the heart. This is strictly speaking a direct feeling of Him, because man also forgets the heart when, gathered in it, he feels himself in the presence of Jesus Christ, in the atmosphere of the Kingdom of heaven, found with it.[138] St. Isaac the Syrian says that then, even the movement of prayer ceases in the mind, because it is enraptured by the divinity and glory of the Master, whose wonderful presence is felt. He writes: "So prayer is interrupted in time of prayer by its movement and the mind is taken and immersed in the astonishment of rapture and forgets the desire for its petition."[139]

---

[136] "Continually shout in your heart the name of the Lord Jesus that the heart might swallow the Lord, and the Lord, the heart, and the two become one. This thing isn't accomplished in a day or two, but over a long period of time and there is need for much effort and toil until the enemy is driven from it and the Lord comes to dwell there." *Ibid.*
[137] "And again the mind will have power to watch over the heart and to keep it with all diligence; it will try to penetrate into its most distant and quietest rooms...which are the dwelling of Christ." St. Mark the Ascetic, *On Baptism, PG* 65.1016D, 1017A.
[138] *Ibid.*, 996.
[139] *The Ascetical Homilies* 32, p. 117.

4. This state is also called the opening of the heart because it is pierced by love for Jesus.[140] The mind begins to feel a pleasure from insistently remembering the name of Jesus and at the same time tries to get to the things within. If not, it is a sign that it hasn't yet found the "heart" or that it hasn't been opened. But it's enough that the mind makes the effort to return to itself and to remember the name of Jesus insistently. Because by so doing, the Lord Himself pushes the wall of the heart aside and shows Himself.[141] He draws the mind to Himself, and plants in it love for Him.[142] St. Diadochos continues:

> Grace itself then thinks together with the soul and cries out together with it: "Lord Jesus Christ."[143] [Because immediately] ... we need His help to unite and gladden all our thoughts with His ineffable Sweetness, that we might be moved with all our heart to the remembrance and love of our God and Father.[144]

So that these two essential requirements, which are suitable in some way also for unceasing prayer, may be more easily realized, certain methods were sought in the realm of Eastern monasticism; they consist of a support for the effort of the mind to return to the interior by certain procedures in which the body is engaged too. These procedures are based in general on the interdependence of the soul and body, or on the unity of their movements. Just as states of the soul are prolonged by exterior bodily attitudes and movements, so too gestures and exterior positions, if they are accompanied by the concentration of thought on them, have a considerable influence on the states of the soul.[145] A humble soul makes the body kneel, but also kneeling accompanied by the concentration of thought on God creates a state of humbleness in the soul. The abstract spirituality of some of Western Christianity, which is seen in the realm of religious practice, is unnatural. Such spirituality has forced its postures; it is realized only by a coerced blockage of the wave

---

[140] "The perfect love of Christ is the innermost opening of the heart, where Jesus has entered as Forerunner." St. Mark the Ascetic, *op. cit., PG* 65.1009C.
[141] *Ibid.*, 996CD.
[142] Diadochos, *op. cit.*, 59, GrPh 1, p. 251; *cf. Phi* 1, pp. 270-1: "But so arduously and unceasingly should you look at this word ('Jesus Christ') in your inner chambers, that it will never stray toward some image.... As a result the Lord will draw the soul to the love of His glory. For when that glorious and much desired name lingers by the remembrance of the mind in the warmth of the heart, the habit to love His goodness is immediately sown in us."
[143] *Ibid.*, 61, GrPh 1, pp. 251-2; *cf. Phi* 1, p. 271.
[144] *Ibid.*
[145] Max Scheler: "The religious act is basically spiritual, but in its performance it is always of a psychophysical nature, not only physical.... He who prays on his knees, prays with an idea of God different from that of the one who prays standing.... Pascal said: 'Just get down on your knees, and you will gain piety.'" *Vom Ewigen im Menschen, pp.* 555-7; *cf.* this same book in English, *On the Eternal in Man* (New York, 1960), pp. 265-6.

of feeling which, born in the soul, moves toward the body, or born in a bodily posture spreads over the soul.

30. Methods for the Facilitation of Pure Prayer

The methods which have been developed in the East to facilitate the elevation of the mind to pure prayer, by certain procedures, or better said by variations of these methods— because the differences between them are a matter of emphasis— are the following:

1. The method which bears the name of St. Simeon the New Theologian.[146] It is called *The Method of Holy Prayer and Attention (Methodos tis ieras proseychis kai prosochis)*, and its old Greek text was edited for the first time by I. Hausherr in 1927.[147] It is the oldest text put in writing that we know of; it was found in a codex from the end of the eleventh to the beginning of the twelfth century.[148] The proof of this was given by M. Jugie, against Hausherr,[149] who taking up once again the view of several previous authors that this method can't be of Simeon, argued for the first time that it belonged to Nicephorus the Monk, who lived in the second half of the thirteenth century.[150] This opinion, however, had to be abandoned for good, as the result of a text which we had the good fortune to find in the unedited writings of Palamas and which we published.[151] Palamas knew the method of Nicephorus the Monk, but he didn't associate it with that known by the name of Simeon the New Theologian; he also knew the latter as the author of a distinct method.[152]

So even if Simeon the New Theologian isn't the author of this method it is older than that of Nicephorus the Monk which dates to the thirteenth century, since Gregory Palamas had received this tradition from his predecessors, some of whom had known Nicephorus.

---

[146] We're not going to refer to the method ascribed to St. John Chrysostom, discussed in the previous chapter, which is probably older than St. Simeon's, because it doesn't have a single technical-physiological procedure. In general it pleads for the essential recommendations analyzed earlier: the return of the mind to the heart and the recitation of the prayer addressed to Jesus. See Staniloae, *The Life and Teaching of St. Gregory Palamas* [in Romanian], pp. 44-5.

[147] I. Hausherr, *"La méthode d'oraison hésychaste"* Orientalia Christiana IX-2, no.36 (June-July, 1927), pp. 54-76. This *method* was previously unpublished except in a modern Greek paraphrase in the *GrPh*, 2nd ed., 2, pp. 512-18, (4th ed., 5, pp. 81-9) from which it was reproduced in *PG* 120.701-10.

[148] Vatican Greek 658.

[149] M. Jugie *"Les origines de la méthode d'oraison hésychaste"* Echos d'Orient (April-June, 1931): 179 *ff.*.

[150] *Ibid.*

[151] *The Life and Teachings of St. Gregory Palamas* [in Romanian], Sibiu, 1938, pp. 54-5. This text, "Against Barlaam," is found in *The Defense* 1.2.12, p. 143.

[152] *Ibid.*

The *Method* of St. Simeon the New Theologian begins by showing that there are three kinds of prayer. The first two are seductive—only the third is a "bearer of light." The first form of prayer is accompanied by the work of the imagination. He who prays raises his hands, eyes and mind to heaven and begins to mentally envision things divine, heavenly blessings, angelic hosts, the dwellings of the saints—all that he has heard from Holy Scripture he thinks about, during prayer; by them he moves his soul to the love of God—yes, he sheds tears too. So he begins to get proud without realizing it and thinks that this state is a gift of God. Sometimes this kind of prayer is accompanied by the pretensions of extraordinary phenomena, such as bright visions, sensations of incense, unreal voices. All these are signs of an error which can drive a man crazy because he hasn't first gained dispassion and the virtues. He is in the ranks of the beginners.

In the second kind of prayer the mind, after it has already turned away from perceptible things and from the sensations which come from outside, now concentrates on the words of the prayer; now it examines the thoughts which rush into the soul and tries to expel them. It is a battle which doesn't allow it to be quiet and to develop virtue. The great danger which is ready to ambush the one who gives himself to this kind of prayer is vainglory, which makes him look down on others. This second kind of prayer, says the *Method*, surpasses the first as a night with a moon surpasses night without stars and light, or as youth surpasses spiritual infancy. This is the phase of psalmody, of delight with tender words. In the first phase psalmody is impossible, because "one can't sing to the Lord in a foreign land, or from a passionate heart." This is the prayer of the advanced.

The third kind of prayer begins by obedience; during it the mind guards the heart and from its depths it sends up its petitions to the Lord. It is the prayer of the spiritual man. This kind is possible, however, only if the soul has already reached perfect dispassion. It has eliminated all affections for the world and by obedience to a spiritual father has gotten used to not having its own way. The soul has mortified every worldly passionate desire. The mind of such a person can no longer be swayed by the devil, by trickery, toward various thoughts, but stays free of them all; he is able to easily reject any thought that comes to him, so that he can pray with a pure heart.

As can be seen, anybody, anytime, even according to this method, can't reach pure prayer all at once, by using certain physiological methods, as Western theologians have taught in derision. Rather it is the coronation of prolonged efforts to be purified from the passions and thoughts. Only after someone has gained a clear conscience before God, men, and the things of the world, can he use these procedures as auxiliary means to gain pure prayer. So it isn't the procedures that are essential, but the permanent state which someone has gained. For him it is easy to offer pure prayer, one way or another. So the one who has attained dispassion and purity will want to be lifted up from time to time to the state of prayer free from every thought; so he must gather his mind in the depths of his heart and from there send up his prayer to God. He can then also use the following auxiliary procedures for the gathering of the mind in the heart:

> Sitting in a quiet cell, alone in a corner, do what I tell you: Close the door and lift up your mind from all that is vain and passing. Then rest your beard on your chest and direct your physical eyes with all your mind toward yourself. And hold your breath a little, in order to keep your mind there and to find the place of the heart, where all the powers of the soul are used to being found. First you will find an intense darkness, impenetrable.[153] But by doing this night and day you will find— what a miracle— an unspeakable bliss. Because as soon as the mind finds the place of the heart, it sees what it has never thought possible: It sees the air in the darkness of the heart and its whole self, full of the power of discernment, and at the same moment, when a thought appears, it rejects it and destroys it, by calling on Jesus Christ, before it can coagulate and take form.[154]

But the *Method* also knows a fourth level of prayer, of the spiritual elder, when the mind no longer has a need of such auxiliary physiological means, of such toils, to reach its state of concentration in the heart, but reaches this state immediately and remains motionless in contemplation. Only this terminates the ladder of prayer. From this it is seen that the physiological recommendations are of use only for those who haven't yet gotten used to pure prayer, but are becoming familiar with it. They are for those who haven't yet become steadfast in dispassion.

Coming back to the third level of prayer described in the above passage, we note three elements taken precisely from Diadochos of Photiki: the gathering of the mind in the heart with the calling on Jesus Christ, the light which the mind sees there, and the easy rejection of every thought.[155] What is unique to the *Method* are the following physiological elements:

---

[153] So it is in the modern Greek text in the *GrPh*. The detail with the "navel" is only in the medieval Greek text published by Hausherr and it seems that it was interpolated by certain adversaries of the Hesychasts.
[154] Symeon the New Theologian, *GrPh* 5, pp. 86-7.
[155] *On Spiritual Knowledge* 59, *Phi* 1, pp. 270-1.

a. The directing of the sight toward the chest, that parallel with this the mind can seek and find the place of the heart.
b. The holding of the breath [breathing very slowly].

For the last detail, the *Method* doesn't give any explanation at all; the other methods explain respiration completely. So it is hard to believe that this *Method* would have made such a recommendation without presupposing that some explanations were known. This makes us believe that although the *Method* attributed to Simeon is older than the others which we know, it isn't the first. It's obvious that there was a practice, a tradition with several variations complete with explanations. He who put this *Method* in writing was editing one of these variations. He also put it down in writing rather informally, and more for his own use and for those around him; so he didn't give detailed explanations. They were known by an oral tradition.

2. During the period of Hesychasm the method which enjoyed the greatest authority was that of Nicephorus the Monk. So even then very little was said of Simeon as the author of any method. We believe that besides that it never had any significant authority, because it didn't give any important explanation in regard to respiration.

The *Method* of Nicephorus the monk is the second oldest that we have. He was born in 1215, and in 1260 he came to Athos where he learned the art of quietness from the most eminent fathers, so that later he in turn could become the guide of the younger.

He put together a collection of patristic explanations for them, which would strengthen them for the battle and show the kinds of warfare and the rewards and crowns of victory. He saw that they couldn't struggle against the instability of the mind so he also drew up for them a procedure by which they could stop the scattering and the fantasy of the mind.[156]

One of Nicephorus' disciples was also the teacher of Palamas. The Hesychast movement at Athos began strictly speaking with Nicephorus so his procedure was also the most practiced. But because he too learned from others the art of prayer, his procedure expresses in depth an existing practice. The first part of his method is a collection of patristic explanations and the second the procedure itself. It was first

---

[156] See the fragment from Palamas, *The Defense,* the Second Treatise of the Second Series, Codex Coislinianus 100, f. 157 r-v, discovered and published for the first time by D. Staniloae, *The Life and Teaching of St. Gregory Palamas*, pp. 54-7.

published in the Greek *Philokalia* where it is entitled *On Watchfulness and Guarding of the Heart.*[157] It was reprinted in *PG* 147.960 *ff.*

Here is the procedure which, according to Nicephorus "quickly leads to dispassion and the vision of God":

> You know that we breathe in air and that we breathe for nothing else, but because of the heart, since the heart produces the life and warmth of the body. So the heart inhales that it can expel its own warmth and obtain a suitable temperature. The cause of this economy, or better said too, is the lung, which having from God a rare fabric, like bellows, inhales and exhales the content without difficulty. So the heart, drawing in by respiration cool air and putting out the warm, properly keeps the order for which it was put there for the maintenance of the organism. You then, sitting and gathering your mind, introduce it, that is the mind, by way of the nostrils, where the air goes to the heart, and force it to go, along with the inhaled air, to the heart. Entering there, the lack of joy and bliss will cease. Like a man who, returning home from being away, doesn't know what to do because of the joy of being worthy to return and to see his children and wife again, so the mind, when it unites with the soul, is filled with unspeakable pleasure and happiness. So, brother, teach the mind not to leave there easily. Because at the beginning it wants to often leave the enclosure and the restraint of what is within. You must also know that, when your mind is there, you must not remain in silence and laziness, but have as an object of constant thought the words: 'Lord Jesus Christ, Son of God, have mercy on me.' And if you toil much and cannot enter the places of the heart, as I have shown you, do what I tell you and with God's help, you will find what you are looking for. Know that every man's power of thought is in his chest, because in the inside of the chest even when our lips are still, we speak, we decide, we pray, psalmodize and so on. Give the 'Lord Jesus Christ Son of God, have mercy on me' to this thinking power; expel every thought from it, because you can if you want to. And force it to shout this within, instead of any other thought. If you do this for a certain time the entrance to the heart will open to you, as I have written to you, without any doubt. We know this from experience. And all the host of the virtues, love, joy, peace and the others, will come to you along with that much longed for and sweet attention.[158]

As can be seen, in this *"Word"* we have not one method, but two: one which recommends that the place of the heart should be sought from the beginning, that the mind should be sent there along with inhalation; another which recommends, for the same result, the simple but

---

[157] *GrPh* 4, pp. 16-28.
[158] *Op. cit.,* pp. 27-8.

persistent recitation of the prayer addressed to Jesus. The second doesn't differ from that attributed to St. John Chrysostom, as proof that the physiological procedures weren't considered necessary at once. And first he says nothing of the position of the body or of the direction of the eyes, but he explains only the reason why the respiration must be disciplined. This proves that it is only the explanation of some recommendations left unexplained in the *Method* of Simeon the New Theologian, or that he presupposes that an existing practice is known. Better said, the observation that the power of thought is found in the chest and that it must recite where it is the prayer of Jesus would justify us in accepting that Nicephorus the Monk presupposes some kind of directing of the sight toward the chest.

In any case, in Nicephorus' *Method*, the only physiological element that is a little strange is that of the breathing. He explains first the purpose which respiration has: It keeps the temperature around the heart moderate. In the organism there is combustion which produces a certain heat. The heart especially feels this warmth. The air which we inhale has the purpose of tempering this warmth. In fact it is a common experience that when we inhale we take in cold air, and when we exhale our breath is warm. This can maintain a calmness and so the possibility of prolonging prayer.

But Nicephorus' *Method* stops here with its explanations; there are no practical conclusions. In other words it doesn't show that from the above premises there is the necessity of having regulated breathing, because if a normal temperature and a natural disposition are maintained this influences the spiritual life for the good; it's known that an accelerated respiration, in other words the intake of insufficient cold air (rich in oxygen) and the insufficient elimination of warm air (loaded with carbon dioxide) promotes warmth in the body and along with it, a state of uneasiness. The man who breathes too fast can't think quietly. Likewise the man full of passion, breathes fire and fury, as we say; he doesn't get enough oxygen nor exhale enough carbon dioxide so he snorts through his nose and mouth. The control of a passion is also obtained by the calming of respiration, as a proof of the inter-dependence between soul and body. In general we know that quietness and self-control go along with keeping cool, with a temperature not fired up by fast breathing, by some passionate movement of the body. A full stomach, for example, heats up the blood, while hunger keeps it cool.

Nicephorus doesn't use the scientific terms of combustion, oxygen, and carbon dioxide, which chemistry gave us later. But his observations are the precise record of a process, according to its empirical side; so they express, in their own way, a scientific truth.

Because he doesn't finish his explanations, but interrupts them before he draws a conclusion, we see that neither does his *Method* express all the elements which made up the basis of the procedures and which surely many were familiar with. In any case we see that the ones who initiated these practices knew about them. So we realize that it isn't based only on Simeon's *Method*, but on an existing practice, as the latter one too. From this point of view Simeon's *Method* is more complete, because although it doesn't give any explanation, it recommends a holding (back) of the breath. On the other hand, that of Nicephorus gives explanations, but doesn't require the holding of the breath. In Simeon's *Method* it says, however: "Hold your breath then, so you don't breathe easily."

It seems that there is a contradiction between the two methods. On the one hand they teach that accelerated breathing disturbs the inner state— it doesn't absorb nor eliminate enough air. So they recommend breathing which does this satisfactorily. On the other hand the breathing is reduced so that respiration isn't easy. This would likewise mean an insufficient intake and elimination of air— as a result respiration would be accelerated. But by taking a closer look we discover that a reduction of breathing— of inhalation and exhalation doesn't mean a lessening of the air received and removed, but only a lengthening of these actions, and so a slower rate. Air is received and expelled more gradually, not all at once, but precisely because of this it is received and eliminated more completely. Only by this reduction does the breathing take place completely; and so the temperature and the normal and steady disposition of the body, and that of the soul too, are maintained. Furthermore, this development of the process of respiration keeps the whole organism in a quiet state and the mind can concentrate undisturbed.

But Nicephorus the Monk, although he gives explanations, stops before he draws any conclusions. He goes on to another idea in connection with respiration; better said he becomes preoccupied with drawing another conclusion in regard to the rhythmic character of respiration. So after he has shown that the purpose of breathing is to maintain "a proper temperature" in the organism, he continues: "You then, sitting and gathering the mind, introduce it into the nasal passages where the air goes to the heart and push it and force it to go, along with the inhaled air, to the heart."[159] This doesn't mean the nature of the mind, as Palamas explains, but its action, in other words it's thought and attention. By this recommendation the attention is stopped from being directed toward outward things and is brought back to the interior. Cer-

---

[159] *GrPh* 4, p. 27.

tainly, attention isn't something physical, that can be sent through the nose with the air of the heart. It isn't any less true that it can follow a physical movement. Here it is recommended that the attention follow the movement of the air as far as the heart. Because we don't feel the movement of the air, however, after it leaves the lungs, our attention must make its way further to the heart by imagery. But neither must it stop at the physical heart, but keep going, to the spiritual heart and overcome all things. Strictly speaking this is the intent: Thought returns to itself; it gives up every definite object, and because it can't comprehend itself, after it has withdrawn from everything it is given a preoccupation: the thought of Jesus Christ. The following of the path of inhalation is an auxiliary means for this withdrawal of the attention from things, for the return of thought to itself.

This imagery plays a great role. The feeling of the course which the air takes to the heart— it attracts our attention to it— makes us imagine, that parallel to it, our thought too is going into us. In fact it does. But not on a material path and it doesn't stop at our physical heart. This material path, followed with attention, is an occasion which facilitates and symbolizes the movement of the thought returning to itself. A comparison is how bringing the hands to the forehead helps the mind concentrate on something. Inhalation must be prolonged, because parallel with it the thought is also going to the interior, until it is completely alone with the thought of Jesus. And this action must last, so that it can become accustomed to going there and staying there. Of course, the retention of the mind in the heart for a longer time isn't realized only by the prolongation of inhalation but also by the retardation of exhalation. But here Nicephorus the Monk doesn't give any details. Gregory of Sinai does, however, in his *Method*. On the one hand he passes on the recommendation from Simeon the New Theologian's *Method* to hold the breath; on the other hand he draws from it the necessary conclusion to slow down the exhalation. He shows how this too is necessary for the mind to stay in the heart longer. If Nicephorus shows how the mind can be driven toward the heart by inhalation, Gregory of Sinai shows how it can be kept there longer by slowing down exhalation.

The *Method* of Gregory of Sinai thus sheds new light on the subject; of course all he did was to write down other explanations from the vast number that went with an existing practice. So if Simeon's *Method* has nothing distinctive, the other two compliment each other, or are completed in the rendering of an existing practice.

3. Gregory of Sinai was born around 1255. He journeyed as a pilgrim through Cyprus, Sinai and Crete where he learned from

the hermit Arsenius, the Hesychast practice.[160] He couldn't have reached Athos before he was at least 35-40 years old, thus before 1290-95, if not later. In other words, after this the Hesychast method of prayer was made known and practiced there by Nicephorus the Monk and by those from whom he had learned it, as well as by his disciples. So it can't be said that Gregory of Sinai introduced this method at Athos; at most he caused a revival of the practice.

The unionist Emperor Michael the VIII Paleologos exiled and killed the antiunionist monks at Athos between 1277-81; the Holy Mountain would have felt this devastation for a long time. Nicephorus the Monk, a very old man, would no longer have made the effort to return to Athos. Arsenius, a Cretan monk who introduced Gregory of Sinai to the Hesychast practice, might have been a refugee from Athos and wouldn't have been totally foreign to the person of Nicephorus the Monk, himself exiled to an island not far from Crete. So Gregory of Sinai doesn't appear to have been an initiator, but only a reorganizer, a zealot and an interpreter in writing of the Hesychast practice. This could also be substantiated because he isn't a target for Barlaam, as was Nicephorus the Monk, or a victim of the attacks that took place at the end of the fourteenth century, as Simeon the New Theologian was. Barlaam with precision attacks the *Method* of Nicephorus the Monk and that which goes by the name of Simeon the New Theologian, but not that of Gregory of Sinai. Palamas never mentions Gregory of Sinai, nor do the Hesychast authors Callistus and Ignatius, in the *Directions to Hesychasts*. Neither do they mention Simeon the New Theologian, but they speak only of Nicephorus' *Method*.[161] It is interesting, however, that Gregory of Sinai in his *Method* mentions Simeon the New Theologian and uses quotations from his *Method*, but he never mentions Nicephorus' *Method*.

Here now is Gregory of Sinai's *Method* :[162]

> Sitting from morning until evening on a stool about as wide as the hand is long, gather your mind from the reason *(ek tou igemonikou)* to the heart and hold it there. With effort *(emponos)* bend the chest, shoulders and neck, so you feel great pain and cry out persistently with the mind or soul *(noeros i psychikos)*: 'Lord, Jesus Christ, have mercy on me.' Then, moving your thought to the other half, say: 'Son of God, have mercy on me.' And saying this half many times, don't change them [the halves] continually because of laziness—

---

[160] J. Bois, *"Grégoire le Sinaïte et l'hésychasme à Athos au XIV siècle"* Echos d'Orient 5 (1901-2), p. 67.
[161] See D. Staniloae, *op. cit.,* pp. 62-3; *Directions to Hesychasts, PhilPH*, pp. 162-270.
[162] *GrPh* 4, p. 72.

plants that are transplanted continually don't take root. Slow your breathing too, so you don't breathe easily,[163] since the gentle air coming out of the heart darkens the mind and abducts the thought. It carries the mind away and makes it a prisoner of forgetfulness or makes it go from one thought to another. Thus it finds itself without realizing it where it shouldn't be. And when you see the unclean things of evil spirits, or of thoughts coming up or forming an image in your mind, don't bother them; even if the pure images of things appear to you, don't pay any attention to them, but slow your breathing as best you can. Enclose your mind in the heart and continually and persistently call on the name of Jesus Christ. And so you will burn them quickly and destroy them, conquering them with the divine name. John of the Ladder says: 'Conquer your enemies with the name of Jesus, because there is no more powerful weapon in heaven or on earth.'[164]

Regarding the recitation of the Jesus Prayer, Gregory of Sinai writes:

... some say that it be said with the mouth, others with the mind. I recommend both, for sometimes the mind can't say it, being overwhelmed with cares, other times the mouth can't. Therefore you must pray with both, with the mouth and the mind. It is necessary only to speak quietly and without agitation, so that somehow the mind doesn't trouble the feeling and attention of the mind and hinder them. This until the mind, getting used to this work will make progress and receive the power of the Spirit to be able to pray fully and persistently. Then it is no longer necessary to speak with the mouth, but neither is it possible; then it's enough to carry on the work with the mind.[165]

This would be what Simeon the New Theologian's *Method* calls the fourth level of prayer. The regulation of breathing is only a means, which helps some to bring the mind back to itself. The divine Spirit brings it there permanently; His work is felt after we have toiled much to gain pure prayer. St. Gregory of Sinai comments:

No one can hold the mind by himself if the Spirit doesn't hold it. Because by disobedience to the commands, the mind backslides and is separated from God; it is carried everywhere as a prisoner. He restrains his mind and holds his breath by shutting his mouth; but he doesn't succeed for long—it is scattered again. When the action of

---

[163] *Ibid.*, p. 71. The idea in this passage is taken from the *Method* ascribed to Simeon the New Theologian. St. Gregory of Sinai's *Method* is published in the *GrPh* 4, pp. 71-9. The reader will also find it in the *PhilPH* as the second half of St. Gregory's *Instructions to Hesychasts*, pp. 84-94, starting with the heading "On Silence and Prayer." *trs*
[164] *GrPh* 4, pp. 71-2.
[165] Fr. Staniloae gives no reference here. *trs*

prayer comes, however, it truly keeps the mind with itself and it fills it with joy and it delivers it from slavery.[166]

In Gregory of Sinai's *Method* we neither find the explanation from that of Nicephorus the Monk as to why we breathe [as a part of the prayer], nor the recommendation to force our thought along with the air toward the heart, but we do find two other details: an explanation of the recommendation from St. Simeon the New Theologian's *Method* to slow breathing and the advice to recite alternatively the words of the Jesus Prayer.

The breath must be delayed, according to Gregory of Sinai, because it slows down the hurried or sudden exhalation of the air from the heart, which would cause a darkening of the mind, or an exit of it from within. In fact, a hasty and noisy exhalation on the one hand, doesn't leave time for the thought to concentrate little by little in the interior; on the other hand, it attracts attention to it, drawing it from within. Therefore it's good that both inhalation and exhalation be slow and noiseless. If the one who prays gets used to this prolonged and quiet rhythm of breathing, it will no longer bother him; it will just help him to concentrate the mind within. Such a person forgets that he still has respiration, although it makes this concentration possible.

Gregory of Sinai is the first who tells us that a short prayer addressed to Jesus must be divided in two and that each half must be said for a time. In fact, if the prayer were said completely each time, it would force the attention to the abundance of words and the mind wouldn't be able to concentrate. Later on, new recommendations will be given in this regard.

4. St. Gregory Palamas, in his writings, defends those who use such auxiliary means; he doesn't consider them absolutely necessary, but only as useful in some measure for beginners. So he doesn't recommend all of them, but only some:

> To teach beginners especially to look at themselves and to bring their mind within through respiration, isn't something reproachable. Because it wouldn't be right for any sensible man to prevent him who hasn't yet the mind capable of contemplating itself, to concentrate by just any method. The mind of those who are at the beginning of this struggle, even when it concentrates, jumps around continually and therefore must be brought back continually; because they are inexperienced their mind, being very unstable, gets away from them all the time

---

[166] *Instructions to Hesychasts* 1, *GrPh* 4, p. 81; *cf. PhilPH*, p. 75. The Greek title is, "How the Hesychast must sit at prayer and not quickly get up."

and contemplates itself with difficulty. For this reason there are some that counsel them to watch their respiration and to hold it a little, their inhaling and exhaling and to thus succeed in concentrating the mind by it [the breathing]. This until, making progress with the help of God toward the good and making their mind inaccessible to what is around it and making it pure, they will be able with precision to bring it back to a 'unified recollection.'[167]

Although St. Gregory Palamas only mentions Simeon the New Theologian and Nicephorus the Monk, the explanation regarding the slowing of breathing could only have been taken from St. Gregory of Sinai's *Method*, or from the practice itself.

5. In the treatise by Callistus and Ignatius new details are given as to how to gather the mind in the heart and to concentrate it completely on the Jesus Prayer. In general the treatise expresses the *Method* of Nicephorus, but neither is it foreign to what goes by the name of Simeon the New Theologian nor to that of Gregory of Sinai; in other words it recommends the sitting on a narrow stool (Gregory of Sinai) and in a corner of the room (Simeon the New Theologian):

> And before these things, or rather before everything, this contest is won in the mind, with the help of divine Grace, along with an insistent, sincere, and focused calling on our Lord Jesus, in faith. But not simply by this natural method, that is by breathing through the nose, or by sitting in a quiet and dark place— God forbid— does the mind succeed in arriving at pure prayer. These were invented by the divine fathers only as auxiliary methods *(synerya pos onta)* for the gathering of thought and for its return to itself from its usual scattering.[168]

The details which Callistus and Ignatius offer are the following:

> After sunset, calling on the all good and all powerful Lord Jesus Christ for support, sit on a stool, in a quiet, unlighted cell. And gathering the mind from its usual exterior loitering and wandering, and pushing it quietly into the heart by nasal inhalation, hold on to the prayer, that is the 'Lord Jesus Christ, Son of God, have mercy on me,' introducing that is, in some way, along with the inhaling, in a unified way, also the words of the prayer.

---

[167] *The Defense* 1.2.7, p. 133; *cf. The Triads*, pp. 45-6.
[168] *Directions to Hesychasts* 24, GrPh 4, p. 224; *cf. PhilPH*, p. 195.

In other words they recommend that, along with the thought of these words, that one should also think of death, judgment, the reward of good works and the punishment of evil; yes, the one who is praying should consider himself a greater sinner than all men and dirtier than the demons. Thus thinking of the eternal punishments which he will have to undergo, he begins to feel his heart pierced and tears start to come. If they don't come yet he should keep on until they do, because this cleanses the passions and stains:

> And if tears don't come, sit and pray with these same thoughts along with the prayer, an hour; and when you stand up, carefully chant the little compline; and sitting down again, keep to the prayer, as much as you can, purely and without distraction, in other words without worry and thought and dreaming, with much soberness, for half an hour.[169]

So too they recommend that in the morning one spend an hour concentrating in pure prayer, then a sung prayer, and again a half-hour of pure prayer.[170]

In general the monk must pray unceasingly. Better to "choose death than to remain a moment without prayer," for "the soul which doesn't move toward prayer is dead" and "he who prays talks with God."[171] But one can't concentrate in pure prayer just any time, lacking any thought whatsoever; the recommendations given above serve this prayer as preparatory and auxiliary means.

On the other hand, one must not wait until he is fully consolidated in dispassion, in order to try to concentrate in pure prayer. Progress in dispassion and in pure prayer come simultaneously. At the start, with great effort, some moments of pure prayer can be won and at once it raises thoughts which must be struggled with. He who, however, has come:

> ... unto the measure of the stature of the fullness of Christ' (Ephesians 4:13) partakes of divine love, by pure and unscattered prayer of the heart, and thus becomes perfect and unbending in spiritual prayer and has a part in unmediated ecstasy and rapture and union with the One longed for, due to perfect love.[172]

So the recommendations of the methods, with the difficulties which they describe, are addressed only to those who are at the beginning of the efforts to gain pure prayer, who consequently haven't reached a full

---

[169] *Ibid.*, 25, *GrPh* 4, p. 224; *cf. PhilPH*, p. 195.
[170] *Ibid.*, 26, *GrPh* 4, pp. 225-6; *cf. PhilPH*, pp. 197-8.
[171] *Ibid.*, 29, *GrPh* 4, pp. 228-9; *cf. PhilPH*, p. 200.
[172] *Ibid.*, 46, *GrPh* 4, pp. 245-6; *cf. PhilPH*, p. 221.

dispassion either. The recitation too of all the words of the Jesus Prayer are suggested only for beginners. The advanced remain only with the name of Jesus, while the perfect, only with its uninterrupted mental commemoration. If the frequent commemoration of Jesus is recommended for all, or the recitation of prayer to Him, only the perfect reach the state of pure, perpetual prayer:[173]

> So prayer which is made within the heart with attention and vigil is beyond any thought or fantasy whatsoever. By the words, 'Lord Jesus Christ, Son of God,' the mind reaches out completely, immaterially and effably, toward the Lord Jesus Christ Himself, and by the 'have mercy on me' it returns and moves toward itself, not being able to suffer nor able to pray for itself. But progressing in the living of love he focuses totally on the Lord Jesus Christ Himself, because he has visible evidence of the second part [of the prayer].[174]

6. Nicodemus the Aghiorite, the learned church writer of the eighteenth century, gives us more detailed explanations of the ancient physiological explanations, which really amount to the return of the vision to the chest and the slowing down of respiration.[175]

In regard to the first Nicodemus tells us:

> You know that everything has a natural relation with the essence and the power which make it go and it naturally returns to this essence and unites with it, and rests. So when the work of the mind is set free from all exterior things of the world by the guarding of the senses and of the imagination, it must be brought back to its essence and power, in other words the mind must be made to enter the heart, which is the organ of the essence of the mind and its power. This return of the mind, the beginner must get used to doing… , bending his head and resting his beard on the upper part of his chest.[176]

By the return of the mind to itself, it becomes one, and by itself it raises its thought to God. The mind, entering the heart, must not be left with nothing to do, but must give itself to meditation on the Jesus Prayer.

---

[173] *Ibid.*, 52, *GrPh* 4, p. 251; cf. *PhilPH*, p. 227.
[174] *Ibid.*, 48, *GrPh* 4, pp. 246-7; cf. *PhilPH*, p. 222.
[175] These explanations are given in *A Handbook of Spiritual Counsel* 10 (New York, 1989), p. 158, "In What Way Does the Mind Return to the Heart and That This Return Is Not a Deception," and p. 160, "Why One Needs to Control His Breath in Prayer."
[176] Nicodemus of the Holy Mountain, *A Handbook of Spiritual Counsel* [in Greek], Athens, 1987, p. 170.

Nicodemus doesn't only repeat the idea of Diadochos; he develops it. But first let's hear from Diadochos himself:

> And when the mind is found in the heart, don't let it just contemplate, and do nothing else; but finding the inner logos *(endiatheton logon)*, that is the inner logos of the heart, by which we think and compose and judge ourselves and examine and read whole books silently, without the mouth speaking; this, I say, your mind finding the inner logos, don't let it say anything else but this short prayer called *monologistos*, 'Lord Jesus Christ, Son of God, have mercy on me.'

And now, let's listen to St. Nicodemus:

> But this alone isn't enough; it also requires that you put into motion the will power of your soul, that is you must say this prayer with all your will and strength and love. I state it very clearly. Let the inner logos say only the above prayer, and let the mind pay attention as much with its mental sight, as with its mental hearing only to the words of this prayer and much more to what the words mean, remaining without images, without forms, without picturing anything, without thinking of any other perceptible thing, within or without, even if it is good. Because if God is beyond all beings perceptible and imperceptible, the mind too, seeking to unite with God by prayer, must go out of all beings, perceptible and mental, and even beyond them, in order to reach divine union.... And let your will be joined completely by love to the words of the prayer, so that the mind, the inner logos, and your will, the three aspects of the soul, may be one, and the one three, because by this means that man, who is the icon of the Holy Trinity, is joined and united with the prototype, as that great teacher and doer of mental prayer and attention said, I mean the divine Gregory Palamas of Thessalonica: 'When the unity of the mind becomes three, remaining united, then it is joined with the threefold monad of the Godhead, closing the door to error, and remaining above the flesh, and the world and the ruler of the world.'[177]

So Nicodemus the Aghiorite starts with the return of sight toward the chest, which is for the beginner a means that facilitates the breaking away of thought from external things and its concentration on itself, on its own unlimitedness. Then he shows how the way to the contemplation of God goes from the freeing of the mind from the narrowness adapted to finite objects to the discovery of the divine infinite. So the concentration on this unlimitedness of the mind is at the same time a concentration with all its facilities on the divine infinite. However, this unification of the mind with its limitlessness doesn't come about all at

---

[177] *Ibid.*, chapter 2, "On Prayer," pp. 173-4; *cf.* Nicodemus, *A Handbook of Spiritual Counsel*, pp. 159-60.

once, but by a previous putting into operation for this purpose of all the mental faculties: the mind, strictly speaking, reason, and will. The mind would be the general supervisor of understandable things, reason would be discursive thought, which brings into relief each element of a whole thought, and stabilizes the relationships between them, while will would be the loving guide of this whole thought toward Jesus. So at the beginning an indistinct meditation on the words of the prayer aren't enough; a bringing out of all the meanings contained in it, existential meanings which awaken the loving attachment of the will to Christ, is necessary. From this rational, but also existential, analysis of all the meanings contained in this prayer, we raise ourselves to an embrace and unitary contemplation of the content of it, directed toward Jesus with all love.

In essence, the unified mind to which Nicodemus the Aghiorite wants us to raise ourselves, so that by it we can see God, is not an immobile abstraction. It is nothing but the mind on fire with the love of God and conscious of its own sinfulness. From this state Callistus and Ignatius and Callistus Cataphygiotis, other authors of the *Philokalia*, want us to raise ourselves. And the sign that we have arrived at there is the shedding of abundant tears.

Likewise the slowing of breathing during prayer must serve this concentration of the mind. Here, Nicodemus the Aghiorite brings, along with the explanation given above, a detail which we haven't encountered so far: We must not breathe in perfect continuity as our nature is used to. The breath must be held a bit until the interior reason says the whole prayer all together. First it must meditate on all its words. A total interruption of the process of inhalation-exhalation can't take place, however, and especially right between the two, where it seems that Nicodemus wants the prayer to be said. So we think that the intent here is likewise just a prolongation of inhalation a bit more than the usual. His refinement consists especially in the fact that the recitation of the words are attached to inhalation and not to exhalation, because, according to the ancient methods, by inhalation the thought returns to the interior. At the time of exhalation it is better to be quiet, in order to also keep the thought within and so that the attention not be a prey to the movement of air.

The prolongation of inhalation, a little beyond the usual also produces a kind of discomfort, pain, a suffering of the heart, says Nicodemus the Aghiorite. First, it humbles it, refines it, breaks it. It throws out from it the poison of pleasure and secondly, it makes it attract the attention of its mental powers to itself. Thus the holding of the breath a bit prolongs the act of the concentration of the mind within. So it also produces this existential state of humility and defeat, and brings on tears, a state which the mind must gain. It must gather in wholeness before Jesus, unseen but felt as present.

Palamas had to speak of this bodily pain too. He showed its use, against Barlaam; the latter conceived the state of mental prayer as a one of pure and comfortable intellectuality, in distinction to the Eastern Fathers. They thought of it as a state joined with existential elements, with affection, with humility, with tears, with pain felt physically and at the same time with joy which overflows from the spiritual depths of the soul. Only in ecstasy, or beyond it too, every bodily feeling whatsoever, ceases.[178]

7. We have seen, however, that almost all authors studied so far, know, along with the more complicated method of controlling respiration, and of the turning of the eyes toward the chest, a more elementary method too: the simple but ever increasing recitation of the words, "Lord Jesus Christ, Son of God, have mercy on me a sinner." This is what makes up the method attributed to St. John Chrysostom and those of St. Simeon the New Theologian and of Nicephorus the Monk. The latter also established the relation between this more simple method and the more complicated ones: He who can't start out from the beginning with them, should begin with the simple and ever more frequent recitation of the Jesus Prayer.

This was put into practice in nineteenth century Russia not only by monks, but also by the so-called pilgrims, or pious people, who giving up everything, walked around the whole country speaking the Word of God; it might surprise us that it was even practiced by people living the usual life in society. This diffusion of the Jesus Prayer among the masses of the Russian faithful comes to us in the form of the confessions of one of the pilgrims, who practiced it. His little book is called *The Way of a Pilgrim*. The author remained anonymous. It was printed the first time at Kazan in 1883, by the Abbot of the Monastery of St. Michael, who had copied it from a manuscript which he found at Athos. The story seems to have taken place between the Crimean War and the freeing of the Serfs, in other words between 1856 and 1860.[179]

According to this account, the whole development of the spiritual life, from the beginning right up to the highest steps, takes place on the thread of the Jesus Prayer. The spiritual life begins with the oral recita-

---

[178] *The Defense* 2.2.7, p. 361.
[179] We have used the German translation, *Ein russisches Pilgerleben* (Berlin: Petropolis Verlag,1925), translated by Reinhold Walter. In French it appeared in the Irenikon collection under the title, *Recits d'un pelerin russe* 4 (1928, 5-7). See also *The Way of a Pilgrim and The Pilgrim Continues His Way*, trans. by R. M. French (San Francisco: Harper, 1991).

tion, within short intervals, of this prayer. It deepens and purifies the person to the extent that he recites the Jesus Prayer more frequently, more interiorly, and more automatically.

In the stories told by the Russian pilgrim, however, the Jesus Prayer goes through three phases. The first phase is that of a simple recitation of it, at the beginning 3000 times a day, later 6000, then 12000, then constantly.[180] After a time the practitioner can go on to the method attributed to Simeon the New Theologian. He tries, with the imaging of the place of the heart, to regulate his respiration, to synchronize the words of the prayer with the beating of the heart and with the rhythm of breathing. But even now he hasn't yet reached mental prayer. He reaches this when the mind by itself makes the prayer, totally without words, as its own permanent movement, parallel with the beating of the heart. If the first two phases are especially called the Jesus Prayer, the third is called in distinction mental or pure prayer. It follows that the Jesus Prayer becomes gradually a mental prayer; also the content of mental prayer is likewise Jesus.

The synchronization obtained in the second phase constitutes a refinement of the ancient methods, although it isn't ruled out that this synchronization also existed in the ancient practices, even if the written methods don't explicitly tell us so. The synchronization with the beating of the heart consists of a recitation or thought of each word of the prayer at the same time as a heart beat. This, after which its practitioner has gotten used to representing the place of his heart and hearing its beating. Here is how the pilgrim initiates a blind man into the teaching of this synchronization:

> After I had read to him what was necessary from the *Philokalia*, he began to beg me to show him how the heart can be found with the mind and how the divine name of Jesus Christ can be introduced into the heart. I began thus to explain to him: 'Now you can't see anything, but you can imagine and picture with your mind what you used to see, for example a man or an object, or one of your members, such as your hand or foot and you can imagine it just as real as when you saw it materially in front of you. Isn't it true that you can in this way direct your eyes, blind as they are, toward something?'
> 'Yes I can,' he said.
> 'Then picture your heart, direct your eyes there, just as though you were looking at it through your chest, and picture it as vividly as you can, and listen very attentively with your ears, how it moves and beats each time. When you have done this, start to recite with each

---

[180] Walter, pp. 16-7; *cf.* French, pp. 13-14. Here we find the unsuccessful attempt to apply all at once the *Method* ascribed to Simeon the New Theologian.

heart beat, looking into it, the words of the prayer. On the first beat say or think the word 'Lord,' on the second 'Jesus,' on the third 'Christ,' on the fourth 'have mercy,' on the fifth 'on me,' and do this as many times as you can.'[181]

After getting used to this synchronization, that with respiration starts too. This takes place in a different way. During inhalation the first half of the prayer, "Lord Jesus Christ" is recited, and during exhalation the second half, "have mercy on me."[182]

This synchronization can't be realized but by prolonging the respiration, that its duration corresponds at least with three heart beats while the first three words of the prayer are being recited. After more or less getting used to it, the practitioner joins as much as possible the respiration and the pulse with the words of the Jesus Prayer, or with the thought of them, so that there is no longer the heart beat or breathing which isn't joined with them. The prayer becomes the breathing of life, of the soul.

If it consisted only in the habit of reciting the words of the prayer simultaneously with the beating of the heart or with respiration, this synchronization could become something mechanical. But the principle accent isn't put on the words, but on the thought of each word, until, in the phase of mental prayer, the recitation ceases— only the repetition of their meanings with thought is left. The repetition with meaning becomes an uninterrupted habit. Parallel with the breathing of the body the uninterrupted thought of Jesus takes place as another respiration, joined with the feeling of the heart. It is the permanent prayer of the totally spiritual person. Then "... the name of the Lord has been planted in the heart," as we read in the method attributed to St. John Chrysostom, or "the heart has swallowed the Lord and the Lord, the heart so much so that the two have become one" and the heart can't beat without the mind seeing Him:

> And finally, after some five months, I felt that the prayer was taking place in me without any prompting on my part and that it kept going by mind and heart, not only during waking hours, but even in sleep,

---

[181] Walter, pp. 149-50; cf. French, pp. 89-90.

[182] The pilgrim, however, was introduced to this practice in the following way: "So first of all I tried to find the place of the heart, as Simeon the New Theologian teaches. I closed my eyes, I looked with my mind, that is with my imagination and I tried to see how it was there in the left side of my chest and I listened attentively to its beats. I occupied myself with this for about half an hour several times a day. At first I didn't observe anything but darkness; later I perceived my heart and the movements within it very clearly. Then I began to introduce and to take the prayer from my heart along with my breathing, as Gregory of Sinai and Callistus and Ignatius teach. In other words looking spiritually into my heart and inhaling, I recited 'Lord Jesus Christ,' and exhaling, 'have mercy on me.'" Walter, p. 60; cf. French, pp. 37-8.

and nothing could interrupt it, not even for a moment, regardless of what I was doing.[183]

Mental prayer is then, when the conditions have been met, truly unceasing prayer:

> Nothing was hindered by this prayer and it didn't bother anything. If I had something to do and the prayer was going on in my heart by itself, the task went on more quickly; if I was listening or reading something, the prayer didn't stop and I felt at the same time both of them, as though I were divided in two or as if I had two souls in my breast.[184]

The effects of this prayer are astonishing:

> After some three weeks, I started to feel a pain in my heart, then a warmth, a peace and a very pleasant quietness. Sometimes it seemed that I felt a quaking in my heart. It was so light, so free, so comforting. Sometimes I felt a burning love for Jesus Christ and for all of God's creation. Sometimes tears full of thanksgiving poured from my eyes by themselves, for God who had granted me, such a sinner, a gift like this. Sometimes my understanding, usually so heavy, was illumined, so that I easily grasped and understood things which previously I wouldn't have been able to even imagine…. I experienced an illumination of reason, a penetration into Holy Scripture, an understanding of the spirit of creation.[185]

> And when… I prayed with my heart, everything around me seemed delightful and marvelous. The trees, the grass, the birds, the earth, the air, the light seemed to be telling me that they existed for man's sake, that they witnessed to the love of God for man, that everything proved the love of God for man, that all things prayed to God and sang His praise.

> Then I understood what the words of the *Philokalia* mean: 'to understand the spirit of creatures.' And I saw the way which must be taken in order to talk with God's creatures.[186]

---

[183] Walter, p. 63; cf. French, p. 39.
[184] Walter, p. 64; cf. French, pp. 39-40.
[185] Walter, pp. 61-2; cf. French, p. 38.
[186] cf. French, p. 30. Here we see what a deepening of our comprehension—of the *logoi* of nature, of our neighbors, of the Scriptures—means. Prayer contributes much to this deepening. We have placed the chapter on spiritual understanding before prayer, for the economy of the work. Even so prayer with its many phases, isn't absent on any step of the spiritual understanding of creation. It too contributes to it. In prayer, when you talk with God, He also answers you by events. They too are His words, and He becomes transparent and is heard through them. But as words of God, they speak at the same time of God; they praise Him; they put to the test our powers of patience, of understanding.

In closing this chapter, we will summarize what has been said in connection with the methods for the facilitation of the concentration of the mind in the prayer of the heart, with the following points:

1. These methods are not considered absolutely necessary, but only auxiliary means for those who haven't been able to gather their minds within and to recite without interruption the words of the Jesus Prayer. The one who tries to say this prayer without interruption, discovers that without a concentration at least of his attention on breathing, he can't concentrate much either on the saying of the prayer, or in any case he will require a much greater attention. Respiration, with its permanent continuation, is a thread of support for the concentration of attention. If we get used to associating the saying of the Jesus Prayer with it, it will be easy for us to continue this prayer permanently.

2. Until we attempt to use these methods, it is necessary for us to get used to saying it in a more simple way, and less systematically, but ever more frequently and with our thought concentrated, either on the whole of the Jesus Prayer, or at least on two or three words of it: "Jesus! Lord Jesus! Lord Jesus Christ, have mercy on me!" At the same time we must be advanced in freedom from the passions and from care.

3. When we begin to apply the recommendation of these methods we are not on the highest steps of the spiritual life. We are, from one way of looking at it, beginners, and as long as we apply these recommendations we go through certain phases. First, we can't apply but one or the other of these recommendations. Some people remain all their lives at that stage. Others, with time, apply all of them.

4. Prayer during these phases isn't yet mental prayer, but the Jesus Prayer. It becomes mental prayer when there is no longer the need for either words, or methods, and the mind is occupied with it unceasingly, along with the heart.

31. To Jesus: By What is Deep Within us

In negative theology we make an abstraction of the world only by reason and not totally even then, because when we negate one of God's attributes we think about what we negate. In mental prayer we turn away from all things and submerge ourselves in ourselves; we make an existential abstraction, total and lasting, by all that we are. In the prayer made by the mind in the heart we not only negate the world and think of it at the same time, but pure and simple we totally forget the world with our whole being. We are left only with ourselves and not with our superficial selves, with our traits and properties which can be seen or thought about in definite concepts. Rather we remain with our "I" from the depths, unconstrained by the thought of things, which can't be seen or defined by any concept whatsoever. We find ourselves only with the simple consciousness of the presence of the self, of its indefinable realities.

The heart in which the mind gathers isn't so much the heart of flesh, as it is the central location of the mind, the center of man, his spirit, his subject, the whole man within, not just the intellectual or sentimental. Here are the innermost chambers of man, "where there are no longer winds of evil thoughts,"[187] the chamber beyond the altar screen, where Jesus dwells from Baptism.[188]

There, by prayer, we try to bring our thought to that place which has no boundaries, but opens up an unlimited perspective; so we must force ourselves to penetrate ever deeper, ever further within.[189] Now our thought does this by forsaking all perceptible images, all definite concepts, all representations. St. Gregory Palamas says:

> In prayer the mind gradually abandons all relations with created things: first with all things evil and bad, then with neutral things capable of conformity to either good or ill, according to the intentions of the person using them. It is to this last category that all studies belong and the knowledge that comes through them. Hence the Fathers warn us against accepting the knowledge that comes from the enemy at the time of prayer, so as not to be deprived of the superior. Thus the mind slowly abandons all relations with these things, and even with those superior to them, in order to be totally sepa-

---

[187] Mark the Ascetic, *On Baptism, PG* 65.1016D.
[188] *Ibid.*, 996C.
[189] *Ibid.*, 1017A.

rated from all beings through pure prayer. This ecstasy is incomparably higher than negative theology.[190]

All the holy Fathers say that the leaving behind of all perceptible and intelligible things is the condition *sine qua non*, the absolutely essential condition for the approach of the mind to the infinite God. For example, in a scholia from St. Maximus the Confessor we read:

Perceptible things and intelligible things are between God and men. The mind, raising itself above them, approaches God unenslaved by perceptible things in activity and unhindered by the intelligible in contemplation.[191]

But this transcendence is realized more completely in prayer than in negative theology. We know that the mind can't remain even for a moment without something to do, thus without content. The big problem is, how can it have at the same time content and yet forsake all that is definite and what defines it, all that is an impression of the perceptible and intelligible world? Negative theology, nevertheless, negates this content imagining it and thinking it, as the smoker who is dissatisfied with tobacco, but at the same time smokes. Prayer alone succeeds in making this work complete by removing from the mind all definite content whatsoever. It occupies the mind with the infinite, with God; in other words, it fills it in a positive and experiential way with the apophatic.

But how can thought leave behind all definite content, to penetrate the chamber of the heart? And how is this the same as drawing near to God?

The holy Fathers make a distinction between the mind *(nous)* and reason *(logos)*. Reason is the faculty which conceives things by putting them in defined concepts, called also reasons or *logoi*, because they can be objects of reason. The mind is the faculty which thinks contents without delimiting them in concepts. Reason comes from the mind, just as the divine Logos is continually born from the Father, who is the first Mind *(nous)*.[192] Therefore as the divine mind is the principle of all things, so too the mind in man is the ultimate principle of all that is in him, so of reason, too. It is therefore the basis of the human subject, which is beyond delimited contents, beyond reason too which grasps them in concepts. It is the unlimited basis of the subject which also uses reason. Reason can't grasp it, by any concept whatsoever, as it is beyond

---

[190] *The Defense* 2.3.35, p. 477; cf. *The Triads*, p. 65.
[191] *Questions to Thalassios* 51, PG 90.485.
[192] *Ibid.*, 24, PG 90.332. "Now the head of Christ, in other words of the Logos, found mystically by negation, as He who surpasses all things, is the Mind, which is infinite beyond all things in every way and absolutely." St. Gregory of Nyssa sees the divine image of man in soul (Father), reason (Son) and mind (Spirit). *On the Image and the Likeness*, PG 44.1340D, 1344A.

reason and every concept. We must leave behind all concepts and raise ourselves above reason which forms concepts, in order to grasp the indefinable basis of our subject. Only then does the mind conceive its own self, and become conscious of itself. Things and concepts are a curtain which shut off our view, not only of God, but also of the basis of our subject. Only the mind can think its own self, but it must lay aside things and concepts, which by its determinable (rational) thought have gotten between it and its thought of itself. The mind should be able to see its own self as in a mirror (so as not to double itself). Yet, images and concepts cover the mirror with a wall which must be pierced with much effort, in order to penetrate the heart, or its own being.

St. Maximus the Confessor also calls the mind *subject*, and the acts which come out of it he calls *accidents*.[193] Lossky has this to say:

> The most personal part of man, the principle of his conscience and of his freedom, the spirit *(nous)* in human nature corresponds most nearly to the person: It might be said that it is the seat of the person, of the human hypostasis which contains in itself the whole of man's nature— spirit, soul and body.[194]

Both from the character of the human mind, as the image of the divine Mind, and from the definition of objects as defined realities conceived by it, we see that God too is a subject and namely one in the highest sense of the word. We discover that things, although they are objects to us, aren't totally so— in the sense that neither do we know all of them in full, neither do we create them by our knowledge. We realize that they can't exist by themselves, and that at the same time they don't exist for themselves. So we conclude that there has to be a supreme subject on which things depend in an absolute way, one that fully knows them and creates them; yet in no way do they diminish His power. This subject, which has all the attributes of God, is the only One who exists in an absolute way by Himself and for Himself; He is the only basis (substance) in the full sense of the word. All created things are phenomena and accidents in relation to Him.

So because God is a subject, it is necessary to forsake all objects in order to be raised to the understanding of Him. Then when we come face to face with our own subject, we can in some manner come to understand Him. Objects are only external things, but concepts of thought likewise. Everything that can be defined in the framework of thought

---

[193] *Questions to Thalassios* 52, scholia 8, *PG* 90.500: "The Mind is called subject *(hypokeimenon)* as one which is capable of virtue and knowledge. And activity and contemplation are considered as being in the subject, being before the mind in the relationship of accidents." *(pros ton noun symbebikoton logon echousi.)*
[194] *Mystical Theology*, ch. 10, p. 201.

has the character of an object, given that no subject whatsoever (whether ours or of our neighbor), can be included in a defined concept.

God doesn't resemble things, or concepts, or that which can be contained in thought or in objects in general, which don't exist by or for themselves. They are by nature inferior to thought, subordinate to it and to the subject which conceives them. Now God can't be subordinate either to a power or to a thing. Our thinking subject (our mind) is the highest sovereign which we encounter in the world; it raises itself over all the order of objects and avoids being grasped in any way. So it is the only entity which is like God. Therefore to raise ourselves in some way to an understanding of God, we must somehow understand the thinking subject in the created world. Strictly speaking there can't be talk of an understanding in the usual sense of comprehension, because only objects can be comprehended. What happens is rather a meeting with it, while it remains uncaptured, sovereign, free and indefinable, before us. This, when we are talking about the subject of our neighbor. But something, in some comparable measure happens too when we are talking about our own subject: Our subject is revealed and lives its own self, it meets itself eye to eye, as in a mirror, it gets to know itself. But when it meets itself, it forgets everything, better said that in order to meet itself it must forget all things. External things and the content of thought, with one word objects, stop the subject from returning to itself; they draw it to everything but itself. Only with great effort, by discipline, does the subject become capable of getting loose for a few moments in succession, from the slavery of contents, which hold it far from home and constrict it as much as they can.

Now this return of the subject to itself is a way which leads closer to God than affirmative or negative theology. They are ways of reason and use in a positive or negative way things and definite concepts. In this return of the thinking subject to itself, we have on the one hand a more complete removal of things and thinkable contents; on the other hand the meeting of the subject with itself reveals a positive datum with an incomparable higher value than all the objects removed. It constitutes the point in which the rational act of the negation of all things changes its structure, and becomes a feeling or a positive experience of the deepening of the reality of our own subject. But this reality doesn't reveal itself to us alone. It reveals the divine reality itself to us, in a more intense and visible way than the world of objects. For the infinite and sovereign depth of the subject isn't left captive in concepts, but, in a more adequate way than objects can, it makes God visible. We feel, however, that the subject doesn't have the attributes of the infinite, for there are so many realities which don't depend on it. Even so, the unlimitedness of the subject makes us follow the scent of the divine infinity. Our subject can have its basis only in the divine infinity, not in the world of objects. Now this sovereignty of the subject, which we feel isn't all-powerful, makes us realize the presence of an absolute Sovereign. In every way, the amazement which the mystery of the subject provokes in us, easily becomes an amazement before the much greater absolute Subject.

The holy Fathers affirm that the mind, when it succeeds in looking at itself, becomes transparent, and it sees God through itself. He "shows Himself in the pure mind as in a mirror, while by Himself He is unseen."[195]

In a passage from the writings of Evagrius, adopted by many Fathers of the Church, we read:

> When the mind, unclothing itself of the old man, puts on that of grace, it sees in the time of prayer its state like that of a sapphire or of the heavenly color. This state Scripture calls the place of God, seen by the elders of Israel on Mt. Sinai.[196]

But more relevant for this transparence of the mind, which makes God visible is a text from Diadochos of Photiki:

> You shouldn't doubt that when the mind starts to be strongly energized by the divine light, it becomes totally translucent, so that it luxuriously sees its own light. And this takes place completely, when the power of the soul conquers the passions.[197]

St. Gregory of Nyssa says the same thing in his commentary on the sixth Beatitude. According to him, the cleansed heart sees God, not as a person apart, but he sees Him mirrored in himself. The heart or "the man within which the heart calls Lord" *(o endon anthropos, on kardian onomazei o Kyrios)*[198] reflects God by its nature. But sin, covering it, has also covered the One mirrored in it. As soon as we cleanse it and it sees itself, it also sees God as some see the sun in a mirror, without turning to Him in order to see Him in His hypostasis.[199]

But of what nature is this transparence, on the basis of which the mind, contemplating itself, at the same time contemplates God? Better

---

[195] *The Defense* 1.3.9, p. 169.
[196] W. Bousset, "Evagrios-Studien," in *Apophtegmata Patrum* (Tübingen, 1923), p. 316.
[197] *On Spiritual Knowledge* 40, GrPh 1, p. 246; cf. *Phi* 1, p. 265.
[198] See *ACW* 18.148-9. So here the subject would be the heart, as the center of the mind. It is the real man.
[199] St. Gregory Palamas says somewhere: "He who has purified his heart of every extraneous content and of every passionate disposition, sees in its beauty the image of the divine nature; so he who sees himself, sees in himself the One longed for."

said, how is the mind capable of being transparent and what "form" does this knowledge of God have by it and how does it realize that it isn't seeing only itself, but God too? Because the intimacy of our heart, when it is found, isn't empty, but in its unlimited contents is reflected the presence of Christ. Christ, Who entered as a forerunner at Baptism, is here.[200] Here within us the King of the heavens is found;[201] this is Christ's home, where none of the things of the world penetrate and the one who goes further and further within the heart comes closer and closer to God.[202] When the mind penetrates its heart, by the casting away of all thought, it meets Christ, the One who dwells in it. This encounter with God, by the mind emptied of all things, we believe is experienced in the following way:

After the removal of every content which by its nature has limited contours, we turn to ourselves as a thinking subject. Then we experience a certain unlimitedness and something which cannot be captured, an opening of an abyss, in the face of which we are dizzied, or are left dumbfounded. First, this dizziness or astonishment in the face of the abyss means a paralysis of the powers of the mind, to the extent that it can no longer move forward. The abyss in front of it is a great darkness. Secondly, it realizes that this abyss isn't entirely a region of our being, neither a void in the sense of an absence of any reality whatsoever. It isn't darkness strictly speaking. Rather, it represents, in continuity or by contact with the unlimitedness of our subject, the infinite depths. For us, it also represents the unlighted depths of divinity. St. Maximus the Confessor calls the wisdom of God an "abyss," and the cleansed mind "the place of the abyss," which as such can also be called an abyss. It is called an abyss because it is made thus *(thesei)*, as something which is capable of receiving the abyss, while wisdom is an abyss by nature.[203] This means that the mind becomes limited when it gathers objects and finite concepts and limitless when, forsaking them, it receives the One "without form," Who gives it no form whatsoever. So, when I feel the mind losing its boundaries I feel at the same time that the divinity is in it too. This also sheds light on how, by grace unlimited, we will become gods in the future age.

Because this moment is one of dumbfoundedness for the mind, it represents a total apophaticism, the abandonment not only of all the contents of the mind, but even of its activity too. After this moment of

---

[200] Mark the Ascetic, *On Baptism, PG* 65.996C, 1008B, 1009C.
[201] *Ibid.*, 1016B.
[202] *Ibid.*, 1017A.
[203] *Ambigua, PG* 91.1112: "An abyss is also called the place of the abyss. So the mind too is known as an abyss by participation, because of its receptive capacity."

the stoppage of the mind, some receive as a gift from above the vision of the divine light. We shall speak about this in a future chapter.

But this astonishment isn't an inertia like the physical, or a sleeping of the spirit. Even in it is implicated a consciousness: the feeling which is at the same time understanding *(noera aithisis)* above the understanding of the boundless and unrestricted depths of God, Who isn't a limited object, but a boundless and sovereign reality. In this freeing of ourselves from our limitations we feel the pressure of a presence which penetrates us and sustains us as a foundation of our unlimited existence. We realize that and nothing more. On the one hand we realize that this boundless and absolute sovereign reality is something other than these two realities; we experience the latter as only indefinitely and relatively sovereign, not as infinite and absolute. But on the other hand we can't separate them in our spiritual experience. We can't distinguish where one starts and the other stops. It is the experience of a union and interpenetration between God and ourself, although it isn't yet the luminous union on the succeeding steps.[204]

We must stress, in equal measure, both these aspects of the experience which the mind undergoes when it is gathered in the heart. If we would accept only the first, we would dissolve the unmediated tie of the heart with God, the presence of Jesus in the heart and implicitly the mystical knowledge of God. If we put the stress exclusively on the aspect of "inseparable and indistinct union," we would slip into neoplatonism and Hegelianism. These systems see the world as a continuity of substance with the absolute and consider that the gathering of the mind from scattering, its simplification, means the rediscovery of the absolute, which is one with its intimate substance; thus, according to these teachings, the absolute isn't distinct from the world by substance, but only by the fact that He is One, while the world is His multiple form. In reality the subject by turning to itself doesn't meet itself; so this experience excludes both the distancing from God, and identification with Him too. Exactly when, taking off all the clothes of the created world, we would expect to see our subject uncovered *(gymnos nous)* and would taste the fullest feeling of sovereignty, we encounter before us another power— its reign over us is seen to be infinite and imposing and more overwhelming than the rule of the world. And nevertheless, we

---

[204] A comment from St. Maximus' *Questions to Thalassios* 33, *PG* 90.376, reads: "When the mind has gained an unmediated union with God, it stops totally its power to think and of being conscious of itself. And when it starts it again and it thinks of the things which are after God, it starts to distinguish [things again], cutting that union which is above understanding." St. Isaac, in turn, tells us that "From pure prayer to the things which are within, after we pass this frontier, the intellect no longer has the power to pray, or move, or cry, or control itself.... But beyond this boundary there is a ravishment and wonder, and not prayer." *Op. cit.,* 32, p. 117.

must make a great effort to arrive under the ray of its reign in a conscientious way and stay there. We fall under the slavery of the world by inertia—we become slaves of God and remain so by the greatest effort, and by this we become at the same time truly free: slaves of a loving supreme person, with the very fullest freedom.

What if this abyss, which our mind experiences in turning to itself, is a total darkness, as Hegel says, and we can say nothing about it?[205] There would still be the possibility of a pantheist ambiguity, of an identification of our subject lost in it. But we said that this abyss lets us experience it as an absolute sovereign. Now precisely in this is shown its character of subject and this is what distinguishes it from our subject. Arriving at our pure intimacy, we experience the infinite but personal presence of God, hidden under the veil of the most complete darkness, just as many times we feel that somebody is near us, because we feel it, but we can't see anybody.

We can also make this fact clear from the circumstances which make it possible: We have seen, in a previous quotation, the self-transparency which the mind gains in time of prayer. Prayer is always what allows the turning away of the mind from all things, from all ideas. But this isn't only an act of the self-contemplation of the mind, but is an ecstasy of the thinking subject, an act by which it transcends itself; it goes beyond itself, to the supreme and infinite Subject. In prayer our subject feels that it isn't alone, but that it is in the presence of God. It would appear that prayer isn't a preoccupation of the subject, with itself, but only with God; therefore the coming close to God in the time of prayer isn't made via the transparence of the subject strictly speaking.

At the beginning, mental prayer tries to find, with the name of Jesus, the place of the heart, or the pure center of the subject. This shows us that the mind, although it is preoccupied in a predominant way with God, seeks God through the intimacy of its own subject. Prayer therefore seeks Jesus in the heart or by the heart, and the more it penetrates it and becomes more firmly established in it, the more it is dominated by the certitude that it has met Jesus, that it is found before Him. By mental prayer, the amazing depths which are encountered in the mind after the removal of all content and after its return to itself, are revealed as

---

[205] In the nineteenth century German philosophy hadn't yet discovered the whole mystery of the person, infinitely superior and on a totally different plane than that of objects, and neither the possibility of union between persons in such a measure that they can form a unity, in which the consciousnesses are not confused and nevertheless each can embrace the whole. Therefore nothingness, night, unconsciousness were considered superior to the light, consciousness, or supraconsciousness, which enhances the value of everything and represents [the person]. So it is the supreme grade of existence, which mirrors and multiplies it to the infinite and is made ever new by the problems and never ending aspects which it creates.

depths of the supreme subject distinct from us, before which we are humbled. The humility of prayer grows from the simultaneous consciousness of our subject and of the supreme Subject, distinct from each other, but in relationship and reciprocal penetration. In prayer, with an absolute certitude, we are following, around us and in us, the trail of the presence of the supreme overwhelming Subject. This experience is truthful and full of certitude to the extent that we feel that the presence of the reality which envelops us is an infinity, before which we are but fragments, and a sovereignty, on which we totally depend. This infinity and absolute sovereignty overwhelms us, so much so that the heart feels overcome, or filled totally with it. A perfect union is realized, the heart "swallowing the Lord and the Lord the heart, the two becoming one."[206]

Only in prayer, and namely in mental prayer by which we contemplate our pure subject, do we experience the presence of God as subject, and don't conceive Him, in an inadequate way, as object. To us, in this prayer, God is no longer an object, but a subject, Who claims us and asks us for a voluntary submission. He makes us feel His greatness before His majesty. We become conscious of our nothingness, and yet this moves us to adore Him even more. God is to us thus *the Subject* Who stands on the first plain of our vision; our subject stands in His shadow. We are in some way received in His sphere, or He penetrates into the content of our subject; He fills it and overwhelms it so much so that we forget ourselves. We experience within us His character of first Subject and the force of Him as supreme Subject, without His being confused with us. At the same time or alternately we also feel our littleness and subordination which continue through Him. In words whispered or unformed, we hear the thought of astonishment and of the prayer being

---

[206] For Hegel, as for Dionysius the Areopagite and St. Maximus the Confessor, the Absolute can't be an object. But he adds that neither can it be subject. Therefore it is necessary for us to raise ourselves not only beyond all objects of consciousness, but even beyond our own pure and empty consciousness. "Reason doesn't touch the absolute except by going out from this varied partial existence. To the same degree that the construction of the intellect is more lasting and brilliant, to the same degree the effort of life becomes more tortured, enclosed here, wanting to uproot itself from these walls, longing for freedom. In the measure in which it penetrates to another horizon, as reason, the totality of limits is disestablished, being related to the absolute by disestablishment. But in this way, being at the same time conceived and put as a simple phenomenon, the rupture between the absolute and the totality of limits has disappeared.... The Absolute is night, and the light is more recent than it.... Nothingness is anterior; therefore every being, every creature is tearing itself off from the finite.... Consciousness itself is torn loose from totality." Faith, being a relation of the limited with the Absolute, is based on the identity between these two, but on an identity from which it is unaware. The unification of the things separated by faith "appears to the intellect an illegality." At a time when the sacred and the divine subsist in its conscience simply as object, it sees in the suppression of the opposition, in the identification on the plane of consciousness, just a disestablishment of the divine. Georg Wilhelm Friederich Hegel, *The Difference Between the Systems of Fichte and of Schelling* [in Romanian], in *Izvoarele de Filosofie* 2 (1943), pp. 127, 131, 137.

repeated: "Lord, how great you are and how little and unworthy I am. Have mercy on me!"

We have followed especially Mark the Ascetic in the preceding. We have seen how the heart of our intimacy has Jesus in it, from the beginning, or in a continuation with it. (It is understood not of substance, but of presence.)[207] It suffices to descend into the heart, in order to contemplate in it or in relationship with it the infinite abyss of the divine presence of Jesus. But the methods of the prayer of the heart give the impression that at the beginning the heart doesn't have Jesus, but we must bring Him there by prayer. But looking closer we see that in this method the meaning is the name of Jesus. With it we must knock insistently at the door of the heart in order to open it and we must make the knocking heard in the heart, repeating it continually. Christ dwells in the heart and opens [the door] for us because we call out His name, because we show our need for Him. But this need is awakened in us by a kind of feeling of His sweetness in our vicinity. He makes us call Him. The name of Jesus is the thought directed to Jesus. Now the thought of one person to the other is a witness to a mystical tie and the means of the intensification of this tie. When I feel the need and I think of somebody, usually this person is the one who causes this thought in me, by an influence from a distance, in the same way that thinking of him in a voluntary way I transmit a signal to him.

The explanation of this apparent contradiction discussed above is also given to us by Mark the Ascetic, who says that good thoughts, thoughts dedicated to Jesus, come from Him, the One present in the heart. Without having at the beginning the consciousness that He is in our heart, He attracts our thoughts to Him, and by them we knock continually at the door of the heart, at His door. Then He too, knocks at the door of our consciousness with these thoughts. He opens the door so that we can go in to Him in the heart. This after we too have allowed Him to enter our consciousness.[208] In the heart we meet Jesus, but in as much as He has gone out by thought of Him before us, as the Father went out to meet the prodigal son, from experience we can't tell that He was previously in the heart, but it seems to us that He has just entered, along with our entrance. But the persistence with which we sought Him by remembering Him can only be explained by the fact that He was there ahead of us, in a hidden way. Actually He was influencing us, first

---

[207] *The Method of St. John Chrysostom*, Staniloae, *op. cit.*, p. 45.
[208] The entrance of Jesus into the heart at Baptism is considered by the holy Fathers as a return, as a reestablishment of the original tie between God and the soul. It puts into operation the work of the cleansing of the image (of the heart) from sin, from the egotistic separation from the infinite God, in the sense of St. Gregory of Nyssa.

TO JESUS: BY WHAT IS DEEP WITHIN US 293

to help us, then to also put our powers to work in finding Him, that they might develop, and be able to understand Him.[209] Thus by seeking and finding Him, we look for and find our intimacy, or vice-versa. Our efforts were stimulated and aided by Him.[210]

---

[209] *On Baptism, PG* 65.1008AB, in connection with the passage, "From your temple kings will bring you gifts in Jerusalem." Psalm 68:29, LXX, 67.30.

[210] Diadochos, *On Spiritual Knowledge* 77: "Grace as I have said, even from the moment in which we are baptized is hidden in the depths of the mind, but it covers its presence from the perception of the mind. And when someone with all his heart begins to love God, then in some way by the perception of the mind He begins to communicate some of His riches to the soul.... Because when someone sells all his worldly riches, he will find the place in which the grace of God is hidden." Worldly riches are not only the material, but all its images and concepts. "The grace of God, on the other hand, dwells in the depths of the soul, that is in the mind.... Thus when we feel the divine longing rising up from the depths of our heart, we remember God fervently...." *op. cit.,* 79, *GrPh* 1, p. 259; *cf. Phi* 1, pp. 279-80. Note the alternation of the terms "mind" [intellect] and "soul." "You shouldn't doubt that when the mind begins to be energized powerfully by the divine light, it becomes entirely transparent, so that it can richly see its own light." *op. cit.,* 40, *GrPh* 1, p. 246; *cf. Phi* 1, p. 265. "The soul then has the same grace to think together with the soul, and to cry out with it the 'Lord Jesus Christ,' as a mother teaches her child, striving together with him to say the name, 'father.'" *op. cit.,* 61, *GrPh* 1, pp. 251-2; *cf. Phi* 1, p. 271.

32. Mental Rest: The First Step of Stillness

From the preceding we have seen that, according to St. Gregory Palamas and St. Isaac the Syrian, mental prayer culminates in the cessation of thought, of the working of the mind. This moment, however, isn't the vision of the divine light, but a feeling of His presence, provoked by His power.[211] The question which we raise here is, "How can this cessation of mental activity be experienced and by what sign is it characterized?" We said in the last chapter that the mind arrives, in the time of pure prayer, face to face with itself. It experiences a certain astonishment as much in the face of its own limitlessness, as it does in the face of the divine boundlessness and sovereignty which it feels to be present.[212] This experience has therefore a negative as well as a positive side.

The negative consists in the amazement mentioned; the positive, in the feeling of the presence of the divine infinitude and sovereignty. In the previous chapter we dwelt more on the positive side of this experience, without forgetting the negative. Here we want to bring out the negative, presupposing naturally its tie with the positive.

St. Maximus the Confessor speaks too of this inactivity of the mind, after it has forsaken all representations, concepts and meanings. Then the mind stands motionless in itself, fixed in a total immobility, invoking the divine wisdom, [before] the abyss truly uncrossable, that it might hear a faint rumble of His cascades, without being shown the cascades themselves.[213] In another place he lists with more detail the steps on which the mind must raise itself until it reaches the total cessation before the "divine infinitude, ineffable and apophatic." One mortifies his sin only by deeds, another the passions too, another also their images, another the thought of them too. Another also discards the tie of the senses with the perceptible. Another stifles all perceptible movement. He no longer has within himself a natural movement:

---

[211] "When every mental action is truly stopped, by what then do the angels and men who are equal to the angels still see God, if not by the power of the Spirit?" *The Defense* 1.3.18, p. 189. And in another place, "The mind...stands entirely apart from all the things that are, during pure prayer. This ecstasy [exit] is incomparably higher than negative theology. But union does not yet take place...nor the seeing of the light." *Ibid.*, 2.3.35, p. 477.
[212] Thus St. Maximus the Confessor interprets Psalm 42.7: "Deep is calling to deep as your cataracts roar." In other words, the mind in discovering its own depths, after the abandonment of all representations and concepts, looks for and pursues the voice of the cataract (of the overflowing) of the divine deep. *Ambigua, PG* 91.1400-1409.
[213] *Ibid.*

MENTAL REST: THE FIRST STEP OF STILLNESS 295

Another totally stops even the working of the mind.... In order to say more, [he goes on], one crucifies himself by active philosophy, becoming dispassionate and passing over to natural contemplation in spirit, as from the body of Christ, to his spirit. Another, leaving behind the symbolic contemplation of things with the mind, is moved from the simple and unitary mystagogy[214] of the knowledge of God, as from Christ's spirit, to His mind. Now another raises himself in a mystical way from this too, by total negation, to the unspeakable and apophatic *(eis tin arriton kai aphairetikin aorisian)*, as from the mind of Christ, to His divinity.[215]

From the preceding we can list the following characteristics of this standstill of mental activity:

1. This cessation is produced because the mind has reached the peak of all objects received by thought and has given up all understanding, no matter how well defined; it has realized that no definite thought whatsoever can see God. Strictly speaking the movement or activity of the mind consists in its effort to define, to precisely state in certain meanings, what it knows. But this is proper only for finite, created, existences. When the mind has given up preoccupation with the created and finite and finds itself before God, it realizes that its activity no longer has any purpose, but on the contrary, that it is harmful because it brings it down once again to finite things.

The cessation is caused by the experience of the divine boundlessness or infinity. Without this, the mind would not discard all finite meanings and would not persist in this state. It isn't realized until the mind has felt in an overwhelming way the presence of the divine infinity. It is superior to negative theology, which still thinks the concepts which it negates.

2. So we can draw two conclusions: First, the experience of God by the motionlessness of the mind is superior to the consciousness gained by affirmative or negative activity. Secondly, this shows that this inactivity isn't a simple inertia or insensibility, but an experience of the divine reality which it doesn't try to define further. It demonstrates that this state is one of prayer, but of prayer full of silent astonishment, of the powerlessness to define

---

[214] The word *mystery* originally referred to the secret religions in ancient Greece. *Mystagogy* was the instruction preparatory to initiation into mysteries, says the *Oxford English Dictionary*. "For Maximus the term mystagogy signifies a liturgical contemplation of the mystery of the Church...." *Maximus Confessor, Selected writings*, p. 214. See the long note there for a discussion. *trs*

[215] Maximus the Confessor, *Ambigua*, PG 91.1360.

what it (the mind) wants and Him from Whom it asks and Who feels that it hears it.[216]

Although it is a state superior to prayer, nevertheless it is called prayer because it is given to the worthy in the time of prayer and it has its source in prayer.[217]

3. The mind has left all things behind, even its own function which it had directed toward these things. It finds itself now before the Master, at the end of the earth, looking intensely and astonished at the ocean of life which is contained in Him.[218]

It can't go ahead on its own power. It can't go back and it doesn't want to. It stands at His imposing and fluid door which it can't enter. Its state can be characterized as overwhelming amazement. The amazement fastens it to this ocean, but at the same time also paralyzes it so it can't function. It wants to go ahead, but it can't. So it seeks the help of God. This shows that this cessation of the mind before the gates of the King, or of the ocean which surrounds Him, isn't the last step of the knowledge of God. Our spiritual ascent doesn't stop either at this apophaticism of the second step, or at this ecstasy in silence in the knowledge of God. But it will ascend further only by the fuller coming of the Spirit, Who will raise the mind to the vision of the divine light.

From the ocean of the divine majesty emanates a charm which makes the mind forget the things behind, which is so overwhelming that it paralyzes its movements, with all its deep longing to go ahead.

4. It has given up all things and stands motionless, praying that a vessel will be sent to bring it into the open sea, which will open the door for it. This reveals a state of great love before the divine infinity. Prayer is always a manifestation of the love of God.[219] And since this love doesn't cease now, nor its long

---

[216] The holy Fathers speak of a prayer beyond prayer, of one which is not in contradiction with the cessation of mental activity. Thus St. Isaac the Syrian writes: "...the works of prayer cease, and the mind is found more in contemplation, and not in prayer." *The Ascetical Homilies* 32 [in Greek], Athens, 1961, p. 117. This is absolute quiet (hesychia). "[Man's] nature remains without motion, without action, without the memory of earthly things." *Ibid.*, 85, p. 303.

[217] This is the quieting of the mind, which is superior to prayer. It is the state "of the age to come," when the saints have their minds submerged in the Spirit of God. They are no longer in prayer, but pray without prayer, or better said they are submerged, amazed in the glory which fills them with joy. This happens when the mind is destined to feel the happiness of the age to come. Then it completely forgets itself. It leaves behind all that belongs to this world and no longer has in itself any movement toward anything whatsoever. *Ibid.*, 32, p. 122.

[218] *Ibid.*, 32, Greek edition of 1895, p. 138.

[219] Mark the Ascetic, *No Righteousness by Works* 95-97, GrPh 1, p. 115; cf. Phi 1, p. 133: "Nothing is stronger than prayer in action; and nothing more useful in winning the goodwill of God. All the work of the commandments is contained in it; for nothing is higher than love for God. Undistracted prayer is a sign of love for God by those who persist in it."

standing desire, this state too is nevertheless one of prayer, of unlimited prayer.

5. In the measure that the warmth of prayer has grown, so has love, that it might reach its fullness in pure prayer, the highest step of prayer.[220] This love also remains after the ceasing of pure but unlimited prayer; love will constitute, together with the coming of the Spirit to help, the bridge of crossing from the coast of created land, to the vastness of the divine ocean. For love, being well established in the created being of man, wants to also launch out on the limitless ocean of the love of God. But this desire will be fulfilled when the mind is ravished by the divine light which descends from the divine being. The bridge, however, is thrown to us by God. It can penetrate our nature, because the latter is full of the desire for the bridge thrown by God, by a work started long before.

Thus the divine bridge is able to get a good footing in the spiritual nature of man. As will be seen in the next chapter, we make a distinction between love as a long process, also due to God, but also to our effort, and love as an unseen wave released all at once from on high. The first has been growing all during the time of asceticism and illumination and especially during prayer, that, in the moment of the cessation of the activity of the mind, it might be astonished in the face of the inexplicable and infinite divine mystery. It is still a state of longing love, which, however, can't go forward any longer by a new effort of ours towards the divine majesty. At the moment of the cessation of mental activity, this love of God reaches the ultimate steadiness and warmth that can be obtained by our effort, that the divine light launched from the other shore and descending to it might ignite it, intoxicate it and by this open for it the light of the divine interior. This astonishing love, which is the positive content of the state of the cessation of mental activity, can't yet be called the ultimate rest of the mind. Because in it is still the longing for union with God, a longing which has reached its highest dimension. It is true that having gone out from finite things and concepts, it no longer needs to go from the one to the other in its unceasing desire to unite with God, but it stops in an unwavering astonishment in the feeling of the still covered Boundless One. But on the other hand, it seeks as an answer the showing of the divine Boundlessness in light. This revelation presupposes, as a preparation on man's part, the love of God won over a long period of time and nurtured especially in the time of prayer until the culminating cessation of the mind before the divine Boundlessness.

---

[220] *The Defense* 1.3.18, p. 189: "Any way of prayer ends in pure prayer."

So the divine light isn't ignited by this firm, alert, warm, love itself, grown by affirmative and negative reasoning about God and by prayer full of feeling and stopped now in astonishment. But in this state long prepared by the soul, the love of God, as an overflowing drink which ravishes the soul, descends all at once as a gift exclusively from above. The first love was a part of the previous phases of the ascent, and due to human effort; so love as an exclusive gift from above, as ecstasy, as intoxication, must take part in the third state of the ascent, in which man prepared by previous efforts no longer does anything by himself, but receives all as a gift of God.

Until now the mind has progressed in a knowledge of God and by its own efforts to return to itself and to love God. Once it arrives at the limits of its interior depths, and directed toward God, at the edge of its powers, it waits to be ravished beyond itself in union with God, in a state of burning, intoxicating, ecstatic love. It waits not only to see God as a sun mirrored in itself— in the sense of St. Gregory of Nyssa— but to be ravished in the very interior of the transcendent Sun itself.[221]

This knowledge of God beyond its own depths, when its own subject is no longer seen directly, and the divine subject indirectly, but vice versa, takes place after the total exit of the mind from itself, beyond itself. It has attained this by the suspension of all its natural activities and by the ravishment of the Holy Spirit. It is a knowledge which is one with love, and is expressed in the East by the vision of the divine light.

6. The experiencing of the feeling of the boundless divine mystery, the state of boundless prayer and the warm and firm love for God are other characteristics which distinguish this apophaticism from negative theology, in which the intellect is more active.

Furthermore, this experience isn't reached without a freedom from all cares, from those intended to produce pleasure, or from all that can cause pain or need. Now once that the feeling of this divine ocean is reached, it controls man with such charm, that he remains quiet in tasting it, unaffected by anything from outside. Nevertheless, a progress is also present in it, and therefore in the peace produced by it. From the divine vastness, even if it is felt as being covered with darkness, the

---

[221] von Balthasar, *Die gnostischen Centurien*, p. 361, sees a contradiction between Evagrius, where God is met by submersion in His most profound depths, and St. Maximus the Confessor, where the mind must go out of itself, in order to see the Transcendent One. We think that these are only two successive steps known by all the holy Fathers, or that, neither when the mind is submerged in itself, is it totally lacking in the going out of itself nor when it is gone out of itself, has it completely abandoned itself.

mind somehow gets more and more meanings. St. Isaac the Syrian writes:

> If you want to find, O brother, the incorruptible life during your short days, let your entrance to tranquility be with discernment. Examine your task carefully and do not be drawn only by its name; but enter, deepen yourself, and struggle,[222] and study to know what is the depth and the height of the living of tranquility ... thus also the work of tranquility becomes a harbor for the mysteries, for the discreet purpose, to which the mind from the beginning of the foundation until the finishing of the whole building is attentive, as well as to all its time-consuming and difficult work; and as the eyes of the pilot watch the stars, so too the monastic watches by his inner sight his purpose during the whole course of his journey, which he had in mind the first day, when he decided to walk the hard road of tranquility, until he would find the pearl, for which he entered the unfathomable depths of the sea of tranquility.[223]

But the spiritual man also reaches a great quietness when he is raised to the vision of the divine light. For although there exists a progress in it too, accompanied by a burning love, on the other hand it is a calm from every work whatsoever of his own being and from every worldly care.

---

[222] By asceticism. *trs*
[223] *The Ascetical Homilies* Epistle 3, p. 316.

PART THREE
PERFECTION

PART THREE

PERFECTION BY UNION WITH GOD OR BY DEIFICATION

33. Love and Dispassion
The Steps of Love

Union with God can only be reached by pure prayer. "The virtue of prayer brings about the mystery of our union with God," says St. Gregory Palamas, "because prayer is the tie of rational creatures with the Creator."[224]

Before attaining the state of pure prayer, man must be cleansed of the passions. But cleansing from the passions is one with the growth of the love of God. Thus the love of God trickles into the soul with anticipation and strengthens it in the quiet of dispassion and in pure prayer. Now by this, more love also comes to him. Better said, now only divine love, or the Holy Spirit, works in him. As Diadochos says, "Just as the troubled sea becomes calm when oil is poured on it, because of the attributes of the oil, so too our souls are filled with a blessed calm, when the sweetness of the Holy Spirit is poured into it."[225]

Thus there is a close tie between love and dispassion. Love presupposes dispassion and in turn it strengthens it too, because it is the opposite of the passions, which represent egotism. Where the passions are, love can't be. So love comes into the soul fully amplified after we have reached dispassion, after we have been freed from the passions. Certainly only then do we gain culminating prayer too, which is higher than prayer by concepts and words. Because the one who isn't peaceful can't pray as he should, and he can't turn exclusively to God, as long as he is preoccupied in an egotistic way with himself. In this sense, love sums up all the other virtues, if by every virtue a passion is slain. But it is the immediate fruit of prayer. "All the virtues work with the mind to attain the love of God, but, more than all, pure prayer. For by this flying toward God it goes beyond everything that is," says St. Maximus the Confessor.[226] If the passions mean in a word the love of self, the love of God is just the opposite. Diadochos comments:

> He who loves himself, cannot love God. But he who doesn't love himself because of the overwhelming richness of the love of God,

---
[224] *On Prayer*, PG 150.1117.
[225] *On Spiritual Knowledge* 35, GrPh 1, p. 244; cf. Phi 1, p. 263.
[226] *Chapters on Love* 1.22, GrPh 2, p. 4; cf. Phi 2, p. 54.

loves God, for such a person never seeks his own glory, but that of God. Because he who loves himself seeks his own glory, but he who loves God, loves the glory of Him who made him. Since it is proper to the sensitive soul to always seek first the glory of God in all the commandments which he is carrying out, and secondly, to enjoy himself in his humility.[227]

But the love of God on the highest step isn't only freedom from passions, but the gift of God which descends to the soul which has reached this state.

If prayer originates below, certainly aided by the hidden grace of the Holy Spirit, culminating love is God's answer from on high. By it the divinity becomes open and palpable. St. Gregory Palamas says this of the Apostle Paul:

> Under the effect of ecstasy he forgot even prayer to God. This is what St. Isaac talks about, when he confirms the great and divine Gregory: 'Prayer is the purity of the intellect which is produced with dread only from the light of the Holy Trinity,'[228] [or again,] 'Purity of mind is what allows the light of the Holy Trinity to shine forth at the time of prayer.... The mind then transcends prayer ... [and is] a fruit of the pure prayer sent by the Holy Spirit. The mind does not pray a definite prayer, but finds itself in ecstasy in the midst of incomprehensible realities.[229]

Thus union isn't strictly speaking prayer, because in prayer the consciousness of the distinction with God is still too clear. It is however the product of prayer, realized at its termination, as the rapture of the mind to God. St. Gregory Palamas makes this comment about the union of the mind with God: "This is what the Fathers have said: 'The end of prayer is to be snatched away to God.'"[230] Union is one and the same with the living of the love of God, which comes down from on high. Now "Love is from prayer," we also learn from St. Isaac.[231]

But here the discussion isn't about the love which grows with prayer and from it, but about the love which is divine, uncreated energy, as a gift from above. Notice how Diadochos of Photiki distinguishes the two:

> One is the natural love of the soul and another that which comes to it from the Holy Spirit. The first is controlled and also put in motion

---

[227] Diadochos, *On Spiritual Knowledge* 12, GrPh 1, p. 238; cf. *Phi* 1, pp. 255-6.
[228] Homily 32, *op. cit.*, p. 122.
[229] *The Defense*, 1.3.21, p. 195; cf. *The Triads*, p. 38.
[230] *Ibid.*, 2.3.35, p. 477; cf. *The Triads*, p. 65.
[231] *The Ascetical Homilies* 35, p. 135.

by our will when we so desire. So it is easily carried off by evil spirits, when we don't hold strongly to our will. The other inflames the soul with the love of God so much that all its parts cling to the ineffable sweetness of this love, in an ineffable and infinite affection. The mind, pregnant then with spiritual energy, becomes like a spring from which love and joy bubble forth.[232]

In distinction to Catholicism, which doesn't admit the uncreated energies of God and which therefore must consider love too as a created gift, Orthodoxy considers love as an uncreated energy, communicated by the Holy Spirit, a divine and deifying energy, by which we really participate in the life of the Holy Trinity. "Love comes from God," says St. John (1 John 4:7). "But this love presupposes," according to St. Basil, "a corresponding disposition in created nature, a germ or potentiality for love *(agapitiki dynamis)* in the human being called to attain his own perfection in love."[233]

Man has the potential capacity to become the subject of divine love and in some way goes in this direction too. In this stands the divine image in him. But he can't have love itself in its fullness by himself; he receives it from God, which means that he can't gain the likeness except in communion with God.

In other words, although the virtuality of the likeness is hidden in the image, this virtuality can't become an actuality by itself, but only under the flame of divine working and love.

We don't find nature in a pure state, but below it, or in one above it penetrated by grace. So neither do we know natural love in its purity. The love which we see in man, besides the ties with God isn't even natural love. The great deficiencies of this love show us that true love can be nothing but a gift from God. When nature has reached its healthy state, divine grace is in its love too.

But man is also active in this natural love. However, he in whom this love of God works exclusively is higher than this step. Strictly speaking, we can distinguish three steps in love: a) The tendency of natural sympathy from the state of nature fallen from grace; b) Christian love, which uses this tendency and grows by divine grace and by self-efforts; this grows and becomes firm. It brings nature to a kind of fulfillment. At the beginning it is less firm, later much more so and intense. Diadochos has in view sometimes the first, other times the second, when he speaks of natural love. In its beginnings, the second love, being unstable, can easily

---

[232] *On Spiritual Knowledge* 34, GrPh 1, p. 244; cf. *Phi* 1, p. 263.
[233] Basil, *The Long Rules* 1, Question 2, Boston, 1950, pp. 18-19, as quoted by Lossky, *Mystical Theology*, p. 214.

be confused with natural sympathy, or better said, with that which lacks grace. But in the measure that it progresses, it is fortified, it approaches love as ecstasy, which is a gift exclusively from above. The second love, or Christian, prepares the soul for ecstasy. Sometimes these two can be again included under the same name, especially when we are talking about the highest steps of the first; c) finally, there is love as ecstasy or as a gift exclusively from above. This comes after a long preparation through the second and lasts for moments, that from the second it might gain new force and continue its growth. If, in the course of the second, man is raised to the state of nature reestablished in grace, love as an exclusive gift raises him above the limits of nature. When we often speak of true love, we mean the second love, in opposition to the first, overwhelmed by egotism. But still neither is it love as an exclusively divine power.

Full love means a man's complete victory over himself, not in the sense that he is belittling himself after some discouragement, but in the sense that he affirms life in a positive way; he considers that true life stands in the exclusive care of others and in the forgetting of self. He who has true love in himself experiences an infinity of the power to give himself, something which evidently he can't have from himself.

Divine love has a firmness which no vicissitude whatsoever can shake, something which is foreign to natural love. He who has this love feels in himself a spring always bubbling over with light and joy. Natural love can't have these virtues; it falls so quickly and every evil that it suffers weakens it.[234]

The divine love which comes down into man presupposes a victory over the egotism manifested by the passions and, being a positive going out of man from himself, it is at the same time the love of God, and love of others. Certainly, the power of love is from God and is gained by the focusing of the soul on God by prayer. Therefore it is just to say that the love of God is the source of love of others, not the other way around. Man's love doesn't suffice for God's love, but God's love suffices for man's; the one prolongs the other. "When someone begins to richly feel the love of God, then he begins to love his neighbor too, with spiritual feeling," Diadochos writes.[235] This doesn't mean that sometimes the love of people can be lacking. The love of others is a necessary fruit of the love of God, just as the fruit of a plant is the necessary effect of the sunshine which it receives by its orientation toward the sun.

---

[234] Diadochos, *On Spiritual Knowledge* 15, *Phi* 1, pp. 256-7.
[235] *Ibid., GrPh* 1, p. 239; *cf. Phi* 1, pp. 256-7.

"He who loves God can't help but love every person as himself, even though he is displeased by the passions of those who are yet uncleansed."[236] "The saints reach perfection and likeness with God when their love overflows for all men."[237] The love of God doesn't admit even the littlest shadow in the love for one's neighbors. "If a person sees a trace of hate in his heart, for any fault whatsoever in anyone at all, he is completely alienated from the love of God."[238]

God, by nature good and without passion, loves each person equally, as His creature, but glorifies the virtuous, as also having made the truth his own, and pities the depraved, and by goodness, in this world seeks to chastise him; likewise, the dispassionate and positive man loves everybody the same, the virtuous for his nature and for his good will; and the evil one for his nature and out of sympathy pitying the one who is foolishly trying to make his way in the dark.[239]

The power of such a love for our neighbors is explained by the fact that it is nothing else than the love of God come down into the soul and directed partly toward God and partly toward men. St. Isaac the Syrian sees, however, an opposition between the love of the world and the love of men. "He who loves the world can't gain the love of men."[240]

Certainly man can't hold all the love of God. But it's no less true that, having it in him, he feels it as something that isn't going to end. It grows in the measure of its exercise and of the will to intensify it. Because in the measure in which he opens his heart to others, he enlarges it for the ocean of divine love. "Many saints have also given their bodies to beasts, the sword, fire, and their neighbors."[241] The unending divine love is communicated through those who have reached such a love, even if the canal of their being is too narrow to be able to manifest it as a whole at the beginning. They feel that it overwhelms them, that a joy and an infinite impulse to embrace everyone floods them. And so it is, on the higher steps like ecstasy. St. John of the Ladder comments:

> Love by quality is likeness with God, in so far as is possible for mortals. By energy it is intoxication of the soul. By attribute it is the fountain of faith, an abyss of longsuffering, a sea of humility.[242]

---

[236] St. Maximus the Confessor, *Chapters on Love* 1.13, *GrPh* 2, p. 5; *cf. Phi* 2, p. 54.
[237] St. Isaac the Syrian, *The Ascetical Homilies* 81 [in Greek], Athens, 1961, p. 271.
[238] St. Maximus the Confessor, *Chapters on Love* 1.15, *GrPh* 2, p. 5; *cf. Phi* 2, p. 54.
[239] *Ibid.*, 1.25, *GrPh* 2, pp. 5-6; *cf. Phi* 2, p. 55.
[240] *The Ascetical Homilies* 81, p. 271.
[241] *Ibid.*
[242] *The Ladder* 30.7, *PG* 88.1156B; *cf.* Moore, p 262.

Here is how St. Isaac the Syrian describes the infinity of love which comes down from God into the heart:

> And love, having God as its cause, is like a spring bubbling up whose stream never stops; and He alone is the cause of love and its material is inexhaustible... for this material which brings him to the remembrance of God is always available to him, so that even in sleep he speaks with God.[243]

Now the ecstatic character of this love is also described by him as follows:

> The love of God is warm by nature, and when it falls on someone without measure, it makes that soul ecstatic; therefore the heart of the one who feels it can't hold or bear it, but according to the measure of the quality of the love which has fallen on him, some unusual changes are seen in him. And these are the perceptible signs of it: The man's face becomes flushed and full of joy, and his body is warmed; shame and fear leave him and he becomes ecstatic. The power which makes his mind function leaves him and he becomes like one out of his mind; frightful death he considers joy, and never again does the contemplation of his mind suffer any interruption in the understanding of the heavenly.... His physical knowledge and vision leave him and he no longer feels it when he moves among things, and even if he does something he doesn't feel it completely, as one who has his mind suspended in contemplation and his thought in a continual conversation with someone.

Calling it as does Diadochos, "a beverage for the soul," here is how St. Isaac characterizes this beverage:

> The Apostles and martyrs, long ago, became drunk with this spiritual drink; the first, traveling all over the world in toils and in shame, the latter having their limbs cut off, shed their blood like water; and suffering the worst things they didn't weaken, but bore it all. [244]

So divine love is a drink, because it floods with its enthusiasm the worldly judgment of the mind and the feeling of the body. It moves the one who participates in it to another plane of reality. He sees another world, whose logic darkens the logic of everyday life; he receives the sense of other states, which overwhelm the feeling of bodily pains and pleasures. So, to this world, the martyrs seem to be crazy, but they are truly wise.[245] St. John of the Ladder states that divine love makes those who share in it no longer feel either pleasure from food, or even to of-

---

[243] *Directions to Hesychasts* 90, *GrPh* 4, pp .283-4; *cf. PhilPH*, p. 258.
[244] *Ibid.*
[245] *Ibid.*

ten want it. "Water under the surface nourishes the root of a plant, and their souls too are kept going by a heavenly fire."[246] Love is thus a force which, nourishing the spirit, also pours power into the body, so that it no longer needs regular food to sustain its vital functions.

But more interesting is another observation by John of the Ladder, that by loving a loved one, we are transformed. How much more when we love the Lord:

> If the face of the one we love clearly and completely changes us and makes us radiant and content and happy, what will the Lord's face invisibly do when He comes to the pure soul?[247]

---

[246] *The Ladder* 30.19, *PG* 88.1157BC; *cf.* Moore, p. 264.
[247] *Ibid.*, 30.16, *PG* 88.1157A; *cf.* Moore, p. 263.

34. Love as a Factor of Perfect Union And as Ecstasy

The great mystery of love is the union which it realizes between those who love each other, without their dissolution as free subjects. And yet, the two are not only thinking pleasurably of each other, but each receives the other into himself.

Between those who love there is no separation. It would be simplistic, however, to conceive of love as only a communication of energy from one to the other, just as it would be totally wrong to think of it as an identification of the egos. The energy which is communicated from the one to the other between those who love doesn't have a physical character and isn't communicated in the same way as physical energy. In a certain sense, the one loved doesn't send only his energy into the being of the one who loves, but his whole self, without ceasing to be in himself too. It is a projection of his whole being by his energy into the soul of the one who loves. And the image of the one loved isn't imposed with force, but is received and kept with joy; and better said, it is absorbed by the one who loves, to the point that you don't know who, along with his image, is sending more energy from himself to the other, the one loved or the one who loves.

Certainly this mutual communication of energy takes place differently between two people than between God and man. Here first of all God sends His energy into man. And the divine Eros descending into man makes him absorb the projection of the image of God in himself. But it isn't less true that the divine energy, once communicated to man, returns to God and in this return it takes the form of the affection of the human subject, alerted by divine energy. For not only does God love man, but man too loves God in turn, or he too sends his own energy toward God, or the divine energy is clothed and stamped by the intention and the affection of his own subject. If, as St. John of the Ladder says, the face of the beloved completely remakes us according to his image and fills our face with joy and charm, it means that an energy of his is transmitted to us and works in us, but not in a physical or subconscious way, but by our will, affection, and conscience, facilitated, however, by that energy that works more deeply in us.

This action of the image of the beloved's nature absorbed by that of the one who loves and vice versa was observed and insistently described by Ludwig Binswanger.[248] He called this absorption and the transformation which it causes, *imagination* in the etymological sense of the word.

---

[248] L. Binswanger, *Grundformen und Erkenntnis menschlichen Daseins* (Zurich, 1942).

LOVE: A FACTOR OF UNION AND ECSTASY   311

This imagination isn't a simple fantasy or illusion, without a real object, but the reception in the soul of the image of a real being, an intimate tie between two beings who love each other. The image of the beloved or of the one who loves received in me, I live as a true sustainer or foundation of my life.[249]

But Binswanger isn't satisfied with just mentioning this "imaginative" love, this joy of having the image of the beloved always in mind, but he also looks for its explanation. He finds it in a fundamental union, realized between people that love one another. We have seen that we experience God in prayer as the absolute sovereign Subject. As such we also experience any neighbor of ours, as we experience our own subject too. Neither our subject, nor that of our neighbor, can be captured, contained, subordinated, made an object. But if our neighbor's subject can't be captured, which happens especially in love when I'm not trying to do such a thing, and so I can't annul his sovereignty—I nevertheless experience him as given to me. I don't feel myself as a single individual in opposition to him, or him in opposition to me, because if this were true, the relationship of love would be broken. In love I don't only live myself or by myself, but also my neighbor or by my neighbor, without his ceasing to be a subject independent from me. This means, nevertheless, that I don't have him as an object of mine, as a part of my individuality, but in a free relationship with me, not of mine, but of ours. His subject is given to me, or is revealed to me as given to me, as my subject too, in a sovereign existence, but nevertheless holding to my existence, lived in one place with my existence. He becomes more intimate to me than anything which I possess; I see him penetrating more deeply in me than anything, and I penetrate him more than anything which he has. The intimacy between us is fuller than between me and anything I possess, but nevertheless I don't possess him as an object. I can't reduce him to something ruled by my own ego and I can't order him around or make decisions for him, by myself.

You give yourself to me freely and without ceasing to be sovereign, insubordinated to me as an object. I likewise give myself to you. Yet this means that neither I, nor you become the exclusive property of the other, but I am yours without ceasing to be mine and you are mine without losing your freedom, without ceasing to be yours. I am thus ours and you are ours.[250] Strictly speaking neither I nor you are "ours" in

---

[249] "Certainly the fantasy of love has two aspects: First, the creation of an image and secondly, a non-theoretical, the blessed or the believing cause and effect." *Ibid.*
[250] "You—the loved one—can only prove positively your independence to me by giving yourself to me and by receiving me as second person and at the same time as first person. In the same way I—the loving one—can only prove positively my independence from you by receiv-

the sense of objects owned together. Instead you and I experience "us" as a unity of free subjects, so connected, that it can't be severed. This unity is lived by each of our two subjects. Your subject is just as intimate to me, just as necessary as my own. Yes it is for me, or for my subject, the center of preoccupation and the source of life, just as my subject is, for you, a similar center and source.

We are two in a unity, and we look to each other. You are necessary to me, you hold to my existence, without being incorporated into my ego,[251] and I to your existence, without being incorporated in you. You are necessary to me, not so that I can make you my subordinate and servant, not because I feel the need for such a thing, but so that you can be for me my center of preoccupation and service. You are necessary to me as an autonomous subject, not as a subordinate object. You are necessary for me in order to replace care for myself with care for you, in order to put you in the place of my ego. You become so intimate to me, so much a part of me—I draw you so much into the center of my existence—that you substitute for my ego. You take the place of my ego, you hold the place of the first person in me. Still you keep yourself independent of me. St. Maximus the Confessor says: "By love each draws his neighbor as much to himself in his intentions and prefers him to himself, as previously he rejected him and preferred himself."[252] You do the same for me and in this is manifested the independence of your subject in regard to me. Precisely by this you make my happiness complete. It is a substitution of the egos. You have taken the place of my ego, and I have taken the place of your ego in you, by your will, not by my constraint.

But you have taken the place of my ego in me while remaining autonomous. So strictly speaking there isn't an absorption of you in me, but a going out from myself, of my living not around my own ego, but around yours, as well as your living around me. I don't experience only your living around me, but also mine around you. I am no longer the center of my life, but you are. So I experience you as a center; but because I am the center of your life, my value, my worth bears fruit through you, so that through myself I experience your worth. At the same time by you I also realize my value; thus even in regard to myself, I

---

ing you as your second person. The independence of this I and You is therefore not based on our existence as sometimes mine and sometimes yours but is based on our life, in other words, on the being of the existence as *Wirheit* [we-ness]. First from the wirheit springs the *Selbstheit* [selfness]. We are earlier than I myself and You yourself." *Ibid.*, p. 126.
[251] ...into my person, who is able to think, feel, act. trs
[252] *Second Letter to John the Valet, PG* 91.400.

know my value through you, or I have complete hold of myself through you. My self-consciousness is inseparable from yours, from "ours."

Dionysius the Areopagite says this about love as a going out from self:

> And the Divine Yearning brings ecstasy, not allowing them that are touched thereby to belong unto themselves but only to the objects of their affection.... And hence the great Paul, constrained by the Divine Yearning, and having received a share in its ecstatic power, says, with inspired utterance, 'I live, and yet not I but Christ liveth in me.'

By this love he is "beside himself unto God, and not possessing his own life but possessing and loving the life of Him for Whom he yearned."[253]

Strictly speaking neither do I belong to you, nor you to me, but both of us to a new common "we." I go beyond myself in the relationship of love with you; no longer am I enclosed in myself, but in some way enclosed between me and you; I have left the circle of my personality as you have too the circle of yours; we create a unity which no longer is reduced to the characteristics of a single ego, of mine or yours, and nevertheless it isn't outside the two of us. This doesn't mean having either both of ourselves in a common personality as we could have different objects in common, but as my ego alone is higher than the qualities of my personality but nevertheless I live it, so our egos are higher than an individual or common personality but we live them in common; and I and you live from the unity of the two subjects, without there ceasing to be two; I live "us" and you "us." So my tie with you can't be expressed as your incorporation into me, or of mine into you, but as an "encounter," as my going out from myself and of you from yourself; I stand open before you and you before me. This reciprocal opening is at the same time a mutual belonging and freedom. I can't exist without living you, and neither can you, without living me. I grow spiritually by living you, and you the same. It is my completion through you and yours through me.

I need to communicate to you certain things and if you listen with understanding, I too gain a new understanding of them. I gain in depth, I become transparent to myself as a subject because I penetrate into the depths of your subject, or because you freely open your depths. You are my hope and strength; I am your hope and strength. Even by considering yourself my hope and strength, you are strengthened, and I am too, because I consider myself your hope and strength. Our belonging to a

---

[253] *The Divine Names* 4.13, pp. 105-6.

common "we" makes it possible, when you cry out for my help, for me to feel that something which holds to me is suffering, and if I hit you it weakens me and I hurt myself in a much more essential way than if I were to lose some good thing which is exclusively mine. Maybe this is why the French say, *"partir c'est mourir un peu."*[254] Leaving your side, I die in some way, as you also die when you leave me. So this explains the sharp rebuke of my conscience when I have done evil to another and the responsibility which I feel for my neighbor. In love your belonging to the circle of my existence is revealed, as part of a "we," as part of a common reality which I belong to, and you too; and in this "we," without which I can't exist in a normal way, I have the role of receiving from you, as you have the role of receiving from me. Such reasoning explains this thing which I feel as a real miracle: You love me. Each subject understands why he loves the other, because he sees in the other a series of attributes and of help; he feels that without him he can't live. But he doesn't understand easily why the other loves him; in the other's love for him he feels worthless, uninteresting, without depth. No one can realize how much he enhances the value of the other, but he realizes how much the other is worth to him.

This is the opposite of pride and of thinking too much of oneself. Here we see that no one can be satisfied with himself without another, that his existence becomes rich and profound only through another. Living exclusively in myself, existence for me loses all content. Binswanger cites for this phenomenon the following words of Jean Paul, who sees the principle miracle not in loving, but in the fact of "being loved":

> The love with which the goodness of the other person receives us is something so mystical, that we can't penetrate its meaning, because we can't share the good idea that he does it for our ego; we can't understand how he can love us, but we reconcile ourselves to the idea, if we remember that the other person from his point of view understands just as little our love for him.[255]

So Christian love is joined to humility. In a way analogous with that of Jean Paul,[256] Dostoevsky has Markel, one of his characters, ask his servants: "My beloved, my good ones, why do you serve me? If God has mercy on me and lets me live, I will serve all of you, because each one must serve the other."[257]

---

[254] "To go away is to die a little." *trs*
[255] Binswanger, *op. cit.*, pp. 115-16, 216.
[256] Richter, Johann Paul Friedrich (1763-1825), usually called Jean Paul, "...the most important German humorist.'" *Encyclopaedia Britannica* 19 (1996), p. 316. *trs*
[257] *See also* F. Dostoyevsky, *The Brothers Karamazov* (New York, 1970), p. 347.

LOVE: A FACTOR OF UNION AND ECSTASY

How much harder it is for us to understand the mystery of the love of God for us and God's desire to respond to Him with our love. The worth which God has given us is amazing. Love is the proof of our eternal existence and the means of our perfection.

Sometimes this sentiment of our lack of importance makes us prepare to give a word of appreciation to someone who seems too far above us that he doesn't need it; other times we direct harsh words to our neighbors, thinking that they can't have any serious impact on them. But later we find with surprise how much the lack of a good word on our part hurt someone, or how much a bad word injured him.

It would seem, at first glance, that what is involved in this failure on our part to acknowledge certain people who seem superior to us is [the lack of] this same humility which must accompany our love. But true humility doesn't hesitate in giving others all the attention they deserve; the sentiment of our own littleness, being overwhelmed with the sentiment of the worth of another, must make us forget the little importance [which we think] our words and gestures can have, and to give the other all our attention without thinking of ourselves any longer, but exclusively of him. In this sense love is also a going beyond ourselves.

The humble feeling of this littleness of our own person doesn't exclude, however, our own growth by means of the love of neighbor.[258] I feel that, if I were to live for myself without the bond of love with someone else, I would be nothing, but in this relationship of love I grow; however, all the plus which I experience I attribute to him. We are going to see that we have the same sentiment when I grow in the love of God.

So love is realized when two subjects meet each other in a full, mutual experience, in their qualities as subjects, that is without the reciprocal reduction of each other to the state of objects, but revealing themselves to each other to the maximum, as subjects; nevertheless with all this they give themselves to each other with complete freedom. Love penetrates two subjects reciprocally in their intimacy, more than the interpenetration between a subject and a thing, without their ceasing to be sovereign and autonomous. By love you penetrate into the intimacy of your neighbor, into the kernel of his being, more than you can pene-

---

[258] This growth is gigantic. Goethe considers it even infinite: The meeting of two persons in love is equivalent to putting them in touch with the infinite source of existence, which has the same characteristics as nature reunified by love: "...your power is endlessly multiplied if you believe that I love you." Goethe to Frau v. Stein, March 12, 1781, in Binswanger, *op. cit.*, p 79. But it is equally true that in living together two or more persons who are not bound by love, keep picking on each other in such a torturous way, that their life is a real hell, from which many times they can't escape.

trate the nature of an object, even if you assimilate it by eating it. You penetrate him without annihilating or belittling him, but, on the contrary, you give him the opportunity to grow. So love is the supreme union and the reciprocal elevation and for that very reason, the supreme way of knowledge in which the neighbor isn't passive, but freer than in any other state or relationship. The more I love him, the more he reveals himself to me. The human subject can actualize such a bond with any subject when he has known him by means of the senses. So he is in such a relationship potentially and is called to actualize it with anyone. But the possibility of this tie being realized is more or less smothered by the attempt of the subjects to reduce each other to the state of objects, or by the lack of attention which one subject has for another. Pride, egotistic passions, waste away the normal relationship which awaits development in each of us. When, however, we develop this tie or we discover it in us, we put ourselves incomparably further into the interior of the other than formerly, and also into our own interior. Now our own depth is realized and becomes transparent to us, as well as the depth of our neighbor. His depth is revealed to us; it gives us a considerable plus of reality. The other person is revealed to us as having an amazing depth, an unsuspected richness. But what is strange is that this plus can't be defined exactly. As long as we remain in a superficial contact with our neighbor, when the great richness of his subject is covered, we can formulate in definite concepts certain characteristics of his and we tend to define them exactly; but, on the contrary, the revelation of his subject puts us in a relationship with an advantage incomparably greater, but impossible to define, in its essence, in concepts.

Love is a gigantic increase of knowledge; at the same time it produces a huge plus of life in the one loved and in the one who loves; it develops to the maximum his being and mine. But this knowledge can't be captured in concepts. Here the whole meaning of the "imagination" of Ginswanger is revealed to us. Realizing by direct experience that a treasure is contained in the subject of my neighbor which can't be delimited by concepts, I make use of imagination for every superiority in him, experienced, but uncaptured in concepts.

This imagination has multiple foundations of truth. First of all everyone's subject hides indefinite potentials, which can be turned to good account by love. So likewise only he who loves him grasps these potentials. This, first of all, because he intercepts in voluntary manifestations and in his spiritual vibrations a multitude of nuances which reveal the sleeping possibilities unobserved by the contemptuous or superficial view of those who are hostile or indifferent. Secondly, because the one who loves beautifies in a real way by his love each trait of the one loved.

Not only because he projects a wave of light over them, but also because in fact the loved one, feeling the love of the other, lives it as a power which brings out from his depths all that is good and at the same time he increases it considerably; in fact by our love we make others better and more beautiful, as we also do to ourselves. And thirdly, the one who loves fashions in himself an image of light of the other. This is due either completely to the potential hidden in the traits of the one loved, or to the ideals to which the tendencies of the one who loves aspires in an unknown way. It could be a synthesis of the aspirations of the one and of the potentialities grasped by the other, which is more probable.

In general, imagination is the product of certain forces, of potentials, of possibilities from the common resources of the two, from the content of the "we." And if the one who also imagines them believes powerfully in them, which happens in true love, the force from their base— in which the will is involved too, and is communicated from the one who loves to the loved one— it makes him also compel himself toward their actualization, making an abstraction of the fact that in him the ideal image which he makes regarding the other, is also working. The indefinableness of the subject loved, so rich in potentials, or the enriched duality of the subjects which love each other, includes as virtualities all that is expressed by their imagination; then the force of this imagination— which is the force of love, if the love is true, stable and powerful— succeeds in actualizing these potentials in each of them. Thus the image of the one loved, idealized by the imagination of the one who loves, becomes a model force which transforms the one loved from day to day, while the one who loves also actualizes more and more his idealized image, fashioned by the other. Strictly speaking, between my idealized image of the other, and his idealized image of me a fusion is produced by reciprocal communication, and I, making myself according to the image idealized by the other, actualize at the same time my idealized image which has started to become the image according to which the other is formed. And looking at the other, in the light of the reciprocally idealized image, in time each becomes very much like the idealized image of the other; for in looking at the other, each sees an idealized image of him according to which he models himself. It's understood that the new image of the two together carries not only the traits of the one or the other, but is a synthesis of the two, so that it isn't an egotistic victory of one ego, but of "ours" over my or your egotism, and my, and your, growth.

If imagination were lacking, the image of each would harden and lose its beauty. Imagination is the force by which the one who loves brings to the surface, as a diver, from the infinite treasures of the one loved, beauty and light and new transparencies for the image of the other and then for his own image, for the common image and in part he enriches it in a real way with them. When the imagination is stopped, love is extinguished. The force of imagination is love and the force of love is imagination. And in so much as love is in contact with a deep, true, reality, it too has a real base. On the other hand, love and imagination have a real creative power.

But we can also take another step forward in the clarification of the integral power of this imagination. As we have already seen, the one who loves, by discovering the indefinite depths of his neighbor's subject also discovers his own. This doesn't mean that he can't also descend by himself into these depths of his own, of course if he isn't devoid of the love of people in general. He can have such a power, however, only if he loves God. But we have seen that the one who descends into the unlimited depths of his own subject, also follows the scent of the divine infinite, in connection with his own unlimitedness too.

Certainly, in this case, the way that the subject goes down into his depths is the way of prayer. Someone might think that when we admit such a descent into our own depths, we contradict our affirmation that without the love of another we can't discover our own subject; so we mention that prayer doesn't stand in contradiction to the way of love, but it likewise is a way of continual growth in love. Because when we go forward by the Jesus Prayer, to mental prayer in the heart, we are sustained by love for Him. It grows continually, and fashions us, in a spiritual imaging of His spiritual image, according to His image. Then we feel Him ever more united with our ego, in a "we" from which I can no longer leave without the danger of being lost. And not only do I receive in me the ego, the "I" of Christ, which makes me according to His image, but also His "I" receives mine in Himself— He accepts even my body in Himself, so that He includes me in His pure senses, in His pure actions. Thus all of us who believe become one "body" with Him and with each other, a fact which will become perfected in the future life.

This is realized especially by the pure prayer addressed to Jesus. And He who carries out this substitution of the egos, between me and Christ and between all those united with Christ, is the Holy Spirit. He is the Spirit of this communion, because the Spirit is communion in the Holy Trinity too. But until I have reached the capacity for such a prayer which fills me with Christ, I must also grow much in love for my neighbors, and in the intervals when this prayer is interrupted I must feel more and more full of love for them. The steps of the spiritual ascent aren't so separate as we have described them previously for methodological reasons. At the same time a number of them coexist and the one who has reached one rung doesn't stay on it, but reaches up for another. With new spiritual riches, however, he is capable of climbing more easily the ones above than he has also descended.[259] As long as he lives on earth, a person can't always be in prayer, or always feel love.

In the line above we answered the common question: "How does our ego reveal itself, by the love of another, or by prayer which isn't connected to the love of another?" But because the opinion also exists that love isn't first, but self-revelation, we want to answer at greater length than we did previously, the question: "Which is primary, the self-revelation of the ego or the love of another?" Kirkegaard gave this answer: Self-revelation is first, and after it, with much trouble, love of others. "He who can't reveal himself, can't love."[260] This is also because we put prayer first, as a means of leaving the external world for the rediscovery of the ego, following the ascetical orientation of Orthodox spirituality. Binswanger, on the contrary, believes that the love of others comes first and after that comes self-revelation. He reverses Kirkegaard's sentence: "He who can't love can't reveal himself." Love comes before self-revelation.[261] Binswanger thus chooses so decisively the latter way, because he is thinking especially of the love between man and woman, which is also aided enormously by physical attraction and which can many times very easily fail. He has in view natural love, which has no need of prayer, of asceticism in order to be born in us as a gift of God.

But true love for any neighbor, the love which never fails, can't be born without prayer and without asceticism to purify the passions. It's true that without the revelation of the subject of our neighbor in true love neither do we discover all the depth of our subject. Thus we don't touch the ultimate perfection in prayer; but neither without prayer can we gain the full love of our neighbors. We believe that prayer as the love of God and the prayer of others progresses in parallel and conditions one another. But faith in God is first. It gives force to the will to love our neighbor, just as it sustains our effort in prayer.

---

[259] It seems that the author is saying that the spiritual person goes up and down, and learns from experience. *trs*

[260] "Every human being has in his inward and outward life various things which hinder him from becoming totally transparent to himself, from understanding himself clearly in his relation to the world, from revealing himself. He who can't reveal himself can't love and he who can't love is the most unhappy of all." Søren Kierkegaard, *Gesammelte Werke,* vol 2., p. 133 *ff.* [this citation was incomplete in the manuscript. *trs*].

[261] "He who can't love, can't reveal himself. Love and selflessness are one.... You are the one who removes those hindrances and helps me to become myself, quite transparent in my relations to the world, clear, evident." *Op. cit.,* p. 129.

We maintain that he who loves another discovers himself, helped too by prayer, or the one elevated to the step of mental prayer, is helped also by love. And discovering the boundlessness of his own subject, he discovers in connection and in communication with it the divine infinite too. This in proportion to how much he also discovers in the depths of his beloved neighbor and in inner communication with him, the divine infinite.[262] If this is so, the "imagination" of love has its infinite source in the adornment of one's neighbor with the features of the most ideal attributes; our neighbor can take hold of everything in a real way, if he has a relationship with Christ, either directly, either through me, whom I love by my relationship with Christ, the source of all the virtues.

This is the full meaning of loving imagination. But the infinity which is opened in the face of love isn't an infinity in substantial continuity with us. It is true that, in the loving form of "we," existence finds its boundlessness which is poured out in each of the two egos as an inundation of joy, as an overwhelming drink. But no matter how much we feel the boundlessness of the subject of our neighbor, at the same time we realize that our boundlessness isn't everything; it stands in relationship with a source distant from it, and infinite. So too the richness of my neighbor, or of the community between us has its source distinct from it, or from "us." Otherwise, the loving community doesn't last; it quickly depletes its source of sustenance. Love puts us in relationship with the infinite, only when this infinite is divine, when it is distinct as a nature from us, thus when it is imparted to us as a gift. In the community of love between me and another, God is present, without this meaning that the love of the other anticipates the encounter with God.

Binswanger thinks that the infinity of love is one of a universal nature and that the road to the meeting with this absolute leads only through a concrete "you." Therefore for him a road doesn't exist which first leads to the Absolute as a Person, because he isn't thinking of an Absolute Person. We Christians believe in the Absolute Person; we consider that we can meet first with this absolute "You" and only He can and wants to send love to us and to persons created according to His image.

The sentiment of fullness, of overflowing, of blessed intoxication, as the Fathers call it, we, too, live in fact in the love for others, in the

---

[262] St. Simeon the New Theologian says in this regard: "Each person, looking at his brother or neighbor the same as his God, should consider himself as small before his brother, as before his Maker." *The Practical and Theological Chapters* 114, *GrPh* 1, 2nd ed., p. 165, *RoFil* 6, p. 96, p. 94, or "We are obligated to look at all the faithful as one, and to reckon that Christ is in each one." *Op. cit.*, 61, in the *GrPh*, p. 158, *op. cit.*, 3; in the *RoFil*, p. 61. In fact from the one who loves you life flows, as from God, because he is in a relationship with God.

measure that the communication of love streams from me and my neighbor. But this plenitude can't have as an ultimate source a natural, universal base. Only the supreme, infinite Person, can be the source of such full love and joy. You realize that the overflowing joy which the other one has from you and the unrestricted will of containing you wholly in himself isn't caused only by you with your relativity. Neither can it come from the content of his being nor from an impersonal source. The other reveals himself to you and you to him as a gift of the infinite Person. So the joy of the one for the other is also a gift from the supreme Person Who is beyond both of you, who by him gives Himself to you and to him too by you. The fact that this conviction only lasts a moment strengthens it for you. If everything would come from nature and would be a part of it, it would last and be permanent. But when we receive it, it seems to us as though it is going to melt our being, as though it were going to break us apart, as though we would faint if it would last longer and become greater in intensity. If this spiritual joy originates from the resources of our being, which both of us have in common, how would we any longer experience our incapacity to live it wholly in continuation, or all the time?

We can spend a longer time in the intoxication of the love of God, at the height of pure prayer. Prolonged prayer, with the abandonment of the narrow forms of the images and interests for the limited objects of the world, has accustomed us to an "amplification of the heart," in order to have room for a joy which overflows its boundaries. Certainly on these culminating steps of prayer the intoxication of love doesn't appear as a product of the preparation by prayer. Prayer leads up to the "cessation" of the mind from every activity directed toward the limited. But the intoxication of the love of God descends all at once from above. Certainly, as we have already seen, it is necessary to specify that outside of this love as spiritual intoxication, as overflowing joy, which expresses the total absorption of your person in the other and of the other's in you, there is also a peaceful love, directed by rational consideration, which grows little by little. This is a preparatory condition for the other. And you gain this with the help of the grace of God, given at Baptism, but without excluding your efforts. The other comes, however, exclusively from above, not as produced by that before, but nevertheless having the need for preparation through it.

In the love for our neighbor, we likewise distinguish this longer stage and overflowing joy of a moment as a gift from above. If once in a while such a joy for a neighbor grips us without our being prepared by a special love for him, this is because our soul was prepared in general for love by prayer as a loving way toward God and consequently what followed from here was to love any person whatsoever. But in any case the moment of the ecstatic joy of a person, not following a special preparation of the amplification of the heart by the forsaking of all images, concepts and limited interests, has to last a much shorter time than the intoxication of the love of God.

A second factor which makes the ecstasy of love for God last longer, is that God Himself is now in a relationship with us and therefore near us. He gives our being an amplification capable of experiencing the infinity of a more stable love. This infinity itself overwhelms our being to such an extent that it seems that our bones, which are the most resistant part of our limited being, melt. The spiritualized person no longer feels, in the love with which he loves God, anything human. He is aware only of the power of the divine love poured out in him: He loves God with this same love with which God loves him.

Diadochos describes this state:

> In the measure in which someone feels the love of God in his soul, and accepts it, he enters into the love of God. Therefore such a person never ceases to go toward the light of knowledge with a love so powerful, that he feels even the strength of his bones being spent. He no longer knows himself, but is completely changed by the love of God. He is in this life and he isn't. Furthermore, living still in his body, by love he goes outside of himself, with the movement of the soul, continually toward God. Burning in the heart unceasingly with the flame of love, he is joined to God by the unweakened power of a great love, as one who has left once and for all self-love for the love of God.[263]

The ecstasy of love, or the sentiment of union with God, the sentiment that he forms with God a "we" actually experienced, becomes longer, producing a joy, a spiritual warmness more and more blessed. Now the prolonged ecstasy makes it so that the periods between one ecstasy and another are ever fuller of the consciousness of the actual presence of God, of peaceful love, joined with the work of the mind, so that man's life gains a continuity of uninterrupted love. This continuity is expressed by the Apostle Paul in this way: "If we seemed out of our senses, it was for God; but if we are being reasonable now, it is for your sake" (2 Corinthians 5:13), implying, however, "but for God too."

We shall have a part in perpetual ecstasy, strictly speaking, only in eternal life. Only then shall we completely leave discursivity, only then shall we continually take part, in our uninterrupted essential penetration of the divine subject, as well as of human subjects, of an eternal substan-

---

[263] *On Spiritual Knowledge* 14, GrPh 1, pp.238-9; cf. Phi 1, p. 256.

LOVE: A FACTOR OF UNION AND ECSTASY 323

tial knowledge, of a union with the very intimacy of divine and human reality.

Here is a question which needs more illumination in this chapter: "How, by union with the Absolute person, or with one or the other human subject, attained by love, is the union of the whole of human nature out of all subjects, and its union with God, realized?" The holy Fathers affirm it. St. Maximus the Confessor says that first of all love unifies the individual man. It replaces anger, falseness, gluttony and all the things in which man has taken part by bodily love of himself. When these things no longer exist, no trace of wickedness can persist; in their place various kinds of virtues are introduced, which integrate the power of love. However, by this unification of the individual man, the unification of individuals between themselves is also realized.

Now love brings together the things that are separated and makes man again a single logos and a single way of behavior and levels all the inequalities and the differences of opinion of all. Indeed, it takes them to a laudable equality, because each draws the other to himself in his intentions and he prefers him to himself, in the measure in which he rejected him formerly and preferred himself. And by love the self is emancipated. It is freely separated from its own *logoi* and preferences, from its thoughts and traits and it comes together in a simplicity and identity, on the basis of which no one can any longer be distinguished in any way, but each has become one with the other and all with all, or better, with God rather than between themselves, manifesting in them the same logos of being both according to nature and will.[264]

How then do we all become by love "a single man," united with God? At least as long as we live on earth, we can experience love as a short ecstatic state, directly in time, rather than only in relationship either with God, or with one or another of our neighbors. Thus too the perfect union realized by it. Especially the ecstatic love for God in mental prayer absorbs us so much in union with God, that we forget people, something which doesn't happen so exclusively in the moment of ecstatic love of a neighbor. For in the latter case, in the engrossing contemplation of a neighbor we realize that in relationship with the boundlessness of his subject stands the divine boundlessness. So by this, in an indirect way, the union between us and God is also realized. But in the moment of this ecstatic love with God, or with a neighbor, we don't experience an actual union with all people.

It follows that only in peaceful everyday love, manifested in fact and in thought, in Christian love in a broad sense, can we experience more

---
[264] *Second Letter to John the Valet, PG* 91.400.

or less, love for all men. My interest, my passions, contradictory opinions, as voluntary manifestations, no longer break the unity of nature between me and my neighbor. Every moment I judge things from the point of view of my neighbor with whom I am connected; I replace my ego with his and give up mine. By doing this right along with various neighbors with whom I come in contact, the sentiment of my union, actual or virtual with anyone, is strengthened. On my part there is no longer a rift between me and them; I no longer see any such thing. If they do, I don't.

This steady behavior strengthens the sentiment of my unity with them and with God. This makes the living of a perfect union easier, in moments of ecstatic love, of contemplation of the subject of any neighbor regardless of what he has that is victorious, boundless, and mystical. And in turn these moments strengthen my behavior, which is full of attention and of self-denial in regard to any neighbor. The energy of my love for another, also nurtured by the effort of will, but especially by these moments of ecstatic contemplation, is easily directed later toward other people. And everywhere I gain a steady disposition of love for anyone, a joy for all, a conviction that in each one I can discover the mystery of enchanting depths. I feel united virtually with everyone and with every concrete opportunity; this virtual and indirect union is easily realized and becomes direct. And the love which I manifest for my neighbors fills them with its energy; this has as a result its return to me and its propagation toward other neighbors of theirs. The energy of love, come down from above, has the tendency of becoming a universal tie between all people and between them and God.

Love for others grows from the habit of love for God and especially from living it as ecstasy on the culminating step of prayer; now love for God is made easier for us by the practice of loving our neighbors. The soul full of love acts the same before God and all men. It feels a part of the universal "we," a partner of God every moment and ready to become a partner every moment with one neighbor or another in the tie of Christian ecstatic love.

In the joy that I have because of you, my love for you, which goes so far that I forget my ego, in order to put you in its place, in the union between you and me; human nature divided up into persons conquers its segmentation and finds itself again in its unity, a fact which gives it an overflowing joy. The allocation into persons was and is necessary precisely because by reciprocal love between them they discover their worth and a beauty which otherwise they couldn't find.

The unity discovered by the love of a nature allocated into subjects is valued in another way and so it nurtures an unending joy and affection.

LOVE: A FACTOR OF UNION AND ECSTASY

Binswanger says: "*Wirheit* [we-ness] in life is a sign, greeting, challenge, expression and embrace of existence with itself: with one word, an encounter."[265] We could better call the meeting through love a "rediscovery." This is a sentiment experienced by two beings who have found their souls in love. Human nature finds again through love its unity divided by sin. So the sentiment of the one who loves, as of the one loved, rediscovers its home after it has gone astray.[266] Its home is interiority, the ultimate base, the hearth of rest. So we can say that man, as long as he is alone, even in the state of "interiority," isn't truly "at home" in himself, in other words in his true "interiority."

The husband's home is where the wife is, the wife's home is where the husband is, or better said "the home" is made up of both, as an expression of "we."

A building where the one loved no longer lives has become a desert, as proof that what made it "home" was the presence of the one loved. Those who love each other receive each other in their hearts; they open their hearts one to the other: That is intimacy.[267] The heart which opens up to the one loved isn't only the self-revelation of the subject in its infinite depths, but also the affection with which this subject opens itself to receive the other.

The joy which we have because of the encounter with God in love shows us that here too we are talking about rediscovery. Human nature, being the work of the creative love of God, finds itself in a relationship and in an original nearness to Him. The Union realized by love gives it the sentiment of rediscovery, of coming home again, of entering into rest, as St. Augustine wrote: "Our heart is restless until it rests in Thee."[268] We have the feeling that in the love of God as ecstasy, God has opened His heart to us and received us in it, just as we have opened our heart so that He can enter it. On the other hand, the coming back to God, to His heart, means to enter His home. God's "home," however, wants to include all people, because in His heart there is room for everybody, and when I enter it I must feel that by being there I am united

---

[265] *Op. cit.*, p. 170.
[266] Love is "to be at home in one another, irrespective of (universal) nearness or distance or presence or absence. Being at home in one another is the necessity for the possibility that, where you are, a place can grow, no matter if you are present or absent." *Ibid.*, p. 46.
[267] *The Openness of the heart* [in German], *idem, op. cit.*, p. 105. The world is no longer an opaque wall before your heart, swollen with cares and egotistic passions, but becomes transparent (*wird die Welt auf dich transparent*). "The penetration of the world of caretaking and provision with the spirit of love on the one hand and transparency of the world of provision of this spirit on the other hand" is produced. *Op. cit.*, pp. 97-8. But the positive character of the opening of the heart to the transcendental and to the beloved, concerned with the good or the salvation of the other, must of analyzed too.
[268] Fr. Staniloae has used the Latin: "*Inquietum est cor nostrum donesc requiescat in Te.*" trs

with everyone there. Coming back to God, we truly come back home where we belong to the supreme parental home, together with all the heavenly Father's children. To be in this parental "home" with all the loved ones is the highest and purest structure of love. We shall see how this structure is revealed to Moses under the image of the "tabernacle" from on high, according to which the tabernacle, the temple and Church below were made. In this "home," which is God Himself, it is possible to progress infinitely, without being able to enter its nature itself, in the "altar" (the Holy of Holies). But those who love each other dwell one in the other. Not only do we enter into God, but also God into us. The intoxication of the love of God, experienced at the height of pure prayer, fills me with the impulse to love all people, to accept all in my heart, who are found in the heart of God, to feel that I am with all in the interior of the same "home" of God, which is the Church.

35. Love, Knowledge and the Divine Light [269]
I. The Role of the Mind in the Vision of the Divine Light

We have seen that the mind— after it has reached, on the highest steps of prayer and thought, the spiritual image of Jesus— is stopped, amazed, before the divine boundlessness; nothing remains but the love which has gradually grown by the diligence of man up to the limits of his powers. In this moment of the dumbfounded standstill of every mental operation, in this moment in which the spirit feels that it is at the limit *(Grenzsituation)* of human powers, the love of God descends over him and ravishes him in ecstasy. It is an exclusively divine work. Our spirit realizes that this experience isn't the result of its own effort. But this doesn't exclude consciousness of self and of Him Who loves this self. Because in this consciousness it sees at the same time its state of astonishment: It realizes its powerlessness to move itself by efforts to understand within the interior of the mystery of the boundlessness which it feels. This will be the state of the soul in the coming life; it is lived here only momentarily on a greatly reduced level. This cessation doesn't mean the overall suspension of every operation of the mind whatsoever, for now the Holy Spirit is working, and the mind is conscious of His work and receives it. Those who reach this state embrace with joy the unspeakable. Therefore, as St. Gregory Palamas puts it, coming out of this state, they communicate their experiences to others. They refute the erroneous idea that everything has stopped in their spirit, that everything is deadened:

> As I have said however, they, who from the love of men say the unsayable, take away the error of those who ignorantly think that after the removal from things there is total rest, but not a rest which is above work.[270]

For in some kind of way the mind also participates in this work, because "a give and take" goes on, says the same saint.[271] The Holy Spirit gives [these unspeakable things], and the mind receives them. The cessation mentioned previously means only that the mind no longer discovers them by its operation, but by that of the Holy Spirit. So it no longer modifies the things received by its own operation, but it receives them as they are. The mind even receives them by the working of the Holy Spirit. We could say precisely because of this that the mind knows now a truer reality, in as much as it no longer modifies it by its activity. The

---

[269] Chapters 35 and 36 are one in the original. They were divided for practical reasons. *trs*
[270] *The Defense*, 1.3.19, p. 191; *cf. The Triads*, p. 36.
[271] *Ibid.*

mind doesn't process knowledge, but it receives it, suffers it. But suffering is also life.²⁷²

The cessation of mental activity, which is caused by the descent into the soul of the divine activity, doesn't make all the previous effort of the mind useless. The toil to be sharpened and broadened in ever more subtle and comprehensive understanding isn't lost. The exclusive activity of God is inaugurated during the moment of the ecstasy in this present life and will alone remain in the future life. This activity is proportional to the stage which the mind has reached by its own efforts, because the mind is also in the process of the purification of the passions.²⁷³ Without it the mind can't be raised to the ecstatic love of God.

The positive role of the mind in the experience which it receives, after the cessation of its mental activity, is also expressed by Dionysius the Areopagite and by St. Gregory Palamas in this way: They attribute to it, along with the power of the natural activity directed toward created things, also the power to enter into union with God, to accept the union and spiritual feeling of uniting with God. It's true that this sense of union is due to the divine activity dwelling in it. But an object couldn't assimilate this spiritual feeling caused by God. The mind has the capacity to appropriate as its own the divine, spiritual operation; it is *capax divini,* capable of the divine, and this capacity has gone from virtuality to actuality, by the cleansing of the passions. St. Gregory Palamas also declares:

> If our mind couldn't surpass its own self, there would be no vision or understanding above mental activities.... And that the mind has the power to surpass itself and by this power to unite with things higher than it, the great Dionysius also says very clearly. And not only that he says it simply, but he presents it to Christians as a knowledge among those most necessary. 'It is necessary,' he says, 'to know that our mind has on the one hand the power to understand, by which it contemplates the intelligible; on the other [it has] the union which surpasses the nature of the mind and by which it is joined to the things beyond it.'²⁷⁴

---

²⁷² The author uses suffering in the old English sense of "patient endurance." *trs*

²⁷³ Note how St. Maximus presents this idea: "The Sabbath of God is the full return to him of all creatures whereby he rests from his own natural activity toward them, his very divine activity which acts in an ineffable way. For God rests from his natural activity in each being by which each of them moves naturally. He rests when each being, having obtained the divine energy in due measure, will determine its own natural energy with respect to God." *Chapters on Knowledge* 1.47, *Maximus Confessor, Selected writings*, p. 136. Perhaps this is the reason why man can no longer do anything for his salvation in the next life.

²⁷⁴ *The Defense*, 2.3.48, p. 503. The quote from St. Dionysius the Areopagite is from The *Divine Names* 7.1 (London, 1979), p. 147.

So even in the mind there is a tendency to surpass itself, that is to surpass its natural activity directed toward created things and to unite with Him Who can't be understood by this activity. Although the realization in fact of this surpassing or of this union can't be attained by the mind by itself, for it can't have by nature a natural and a supernatural activity, nevertheless God, raising it to a union with Him, also used this mental capacity. (A comparison: The human organism needs air, but air isn't produced by this need; however, without the need for it, air would try in vain to enter the organism.)

Another thing which points to the positive role of the mind in the union with God, in the vision of the divine light, is the fact that the mind, in the beginning, doesn't receive the same [amount or intensity of] divine light, but there is a continual progress in its vision.[275] This must depend on an unceasing amplification of its power to see, to contain, to appropriate the ever higher understanding of that which dwells in it as a divine activity. We have said that its function is from above, but the subject of the function is, together with God, the mind. This means that not the subject or the human organ produces this function, but that it comes from above; it also means that the organ must prepare itself previously, to keep growing by its natural function, to be able to handle more and more functional power which comes from above. According to the holy Fathers the connection of the mind with divine light is comparable to the relationship of the eye to the light of the sun. The eye can't see without it, but it must be capable of receiving the light. In this sense it must also be exercised and must continue to be exercised in the measure in which it receives it in ever-larger quantities. St. Gregory Palamas comments:

> ... which creature could contain in itself all the infinite power of the Spirit, in order to observe by it all that is of God?... Even the radiance of that light, which paradoxically has for material the sight of the seer, enlarges that spiritual eye by union and makes it continually able to contain more and more of it, even it, I say, doesn't cease forever: It enlightens the eye with ever more brilliant rays and always fills it with an ever more hidden light and reveals to it by itself things never discovered previously.[276]

---

[275] St. Gregory Palamas speaks of a "continuous progress of the angels and of the saints toward ever clearer contemplations in the age that never ends." *The Defense*, 2.3.56, p. 521.
[276] *Ibid.*, 2.3.31, pp. 469-71.

The Meaning of the Divine Light

But what is the divine light revealed to the mind on the highest steps of pure prayer?

It is, from one point of view, simply the happy radiation of divine love, experienced in a more intensive form in moments of ecstatic focus on God.

We have seen that in moments of ecstatic love the depths of a beloved subject are opened and become loving and smiling to our view. It is a knowledge higher than knowledge, when our subject or mind has gone out of itself. In these moments we submerge ourselves in the loving boundlessness of his heart, forgetting ourselves. This re-finding of nature, in the loving unity of "I-you" fills both of us with an unending joy. In the presence of the loved one, who no longer, strictly speaking, is only a material image, it seems to us that this joy fills everything and that from it radiates a charm and a light which also fills us with light. Who hasn't noticed that in an ecstatic gaze two beings are illuminated by a smile? The experience which characterizes this state could be expressed by three terms: love, a knowledge by experience, higher than the conceptual, and the light which is the expression of joy. The spiritual light is always the expression of the subjects that love each other. But it is projected also on a material level, making it luminous too. The mutual discovery of subjects is a work of love, and is equivalent to their luminous or smiling radiation.

All this expresses what happens on the supreme steps of pure prayer, when the divine light is seen, which is described and experienced by people who live it, on the above terms. Therefore, the love of God, knowledge and light are always presented to us in a close relationship. Sometimes only two of these terms are mentioned, but always the third is presupposed. Note for example a passage from St. Maximus the Confessor, where he speaks only of love and of the divine light:

> When the mind borne by the eros of love goes out of itself to go toward God, it knows neither itself, nor anything else that exists. For illumined by divine and infinite light, it no longer perceives things created by Him, just as the physical eye no longer sees the stars when the sun comes up.[277]

But even here we see that the light which it mentions is at the same time knowledge because its appearance is as the appearance of the sun

---

[277] *Chapters on Love* 1.10, GrPh 2, p. 4; cf. Phi 2, p. 54.

which makes the stars invisible; in other words when the mind is absorbed in the vision of God, it no longer sees created things.

The light is always knowledge, and the light of knowledge is the fruit of love. But a light or a knowledge which arises from love, which is nothing but an expression of the state of love, is at the same time life. Here is another quotation from St. Maximus: "If the life of the mind is the light of knowledge, while the love of God creates it, it's good to say that nothing is greater than love."[278]

The knowledge understood as light, as life in love, has thus an existential character. It isn't only a part of life, or something foreign and opposed to life, as it often appears to us on this level, but it is life itself. "And eternal life is this: to know you, the only true God, and Jesus Christ whom you have sent."[279] Wanting to bring out the existential character of this knowledge experienced in love, St. Maximus compares it with the warmth of fire, actually felt by the body, in distinction to the knowledge by faith without love, whose content isn't experienced, but is found at a distance, which he compares with the fire imagined or remembered: "Just as the memory of fire doesn't warm the body, so faith without love doesn't energize the light of knowledge in the soul."[280]

So St. Maximus, a little further on, presents love in a relationship to knowledge: "As the light of the sun attracts the healthy eye to it, so the knowledge of God naturally draws the clean mind to Him, by love."[281] The term "love" is missing here. But in the sentence immediately following he presents the tie between light and knowledge, omitting love: "A pure mind is one separated from ignorance and illumined by the divine light.."[282] Finally, in the text which follows, the love of God and joy are put together, in some way substituting the term "light" with that of "joy": "The pure soul is one freed from passions and unceasingly filled with the joy of divine love."[283]

We have followed the mind in its journey toward itself by prayer; we have understood how in seeing itself, it indirectly is following the scent of the nearness of God. Then we have seen it being stopped for a moment, dumbfounded, from every activity. Then divine love descends from above as a fire over a sacrifice passively laying on a mountain peak or on an altar before the unseen God. Then divine love can ravish it that it might by itself go beyond the curtains of darkness which hide God

---

[278] *Ibid.*, 1.9.
[279] John 17:3.
[280] *Chapters on Love* 1.31, *GrPh* 2, p. 6; *cf.* Phi 2, p. 56.
[281] *Ibid.*, 1.32.
[282] *Ibid.*, 1.33.
[283] *Ibid.*, 1.34.

from men when it goes forward only on its own efforts. The mind which no longer sees even itself and which now functions not by its own activity, but exclusively by the divine, has penetrated into the zone of the divine light which radiates from the bosom of the divine subject, that is, from the bosom of the Holy Trinity.

Note how St. Gregory Palamas describes the steps of this ascent:

> The one who desires union with God... frees his soul as much as possible from every impure tie, and dedicates his mind to unceasing prayer to God, and by this becomes wholly himself; he finds a new and secret ascent to the heavens, an unapproachable ascent to the silence of the initiate, as someone might say.[284] With an unspeakable pleasure, he submerges his mind in this deep night full of pure, full, and sweet quietness, of a true tranquility and silence and he is lifted up above all creatures.[285] In this way, he completely goes out of himself and becomes wholly of God; he sees a divine light inaccessible to the senses as such, but precious and holy to pure souls and minds; without this vision the mind couldn't see by being united with the things above it, only by its mental sense, just as the body's eye can't see without perceptible light.[286]

In the time of prayer the mind still knows itself as in some way separated from God; it doesn't see Him, but it just feels Him present in the shadows, as the one through Whose grace his own subject exists. In other words, if in the time of prayer the mind sees itself directly and God only indirectly, from the moment that it is carried off from itself it sees God directly, and it no longer knows itself. This is the experience of love in moments of ecstasy: I no longer see myself, but only you; in the horizon of my sight you take the place of my ego. In fact the divine light is considered as being a reflex of the loving face of God or of the faces which love each other or love us, of the Holy Trinity. Where light is seen, God is no longer covered with a shadow; His presence is no longer just supposed, but He has uncovered His face, which radiates light. St. Simeon the New Theologian writes:

---

[284] The picture is of one newly initiated into the mysteries of an ancient religion of Greece. He is finally inside, but so awed that he can't move or touch anything. *trs*
[285] First is the night, or the cessation of the natural mental activities. Next the flight from the self, or beyond it, which isn't its own doing, but of God, that is a ravishment after which the place of his work has received the divine work. First is the "rest" of the mind, or the "Sabbath," then the "Resurrection," or "the Lord's Day," as St. Maximus the Confessor says in *Chapters on Knowledge* 1.53, etc. *cf. Maximus Confessor, Selected writings*, p. 137 *ff.*
[286] *The Defense*, 1.3.46, p. 247.

For the light of His glory goes before His face and it is impossible that He should appear otherwise than as light. Those who have not seen this light have not seen God: for God is Light.[287]

But this exit of the mind from itself couldn't take place if God hadn't also gone out from Himself. This fact is illustrated for us again by the comparison of the moment of ecstatic love between two human beings. If the loved one doesn't open himself up with a smile, but stays enclosed [in himself], the unifying ecstasy of love can't take place. The lack of light on his face is a sign that he wants to stay locked up, a sign that he isn't going out from himself, or that he doesn't receive the other in himself. Ecstasy between people takes place in a mutual exit of the one to the other. This might also be called exaltation, in the same way that the going out to meet the loved one could be called descent, and the entrance into the other, when he opens up too, exaltation. The exit of God from Himself, however, in order to receive man, is on a kenotic descent.[288] God must open Himself to us through love, for us to be able to enter into a vision of Him. If He were to stay enclosed in Himself, we couldn't penetrate into Him. For us humans the enclosure of ourselves within ourselves is egotism; therefore it is an unnatural state. For God, however, a descent to man isn't necessary and the lack of this descent doesn't mean egotism, because God has a life of love and of light in inter-trinitarian relationships. Therefore when a man goes out in the meeting of another by love, that which he does isn't only a gift, but also an inner necessity for fulfillment. The descent of God to man through love is, however, exclusively a gift. So divine love for man is something else than a necessity of the nature of God; it is only a benevolent act of His. It follows that our union with God in love isn't a union imposed by His nature; this would bring God down to our level, in a pantheist sense.

From the above we see that the love with which God loves us and we Him isn't an essential love with which the divine hypostases [persons] love each other. It is nevertheless an uncreated love, with its source in God's essence. So neither the opinion of Peter Lombard, who says that we love God with the love of God, is just, if by "the love of God" we understand the love with which God loves us, and not the simple love of God; nor the opinion of Thomas Aquinas, according to whom our love for God is created.[289]

---

[287] Homily 79.2, Russian ed. from Mt. Athos, 2.318-19, as quoted in Lossky, *Mystical Theology*, ch. 11, pp. 218-19.
[288] The reference is to Philippians 2:7, where we read that Christ emptied Himself when He became man. Theologians use the Greek, *kenosis*, which means an emptying. *trs.*
[289] Lossky, *op. cit.*, ch. 10, p. 213. Lossky also sees here the error of S. Bulgakov, who would identify the divine energy *(Sofia)* with the essence of God. Stating the Orthodox point of view in this regard he says: "When we say that God is Wisdom, Life, Truth, Love—we understand the

So by making a way for us to His interior, God doesn't give us His essence, but only an operation of His. Therefore we don't become gods by essence. God descends to man in two senses, although simultaneously. By one descent He places in us an activity of divine love for Him, by the other He opens Himself before our love, which is from Him, and which He now seeks. God first loves us with such a love, that it makes us also love Him. First God seeks our heart, that later we can try too to enter into Him. Regarding this second descent of God from Himself, St. Gregory Palamas writes:

> So our mind goes out of itself and so is joined to God, but becomes above itself. On the other hand God too goes out of Himself and so unites Himself thus with our mind, but He does this by condescension. In other words it's as though He were driven by Eros and by love and goes out of Himself, not, however, communicating His depth, not leaving His transcendence, by the abundance of His goodness and unites Himself with us by that union above understanding.[290]

In other words, this descent has as its effect the carrying away of the mind from relations with created things and from the order of its natural activities to the transcendent plane of the divine; therefore it isn't strictly speaking a descent, but an attraction of the seer into the darkness which separates the divine transcendence from the order of created things. It's a descent only in so much as it's a willingness to raise to His bosom a created mind. Palamas describes the entrance of Moses into the divine darkness on Sinai, that is, the raising of his mind to the vision of the divine light, after the cessation of all mental activity:

> But how? Is the divinity no longer hidden, someone might ask? Of course it is. God doesn't go out of His hiddenness, but He gives Himself also to others, hiding them under the divine darkness. But what is more, by raising him above himself and unfastening him in a mystical way from himself and putting him above all perceptible and mental activity, He hid him from himself (what a miracle!) The same thing happened to the divine Paul.[291] He didn't know what he was seeing and he asked himself: Who is it that is seeing? And again that which exceeds all amazement is that in this ineffable and supernatural showing He also remains hidden.[292]

---

energies, which are subsequent to the essence and are its natural manifestations, but are external to the very being of the Trinity." *Ibid.*, pp. 80-1. We don't know if the word "external" is wholly suitable.
[290] *The Defense* 1.3.47, p. 249.
[291] The reference is to 2 Corinthians 12:2 *ff.*, where the Apostle talks of a vision.
[292] *Ibid.*, 2.3.56, p. 521.

But neither is the exit of the mind from itself one that we can call ontological. This going out means that the mind no longer sees itself in a direct way, but it searches by stretching out beyond itself. The vision of external objects is also a kind of exit of the mind from itself. But while the one is a going out to the exterior, the other is a going out to the interior. The going out means that it isn't enclosing itself in its self-contemplation. But it also means the leaving of its natural function and replacing it with a divine one. This going out in its two senses brings about the union of the mind with the divine light which it sees. Seeing by the light of divine love which descends into it, and looking at this light gone out from God which is reflected over it and in the mind itself—this fills it and makes it light. Whoever looks at a light which is shining from the face of a loved one is also filled with it. The light and brilliance from the face of the beloved also reaches the face of the one who loves, and envelops both in a common light and joy. In time, this imprints them with common values and traits and makes the two alike.

The Vision of the Light and the Self-perception of the Mind

So the mind doesn't only see the divine light beyond itself, but also within. From beyond the mind, this light reaches to its interior. But its intention must not be to see itself, but that which is higher than itself and beyond itself, so that it can see it even in itself. We could say that when the mind sees itself, it does so directly, and God indirectly; now it sees God directly and itself indirectly, or in union with Him. Looking at God and forgetting itself it realizes at the same time the blessedness that fills it, which comes to it from God, and this blessedness is the light which it feels in itself, even if it isn't preoccupied in a direct way with itself. The mind, going out of itself has gone, or has let itself be taken, to God, but looking at God and seeing Him as light it also sees itself filled with light. Maybe this is what St. Gregory Palamas means by the words, "the mind sees itself as something else."

St. Gregory Palamas, although he continually sustains that the mind goes out of itself when it sees the divine light, also admits its self-perception during these moments:

> But seeing itself, it sees more than itself: It does not simply contemplate some other object, or simply its own image, but rather the glory impressed on its own image by the grace of God. This radiance reinforces the mind's power to transcend itself, and to accomplish that union with those better things which is beyond un-

derstanding. By this union, the mind sees God in the Spirit in a manner transcending human powers.²⁹³

In another place he says that this reflection of the divine light in the mind makes it become by participation what the original, as cause is:

> The mind is an immaterial nature and so to speak a light related to the first and supreme light which is imparted to all. It remains separate from all things, and its integral tension toward the true light urges it to look intensely toward God, by unceasing, pure, immaterial prayer. It arrives thus in the angelic state and is illumined by the First Light in a way proper to the angels. So it becomes by impartation that which the original is because of its attribute of cause and the mind discovers in itself that brilliant, hidden, all enlightening and unapproachable beauty, a brilliance which the divine chanter David feels in himself with the mind; and so he joyfully reveals to the faithful this great and unspeakable good, saying, "And may the splendor of the Lord our God be upon you."²⁹⁴

So what Lossky says is right: The vision of the divine light means a growth of self-consciousness, better said, the supreme step of self-consciousness, just as unconsciousness or "sleep of the soul" is a sign of sin. "Whereas the life of sin is sometimes willfully unconscious (we shut our eyes in order not to see God), the life of grace is an increasing progress in knowledge, a growing experience of the divine light."²⁹⁵ The divine light is this without being only this. And this consciousness of self is at the same time a consciousness of our littleness, or the other way around: Humility means the consciousness of self, just as pride is the lack of it.

St. Maximus the Confessor says:

> When the mind is ravished through love by divine knowledge, and goes out from all beings it feels the divine infinity; then according to the divine Isaiah it comes by surprise to the feeling of its own humility and with all earnestness repeats the words of the prophet: 'Woe is me ... because I am a man of unclean lips ... for mine eyes have seen the King, the Lord of hosts.'²⁹⁶

Self-consciousness, or the consciousness of our own littleness, however, agrees with the fact that the mind sees itself not as a source of

---

²⁹³ *Ibid.*, 2.3.11, p. 431; *cf. The Triads*, p. 58.
²⁹⁴ *Ibid.*, 1.3.39, pp. 231-3; Psalm 90:17.
²⁹⁵ *Mystical Theology*, ch. 11, p. 219. "Gnosis, the highest stage of awareness of the divine, is an experience of uncreated light, the experience itself being light." *Ibid.*, p. 218.
²⁹⁶ *Chapters on Love* 1.12, GrPh 2, pp. 4-5; *cf. Phi* 2, p. 54; Isaiah 6:5.

light, but as a simple receiver, as the bearer of a spiritual power given to it.

The mind's self-perception, not as something that has its own content, but as a container emptied of everything, through whose transparent walls the divine light has penetrated and shines brightly, confirms this truth: The mind sees first of all that light. Even when seeing itself, it is also in tension toward that which it is not, toward the divine light, which fills it and embellishes it. It sees itself only as a reflector of the divine light, a reflector which doesn't put any content of its own in the field of vision; yes it has the consciousness that even the power by which it sees, even the function of sight is of God.[297] It is only the subject which partakes of the vision. At the same time, in which it sees itself, the mind is surpassing itself. Its own vision under these conditions doesn't limit it to a plane of subjectivity. Rather its vision holds the mind beyond itself. This beyond, however, has penetrated even into the mind's interior, without identifying itself with it, or the mind has penetrated wholly into this beyond. Thus, seeing God it sees itself, or seeing itself it sees God without it being confused [with Him]. A comparison is that when I see you in a moment of ecstasy of love I see myself in you too. I have surpassed myself by penetrating you. Also by looking into myself I see you and this fills me and imprints me completely.

The Divine Light is Spiritual

From all the above we understand that the divine light seen in ecstasy at the height of pure prayer isn't a physical light, but spiritual, seen within. St. Gregory Palamas brings this out in detail.

Palamas considers that this light radiates eternally from the presence of Jesus Christ, and clothes in light the souls of the righteous after death. So he asks:

> And ... when we offer prayers for the departed we cry out at length to the goodness of the Godhead, 'Put their souls in a place of brightness.' What need then do souls have of perceptible light? And what difficulty will there be for them from the contrary darkness, perceptible however? Do you see that none of these things is principally perceptible?[298]

---

[297] St. Gregory Palamas says that, when some sense of ours is working, or the mind, we are aware of it. So too, when something superior to our powers is working in us, we are aware of it. "So this sense is above sense and mind, for when each of these two is working and because it is working, it is felt and understood." *The Defense* 2.3.24, p. 457.
[298] *Ibid.*, 1.3.28, p. 209.

And a little further on he asks again:

> I wonder if the body of Christ shines there for nothing, when there is no one to see that light? Because it would shine for nothing if it were perceptible. Or is it truly the nourishment of spirits, as much for angels as for the righteous? This is why we ask Christ, when we are praying for the reposed, to put their souls where they see the light of His face. How then will their souls rejoice in it, if it is perceptible? How will we rest in general in a light which is perceptible?

Recalling a line from Macarius the Great, who describes this light as the garment of the glory of Christ, in which God will clothe the souls of the righteous after death, Palamas asks again: "How then will this become a garment for the soul, if it is perceptible?"[299] And in a long passage, he states in connection with one of the affirmations of Dionysius the Areopagite regarding the divine light, which will be everything for us in the future age:

> Because really he is saying that we will glow with that same light in the future age, where there is no need of light or air or any other of the elements of this present life, as we are taught from Sacred Scripture, "because then God will be all in all," according to the Apostle.[300] Then we won't need of course perceptible light either if really God will be everything for us, and that light will be divine too. So how will it be by principle perceptible? [Now what Dionysius adds regarding the more divine imitation of the angels, which can have three meanings, shows that the angels too perceive this light. How can this be if it is perceptible?][301]
>
> And if it is perceptible, it will be visible by means of air; consequently each one will see the light brighter or dimmer, not according to the measure of his virtue and its purity, but according to the measure of the purity of the atmosphere.
>
> [So its clearer or darker view depends on the latter and not the former.][302]
>
> And if 'the righteous will shine as the sun,' then each of them will also appear brighter or darker not according to his good deeds, but according to the cleanliness of the atmosphere. Moreover, the things of the future age will be now and henceforth comprehensible to physical eyes, things which 'eye has not seen, nor ear heard,' and have not even 'entered into the heart of man,'[303] and will be penetrated by intellectual assaults. And how will it be invisible to sinners,

---

[299] *Ibid.*, 1.3.29, p. 211.
[300] 1 Corinthians 15:28.
[301] Fr. Staniloae's text has this which is in addition to Hristou's. trs
[302] Here is another textual difference between Staniloae and Hristou. trs
[303] 1 Corinthian 2:9.

if it is perceptible? Or will there be partitions then too, and shadows, and cones of shadows, and as a result ecliptic connections and various circles of light, so that then too the futile pedantry of astrologers will be required in the contemplative life of the age without end?[304]

How then is that light not higher than the senses, when it is above the mind, when it shows itself only after the cessation of every natural activity of the human spirit?

Describing the experience of Moses on Mt. Sinai, Palamas has this to say:

> Because he was able to see, after he had surpassed himself and arrived in the darkness, he didn't see either by the senses or by the mind; so that light is self-visible and fills minds become blind in the sense of surpassing. (For how can a light which is seen and understood by itself *(To autoptikon)* be seen in some image by the function of the mind?) But when the mind is raised above all mental activity and is found without eyes in the sense of being surpassed, it is filled with a brilliance higher than all beauty; it is found in God by grace and has that self-visible light mystically and sees by the union above mind.[305]

It is true that the saints also call the light of grace intelligible, but not in its own sense. Because they consider it also above the mind, being produced in the mind only by the power of the Holy Spirit, when every function of the mind stops.[306]

But this light, although it isn't physical, although it is spiritual, is spread from the soul to the outside, to the face and the body of the one who has it inside. Everyone knows that a joy from the soul fills the face and eyes with a light which is distinct from the physical one produced by the radiation of the sun. "Thus the face of Moses shown with the inner light of the mind which also flowed over the body."[307] As such, the light on the face of Moses was also seen with the bodily eyes of those who were looking at him.

And it shown so much, that it was impossible to look steadily at the abundance of this overwhelming light. So appeared the physical face of Steven, as the face of an angel.[308]

There is a difference, however, between the diffusion of this light on the face of those who see it in their spirit, and the light itself seen by them. The spreading of this light on the face of these people might be

---

[304] *The Defense* 1.3.35, pp. 223, 225; *cf. The Divine Names* 1.4, p. 56 *ff.*
[305] *Ibid.*, 2.3.56, pp. 519, 521.
[306] *Ibid.*, 2.3.31, p. 471.
[307] *Ibid.*, 1.3.31, p. 215.
[308] *Ibid.*, p. 217.

seen also by those who aren't found in a state higher than the natural activities of the mind. Thus by the natural power of the eyes, this light itself, shown in the spirit of those raised above themselves, even if it is seen also with bodily eyes, isn't seen by the natural power of the eyes, but by the Holy Spirit Who also works by their mind and eyes. Therefore if the reflex of the divine light spread on the face of some saints in ecstasy is sometimes seen by just anybody, the divine light itself isn't. For example, the light of the birth of the Savior isn't seen by the eyes of the animals, and the light on Tabor, although it radiated more strongly than the sun, so that just anybody should have been able to see it from anywhere, was seen only by the three Apostles, in whom the power of the Holy Spirit was working. So even if this light is also seen by physical eyes, it isn't seen by them with their natural power; it isn't physical.

How then is that light physical which isn't seen by the eyes of dumb animals... even if they are present with open eyes when it shines? [asks St. Gregory Palamas.] And if it isn't physical, although the Apostles were made worthy to receive it with their eyes, this happened by some other power and not by the physical.[309]

> But if they don't see it with the natural power of their eyes, it means that it isn't like physical light, from space, or from the air, but is part of a spiritual region. Those who see it are able to penetrate by the power of the Spirit in them beyond the plane of physical realities. They find themselves raised to an order of the Spirit. Their eyes are open and they seek a target somewhere outside. But this means only that the light from the order of spiritual realities has overwhelmed the surrounding realities; their senses have become full of the power of the Spirit. We might use a colorless comparison: For those who love each other, all nature is filled with the light which seems to radiate from the other.

---

[309] *Ibid.*, 1.3.27, p. 207; 1.3.28, p. 209.

36. Love, Knowledge and the Divine Light
II. The Vision of the Divine Light, a Knowledge beyond Knowledge

This light is of a spiritual nature, fills the mind, and reveals the mystical realities of God. Therefore it is often given names borrowed from the order of knowledge. But at the same time since it eclipses all that the mind can know by its natural function, it surpasses knowledge and is higher than man. It is a knowledge beyond everything which we experience within the limits of our natural powers of knowing. It is a knowledge which we can never reach by the powers of our spirit. No matter how much the mind develops, no matter how much it evolves, by no evolution whatsoever is it able to unite with God, Who is transcendent to creation and its powers. Palamas does call this result of the union of the mind with created things "knowledge," but he also calls it a vision of the divine light and "ignorance"—not because it also lacks the minimum of perception, but because it surpasses knowledge to the maximum—not because it is an absence of all intelligibility, but because it surpasses the maximum of intelligibility which the mind can attain and comprehend.

But let's listen to St. Gregory Palamas himself:

> Because this union surpasses the power of the mind it is higher than all mental functions and it isn't [a kind of superior] knowledge, *(kath'hyperochin)* and because it is a relationship of the mind and God, it is something incomparably higher than the power which ties the mind with things created, that is than knowledge.[310] Such a union with God is thus beyond all knowledge, even if it be called "knowledge" metaphorically, nor is it intelligible, *(noiton),* even if it be called so. For how can what is beyond all intellect be called intelligible? In respect of its transcendence, it might better be called ignorance than knowledge. It cannot be a part or aspect of knowledge, just as the Super-essential is not an aspect of the essential. Knowledge as a whole could not contain it, nor could this knowledge, when subdivided, possess it as one of its parts. It can in fact be possessed by a kind of ignorance rather than knowledge. For by reason of its transcendence, it is also ignorance, or rather it is beyond ignorance. This union, then, is a unique reality. For whatever name one gives to it—union, vision, a sense perception, knowledge, intellection, illumination—would not properly speaking, apply to it, or else would properly apply to it alone.[311]

---

[310] *Ibid.*, 2.3.48, p. 503.
[311] *Ibid.*, 2.3.33, p. 473; *cf. The Triads,* p. 64.

So the vision of this light can never be put in the framework of the pantheist idealism of Plato, Plotinus, or Hegel. It isn't the natural coronation of an effort of the spirit, or of a development of its powers. But one reaches it by a leap, which the mind doesn't make by itself, but by being carried away by the Spirit. As such we can say that this vision doesn't represent only a qualitative plus of the same nature as compared to the knowledge gained by the efforts of the human spirit. It is also a qualitative superiority, a *ganz Anderes*, just as, everywhere, the divine energies are not only a quantitative plus in regard to the things of the created world, obtained by amplification, but totally distinct. This makes it necessary for us to negate the things of the world so that we can take a step forward to the understanding of uncreated things. The vision of the divine light is a vision and a knowledge [caused by] a divine energy, and received by man by means of a divine energy. It is a vision and a knowledge according to the divine way. Man sees and knows qualitatively as God, or "spiritually and divinely," as Palamas says.[312] This means that an infinite progress in this knowledge of Him is quantitatively possible. But both the name positive as well as negative too must be applied to such a knowledge, for an indication as true as possible.[313] This is true of all the divine energies, not to mention the divine essence. Thus this knowledge has, in connection with the usual categories and terms, an apophatic character, but not because of its minus compared to ordinary human knowledge, but because of its quantitative and qualitative plus.

"Indeed, this contemplation is not knowledge, [says Palamas,] and not only should one not think or speak of it as such, but it is not in fact knowable (unless this term is employed in an improper and equivocal sense). Rather, employing the word 'knowable' in its strict sense, but giving it a transcendent meaning, one should believe it to be superior to all knowledge, and to all contemplation which depends on knowledge."[314]

The inability to put it in the categories and terms of some possible natural knowledge must not make us understand the apophatic character of this experience at the expense of its positive content.

"But the one who reaches this light, [says Palamas, commenting on Dionysius,] sees and doesn't see. How does he see and not see? Because, he says, he sees beyond sight, so that literally on the one hand he knows and sees, and on the other he doesn't see by superiority *(ouch ora hyperochikos)*. He does not see with any mental function and sense, by the

---

[312] *Ibid.*, 2.3.50, p. 505.
[313] Palamas comments on Dionysius the Areopagite: "So here he says that the same thing is both darkness and light, seen and not seen, known and not known." *Ibid.*, 2.3.51, p. 507.
[314] *Ibid.*, 2.3.17, p. 447; cf. *The Triads*, pp. 61-2.

very fact that he doesn't see and know, in other words by the very fact that such a person has surpassed the whole function of knowing. He has arrived at a state higher than sight and knowledge. In other words, he sees and functions in a way higher than we do, because he becomes higher than man and is already god[315] by grace and is united with God and through God sees God."[316]

This light is incomparably more brilliant than ordinary knowledge, as Palamas puts it:

> The light of knowledge may be compared to 'a lamp that shines in an obscure place,' whereas the light of mystical contemplation is compared to the morning star which shines in full daylight, that is to say, to the sun.[317]

And by knowledge, he means not only that from the sciences of nature and reason, but also that from Holy Scripture.

The Vision of the Divine Light, a Supra-conceptual Knowledge

This experience is superior to knowledge and we could even call it unknowing, not only because it is received by the power of the Spirit and represents a quantitative and qualitative plus which exceeds our natural intellectual capabilities but also because it isn't a knowledge by concepts.

Neither can the subject of a human "you," which reveals itself to me in the ecstasy of love, be caught in concepts. The knowledge of moments of ecstasy is superior to concepts. It is a direct, broader vision, of that which is the indefinite subject. Faced with it, concepts are like spoonfuls of water compared to a river or the sea. So the experience of such a reality is more like a vision, a discovery, a union, because of its character of direct and non-discursive contact with unspeakable and supreme personal reality. This is why the holy Fathers prefer to call this knowledge a "vision," and that which is known, "light," as something which is seen directly, which spreads light by its presence. Pure prayer has taken my mind right up to the presence of the divine subject, that in a moment the Eros from above might carry me away and put me in an ecstatic, unmediated contact, with Him. This direct experience or this experience of His unmediated presence appears to me as light which fills everything.

---

[315] The Greek here is capitalized, the Romanian not. *trs*
[316] *Ibid.*, 2.3.52, p. 509.
[317] *Ibid.*, 2.3.18, p. 449; *cf. The Triads*, p. 63.

L. Binswanger makes a distinction first, between knowledge by love, which is an indefinite knowledge of the whole "you," and second, the knowledge determined by some parts of "you," which is produced when I want to take you and subordinate you to me by my thoughts. When I annul the relationship of "I-you," or the state of "we," I forsake the communion and the going out from myself (ecstasy); I do this in order to reenter myself and to draw you too into the sphere of my egotistic ego. And so I transform you into an object.[318] The first does not know reality as "something," as an object, and isn't strictly speaking knowledge either. It receives a revelation of fundamental personal reality in its quality of mystery and intimacy.

It is an unknowing knowledge.[319] Knowledge is strictly speaking only the second, because "knowledge is only a perceptive possessing of something, as something."[320] One person wants to possess the other, so he makes him into an object. But his subject strictly speaking escapes from this will to capture. All that remains in the hands of the captor are veils, or only shreds from them, as in the incident between Joseph and Potiphar's wife.[321]

In love I experience you beyond any attribute whatsoever defined in concepts. When love ceases, I am left with your attributes, your characteristics; when I love you, I see only light from you, not shadows too. I see your traits when I start to judge them.[322]

The moment I encounter you as a whole, you are a light to me. When this ecstatic relation stops, I am left with some superficial bits of you, poured into the drawers of concepts. We have mentioned earlier the smile which illuminates two people when they look at each other with love. This is the joy of nature to rebind itself in its intimacy, beyond

---

[318] Binswanger, p. 504: "If love is lovingly being with one another, a faithful existing in the being, or better expressed, a believing way of living in being-security, then the being is not conceived and known as 'something,' but in its essence revealed as security and being at home."
[319] "A not-knowing knowledge," says Binswanger, *Ibid.*, p. 572.
[320] Max Scheler, *Die Formen des Wissens und Bildung*, p. 30: "Recognition is in itself only a knowledgeable having of something 'as something.'"
[321] "Entireness itself, in the sense of love, the entireness 'You,' can therefore as the absolute entirety, not also be thought of as definiteness. You are absolutely unrecognizable for the discursive or abstract perception, a truth which usually is veiled.... From this it follows that every definiteness, every substance of an idea is only possible as a part." Binswanger, *op. cit.*, p. 570. "Objective perception rests on cognitive grasping of something and a thinking assimilation of something. Thus it (the objective perception) is restricted, as we have seen, to being as existence, to all of the existent...or its qualities." *Ibid.*, p. 573.
[322] "Loving you, I abstain not only from the judgment 'where there is much light there is much shade,' but also from the judgment 'light and shade are opposites,' because, since I love, not only do I overlook light and shade in your case, but I do not see this contrast at all; it does not exist for me, because what exists for me is you, beyond your qualities or eccentricities.'" *Ibid.*, p. 578.

the separation into distinct hypostasis [persons] or precisely because of this, because only in this way can love be manifested in it. It is the joy of nature in a person finding himself again in another. It is the joy produced by the consciousness of this rediscovery, or of the consciousness of unity in love, or of unity reflected and enriched in two minds. Any being, any nature found in a normal existence, reflects a certain light.

Human nature in its normalcy is harmony and harmony radiates light. But its integration into the whole of its existence depends on its normalcy. Therefore the whole of things outside of us we call the world, because it appeared to our ancestors as light.[323] Darkness is produced by non-existence, or by a disorder and so by a weakening of human nature. Darkness is only known to us as night. We know disorder as a suffering in existence, which appears in faint light, or mixed with darkness, or as a false light. It seems that within this nature a darkness flows which stings and wounds the common light.

But a major disorder in a human and between humans is a passionate division produced by sin. People who are enemies are darkened: The light of simulated friendship is a false light. Only the living of unity by love opens the springs of light suffocating in the depths of human nature. My concepts of you as the products of the ego are a sign of the lack of love. They put a distance between me and you and separate us.

If created nature radiates light, how much brighter must be the light that the uncreated being, inexhaustible in existence and in perfect triune communion, radiates. Its perfect unity and its infinite being, lived as perfect love between the three Persons, radiates a light not only among them ("light of light"), but also to conscious created beings. This light, however, can be seen only by those who, by prayer and the purity of love, pray it continually; it is seen only by those to whom it is revealed in love, for this vision also means the culminating union in love with the triune communion.

The reintegration of human nature by love in relationship to intimacy with God, based on the original relationship, takes place along with its unification within itself. Now this fills it too with light.

The smile of God and of man, meeting in the ecstasy of love, fills all things with light. Therefore the encounter with God is experienced as light. Only when we don't have this unmediated experience of God, does our mind forge concepts as a surrogate of this experience. Whoever takes a concept of God as the reality of God, makes an idol for

---

[323] Romanians call the world *lume*, which comes from the Latin *lumen*, light. trs

himself. And the result is his spiritual death, as St. Gregory of Nyssa interprets the verse: "For man cannot see My face and live."[324]

In this sense we must harmonize the apparent contradiction between the insistent recommendation of the Fathers not to consider divine any apparition of light whatsoever, as well as the other affirmations, that the grace of God fills the soul with light.[325] Apparitions which we must face with disbelief are definite "forms," definite images, even if they are luminous; even the light which bears the attributes of physical light, or is enclosed in certain limits can be considered as such. But the light which fills the mind, and which flows from the mind over everything, a light which we realize has a spiritual character, one of reality, of joy, of a universal celebration, no longer has a definite form. It's not an idol, but rather a "feeling" and an "understanding" spread through our whole being. Diadochos, Isaac the Syrian, Simeon the New Theologian, Palamas call it a "mental feeling," caused, however, not by a subjective state, but by the presence, or by the experience of the divine presence.

St. Gregory of Nyssa considers any concept or definite image, taken as God, as the cause of spiritual death, among other things because it suppresses the desire of the mind to move ever higher than anything that can be known in a definite way, and this is an additional motive why it maintains life as a tension, as spiritual progress in man.

"The generosity of God consented to fulfill his [Moses'] desire but He did not promise the cessation or the satisfaction of the desire. For He did not show Himself to His servant... in order to stop the desire of the beholder, because the vision of God consists in never stopping the desire of the one who looks on Him. For He says, 'You cannot see my face, for man cannot see me and live.' Scripture doesn't say this in the sense that the face of God causes the death of those who see it. (For how could the face of Life cause death for those that draw near to it?) It says this exactly because the Divine by nature is life creating, and the characteristic proper to the divine nature is to be situated above everything which can be known. He that imagines that God is something that can be known, no longer has life, as one who has deviated from Him who exists, to something which seems to exist in his fantasy. For He

---

[324] Exodus 33:20.
[325] Even Diadochos, who is more skeptical of such apparitions, speaks more of the light of grace that fills the soul. Sometimes we encounter this apparent contradiction in the same chapter. For example in text 40 he says, "You shouldn't doubt that when the mind begins to be strongly energized by the divine light it becomes completely transparent, so that it abundantly sees its own light. All this happens when the power of the soul gets mastery over the passions. And that everything that appears to it, if it has a certain form, whether light or fire happens by the machinations of the enemy, the divine Paul clearly teaches, saying that he is changed into an angel of light (2 Corinthians 11:14)." *On Spiritual Knowledge* 40, GrPh 1, p. 246; cf. Phi 1, p. 265.

who truly exists is true life; but He is inaccessible to knowledge. If then the life giving nature surpasses knowledge, that which can be understood of course isn't Life. And that which isn't Life, doesn't have a nature which can produce life.... By what has been said, Moses learned that divinity is indefinite, not enclosed by any margins."[326]

But not only is the divine essence unbounded, but also the light which it radiates, as the light of its being. Therefore it isn't a definite form and doesn't stop the longing of the one who sees it to see more and more of it. For he has the certitude that he isn't seeing all, that the divine reality is much, much more than he sees, and no matter how much he progresses, he will never be able to know it all. Thus Palamas talks about:

> ... continual progress in the ever clearer vision of the angels and of the saints in the age without end.... So if, in seeing with this same sight, they behold that light which is beyond sight, how much more then [do they see] God Who appears through it.[327]

On the other hand, when the seer of this light comes out of the state of ecstasy, he is compelled to put what he has seen into concepts and images. He realizes, however, that he can catch only bits of his vision. So he expresses it in contradictory concepts (seeing and not seeing, knowing and not knowing, etc.) Thus this light is supra-conceptual, but it suggests concepts and images, just as the contemplation of a beloved person in moments of ecstasy is above concepts. Still, later, it makes us want to put it in concepts, accompanied by the consciousness of the transparence [of these concepts], or their symbolic character. The indefiniteness of the beloved subject or the infinity of the divine light doesn't make us experience a void, pure and simple, brought about by the indefiniteness of nothingness, but we experience a fullness which as long as we stay under its power, we don't know where to catch it, not that we have nothing to catch. St. Gregory of Nyssa himself, as we have seen, accentuates so much the indefiniteness of the divinity experienced in the divine darkness by Moses, as the prototype of any soul that has been purified of the passions. This makes him observe later that in this darkness Moses received the suggestion for the tabernacle with all its details.[328]

---

[326] *The Life of Moses*, PG 44.404; cf. *The Life of Moses* (New York, 1978), p. 115.
[327] *The Defense* 2.3.56, p. 521.
[328] According to St. Gregory of Nyssa, even the divine voice which refuses to show its face to Moses indicates an immensity of meanings: "Now the divine voice gives the things requested through that which it refused, indicating in a few words an immeasurable abyss of meanings. *PG* 44.404; cf. op. cit., pp. 114-15.

It is impossible to explain the exact nature of this suggestion in a satisfactory way. St. Gregory Palamas just calls it a vision, but a vision of something immaterial. Answering the arguments of Barlaam, that there is nothing beyond negative theology, that the vision of the divine light is nothing but theology by negation, he says:

> Now did Moses, freeing himself from all visible things and from all thoughts and going beyond the sight of the place and penetrating the darkness, see nothing in it? But precisely there he saw the immaterial tabernacle which he showed to those below by a material imitation. Now this tabernacle, according to the words of the saints, could be Jesus Christ,[329] the power and the immaterial autohypostatic wisdom of God, which being immaterial and uncreated by nature, He showed in anticipation by the Mosaic tabernacle that He, the super-essential and formless Word, would someday accept a structure and would come in form and essence. [He would become] the tabernacle which is above and before all things, in which all things were created and are sustained, both visible and invisible....[330]

All the heavenly mysteries were shown to him then as simple and uncovered, he says himself.

---

[329] Fr. Staniloae has rendered this freely, and put "Jesus Christ" into the Greek. *trs*
[330] *The Defense* 2.3.55, p. 517.

The Concept and Structure of Love.
The Immaterial Tabernacle

Maybe this vision of the divine mysteries viewed in their immateriality and simplicity through the transparency of spiritual light comes because this light is experienced not as the commonplace, or as luminous confusion, but as an absolute fullness. The loving relationship between two persons offers us a pallid analogy. In this experience the beloved subject, no matter how indefinite he seems to me, appears to me as a harmony of infinite spiritual and personal richness.

This makes it possible that in God the *logoi* of all the existences implicated or involved eternally can be contemplated and explains the necessity of the previous knowledge of these *logoi* in a distinct way, in order to make our mind capable of the most advanced knowledge of God as the bosom of these *logoi*.[331]

Binswanger has remarked that the reality of the "we" brought about by love also has a certain organization, of which the two subjects are conscious, or, in other words, each subject experiences the other as having a treasure full of harmony, with all his indefiniteness. This organization or harmony he calls "structure" *(Gestalt)*. For example, one is the organized experience of the structure of "we" *(Wirstrucktur)* in love and another is the experience of this same "we" as a simple association of interests, or as a clash of contradictions, when we no longer experience a unitary "we" strictly speaking, but an "I" and "you," or an "I" against a "you."

The "structure" isn't yet a concept, but the seed of concepts. The structure is a form of living, of experience, which by reflection, becomes concepts.[332]

Certain analogous structures also characterize the experience of the one who sees the divine light, or has the feeling of the actual and loving presence of Jesus Christ. He who sees the divine light experiences it in the most general way, as an infinite vastness, as an intimate and holy shelter of love. Maybe this is why St. Gregory Palamas says that, like Moses, the one who enters into the zone of the divine light feels cov-

---

[331] For a discussion of the *logoi*, see Chapter 24, "The Contemplation of God in Creation."
[332] "In the pure form of love, the glance, the greeting, the wave, the word, the kiss and the embrace of love, already the origins of the perception of existence, show themselves in the well known double meaning of the word, namely in the meaning of the actual gaining of knowledge.... From the greeting until the embrace we recognize each other as loving.... So *Gestalt* is not the abstract fixation of contents. *Gestalt* is not already a certain conception but the foundation of certain conceptions. (The same is true for the substance—*Gestalt* of certain people.)" *Op. cit.,* p. 504.

ered by it; he is removed from the scattering which weakens his being, hidden from the sight of those left outside. The loving relationship between him and light is structured in this way, or this is the form by which he experiences it. The more he progresses in light, the more he feels that he is going further and further into a holy temple, into a beloved intimacy. But he senses that in it a deep mystery will remain eternally. From it all the light, all the love, comes as a mysterious infinite spring which makes possible an infinite progress of our knowledge, of love between Christ and us. Thus the divine light is lived as a temple with a number of parts. It begins with the one furthest out and ends with "The Holy of Holies," or with the intimacy of the divine essence, which is hidden eternally, enclosed in the shadows of the mystery; from it waves of light and of love, one after another, come in a procession without end, as from an altar, which appears to the faithful in the temple drowned in obscurity. From it, nevertheless, rays break loose from flickering lamps which spread their light playfully.[333]

Therefore we read in Exodus that Moses, entering into the divine shadows, saw the archetype of the holy tabernacle. St. Gregory of Nyssa affirms that anyone who enters into the divine light experiences the entrance into the tabernacle, not made by hands, of the divinity, which is the eternal Son of the Father, the wisdom and power of God. Precisely this same holy Father categorically forbade man to liken God to any concept, or to some image of human fantasy.[334] He says a little further on that, after Moses purified himself, "... he entered into the tabernacle not made with hands." Perhaps he wanted to indicate that this structure which he saw doesn't have just a theoretical character, but is an existential experience of the divine intimacy by the whole man, an experience and not theoretical knowledge, a structure of love and not a concept. This ascent of man doesn't means only a progress in God, but also in himself, because he is always ascending personally. As St. Gregory Palamas, St. Gregory of Nyssa accentuates that the entrance into the temple not made with hands isn't an apophaticism pure and simple, but that it is a positive vision and an experience in a reality superior to any knowledge:

> After the trumpets sound he penetrates to the unseen depths of the knowledge of God. But he doesn't stay there either, but goes on to

---

[333] The Eastern Orthodox keep the iconostas, which encloses the altar, and so continuously hint that the divine being remains hidden and incommunicable to the faithful. Westerners have taken down the iconostas, because they don't know the difference between the divine energies, which are communicated to the world and the divine being which remains forever incommunicable, as an inexhaustible reservoir of mystery.

[334] *PG* 44.377; *cf. The Life of Moses* 170, p. 97.

the tent not made by hands. In fact, at this point he reaches the limit of one who is lifted up in this manner.³³⁵

Anyone who goes up as high as possible on the spiritual steps must arrive in the Church not made with hands, which is Christ. Of course, neither is the word "tabernacle" completely adequate for indicating this divine mystery. But it is the best:

"For the power which encompasses all that exists, in which all the fullness of the Godhead dwells, the protection of all, which contains in it everything, in the proper sense is called 'tent.'"³³⁶

It is the tabernacle which embraces all things with love, and this tabernacle is the very Person of the Word made flesh.

The Apostle Paul, too, saw the heavenly mysteries, in the general form of a tent, which contains all that exists, says St. Gregory of Nyssa; man is not allowed to utter these mysteries.³³⁷ In it we shall completely rest in the life to come, when our visible tabernacle, this body, is set free,³³⁸ and we shall be clothed in the house not made with hands, in the heavens, in other words, in Christ. This is:

... the greater, the more perfect tent, which is better than the one made by men's hands, because it is not of this created order, and he has entered the sanctuary, [the Holy of Holies], once and for all.³³⁹

It is the divinity in which Christ as man entered fully, as our Forerunner. It is the only begotten Word of God, in Whom "... were created all things, everything visible and everything invisible, Thrones, Dominions, Sovereignties, Powers, or forces."³⁴⁰

The heavenly tabernacle in which we will be clothed in the future life can be nothing but the hypostatic and all comprehensive, but also all the loving Wisdom of God, for the Apostle Paul calls the body which He took, His "curtain,"³⁴¹ through which we will enter His divine infinity. In general St. Gregory of Nyssa considers the body [of Christ] as "the curtain of the lower tabernacle."³⁴² So our soul would be the tabernacle below, made according to the image of the tabernacle above, because— in comparison to the Word, in Whom the *logoi* of all things are con-

---

³³⁵ *Ibid.*, 167.
³³⁶ *PG* 44.380; *cf. The Life of Moses* 177, p. 99.
³³⁷ *PG* 44.381; *cf. The Life of Moses* 178, p. 99; 2 Corinthians 12:4.
³³⁸ *The Jerusalem Bible* translates this literally: "When the tent that we live in on earth is folded up, there is a house built by God for us ... in the heavens." 2 Corinthians 5:4. See 5:1-10, for the whole passage.
³³⁹ Hebrews 9:11-12.
³⁴⁰ Colossians 1:16; *PG* 44.384A; *cf. The Life of Moses* 179, pp. 99-100.
³⁴¹ Hebrews 10:20.
³⁴² *PG* 44.381D; *cf. op. cit.*, 178, p. 99.

tained from the ages, and at the end, all creatures— it, too, is destined to put on with love the *logoi* and the images of all things, not as a source of their being, but as the receiver. Another time, however, the holy Apostle Paul calls the body itself "tabernacle," from which we don't want to be separated when we put on the other, but to put it over the other, "... to have what must die taken up into life."[343] Because nothing of our nature, thus neither the body, will be lost, but will be overwhelmed by light and appear as light.

Does the tabernacle below mean only the body or only the soul or does it mean the whole man, made up of soul and body? The latter is more probable. In any case the fact is that just as our tabernacle here below will someday put on the tabernacle above, so the tabernacle above has put on the one below, showing by this the conformity between them. The reason why the tabernacle above permitted Him to be clothed in a tabernacle below, which was in the process of collapse, was the will to reestablish and consolidate it. Better said, by this two tabernacles were not laid aside, but one and the same tabernacle, uncreated and eternal was also made created. Because Christ is a single tabernacle uncreated and created, in His quality of a unique divine-human Person.[344] The putting on of the tabernacle from above also serves the same purpose of consolidation and reestablishment and full realization, by the entrance into light, in this life for short intervals and incompletely, and in the life to come, forever and completely. Strictly speaking, by our entrance into the light the work begun at creation is perfected. This begins by the descent of "the Light" into the world, where it shines as in a darkness which still doesn't contain it.

The purpose of "the Light," of the tabernacle from above, is to penetrate or to gather again in itself, those who have left. This work begins by the descent of the Light on earth, at the Incarnation; it continues by the Resurrection and is completed for each one when he is raised to its vision, when he enters the tabernacle from on high, at the end of purification. By this light or created consciousness he enters the uncreated, all luminous "Light" or "Life" or "Consciousness" and is penetrated by it. Strictly speaking, we have weakened our full "being"— the power to exist and shine eternally— by the leaving of the Tabernacle on high. By regathering in Him, the power to exist and shine is made anew for us. Everything that exists is able to exist and shine only if it stays in the "house" illuminated by God, and is nourished from the spring of existence and of light which this "house" is; anything that leaves it, leaves

---

[343] 2 Corinthians 5:4.
[344] *PG* 44.381-384; *cf. The Life of Moses* 175-77, pp. 98-9.

the sphere of the existence of the unending light. Our tabernacle here below is restored, consolidated and illuminated for eternity only if it penetrates the true existence and light, or if the true existence (to on) penetrates it. "This one is the Only Begotten God, who encompasses everything in himself but who also pitched his own tabernacle among us."³⁴⁵

This is the great mystery which Moses saw before it was realized; this too is the great mystery which any purified mind, that penetrates the light, after it has been realized, experiences.

Thus, man's ascent to God begins in the Church and ends there. The process of man's perfection begins and ends in the Church; man begins in the Church and finishes in the ages. Within it, within the very bosom of God, he continues to progress forever. He starts out and stays in the visible Church; he climbs on its unseen steps, as in a visible tabernacle on the steps of the unseen, this being one and the same. This is true if, in putting on the invisible tabernacle we don't take off the visible, but put the former over the latter, so that it will penetrate the other more and more. Therefore, the saints don't leave the Church, but are found on the highest steps of it and of their life in God.

We have already seen that man doesn't feel at home when he is alone, even if he finds himself in the same building for a long time. His home is where loved ones are, the place where those who make up a spiritual family live together. The finding of home or of loved ones again, gives an infinite or indefinable feeling of rest. It is one of the structures of an experience which doesn't lose its infinity or mystery.

An analogous sentiment, but infinitely more infinite,³⁴⁶ of rediscovery, of rest, of happiness, of coming home, must also structure the experience of the vision of the divine light, or the entrance into the heavenly tabernacle, which brings all things to the supreme Father. The one who has entered this light feels his intimate and loving dwelling in Christ. At the same time he realizes that he isn't alone with Christ, but that all are there and therefore an infinite love of all and of all things fill his soul. He must experience the light as an unending wave of love which, coming from Christ and from all in Him, draws him within it. At the same time it also overflows from him.

But to describe all the structures which shape the experience of those who are deemed worthy to see the divine light is given only to them. We

---

[345] *Ibid.*, 175, p. 98.
[346] St. Maximus the Confessor often uses the expression, "the infinite times the infinite" *(apeirakis apeiros)*, when he wants to express the experience of the unmediated presence of God. In a paradoxical way the infinite also has infinite levels and aspects.

point out, only in a general way, that these structures must be unending and unspeakably, delicately varied. They must always progress in their nuances, and each must have at the same time an infinite depth and be found in a perfect unity with all the others. Thus we see, on the one hand, that they who return from such an experience are able to tell others so many things about God and His will, or that such supraconceptual experiences are an inexhaustible source for their, and others, spiritual enrichment; but on the other hand we realize that in the life to come we will eternally contemplate in God, accompanied by ever new experiences, the *logoi* of all things, in a perfect unity. Moreover, we bear in mind the measure in which man becomes capable for ever more select structures, because they progress in a certain way. This also explains their need for the sharpening of the mind and the purification of the heart during this life, by and for more satisfactory knowledge of the *logoi* of things. Thus, the moral and intellectual effort of man during the course of earthly life and in general creation with its *logoi* and the relations they impose, appear to us as having not only a passing role, but an eternal value. We will be in the ages with the *logoi* of all things; we will profit and be perfected, by the moral and intellectual endeavors on earth.

But, however useful the idea of these structures might be, we wouldn't dare to use it to illustrate certain elements of the experience of the divine light, if we hadn't discovered in it the modern formulation of one of the ideas of St. Gregory Palamas. He develops it in relationship with some texts by Dionysius the Areopagite. Here we find, instead of the term "structure," that of *typos,* "an impressed image," or the verb *typoun,* "to impress an image." This refers to an immaterial, incorporeal impression, of the mind as the most spiritual part of man, but also of our whole being, as it is distinct from the impressions of the imagination. But what can this shaping be, which the angels too are subject to, if not our continually new structure, of a spiritual nature, which we tried to describe earlier? Barlaam admitted only the impression of perceptible images, and so considered that the divine light too is such an image. In opposition to him, St. Gregory Palamas states more precisely:

"The divine imagination differs greatly from our human imagination, and namely, the former impresses our truly intellectual and bodiless side. Human imagination, however, develops in that part of the soul appropriated by the body. The material in which the impression is made there is the very highest part of the soul, while here what is impressed in us is almost the last of the psychic powers. The impression is made here by the movements of the senses; there, if you want to know who makes the impression in the intellect of the prophets, listen to the great Basil, who comments: 'The Prophets saw with their intelligence imprinted by the Spirit.' So the Holy Spirit is the one that takes up His abode in the minds of the prophets and uses the intelligence as a material, and in it he foretells to them the things to come by Himself and through them to us too. How then, is this simple imagination analogous and of equal value with ours?.... So this refers to visions which are neither perceptible, nor imagined, but totally other than knowledge by thinking."[347]

As proof that there is a shaping of a purely spiritual order of the mind or of the subject, and so of our being too, Palamas cites the following passage from Dionysius the Areopagite, in which he speaks of a moulding of the holy Lordships:

> ... elevated above every dissimilarity, ever seeking the true Lordship, and source of Lordship; and moulding *(diaplattousan),* as an image of goodness, itself and those after it, to His Lordly likeness.[348]

And a little further on he uses an even clearer citation, where Dionysius talks very clearly about "spiritual impressions" *(typous noitous),* about "moulding" and "formation" of the mind.

"The holy ranks, then, of the heavenly Beings share in the participation of the Divine gifts in a higher degree... by moulding themselves intellectually *(noitos eautas apotypousai)* to the Divine likeness... and striving to mould their own spiritual likeness *(morphoun ephiemenai to noeran auton eidos)* after its example, they naturally have more ungrudging communications with it."[349]

Barlaam, admitting only perceptible impressions— inferior abstract thought— states that the visions of the prophets also represent an ecstasy inferior to thought. Palamas, on the basis of the passage above, asks:

> You see that there are also spiritual forms and models *(typous noitous)?* How then, basing your argument on these words, do you conclude that the prophets experience an inferior ecstasy? Because I, from these words am led to think that what the prophets see isn't inferior to human thought, but superior to our mind; and I am taught by these words to recognize their visions as equal to those of the angels.[350]

---

[347] *The Defense* 2.3.59, pp. 525, 527.
[348] *Celestial Hierarchy* 8, in *The Celestial and Ecclesiastical Hierarchy*, p. 31; *The Defense* 2.3.60, p. 529.
[349] *Celestial Hierarchy* 4, *The Celestial and Ecclesiastical Hierarchy*, p. 24, quoted in *The Defense* 2.3.61, p. 529. The sequence of the clauses from this old English translation isn't quite the same as in St. Gregory Palamas' quotation from Dionysius. *trs*
[350] *The Defense* 2.3.61, p. 529.

Palamas, in contrast to Barlaam, admitted spiritual changes and conformations by the knowledge of God, which he understood as a communication with Him, not as a simple speculation from a distance.

Palamas considers even the cleansing of the soul from passions and of the mind from images and concepts a "moulded form." Today we would call this their new "structure." By this we would show the existential, experiential and transforming character, of these structures, their character of lived states, which represent certain relations with God. Palamas continues:

> For the prophets making themselves by purity fit for angelic union and by joining with the angels for the reaching out for the divine, they too are moulded and stamped by them as they [the angels] are by the higher ranks of angels, and they reshape their spiritual image to make it appear in a more god-like form, and by this formation they deepen and cultivate within themselves the holy knowledge descended from there. And the surprising thing is that the purity of the prophets achieves the angelic patterns and forms, at the same time as it is concelebrant with them, as theology says, in so much as it can also receive the impressions of God *(kai autous tou theou typous auti dechesthai).*[351]

The structures stamped in the being of the one who sees the light of God, far from being like the impressions which leave images and concepts of created things in the mind, require as a previous condition the complete purification of the heart. Nevertheless, the experiencing of them [the structures] is not the feeling of emptiness, or of a wave without form, but of certain divine structures. Palamas gives us in this sense the following quotation from a more ancient writer:

> The pure heart is that which presents the mind to God without any form whatsoever *(aneideon),* and ready to be marked by His impressions *(tois autou etoimon ensemainesthai typois),* by which He is accustomed to making Himself known.[352]

The apparent contradiction contained in these words, or in general, between the diligence with which the Fathers require that the mind abandon every image and concept which give form to the mind, if it wants to know God, and the affirmation that God gives the mind certain forms, can't be solved but in the following manner: Images and concepts, fashioned according to created things, give the mind a limited form, which doesn't permit it to be in the habit of thinking about God

---

[351] *Ibid.,* p. 531.
[352] *Ibid.*

the unlimited One. Therefore the mind must leave all images and concepts as finite forms and get used to thinking of indefinite reality, doing this exercise first of all by returning to itself, as the subject of thought. In this way the mind becomes unlimited. But the experience which it has about unlimited realities (itself, the subjects of neighbors and especially God) has its organization, and it too is lived in the form of certain structures. It is the experience of the love of God and of its own love of God, the experience of the glory of God and of its own humbleness, the experience of joy and of happiness. These structures no longer hold it in the finite form of images and concepts, because each of them is boundless, infinite. God experienced as a personal loving dwelling doesn't exclude the sentiment of His infinity. Rest, which is another structure in which we experience God, is also lived as a blessed tranquility in the infinity of the love of God. Among other things, the structure experienced in the loving relationship between two people fills them with bliss precisely because they no longer feel the limits of the senses which they are living— the senses give them no worry whatsoever that the relationship will end. So the contradiction is overcome that on the one hand the mind must leave all finite forms in order to experience God, and on the other, that God impresses on it His infinite forms. These forms have an existential character which mould man's whole nature, in the sense that he experiences them as an inexhaustible existential relationship between him and God.

    The forms of these relations, although they offer from the beginning the experience of the infinite, don't stay the same, but continually progress to the degree that the union between the human subject and God becomes closer, more intimate, by which God becomes more interiorized and according to how the human subject too is made more capable of receiving Him. This is the ceaseless shaping of man by the Holy Spirit, Who makes him ever more like God. But the ontological distance between creature and Creator being infinite, this way of drawing near to God in likeness will never end, or this work of his being moulded according to the divine archetype; so never will he arrive at knowing God as He knows Himself. This road is full of the pilgrims of eternity, strung out according to their ontological distance from God, and according to their voluntary efforts.

    The Cherubim and the Seraphim are near, people are farther away. But neither will the Cherubim ever reach the end of the road of perfection. The steps of the angels are always ahead of us, but neither do they reach the end. The work of their being shaped according to the divine archetype will never be finished, even though they continually come closer to the divine model. The growth in likeness by this unceasing moulding is a lessening of unlikeness, because the increase in the vision of the light presupposes the continual surpassing of a certain kind of darkness mixed into the light on the lower steps; so angelic progress is also called purification, or "purification from unknowing." For the man who made the effort in earthly life to purify himself from the passions, eternal life opens the perspective, not of petrification, but of unending spiritual progress. But progress by spiritual moulding, or by the experience of unlimited blessing in the form of lived structures, begins for man even before entering the zone of the divine light. In the form of contemplation or of intuition and spiritual experience, it accompanies, almost continually, man's rational and conceptual knowledge. Along with precise, delimited forms and meanings, the spiritualized man lays hold too to the depth of the mystery of transcendent realities. But he doesn't do so in a chaotic way, but in a way structured by the different modes and steps of love.

The Vision of the Divine Light
The Supreme Spirituality of Him who sees it

The one who has purified himself of the passions and has reached a burning love for God on the steps of the virtues can attain the vision of the divine light; this means that he has spiritualized his nature to such an extent that it itself has become warmth and a light of the love of God and of men. He no longer has in himself any coldness or shadow of care for himself. This state is the result of his own efforts and of the Holy Spirit.

St. Simeon the New Theologian, in his *Hymns of Divine Love,* and to a certain extent St. Gregory Palamas, have described these three elements: a) that the light is a manifestation of love, b) that this love is the work of the Holy Spirit and that, c) he that raises himself to this state of light or of culminating love forgets bodily sensation, produced by the world through the body, and even himself.

Regarding the mutual tie between the warmth of love, which comes after the purification of the passions, and light, St. Simeon writes:

> Set fire again, my Christ, to the ardor of my heart
> Which the laziness of my sinful flesh has smothered—
> Sleep and the filling of the belly and the drinking of much wine:
> These have completely put out the flame in my soul
> And have dried up the spring of tears.

For warmth makes fire, and fire again, warmth.[353]

Or:

> Love is greater than everything...
> It is fire, it is also a ray,
> It becomes a cloud of light,
> It turns into the sun.
> So, as fire, it warms my soul,
> It sets my heart on fire,
> And gives birth in it to a longing
> And love for the Creator.
> And when it is sufficiently ignited
> And full of fire in my soul,
> A light bearing ray
> Comes to me and entirely surrounds me,
> Casting sparks of light into my soul,
> Lighting up my mind
> And putting it into a state
> To see the heights of contemplation.[354]

The warmth of love which becomes light has at the same time its source in the working of the Holy Spirit. The Spirit cleanses the soul from everything which draws it to the baser pleasures and fills it at the same time with delicate feelings kindled with love; better said He Himself, as the source of them, transforms these feelings into sparks of light, or He Himself appears as light. The light is thus a state of the spiritualized human nature, improved, transparent. The soul is filled with purity, with goodness, with love; it feels a great impulse to open up, to communicate its feelings of love, to communicate itself. And the One who communicates Himself by it in this total sincerity of love is the Holy Spirit:

> O Drink of light!
> O Movement of fire!
> O Stirring of flames,
> Which burn in me a sinner,
> Which come from Thy glory!
> This Glory, I say it and I proclaim it,
> Is Thy Spirit, Thy Holy Spirit,
> The Partaker of the same fire and glory with Thee,
> O Word![355]

---

[353] Hymn 28, in *Simeon le Nouveau Theologien, Hymnes,* Volume II, published by J. Koder, in *Sources Chrétiennes* 174, p. 305. *cf. Hymns of Divine Love* 28 (Denville, NJ, 1976), p. 150.
[354] *Ibid.,* 17; *cf. op. cit.,* pp. 66-7.
[355] *Ibid.,* 25; *cf. op. cit.,* pp. 135-6.

The intensity of this love, the blinding level of light with which it overflows, makes the body of the one who experiences it totally transparent for others, and for himself, as though it didn't exist.

In the measure in which his spiritual sensitivity has been accentuated, his bodily sensations, produced in him by contact with the world, have been overwhelmed. This is the supreme spiritualization. The body and the world are not done away with, but they become the medium by which the interior light is made known. A paradoxical thing happens. First, exterior things are overwhelmed; secondly, a great love is poured out through them, to everybody. Light radiates from everything:

> It's in my heart, it's in the air;
> It reveals the Scriptures and makes my understanding grow;
> It teaches me mysteries which I can't explain;
> It shows me how much I have been detached from the world;
> And at the same time it commands me to have mercy on all that are in the world.
> Walls surround me and I'm detained in the flesh,
> But I am, really and truly, beyond them.
> I no longer hear noise, or voices either...
> For me, pleasures are bitter, all the passions have fled.[356]

He that sees the light has been united to such an extent with it, that he no longer is aware that he is separated and distinct from it. And if the light is beyond any ability whatsoever to understand and interpret, he too has gone beyond any understanding of himself. Everything has become a light, pure joy, an unspeakable bliss, which fills all things. Ontological distinctions remain, but they are no longer felt. Or, the one that sees the light and feels the joy knows by himself only this—that he sees it and feels it and that it isn't from him.

St. Gregory Palamas says:

> Now the one who sees, if he doesn't function in any other way, having left everything else, becomes himself wholly light and is made like that which he sees; better said, he is joined too in an unconfused way. The light is also light and is seen by light.... This is union: that all these things be one, that the person who sees no longer be able to distinguish between himself and that through which he is seeing, but he only knows this much: That it is light and he sees a light, distinct from all creatures.[357]

---

[356] *Ibid.*, 18; *cf. op. cit.*, p. 81.
[357] *The Defense* 2.3.36, p. 479; *cf. The Triads*, pp. 65-6.

The great saint of Mount Athos has frequently repeated that this doesn't mean a material light, no not even a light of natural intelligence. It is a light of love beyond nature, in which the very being of the one who sees it has been transformed. It is the state of culminating spiritualization, or of purity, of the overwhelming of bodily sensations, of the surpassing of the severe impulses of egotism; it is a state of supreme goodness, mildness, understanding, love; it is a feeling of spiritual delicacy and ease. This is the state of deification, of likeness to the divine Spirit.

37. Deification in a Broad Sense [358]

Deification is God's perfect and full penetration of man, granted that he can't reach perfection and full spiritualization in any other way. To a great extent, sin has dulled and chained and put an evil spell on the powers of human nature. We don't know the full scope of the powers which our nature is capable of. Envy, care, hate, have clipped its wings. The love which we have for another, or which someone has for us, the trust which people have in us or we have in them— any exit from sinful egotism— unchains unimaginable powers in us, like Prince Charming's kiss which roused Sleeping Beauty from her unnatural paralyzing sleep.

Sin has thrown human nature into a state contrary to it. So we might say that the first step it is raised to, by restoration, is that of its true nature. But concretely, we can't distinguish a state of pure nature, because even the raising of nature to this state can't be realized by its own powers; nature alone isn't able to shake them out of their sleep, and get along only with them. Only by cooperation with divine powers is it raised and stays in this state. Thus, in the process of deification, for a long time, man, in certain ways doesn't yet attain the level of the complete health of his nature, but in other ways he has surpassed, by divine grace, the purely natural level.

Because he is near the normal level of his nature, or in certain aspects he has reached it too, he has been raised to certain natural virtues; or even in a state contrary to nature, he keeps in himself, somewhat diminished and dulled, the natural virtues. At the same time, in other aspects, in the person who has received the grace of Christ, but lacks complete dispassion, supernatural virtues are found. They can no longer be explained by the resources of his natural powers, but represent a plus.

As St. Gregory Palamas says:

> In fact we have in us a wisdom from nature which by effort we can develop. But the wisdom of the Spirit, Who speaks by it, is given to the Saints, according to the Gospel promise.[359]

The light shines a long time in the dark. The new man grows in the struggle with the remains of the old man. Since the seeds of the new

---

[358] Sometimes known by the Greek word *theosis*. The English divines of centuries past spoke of *godification*. trs
[359] *Against Akindynos* 5, Cod. Paris, gr. 1238, f. 152; also in Staniloae, *The Life and Teaching of Gregory Palamas* [in Romanian], p. CLX.

man were planted in him, in other words at Baptism, he lives both a supernatural life, and one that is still below nature too.[360]

Deification in a broad sense begins at Baptism, and stretches out all along the whole of man's spiritual ascent; here his powers are also active, that is, during the purification from passions, the winning of the virtues, and illumination. In this ascent the natural powers of man are in continual growth, and reach their apogee the moment they become capable of seeing the divine light— the seeing power is the working of the Holy Spirit. Therefore we can say that the deification by which this revival and growth is realized, coincides with the process of the development of human powers to their limit, or with the full realization of human nature, but also with their unending eclipse by grace.

Deification never stops, but continues beyond the ultimate limits of the powers of human nature, to the infinite. The latter we can call deification in a strict sense.

For the justification of this statement we could use the example of the deification of Jesus Christ's humanity. It likewise begins, strictly speaking, after the Passion and by the Resurrection, when according to St. Gregory of Nyssa, the attributes and energies of human nature are overwhelmed by the divine attributes and energies. It is perfected with the Ascension of Jesus into heaven, as man. This also made possible our personal deification, understood likewise as an elevation above human attributes and energies, to the divine.[361]

So, if deification in a broad sense means the elevation of man to the highest level of his natural powers, or to the full realization of man,[362] because all during this time the divine power of grace is active in him, deification in a strict sense involves the progress which man makes beyond the limits of his natural powers, beyond the boundaries of his nature, to the divine and supernatural level.[363]

---

[360] Diadochos likewise recognizes a natural love and another of the Holy Spirit. *On Spiritual Knowledge* 34, *GrPh* 1.244; *Phil* 1.263. The first is a sign of a nature made healthy by self-control. *Ibid.*, 74. But it is "...easily taken over and perverted by evil spirits...." *Ibid.*, 34. On the one hand the recovery of nature is realized by self-control and with the help of divine grace, and on the other, natural love is easily subdued. Therefore nature isn't firmly consolidated in its healthy state, but is still unstable; thus it is a state which alternates with that contrary to nature. In texts 76-86, and 88, Diadochos describes the battle between the supernatural virtues of grace and the remains of the old man.
[361] *Against Eunomius* 5.5, (Answer to Eunomius' Second Book), *PG* 45.693; *NPNF* series 2, 5.180, col. 2. [Fr. Staniloae is not following the text here exactly. *trs*]
[362] St. Maximus the Confessor, *Chapters of Five Centuries* 1.28, *PG* 90.1189: "If we are [made] according to the image of God, let's become ourselves and of God, better said only of God alone and wholly and not having anything earthly in us; let's draw near to God and become gods, receiving from God an existence of God."
[363] St. Maximus says very clearly that the natural powers of man cease when he has reached their limits, in other words, the maturity of the fullness of Christ. Until then, he is fed with an-

These two kinds of deification differ, but nevertheless a continuity exists between them as between two stages of the same ascent. For the passing from the first stage to the second, however, a leap is necessary, because man too works during the first stage, but during the second, only God.

If in the course of man's spiritual ascent, right up to the full development of his natural powers by their cooperation, divine grace wouldn't give any other help except [to see] that they develop to their limits, the name of deification for this process would hardly be justifiable, although it is realized with the help of divine power. Grace also produces in man, even in the course of this ascent, effects which surpass the limits of pure nature. This is also a more important reason why the name of deification can't be refused for this spiritual ascent before the ultimate attainment of man's natural powers.

On the other hand, we have seen in the previous chapter, that the cessation of the natural activities of the spiritual powers of man doesn't mean a total halt of their activity and development. They continue to work but not because they can any longer contribute their natural resources, but exclusively by the reception of divine energy. Man stays active somehow but as the receptor of the continually growing power of God. Therefore, deification is considered as an experience of which only man is capable. Now this receptivity of man is part of an unending development. It doesn't mean a growth of the power of natural activity, or an enlargement of human nature as an intrinsic source of power and activity. Nevertheless it means a growth of its receptive power, of the power to receive and use the divine energies in ever larger measures.[364] This growth of power to partake of divine grace also takes place by grace; it presupposes, however, the potential for such a growth and is in a certain sense the development of a receptive potential of nature.

---

other kind of food, which we could call finite, which he can prepare with his own powers, with the virtues and contemplations, with the things in the middle, as the saint would also say. After this, he is nourished with "imperishable food," that is with God Himself. Then he becomes the man [who is] god. See *Chapters on Knowledge* 2.88, *Maximus Confessor, Selected writings*, p. 167.

[364] St. Gregory Palamas shows how the one who sees the divine light doesn't see the essence of God—not even all His light—but progresses endlessly in the vision of it: "For what creature would be able to contain all the infinitely powerful power of the Spirit, that by it he might see the whole of God? And to what do I ascribe that hiddenness? The very brilliance of that light, which paradoxically has as material the sight of the seer, enlarging by union that spiritual eye and forever increasing its capacity, will never stop surrounding it with brilliant rays and filling it continually with the most hidden light and by it revealing things as never before." *The Defense* 2.3.31, p. 469. In regard to this receptive function of the mind in the future life too, see St. Cyril of Jerusalem, in St. Maximus the Confessor's *Minor Theological and Polemical Words*, PG 91.101.

This, of course, must not be understood as a capacity to enlarge itself in a physical, but in a spiritual way. It is based on an interior impulse, and exists at least virtually in human nature, before the attainment of what it receives as a gift. This gift is described by all the holy Fathers as lasting and growing in the ages of ages, therefore the power of its reception grows too. On the other hand, man will "suffer" deification; he will endure it passively; he won't produce it, for he has entered into the unending rest. In the vision of Dionysius the Areopagite all the angelic grades are found eternally in a dynamic tension around God, continually progressing in deification. And St. Gregory of Nyssa compares this continually growing gift and its reception, to Moses' ascent on Mt. Sinai.[365]

So, when we said that human nature also ceases to function by means of its powers, even in the slightest way, we meant that it has reached the limit of its development by nature. It has attained its limit as a source of power and of activity, not, however, as a receptive potential. The process of the development of human nature isn't over, although as a source and as a subject of its own power it no longer has any development whatsoever and in this sense its whole growth in divine activity is by grace, not by nature. But the fact that even growth without end in deification also has as a base the receptive potential planted in man's nature, it is expressed in the East by the doctrine that man is made in the image and likeness of God. By sin the image hasn't been lost, but the process of becoming like God has stopped. This, taken over in Christ, will no longer have an end. Man becomes more and more like God, without identifying with Him. Man will continue to become like God forever, in an ever fuller union with Him, but never will he reach full identification with Him; he will be able to reflect God more and more, but he will not become what God is.

This distinguishes likeness from identity, or the quality of god by grace, from God by nature. In as much as in general the knower becomes more and more like the one known, man becomes and tends to become more and more like God, ever more like that which God is, or god by grace. Madame Lot-Borodine comments:

---

[365] "This is truly what it means to see God—to never lack the longing to see him." *PG* 44.404A; cf. *The Life of Moses* 239, p. 116. He who has become close to God, on the one hand, moves ahead, on the other, he "stands," because he has become unbending in virtues. The more he "stands" unbending in virtues, the more he surpasses himself. Virtue is by nature progressive. *Ibid.*, 405C; 243, p. 117. Certainly, neither is the longing of human nature a reality in itself, but is due to an attraction from a distance on the part of God, as the nature of good. "The soul moves toward God," says St. Gregory of Nyssa, "and God doesn't hinder it, on the contrary, He attracts it." *Ibid.* This reference wasn't found. *trs.*

The old axiom, 'Only the like knows the like,' must be taken in the deepest sense, and understood as the assimilation of the knower by the known. The like becomes the like, even his model, by free or charismatic participation.

In her study the author emphasizes the idea that in the East, "the mind" has by nature the tendency and power to contemplate the uncreated One, not by an infused grace, as is said in the West. The grace of Jesus Christ has only reestablished this natural power:

> On the contrary, among the Greeks, the first passage of the created spirit to the Uncreated is a natural, not infused, contemplation. This is by virtue of the divine life in us.

Nevertheless it shouldn't be concluded that the mind by itself goes to what is by nature proper to it and progresses in the knowledge without end of deification. Even after the cleansing from sin, we have seen that deification is "experienced," not conquered by the mind or by human nature. Madam Lot-Borodine herself says that the mind-heart must be lit by the fire of the uncreated Sprit:

> The depths of the *nous-kardia* [mind-heart], from which the intelligence and desire come, together.... The shining refuge of the *theia gnosis* [divine knowledge], bright sparks from the fire of the uncreated Spirit are communicated to the human spirit.

From these very accentuated considerations of Madam Lot-Borodine we must remember only the fact that deification, which is nothing but the never ending progress of likeness, is at the same time also the realization of a tendency, of a potential planted in man's nature.[366]

The process of deification is then the same as the process of becoming like God. From one perspective it is a development by grace of a potential planted in man, especially since "the likeness" is nothing but a development of "the image."[367]

This development of nature, whether it be only as receptivity, also shows why there is no interruption between the first and second stages of deification. At the same time, the above observations have brought out, and incontestably so, the distinctions between them and the leap from the first stage to the second, which also means an exit from the laws of nature in general.

---

[366] "The God-centered anthropology of the Christian East as a basis for its spiritual experience" [in French], *Irenikon* 16 (January-February, 1939), pp. 15, 13.

[367] "Just as it is in painting portraits, if the most vivid color is added to the outline it brings out even the smile; so it is too with those who possess the grace of God—if the light of love is added, the image is raised totally to the beauty of the likeness." Diadochos, *On Spiritual Knowledge* 89, *GrPh* 1, p. 266; *cf. Phi* 1, p. 288.

But deification in a strict sense, as a process of the perfection of man after the natural has reached the limits of its powers of activity and after it has stopped all active contribution on its part, belongs only to the ages to come. During this life here it is only anticipated for brief moments, in the form of an earnest.

38. Deification in a Strict Sense

We will concern ourselves here with deification in a strict sense because it shows more clearly way just exactly what it is.

The most important problem is the connection between it and human nature. As we have seen, the holy Fathers say that by deification, the operations or energies of human nature cease. They are replaced by divine energies; natural attributes are overwhelmed by divine glory. So St. Maximus the Confessor writes:

> The soul becomes god and rests from all its mental and physical works by participation in divine grace; at the same time all the natural operations of the body rest with it. They are deified along with the soul in proportion to its participation in the deification, to the extent that then only God will be visible, through the soul as well as through the body; the natural attributes are conquered by the overabundance of glory.[368]

St. Gregory Palamas states, practically repeating St. Maximus, that when God makes Himself visible to the saints in light:

> ... all power of knowledge whatsoever ceases.... God unites Himself with them as with gods. Because by participation in the perfect One they too are transformed for the good; so, to speak as the prophet,[369] their power changing, they stop all activity of the soul and body, to the extent that they no longer appear and only He is seen through them. The natural attributes are overwhelmed by the abundance of glory.[370]

In this sense, St. Gregory Palamas can say that they who are worthy of the vision of the divine leave the realm of time.[371] He affirms, based on St. Maximus, that deification takes nature beyond its boundaries:

"Only the angels who have kept their place and those people who have arrived at the honor above nature, given to rational beings, also partake of the energy and of the deifying grace of the divine and unspeakable light itself. For it is proper only to divine grace, according to Maximus the Confessor, to grant creatures deification proportional to

---

[368] *Chapters on Knowledge* 2.88, RoFil 2, p. 203; *cf. Maximus Confessor, Selected writings*, p. 167.
[369] Isaiah 40.31: "But they that wait upon the Lord shall renew their strength...they shall run, and not be weary; they shall walk, and not hunger" (LXX).
[370] *The Defense* 2.3.31, p. 471.
[371] According to Lossky, *Mystical Theology*, ch. 11, pp. 223-4. St. Maximus says the same thing in *Ambigua*, PG 91.1144.

DEIFICATION 369

their grade, enlightening nature with the supernatural light and raising it, by the abundance of glory, beyond its boundaries."[372]

St. Gregory of Nyssa likewise considers deification as a raising of human nature beyond its limits. True, he is speaking of the deification of the human nature of Christ, but it is the beginning of the deification of human nature in general. Thus St. Gregory affirms with boldness that after going through the Passion, the body of Christ was made by "interpenetration" with divine nature "... that which the nature which received it also is."[373] He states that the right hand of God or His creative power, which is the Logos Itself, raised man joined with it [Christ's nature] to its own height, making him by "interpenetration" that which it also is by nature.[374] This act was a "remaking" or restoration *(metapoiisis)*. Based on this fact, human nature, found within the divine nature, became everything that it was:

> Immortal in the Immortal, Light in the Light, Incorruptible in the Incorruptible, Invisible in the Invisible.... For even in physical combinations, when one of the parts exceeds the other to a greater degree, the inferior is wont to change completely to that which is more potent:[375] ... that lowly nature... remained no longer in its own measures and properties, but was... raised up... and became... god instead of man.[376]

Certainly, seen alone, human nature isn't made one with the divinity, by essence:

> ... but when mixed with the Divine it no longer remains in its own limitations and properties, but is taken up to that which is overwhelming and transcendent.[377]

This happens, however, only after the resurrection, but not with the essence. The true life found in the body, wasn't able to remain in death; it raised the body by resurrection from corruption, to incorruption. Fire is hidden in wood, but later breaks out on the surface, warming it and

---

[372] *Against Akindynos* 5, Codex Paris, gr. 1238, f. 152; also in Staniloae, *The Life and Teaching of St. Gregory Palamas* [in Romanian], p. CLIX; also in Hristou 3.375.
[373] *Against Eunomius* 5.2, *PG* 45.693; *NPNF*, series 2; 5.176, col. 2. "We...assert that even the body in which He underwent His Passion, by being mingled *(anakrathen)* with the Divine Nature, was made by that commixture *(dia tis anakraseos)* to be that which the assuming Nature is."
[374] The word *anakrasis*, used by St. Gregory of Nyssa, strictly speaking means a "mixing," but another mixing than fusion *(synchysis)*. It is a mixing in the sense of imbibition which saves the identity of the things mixed, or reciprocally imbibed, as fusion doesn't. Iron imbibed by fire, or mixed with it doesn't cease to be iron. A mixing in the sense of fusion is excluded in the definition of Chalcedon *(asynchytos)*, not a mixing in the sense of imbibition *(anakrasis)*.
[375] *Ibid.*, 5.3, *NPNF*, series 2; 5.178, col. 1.
[376] *Ibid.*
[377] *Ibid.*, 5.5, *PG* 45.705; *NPNF*, series 2; 5.180, col. 2.

making it burn; so the divine was hiding in the body, until death and in the time of death, so that later it might fill it with its life, as a maturation of our nature, to the extent that each nature of His can no longer be distinguished. The human nature of Jesus is then remade by interpenetration with the divine, and receives the latter's attributes, or the divine power.[378]

On the other hand, the Fourth Ecumenical Council (of Chalcedon), and the Sixth (of Constantinople), defined that the two natures and two energies were united in the person of Christ "unconfusably" and "inseparably identifiable,"[379] condemning as Monophysitism any contrary opinion. And St. John of Damascus understands the deification of the human body and will of Christ in the sense that they were not taken beyond their limits, that it produced no change in their attributes or energies:

> It is worthy to note that the flesh of the Lord is not said to have been deified and made equal to God and God in respect of any change or alteration, or transformation, or confusion of nature... but through the permeation of the natures through one another, just as we saw that burning permeated steel. For, just as we confess that God became man without change or alteration, so we consider that the flesh became God without change. For because the Word became flesh, He did not overstep the limits of His own divinity nor abandon the divine glories that belong to Him; nor, on the other hand, was the flesh, when deified, changed in its own nature or in its natural properties. For even after the union, both the natures abode unconfused and their properties unimpaired. But the flesh of the Lord received the riches of the divine energies through the purest union with the Word, that is to say, the union in subsistence, without entailing the loss of any of its natural attributes. For it is not in virtue of any energy of its own but through the Word united to it, that it manifests divine energy: for the flaming steel burns, not because it has been endowed in a physical way with burning energy, but because it has obtained this energy by its union with fire. Wherefore the same flesh was mortal by reason of its own nature and lifegiving through its union with the Word in subsistence. And we hold that it is just the same with the deification of the will; for its natural activity was not changed but united with this divine and omnipotent will, and became the will of God, made man.[380]

---

[378] *Ibid., NPNF*, series 2; 5.181.
[379] "One and the same Christ, Son, Lord, Only-begotten (composed) of two natures unconfusably, inconvertibly, indivisibly, inseparably identifiable." Prolegomena to the Fourth Council. *The Rudder (Pedalion)* (Chicago, 1957), p. 243. You will find here too a long note by St. Nicodemus of Mt. Athos. *trs*
[380] *Exposition of the Orthodox Faith* 3.17, *NPNF*, series 2.9, 1899, pp. 65-6.

How can we reconcile the affirmation of some, that deification took human nature beyond its limits, with the affirmation of others, that it didn't?

A closer look shows us that there is a contradiction only in words. St. John of Damascus himself gives us the ability to reconcile the two points of view, when he says that human nature would have been changed only by becoming the source of divine attributes and energies. Here is how he characterizes the divine essence: It is the ultimate source of divine energies. Human nature didn't become the source of divine energies (workings), (which neither Gregory of Nyssa nor St. Maximus affirm) but they are imparted to it from a source distinct from it, with which it is united by hypostasis; it didn't leave its boundaries, and so St. John of Damascus is right. On the other hand, precisely because the human nature of Christ is manifested already before the Resurrection, but especially after it, by certain functions (energies) and attributes which can't be explained by its natural resources, means that functionally, human nature is beyond its limits; by energy, whose origin we made an abstraction of, it is found there. In other words, when we look for the source of the energies of deified nature, we realize that it hasn't gone beyond its limits, because we must answer that it itself hasn't become the ultimate source of this energy. But when we don't look for the source of this energy, but ascertain purely and simply that it is beyond the possibilities of human nature— and St. John of Damascus too recognizes such an energy— we can say that practically, functionally, human nature is manifested beyond its natural limits.

Because red-hot iron doesn't burn by itself, its nature isn't changed into fire, but because it is burning, no matter what the cause, it is functionally beyond the limits of its powers. Roman Catholicism many times claims that the Eastern doctrine of deification is Monophysitism. But because all the Fathers of the Church accentuate that deification is "by grace, not by nature," it is cleared of this accusation. God "by grace," not by nature, means precisely that the nature of deified man remains unchanged, in the sense that it doesn't itself become the source of divine energies; it has them by grace received as a gift. No matter how much the divine energies grow in it, it remains only a channel, a medium which reflects them— never will it assume the role of the source.

Roman Catholicism can't understand this doctrine, because it doesn't know the difference between the divine essence and energies. Man can't be deified except by merging with the divine essence. In any case, what would be manifested, what would be reflected in it would be the divine essence. Catholicism can't admit this. It keeps man in an existence absolutely separate from everything that is divine. In Orthodoxy, even so, the nature of man united with the divine energies becomes the medium by which these energies are manifested; it, however, remains undulled, just as the warmth and light of the sun penetrates and is manifest through so many mediums without their being canceled out, without their being identified with the solar rays. So the human nature of Jesus wasn't modified into the divine nature, after the Resurrection and the Ascension. But the fact is that after these events, His human nature received new divine energies. The question is whether the human energies and attributes were suspended and if this suspension meant their abolishment or only their overwhelming and how we understand this overwhelming.

St. Maximus the Confessor and St. Gregory Palamas use the term "overwhelm" and apply it to all human energies and attributes. St. Gregory Palamas declares:

> According to the divine Maximus, everything that is God is also what is deified by grace, except for the identification by essence. This distinction comes because those who partake of the deifying graces of the Spirit do not also partake of the essence.[381]

We must also understand the affirmation of St. Maximus the Confessor, that deification means a transformation of the whole nature into a passive state, or that "in God and in the deified there will be a single operation," likewise in the sense of an overwhelming of all human operations.[382]

We draw this conclusion especially from the assertion of St. Maximus, that human nature must pass through a state of deification by its "death," or that the deification of the age to come is separated from the workdays of this age, by the Sabbath of rest.[383]

This overwhelming doesn't mean that man becomes insensible. He himself lives his new state of "god by grace," conscious at the same time of his creatureliness by nature. He tastes a divine bliss, but with the gratitude of a creature; he experiences in himself divine powers, but with the amazement of one who realizes that they don't come from him. In other words, he is god, but he doesn't stop being man at the same time; he is god by the things that he does, by his functions, but conscious that he is a god by the mercy of the one and great God. This is the sentiment, so comprehensive of the human, which accompanies the

---

[381] *Apology*, in Staniloae, *The Life and Teaching of St. Gregory Palamas* [in Romanian], p. LXVIII.
[382] *Minor Theological and Polemical Works*, PG 91.33.
[383] *Chapters on Knowledge* 1.55, RoFil 2, p. 143; cf. *Maximus Confessor, Selected writings*, p. 138.

manifestation of divine energies, which God grants to his subject. The latter lives pure love, or the spiritual relation with God in the measure in which the bodily sensations of pain, pleasure, envy or pride, have been overwhelmed. He lives the pure joy of everything that is good, decent, harmonious. He is as God, yes even god, but not God. He is a dependent god, to say in another way that he is a "god by participation." The consciousness of this dependence excludes the pantheistic identification of man with God.

Deification is the passing of man from created things to the uncreated, to the level of divine energies. Man partakes of these, not of the divine essence. So it is understood how man assimilates more and more of the divine energies, without this assimilation ever ending, since he will never assimilate their source itself, that is, the divine essence, and become God by essence, or another Christ. In the measure in which man increases his capacity to become a subject of ever richer divine energies, these energies from the divine essence are revealed to him in a greater proportion too.

We never receive the divine energies in their totality, because they never cease to be manifested in newer and newer proportions; and along with them the power, which is shown through us and our understanding, is growing. In this earthly life the divine energies descend to us, to the lowest level where we find ourselves from the spiritual point of view. They condense their infinite treasures, into a potentiality. So, in the measure in which we grow in spirit, something of the infinity hidden in them becomes real to us. And our eternal ascent is at the same time an eternal lifting up of the divine energies from the potentiality to that from which they descended.

Not only did Christ descend to us, to later be lifted up in us, but all the order of His uncreated truths. From their contemplation through the curtains of the physical world in this life, we are raised to their unmediated contemplation, but neither then will we cease to go forward on its unending steps. Their order reveals the Kingdom of the heavens. It is the divine medium which unites us with God, but at the same time distinguishes us from Him; it also unites us, but it also keeps us distinct from the essence of God.

It is an infinite world, of infinite steps and reliefs of the spiritual life. This doesn't mean that being in it we won't be in God, for God is everywhere where the medium of His energies are. But nevertheless, we won't be united with His essence. We will be, however, ever closer to it, in the measure in which we become greater in spirit in order to be the subjects of ever increasing divine energies.

The divine energies are nothing but the rays of the divine essence, shining from the three divine Persons. And from the time that the Word of God took flesh, these rays have been shining through His human face.

It can also be said that the things of the world are images of the *logoi* of the divine Logos which are at the same time energies. By creation God put a part of His infinite possibility of thought and of energy into existence, in the form specifically at the level of the understanding of human creatures. He did this to permit a dialog with men in which they might go up higher and higher toward the likeness with God and toward union with Him.

The incarnation of the Word confirmed the value of man and of these images of reason and of energy measured by him. But it also gave man the possibility to see in the face of the man of the Logos, concentrated anew, all the *logoi* and divine energies. Thus final deification will consist of a contemplation and a living of all the divine values and energies conceived in and radiated from, the face of Christ, according to the supreme measure of man. But by this, in the face of each man, by the *logoi* and the energies gathered in him, the *logoi* and the energies of the Logos will be reflected luminously. Eternal bliss will be the contemplation of the face of Christ.[384]

So all will be in God and we will see all things in Him, or God will be in all things and we will see Him in all things; and the unitary presence of God in all things will be real to the extent that all creatures gathered in Him remain real and unmingled in God.

This is the eternal perspective of deification.

---

[384] Revelation 22:4.

BIBLIOGRAPHY [1]

Amman, A. *Die Gottesschau im palamitischen Hesychasmus. Ein Handbuch der spätbyzantinlicher Mystik (The Vision of God in the Hesychasm of Palamas. A Handbook of Late Byzantine Mysticism).* Würzburg, 1938.

Ancient Christian writers, the works of the Fathers in translation (ACW), ed. Johannes Quasten and Joseph C Plumpe. Washington, D.C.: Newman Press, 1946-1997.

Ante-Nicene Fathers, translations of the writings of the Fathers down to A.D. 325 (ANF), eds. A. Roberts and J. Donaldson. Edinburgh: T. and T. Clark, 1867-1872. Reprinted by Wm. B. Eerdmans, Grand Rapids, MI, n.d.

Anthony the Great, St. *On the Character of Men, Phi* 1.

Athanasius, St. *Second Letter to Castor, PG* 28.871-906.

Balthasar, Hans Urs von. *Die gnostischen Centurien des Maximus Confessor (The Chapters on Knowledge of St. Maximus the Confessor),* Freiburger Theologische Studien, 61. Freiburg im Breisgau: Herder, 1941. In *Maximus Confessor, Selected Writings*, this work is called *Two Hundred Chapters of our Holy Father Maximus the Confessor on Theology and the Economy in the Flesh of the Son of God.*

— *Présence et pensée. Essai sur la philosophie religieuse de Grégoire de Nysse (Presence and thought. Essay on the religious philosophy of Gregory of Nysse).* Paris: G. Beauchesne et ses fils, 1941.

Basil the Great, St. *Against Eunomius. PG* 29.497-669.

— *The Long Rules*, 2 vols., trans. Sister M. Monica Wagner. Boston: St. Paul Editions, 1950.

Berdyaev, Nicholas. *Freedom and the Spirit*. New York: C. Scribner's Sons, 1935.

Beret, L. "Les etats affectiffs" (The Affective States) in G. Dumas, *Traite de Psychologie*, vol. 1. Paris: Alcan, 1923.

Binswanger, Ludwig. *Grundformen und Erkenntnis menschlichen Daseins (Basic Forms and Knowledge of Human Existence).* Zürich: M. Niehans, 1942.

Blaga, Lucian. *Cenzura Transcendenta (Transcendental Censorship).* n.d., n.p.

Blondel, Maurice. *L'Action, Essai d'une critique de la vie et d'une science de la pratique*, 2 vols. Paris: Alcan, 1936.

---

[1] Not all the bibliographic data was given by Fr. Staniloae, and not all of it was found in other sources by the translators. Hence the incompleteness of some entries.

— *Action. Essay on a Critique of Life and a Science of Practice*, transl. Oliva Blanchette. Notre Dame, IN: The University Press, 1984. Originally published in 1893.

Bohnenstadt, E. von. *Das Schauen Gottes.* Leipzig: Meiner, 1942.

Bois, J. "Grégoire le Sinaïte et l'hésychasme à Athos au XIV siècle" (Gregory of Sinai and hesychasm at Athos in the 14th century). *Echos d'Orient* 5, l901-1902.

Bousset, Wilhelm. "Evagrios-Studien", in *Apophtegmata Patrum (The Desert Fathers, in German)*, Tübingen: 1923.

Brunner, Emil. *Wort und Mystik (Mysticism and Word)*, Tübingen, 1928.

Bulgakov, Sergei N. *Tragœdie der Philosophie (The Tragedy of Philosophy)*. Darmstadt, n.p., n.d.

Cabasilas, Nicholas, St. *The Life in Christ.* Crestwood, NY: St. Vladimir's Seminary Press, 1974. Quotations used by permission.

Callistus and Ignatius, Sts. *Directions to Hesychasts. PhilPH.*

Callistus Cataphygiotis, St. *On Divine Union and the Contemplative Life. GrPh* 5.4-59.

Clement of Alexandria, St. *Carpets. PG* 9. *ANF* 2 (1885) 299-567.

— *The Tutor, ANF* 2, 1885, 209-296. Also in *ANL* 4, 1868.

Clemént, Olivier. *Le Visage interieur (The Inner Face)*. Paris: Stock, 1978.

Daniélou, Jean. D. "Le Symbolisme des rites baptismaux" (The Symbolism of Baptismal Rites). *Dieu vivant* (Paris), vol. 1.

— *Platonisme et théologie mystique. Essai sur la doctrine spirituelle de saint Grégoire de Nysse (Platonism and mystical theology. An essay on the spiritual doctrines of St. Gregory of Nyssa)*. [Paris] Aubier: Édition Montaigne, 1941.

Diadochos of Photiki, St. *On Spiritual Knowledge and Discrimination. Phi* 1.

Dionysius the Areopagite, St. *Epistle 1. PG* 3.1065.

— *The Celestial Hierarchy. PG* 3.119-370.

— *The Celestial and Ecclesiastical Hierarchy*, trans. John Parker. London: Skeffington and Son, 1894.

— *The Divine Names. PG* 3.585-996.

— *The Divine Names and Mystical Theology*, trans. C.E. Rolt. London: SPCK, 1979.

— *The Ecclesiastical Hierarchy. PG* 3.369-584.

— *Mystical Theology. PG* 3.997-1048.

Dostoyevsky, Feodor. *The Brothers Karamazov.* New York: Bantam Books, 1970.

Eckhart, Meister. *Predigten (Sermons, in German).* Jena: Ausgabe von Buttner, 1934.

Evagrius Ponticus. *Kephalia gnostica (Chapters on Knowledge),* trans. from Syriac into Greek by Frankenberg. See below.

— *On Prayer. Phi* 1.

— *The Prakticos, Chapters on Prayer,* trans. Bamberger. Cistercian Studies, Series 4. Kalamazoo, MI: Cistercian Publications, 1978.

— *Texts on Discrimination. Phi* 1.

Frank, S. L. *Connaissance et Etre (Knowledge and Being).* Paris, 1931.

— *Die Krise des Humanismus, Eine Betrachtrung aus der sicht Dostoevschys (The Crisis of Humanism. A Contemplation According to the View of Dostoyevsky),* in *Hochland* (28 Jahrgang, Heft 10). Cited in Binswanger.

Frankenberg, W. *Evagrios Pontikos.* Berlin, 1912. In German. Includes the *Kephalaia Gnostica.*

Gandillac, Maurice de. Review of J. Daniélou's *Platonisme et théologie Mystique. Essai sur la doctrine spirituelle de Saint Grégoire de Nysse* in *Dieu Vivant* 3 (Paris).

Grandmaison, Leonce de. *La religion personnelle (Personal Religion).* Paris: Gabalda, 1927. Also in English, translated by Algar Thorold. London, 1929.

Gregory of Nyssa, St. *Against Eunomius. PG* 45:237-1122. English in *NPNF* 5.33-248.

— *Commentary on the Beatitudes. PG* 44.1193-1302. English in *ACW* 18, pp. 85-175.

— *On the Image and Likeness of God. PG* 44.1527-1546.

— *The Life of Moses.* New York: Paulist Press, The Classics of Western Spirituality, 1978. *PG* 44.297-430.

Gregory of Sinai, St. *On Quietude and the Two Ways of Prayer. PG* 150.1313-1330. *GrPh* 4.71-9.

— *Instructions to Hesychasts. PhilPH.*

Gregory Palamas, St. *Against Akindynos* 5. Codex Paris, gr. 1238, f. 152. Also in Staniloae, *The Life and Teaching of St. Gregory Palamas.*

— *Apology* (included in Staniloae's work listed above).

— *For the Defense of those who Practice Sacred Quietude,* ed. Panayiotes Hristou, The Greek Fathers of the Church, vol. 54, [in Greek]. Thessalonika: Gregory Palamas Patristic Publications, 1982.

— *Gregory Palamas, The Triads*. The Classics of Western Spirituality, ed. John Meyendorff. Mahwah, NJ: Paulist Press, 1983.

— *On Prayer*. PG 150.117-1121.

— *The Writings of Gregory Palamas*, ed. Panayiotes Hristou [in Greek] 2 vols. Salonika, 1982.

Hartmann, N. *Grundzüge einer Metaphysik der Erkenntnis. (The metaphysics of perception)*. Berlin, Leipzig, 1925.

Hausherr, Iréné. "La méthode d'oraison hésychaste" (The Method of Hesychastic Prayer). *Orientalia Christiana* 9/2, no. 36 (June and July, 1927).

— "Les Orientaux connaissent-ils les 'nuits' de Saint Jean de la Croix?" (Do the Orthodox Know the 'nights' of Saint John of the Cross?). *Orientalia Cristiana* 12 (1946).

Hegel, Georg W. H. "Diferenţa dientre sistemele liu Fichte si Schelling" (The Difference Between the Systems of Fichte and Schelling). *Izvoarele de Filosofie* 2 (1943).

Heidegger, Martin. *Being and Time,* trans. Edward Robinson. New York: Harper and Row, 1962. Translation of *Sein und Zeit*. Halle a.d. S.: Niemeyer, 1935.

Heim, Karl. *Jesus the Lord, the sovereign authority of Jesus and God's Revelation in Christ,* trans. D. H. van Daalen. Edinburgh and London: Oliver and Boyd, 1959. Translation of *Jesus der Herr*. Berlin: Furche Verlag, 1935.

Hesychios, St. *On Watchfulness and Holiness. Phi* 1.

Irenaeus, St. *Against Heresies. PG* 7. English in *ANF* 1.315-578.

Isaac the Syrian, St. *The Ascetical Homilies* [in Greek]. Athens: Astir, 1961.

— *The Ascetical Homilies of St. Isaac of Ninevah.* Boston: Holy Transfiguration Monastery, 1984.

Isaiah the Solitary, St. *On Guarding the Intellect. Phi* 1.22-9.

John Cassian, St. *A Useful Word for Abbot Leontius*, from the first two Conferences. *PL* 49.477-558. Also in *NPNF* 11, 1894, pp. 161-641.

— *On the Eight Vices*, *Phi* 1.

John Climacus, St. *The Ladder of Divine Ascent.* Willits, CA: Eastern Orthodox Books, 1973.

John of Damascus, St. *On the Orthodox Faith*. *NPNF* 9, 1899.

— *Dogmatics*, trans. into Romanian by D. Fecioru. Bucharest, 1938. English in *NPNF*, series 2, 18, 1899.

— *On the Virtues and Vices*. *Phi* 2.334-342.

Journet, Ch. *Connaissance et inconnaissance de Dieu (The Knowledge and Ignorance of God)*. Fribourg, 1943.

Jugie, M. "Les origenes de la methode d'oraison hesychaste" (The origins of the Hesychast methods of prayer). *Echos d'Orient* (April, June, 1931).

Koyré, A. "Gotteslehre Iacob Böhmes" (The Theology of Jacob Bohme). *Jahrbuch für Philosophie und phenomenologische Forschung*. Niemeyer, 1929.

Kierkegaard, Søren. *Gesammelte Werke (Collected Works)*, v. 2. [no further information was provided by the author. *trs*

Koepgen, Georg. *Gnosis des Christentums (The Gnostic of Christianity)*. Salzburg, 1939.

Krumbacher, K. *Byzantinische Literaturgeschichte (History of Byzantine Liturature)*, 2 Aufl. München, 1907.

Lavelle, Louis. *De l'Acte (Concerning Action)* [no further information was provided by the author. *trs*

"Liminaire" [several anonymous authors]. *Dieu Vivant* 1/8. (Paris, 1946).

Lossen, Josef. *Logos und Pneuma im begnadeten Menschen bei Maximus Confessor (Logos and Pneuma in the blessed human being in the works of Maximus Confessor)*. Münster, 1941.

Lossky, Vladimir. *The Mystical Theology of the Eastern Church*. Crestwood, NY: St. Vladimir's Seminary Press, 1976. Quotations used by permission.

— *Orthodox Theology*. Crestwood, NY: St. Vladimir's Seminary Press, 1978. Quotations used by permission.

Lot-Borodine, Madam. "L'anthropologie théocentrique de l'Orient chrétien comme base son expérience spirituelle" (The Theocentric anthropology of the Eastern Christian as the Basis of his spiritual experience). *Irenikon* 16 (January, February, 1939).

Mark the Ascetic, St. *On Baptism*. *PG* 65.985-1028.

— *On Repentance*. *PG* 65.965-984.

— *No Righteousness by Works*. *Phi* 1.

— *On The Spiritual Law*. *Phi* 1.

— *Letter of Nicolas the Solitary*. *Phi* 1.

Maximus Confessor, St. *Selected writings*. Mahwah, NJ: The Classics of Western Spirituality. Paulist Press, 1985.

— *Ambigua.* PG 91.1031-1418.

— *Chapters of Five Centuries.* PG 90.1177-1392.

— *Chapters on Knowledge:* "Two Hundred Chapters of Our Holy Father Maximus the Confessor On Theology and the Economy in the Flesh of the Son of God" in *Maximus Confessor, Selected writings.* pp. 127-180, and PG 90.1083-1176. Also called *Theological and Economical Chapters,* or *Theological Chapters,* or *Chapters of Two Centuries.*

— *Chapters on love.* Phi 1.

— *Life and Asceticism of Maximus.* PG 90.

— *Minor Theological and Polemical Works.* PG 91.9-286.

— *Mystagogy.* PG 91.657-718. Also in *Maximus Confessor, Selected writings,* pp. 181-225.

— *Questions and the Dubious.* PG 90:785-856.

— *Questions to Thalassios.* PG 90.243-784.

— *Second Letter to John the Valet.* PG 91.392-408.

Migne, J. P. *Patrologiae cursus completus, series graeca (PG).* Paris, 1857-1866. 161 vols. The writings of the Greek Fathers in Greek with parallel translations in Latin.

Neilos the Ascetic, St. *Peristeria.* PG 79.812-968.

— *On Asceticism.* Phi 1.

Nicephorus the Monk, St. *Watchfulness and Guarding of the Heart.* GrPhil 4.18-30.

Nicodemus of the Holy Mountain, St. *A Handbook of Spiritual Counsel.* New York: Paulist Press, 1989. Greek edition, Athens, 1987.

— *Unseen Warfare. The Spiritual Combat and Path to Paradise of Lorenzo Scupoli,* edited by Nicodemus of the Holy Mountain and revised by Theophan the Recluse. Crestwood, NY: St. Vladimir's Seminary Press, 1987.

Nicholas of Cusa. *De visione Dei (Das Schauen Gottes),* trans. E. van Bohnenstadt. Leipzig-Meiner, 1942.

Origen. *Against Celsus,* quoted in von Balthasar. English in *ANF* 4.395-669.

— *Homilies on Jeremiah.* PG 13.518.

— *Homilies on Leviticus.* PG 12.468 ff.

Pachymeris. *Paraphrase of The Ecclesiastical Hierarchy.* PG 3.

Peter of Damascus, St. Phi 3.

The Philokalia. The complete text compiled by St. Nikodemos of the Holy Mountain and St. Makarios of Corinth. *(Phi)* trans. from the Greek and ed. G.E.H. Palmer, Philip Sherrard, Kalistos Ware ... [et al.]. London, Boston: Faber and Faber, 1979. 4 vols.

    The Philokalia in Greek *(GrPh).* 2nd ed. Athens, 1893; 3rd ed. Athens: Astir, 1961. 5 vols.

    The Philokalia in Romanian *(RoFil),* trans. D. Staniloae. Sibiu, 1946. 12 vols.

    Writings From the Philokalia on the Prayer of the Heart. (PhilPH) London: Faber and Faber, 1975.

Plotinus. *Enneads,* trans. Michael Atkinson. Oxford: The University Press, 1983.

— *Sermons* [In German]. Jena, 1934. [no further information was provided by the author. *trs*

Ribot. *Essai sur les passions (Essay on the Passions).* Paris: Alcan, 1907.

Scheler, Max. *Die Formen des Wissens und die Bildung (Forms of knowledge and education.* [no further information was provided by the author. *trs*

— *On the Eternal in Man,* trans. Bernard Noble. New York: Harper, 1960. Translation of *Vom Ewigin im Menschen.* Berlin, 1933.

Schmidt, W. *Zeit und Ewigkeit (Time and Eternity).* 1927. [no further information was provided by the author. *trs*

Scupoli, Lorenzo. *Unseen Warfare.* See Nicodemus of the Holy Mountain.

Select Library of Nicene and Post-Nicene Fathers of the Christian Church *(NPNF),* eds. Philip Schaff and Henry Wace. Buffalo and New York: The Christian Literature Co, 1886-1900. 28 vols. Reprinted by Wm. B. Eerdmans Publishing Company, Grand Rapids, MI, nd. Also reprinted by Hendrickson, Peabody, MA.

Simeon the New Theologian, St. *Ethical Discourses.* in *RoFil* 6.119-202. Also *Sources Chrétiennes,* 129.

— *Homilies,* Russian ed., Mt. Athos, n.d.

— *Hymns of Divine Love by St. Symeon the New Theologian.* Denville, NJ: Dimension Books, 1975.

— *On the Three Ways of Prayer, GrPh* 5.

— *The Practical and Theological Chapters and The Three Theological Discourses.* Kalamazoo, MI: Cistercian Publications, 1982.

— *The Life and Teaching of St. Gregory Palamas* [in Romanian]. Sibiu, 1938. It also contains the *Triads*.

Tillich, Paul. *Die geistige Lage der Gegenwart (The Spiritual Condition of the Present).* [no further information was provided by the author. *trs*

Visheslavtsev, B. "The Meaning of the Heart in Religion" [Romanian translation by D. Staniloae]. *Revista Teologica* (1934).

Volker, W. *Das Volkommenheits-ideal bei Origennes (The idea of perfection in Origen).* Tübingen, 1931.

The Way of a pilgrim and, the pilgrim continues his way, trans. R.M. French. New York: Harper Collins, n.d.

Zarin, V. *Fundamentals of Orthodox Asceticism* [in Russian]. Saint Petersburg, 1902.

INDEX

See also Contents.

- A -

Angels. 66 *ff*. We will be like a., 86; fallen a., 88; meekness is the property of a., 180; for them dispassion is inalienable, 186; come with the Son of God, 203; also progress in the truth, 211; need ecstasy, 239; are illumined by the First Light, 336; also perceive the Divine Light, 338; see God, 347; are impressed, 354; visions of prophets equal to that of a., 355; their perfection is endless, n. 364, p. 364; partake of deifying grace, 367; soul in contemplation moves among a., n. 55, p. 222; how they see God, n. 211, p. 284; make continuous progress, n. 275, p. 329.

Anger. One of the passions, 80; develops from natural passion, 88; how it is a sin, 92; can also be good, 96-7; is a psychic factor, 100 *ff*.; St. John Climacus on, 120; how explained, 149; and subjugated, 151; connected with gossip and hatred, 154; trials help to conquer, 171-2; love replaces, 323; peaceful man is free from, n. 8, p. 80; isn't reasonable, n. 35, p. 97; rational soul knows no a., n. 36, p. 97; love restrains, n. 76, p. 112; demolished by psalmody, longsuffering, and mercy, n. 78, p. 113; can be gotten rid of, n. 136, p. 151; must be a major concern, n. 146, p. 157; quick delivery from, n. 189, p. 175.

Angst. ...the phenomenon of fear, 116; as various fears, 130-2; n. 81, p. 116.

Apophatic theology *in general;* **Apophaticism.** *See* chapters 26-28. Is justified, 220; pure prayer realizes, 255; a description of, 288, 294 *ff*.; the a. character of the knowledge of Christ, 342; is positive, 244; exists for knowledge, n. 14, p. 27; reveals boundless horizons, n. 50, p. 220.

Asceticism. St. Paul alludes to, 23; Origen introduces term, 23 *ff*.; is positive, 25 *ff*.; negative aspect of, 62; is our paricipation in death and resurrection of the Lord, 62; mystical knowledge meets, 72; ascetic sometimes proud of, 81; must not erradicate natural passions, 85-6; aids guarding of the mind, 93-4; things discarded by, 113; its problem 115; taught by great teachers, 125; teaches us to meditate on last judgment, 133; is to slay the passions, 187; contributes to purity of mind, 187; prelude to mental rest, 291-2, necessary for true love, 319; Binswanger's idea of, 319; is really positive, n. 6, p. 80; can't do away with stomach, n. 136, p. 151; helps to find incoruptible life, n. 222, p. 299.

Avarice. One of the passions, 80.

- B -

Baptism. Asceticism is an extension of, 26; the Lord is concealed in us from, 59; Christ penetrates us by, 61; for our salvation, 66; the first of the hierarchy of graces, 66; Christ comes into our hearts at, 97; grace comes at, 121; our goodness starts at, 124; repentance renews, 135; Christ dwells in us from, 160-1; makes us Christ's house, 163; relationship to gifts of Holy Spirit, 195-6; He hid in me at, 227; Christ has been in our transconscious since, 259; deification begins at, 362-3; the symbolism of, n. 68, p. 61; reestablishes tie between God and man, n. 208, p. 292.

- C -

Care. (As anxiety), ties us to things, 115; fear and waiting produce, 115; is a motive of fear, 116; Heidegger's and author's analysis of, 116-18; thought of death helps free us from, 133; two kinds of, 143; contrasted with hope, 177-9; trust in God takes away, 190; pure prayer keeps us from, 255; Jesus Prayer requires freedom from, 282, as does the experience of apophaticism, 298-9; clips our wings, 362; Being-in-the-world is essentially care, n. 86, p. 116; a definition of, n. 193, p. 177.

Catholic, Catholicism. C. theologian describes spirituality, 46; C. theology works almost exclusively with philosophy, 47-9; attitude toward faith, 127; usually knows only negative theology, 230; doesn't admit uncreated energies, 305; claims that Orthodox deification is Monophyticism, 370-1.

Church. Spirituality best preserved in Eastern, 46 *ff.*; invokes Holy Spirit, 55; only she imparts Christ, 62; has hierarchical character, 63; c. hierarchy has broad meaning, 63-6; continues in heaven, 66; reestablishes human unity, 82; her living norms and models sharpen discernment of Scripture, 226; her dogmas seem to be antinomies, 235; is our home, 325; c. not made with hands is Christ, 351; ascent to God begins and ends in, 353.

Confession, *see* **Repentance.**

Contemplation. Asceticism helps attain, 24, 60; direct, 28; perfects our spiritual energies, 44-5; angels too enjoy, 64; Baptism necessary for, 66; as is dispassion, 69, 188; a phase of the spiritual life, 69-71; natural reason and, 127; faith and love are c. of God, 128; pride deforms, 181; leads the saints, 187; gifts of Holy Spirit lead to, 197; of God in creation, ch. 24, p. 203 *ff.*; 256; natural, 204, 207; long preparation necessary for, 217 *ff.*; absolute need for, 224; darkness a way to, 234; not of concepts, 235; the light of, 238; is darkness, 240; by negation, 241; terminates ladder of prayer, 264; Nicodemus the Aghiorite and, 276; approaches God unenslaved, 284; natural, 295; can be uninterrupted, 308; of a neighbor, 323-4, 347; not knowledge, 342; as the morning star, 343; part of spiritual progess, 358; a light bearing ray, 359; of uncreated truths, 373; as final deification, 374; eternal bliss, 374; natural, n. 86, p. 70; and faith, n. 110, p. 127.

Creation. First cause of, 33; from nothing, 38; all must share in it, 40; ultimate goal of, 45; of man, 54; how raised, 55; angels' responsibility for, 63; logoi in, 70; contemplation of, 71-2; world is a transparent c. of God, 115; freedom from, 134; has a positive purpose, 148; contemplation of God in, 203 *ff.*; and Scripture, 228; God manifests Himself in, 235; love for, 281; God transcendent to, 248; work begun at, 352; has eternal value, 354; what happened at, 374; raised by hand of God, n. 36, p. 41; all are compatible with, n. 37, p. 42; ignorance of God deified, n. 23, p. 90.

- D -

Darkness. Mind feels infinite reality as, 33; in approach to God, 231-4; divine, 238-43; an intense, 264; an abyss, 288-90; covered with, 298; which hides God, 331; on Sinai, 334, 339, 347; n. 84, p. 236; supraluminous, n. 98, p. 243; Nicholas of Cusa on, n. 99, p. 244; of the soul, n. 119, p. 252; and light, n. 313, p. 342.

Death. Asceticism slays, 24, 26; two kinds, 24; Baptism a sharing in, 62, 135; fear of, 92, 118, n. 182, p. 172; spiritual, 93, 139, 346; thought of, 133, 146, n. 117, p. 133; as joy, 308.

Deification. The goal of, 21, 46-7, 72; the Eucharist and, 55; shown full on Mt. Tabor, 60; definition, 64; in a broad sense, 362 *ff.*; in a strict sense, 368 *ff.*

Dejection. One of eight passions, 80; in mood swings, 94; a disease of incensive power, 102; revolt against pain, 115; explained, 149; how cut off, 151, 169, 171, and the monk, 151; n. 8, pp. 80-1.

Devil, *see also* **Satan.** Pride comes from, 81; temptation from, 111; when he attacks, 164; his throne, 180; and prayer, n. 59, p. 109, dispassion and, 263.

Dialectical Protestant theology. Rejects union with God, 30; distinguish words from idea, 35-7; dialectic and repentance, 139.

Discernment. And the mind, 87, n. 101, pp. 245-6; of thoughts, 120; how won, 196; and knowledge, 196; its scope, 215; rapid, 219; how sharpened, 226; and the gathering of the mind, 264; and tranquility, 299.

Dispassion. Of the second coming, 59; an accessible goal, 69; as a virtue, 71-2; leads to love, n. 81, p. 69; meaning of, 80; escape from passions means, 118; Step 29 of *The Ladder*, 120; Callistus and Ignatius on, 122-3; and Maximus the Confessor, 123; the true sign, 133-4; four kinds, 153; and the good heart, 160; the spiritual force of, 174; follows humility, 181; ch. 22, p. 185 *ff.*; the peak of, 196; reason sharpened by, 211; Christ is resurrected in me by, 227; and ecstasy, 239; and pride, 263; and physiological recommendations, 260;

and Nicephorus, 266; and prayer, 274; ch. 33, p. 303 *ff.*; lack of complete, 362; can lack prayer, n. 125, p. 256.

- E -

Ecstasy. Sterile, 28; as deification, 72; mind transcends itself, 184; Gregory Palamas on, n. 110, p. 127; in Dionysius and others, 234 *ff.*, 255, 274; bodily feeling ceases, 278; higher than negative theology, 283-4; self is transcended, 290; precedes divine light, 296; as love from above, 298, 305, 322, 324, 345; even prayer forgotten, 304; on the face of saints, 337; as your revelation, 343; with divine light, 337, of the prophets, 355. *See also* ch. 34, p. 310 *ff.*

Egotism. Jesus free from e., 61; expression of passions, 79, 94; a rupture with God, 81; of others, 82; when bitten by pain, 102; love can overcome, 141, 317; tears against, 146; fasting against, 152; love is opposite of, 180; as pride, 171; the worst thing, 188; dispassion destroys, 189; and vainglory, n. 6. p. 80; is unnatural, 333; divine light overcomes, 361.

Epiclesis. Brings divine life, 55.

Evil. Fear of future e., 132; e. thoughts, 136; virtues overcome, 141; e. empire, 141; self-control helps against, 148; control of, 158-9, 164; 167; e. person, 181; dispassion means absence of, 185-8; e. suggestion, n. 132, p. 258; perversion by e. spirits, 362.

- F -

Faith. *See* ch. 14, p. 124 *ff.*; Working, 26-8, 35; dialectical idea of, 36; works helps f. in God, 45; in Holy Trinity, 48, 50; how gained, 62; first of the virtues, 71-3; healing of passions begins with, 81; helps to ascend to perfection, 108, 113; combines with hope and love, 120; reason stabilized by, 122; becomes fear of God, 130-3; repentance is born of f. and fear, 134; two roads, 159; a certitude of unseen realities, 177; knowledge born from, 198, 220; as a return to truth, 212-4; as intuition, 217; progress of spirit, 220; and Jesus Prayer, 273; love the fountain of, 307; precedes prayer, 319.

Fasting. Connected with virtues, 73; recommended, 151-2; n. 136, p. 151; overcomes desire, n. 146, p. 157; and love for God, n. 222, p. 190.

Fear, Fear of God. *See* ch. 15, p. 130 *ff.*; of death, 26, 92; of God, 73, 82, 123; a natural passion, 85; to evade sin, 85; of pain, 115; as angst, 116; in Callistus and Ignatius, 121; of our day, 228; dispelled by love of God, 308.

Filioque. Cause of, 47.

- G -

Gestalt. As structure, 349. *See also* n. 332, p. 349.

Gluttony. Makes the stomach impossible to fill, 77; no food ever satisfies, 80; first of the passions, 80-1; caused by self-love,

INDEX 389

102; a passion, 120, 148, 169; in *The Ladder,* 120; monks protected from, 150; conquering is extremely important, 153, 169; definition, 186; digs a canal to the stomach, n. 3, p. 77; a prelude to unchastity, n. 8, pp. 80-1.

Gossip. The nephew of laziness, 120; a hatred for our neighbor, 154; control of, 155.

- H -

Heart. How to move, 43; innermost part of mind, 97-8, 190; where sin starts, 111-2, 158 *ff*.; and Holy Spirit, 121; dispassion and, 133; repentance and, 135; constraint of, 152; as supraconscious, 158 *ff*.; as subconscious of the passions, 159 *ff*.; mind is activity of, 258-9; purification of, 354, 356. *See also* chs. 18, and 29-35.

Hegel, Hegelianism. Defined, 289; says mind is total darkness, 290; pantheist ideal of, 342; his views, n. 206, p. 291.

Hell. Pride drags us down to, 181; world as road to, 205; travelers to, 211; life can be a, n. 258, p. 315.

Hesychasm, Hesychast. Directions to, 119-21; 270; its beginning, 265; practice of, 270; method of, n. 147, p. 262; origins of, n. 149, p. 262; adversaries of, n. 153, p. 264.

Hierarchy. Our Lord gave it to the Church, 63; of blessings, and of all in the Church, 63-66; of angels, 211, 354.

Holy Mysteries, *see* **Mysteries.**

Holy of Holies. As altar of God, 326, 350.

Holy Spirit, Gifts of. *See* ch. 23, p. 195 *ff*.

Hope. *See* ch. 20, p. 177 *ff*.

Humility. *See* ch. 21, p. 180 *ff*.

Hypostasis. Relationship of divine and human, 26, 56, 371; of Father and Son, 54; as repentance, 137; the human, 285, seeing God's, 287; how love unites human, 345.

- I -

Image, *see also* **Likeness.** Human i. of Christ imprints us, 21; of Holy Spirit, 54; man created as i. of Christ, 54, 320; of God hidden in commands, 59-60; we must live accoding to His, 225; God is beyond all, 241; divine light seen as an incomprehensible, 243; mind must give up, 257, 259; ignore i. in prayer, 271 *ff*.; of God in man, 305, 310; one who loves remakes i. of the loved, 320 *ff*.; spiritual i. of Jesus, 327; prophets reshape their, 356; man made in i. and likeness of God, 366.

Imagination. In Callistus and Ignatius, 121; of God, 246; to the infinite, 248; seductive in prayer, 263; to be abandoned in prayer, 275; absorption and transformation of those who love, 310 *ff*., 316-8; divine and human, 354.

Intuition. In the subconscious, 98; of a higher authority, 345; to extract logoi, 206-7; 217; of the truth in us, 214; opposed to reason, 245, 358.

- J -

Judgment. *See* ch. 15, p. 130 *ff*; Reason as a function of, 91; repentance is the hypostasis of, 137-9; in *The Ladder*, 155; as punishment from God, 168; Providence and, 170; world and time as, 176; pride deforms, 181; our, 209 *ff*; don't trust our own, n. 39, pp. 212-3.

Jesus prayer. And the heart, 98; in Callistus and Ignatius, 122. *See also* chs. 29-32.

- K -

Kenosis, Kenotic. Christ's emptying for us, 62; in us at Baptism, 227; n. 288, p. 333.

- L -

Likeness of God. 22, 58; deification is l. to and union with God, 64; communion with God necessary for likeness, 305-7; His Lordly l., 364; will never end, 357; is deificaion, 361.

Listlessness. One of the passions, 80; a discussion of, 107 *ff*.

Logos, logoi. Knowledge of, 28; primary, 40; particular, 40-1; in all things, 57; of the mysteries, 65; in creation, 70-2; n. 12, p. 25; n. 32, p. 40; n. 40, p. 42; n. 60, p. 59; the basis of rationality, 79, 93; the divine, 148, 153, 157, 168; of persons and things, 189; of the virtues, 197, 200; in Scripture, ch. 25, p. 224 *ff*; of Him, 232, 237;

and energies, 248; as concepts, 284; personal, 238; of all existences, 349 *ff*., 354; as images of the Logos, 374.

Longsuffering. *See* ch. 19, p. 168 *ff*.

Love. Perfection culminates in love, 21, 69; is likeness of God, 22; our works prove our, 44 *ff*.; God is source of, 46; perfect commuity (the Trinity) nourishes, 51 *ff*., 57; understands others, 61, 63, 64; is the highest virtue, 71; gained by asceticism, 73. *See also* chs. 33-36.

- M -

Meekness. *See* ch. 21, p. 180 *ff*.

Monks. Live perfect life, 119; take one road, Christians in the world another, 150-2; are ascetics, 156; non-monastics can reach same spirituality, n. 135, p. 150; killed at Athos, 270.

Mysteries. Christ saves us by, 61-3, 65-8; n. 77, p. 67; purification realized by, 135.

Mysticism. Two extremes, 31; a single goal, 49; Neo-Platonic, 49; Eastern and Western, 48-50; n. 11, p. 25; n. 14, p. 27.

- N -

Nature, human. Asceticism confronts negative element in, 24-6; of Christ, 26; requires divine help, 28; can't be absorbed by God, 38; pantheism offers nothing to, 48; Jesus Christ the bridge to, 56; union with God, 73; passions bring to lowest level, 77-8;

INDEX 391

how sin started in, 90; fundamental fear, 131; has bridle, 148; passions entenched in, 150; weakness shown, 172; shares hope and care, 177 *ff.*; unification of, 181, 323 *ff.*, 345; can reach dispassion, 190, 362 *ff.*; restoration of, 213.

Negative theology *in general;* See ch. 26, p. 230 *ff.*

Neoplatonism. 49.

Nous. The mind, 96, 284; soul, 97-9; spirit, 285; mind-heart, 366.

- O -

Obedience. In *The Ladder*, 120; a monastic vow, 150-1, 154; meekness the aid of, 180; n. 94, p. 120; to Him, 214; as beginning of prayer, 263.

- P -

Pain. Human nature defeated by, 26, 87. See chs. 9-12.

Pantheism. Protestant theologians and, 30; if rejected, 47; is gnosticism, 50.

Paradise. Two trees in, 87, 90; blessed, 140, 143.

Passions, see *also* **Gluttony, Unchastity, Avarice, Anger, Dejection, Listlessness, Self-esteem** and **Pride.** Cleansing from, 21, 23, 27, 48, 65, 69, 71; supplanted by virtues, 25, 71. *See esp.* chs. 7-12.

Passions, natural. *See* ch. 8., p. 84 *ff.*

Perfection. The road to, 21, 57; ultimate step, 22, 62; required, 28, 40, 43; His supreme, 45, 58; progress in, 68, 72.

Pleasure. We are attracted by, 26; Jesus Christ conquered, 26; uses others, 82; can be pure joy, 85; bridling, 86; St. Maximus and, 87; pain follows, 88; 92 *ff.*; sloth connected with, 101; senses preoccupied with, 101 *ff.*; passion reaches high point in, 115; and Heidegger, 117; we chase after, 130; repentance not fooled by, 143; and our neighbor, 150; and youth, 152; providence and, 170; and temptation, 171 *ff.*; spiritual, 260, 266, 332; Spirit cleanses from, 359; is bitter, 360.

Positive theology. *See* ch. 28, p. 245 *ff.* The p. way, 168; the p. law, 203; p. forces, 228; p. terms, 230, 246; Dionysius and, 231; and St. Gregory Palamas, 238-41; and Nicholas of Cusa, 244; p. role of the mind, 328 *ff.*

Prayer. *See* ch. 29, p. 255 *ff.*

Pride. One of the passions, 80 *ff.*; analysis of, 88, 94; and St. Maximus, 102; conquered by obedience, 120, 150 *ff.*; fostered by judgment of others, 137; of satisfaction, 138; how wounded, 142; and confession, 145; how weakened, 170, 182; humility opposite of, 181, 183; destroys us, 316.

Prophets. And their listeners, 36; Moses and Elijah, 203; and the spiritual man, 229; Holy Spirit inspired, 355 *ff.*; n. 46, p. 218.

Providence. God rules by, 40, 43; God leads by, 168, 170, 176; n. 109, p. 127; the logoi of, 228; n. 11, p. 199.

- R -

Repentance. See Ch. 16, p. 135 *ff*.; 81; in *The Ladder*, 120-1.

Revelation. Of God, 29; Protestant idea of, 35 *ff*.; Son has revelational purpose, 56; role of in the soul, 98; necessary for contemplation, 188; logoi reveal, 216; Scripture and, 225, 235; and prayer, 239; world and Scripture as, 247; Holy Spirit imparts, n. 46, p. 218.

- S -

Satan, *see also* **Devil.** Man influenced by, 90, 109 *ff*., 158, n. 61, p. 110, n. 151, p. 158; evicted, 97, 117.

Scholasticism. Impregnated with Aristotelianism and pantheism, 47; and intuition of logoi, 206. *See also* **Thomas Aquinas.**

Self-control. See ch. 17, p. 148 *ff*.

Self-esteem. One of the passions, 80; deception and, 146; in *The Ladder*, 155. *See also* **Pride.**

Sleep. Prayer during, 125, 280, 308; too much, 155, 156, 358; fasting and, n. 146, p. 157; of the soul, 336; talkativeness is precursor of, 156.

Soul. Union of with God, 22; cleansing of, 32; a clean, 69-70; and the Bridegroom, n. 68, p. 61; and passions, 80; and body, 87; and natural passions, 89; and mind, 91; faculties of, 96 *ff*.; Baptism removes Satan from, 111; tranquility of, 120; and repentance, 136; and body, 152.

Structure. The Holy Trinity is a dynamic s., 53; church hierarch is a necessary s., 65; care is a s., 116; is proper to each person, 201; of world a symbol, 205; God's home is a s. of love, 326; formless Word accepted a s., 348; of love *(Gestalt)*, 349.

Suffering. Theology knows, 24; Jesus knows our, 60 *ff*.; death joined with, 62; mysticism goes beyond, n. 14, p. 27; and repentance, 144; in general, 170 *ff*.; suffering wrong, n. 146, p. 157; involuntary, n. 177, p. 168; good times followed by, 228; and Jesus prayer, 277; Apostles' and martyrs', 308; and others, 313-4; is life, 328; disorder as, 345; joy and, n. 98, p. 243.

Supraconscious. Hidden center of the mind, 159; n. 205, pp. 290.

Symbol, symbolism. The Lord appears as, 58; mysteries are, 64; are intermediaries, 67; world structure as 205 *ff*.; leaving behind, 295; concepts are, 220, 347, n. 119, pp. 252-3; spiritual experience and, 201 *ff*., 229; Scripture and nature are, 225, n. 60, p. 227; ark of the covenant as, 242; mirror God, 245; material as, n. 55, pp. 222-3.

- T -

Tabernacle. As "home," God Himself, 325-6; Moses and, 347-8; as structure of love, 350 *ff*.; vision of, n. 55, p. 222.

Talkativeness. Child of lying, 120; proof of ignorance, 155-6.

INDEX 393

Tears. And listlessness, 108; meekness follows, 120; in Callistus and Ignatius, 121; in *The Ladder*, 134, 155, 182; gift of, 145; and Diadochos, 170; and Isaac the Syrian, 256; and pride, 263; and eternal punishment, 274; love of God and, 277; and Jesus Prayer, 281; and St. Simeon, 358, sign of mercy of God, n. 126, p. 256.

Temptation. Jesus helps us in, 60; the first, 90; the onslaught of, 112; and repentance, 136; combatting, 154, 255; discussion of, 169 *ff.*; dispassion defeats, 185; n. 59, p. 109; our Lord's victory over, n. 182, p. 172.

Theosis, *see* **Deification.**

Thomas Aquinas. Misunderstood Trinity, 51; had nervous breakdown, 51; made negative theology a corrective, 231. *See also* **Scholasticism.**

Trinity. *See* ch. 4, p. 46 *ff.*; soul compared to, 97; ultimate level of truth, n. 109, p. 127; man is icon of , 276; light of t. during prayer, 304; Spirit in, 318; divine light radiates from, 332; and energies, n. 289, pp. 333-4.

- U -

Unchastity. One of the passions, 80; gluttony leads to, 80, n. 8, pp. 80-1; monks refrain from, 151; self-control aimed at, 169.

Uncreated energies. God communicates Himself to us by, 48; absent in Western theology, 50; proper to Holy Trinity, 52.

- W -

Watchfulness. Recommended by Fathers, 156; *see* ch. 18, p. 158 *ff.*

Will. Essential element of our nature, 26, 30-1, 104 *ff.*, 276; our, 41; passion a product of, 79, 84, 92, 103, 150; two wills in us, 105 *ff.*; man's reestablishment is a question of, 113; simple, 124 *ff.*; vigil victory for, 156; and hope, 179; virtue makes w. grow, 181; dispassion sustained by, 186; love affected by 312, 317.

Postscript

Since first being asked, in the sixties, to translate several articles of our beloved professor and friend, Fr. Dumitru Staniloae, from Romanian into English,[1] and then to write a thesis under his direction in Bucharest in 1971, it was my privilege to get to know him and his writings well. It has been a joy to translate *Orthodox Spirituality* for the Orthodox faithful and others.

Fr. Dumitru Staniloae was born in 1903, in Vladeni, Romania. He received his degree in theology at Cernauti in 1927, and his doctorate there in 1928. He then studied in Greece, Germany, France, and Serbia, and became especially adept in the Greek and German languages. He began to teach theology in Sibiu, Romania in 1929, and following marriage was ordained a priest in 1932. After World War II, he accepted his years of suffering in a communist prison as an opportunity to pray and grow in virtue and to reach the highest level of Christian love.

A contemporary of both Vladimir Lossky and Fr. John Meyendorff, Fr. Staniloae spent his life immersed in the mystical (or "spiritual," as he would say) theology of the Church. He was a follower of St. Dionysios the Areopagite and a disciple of St. Maximos and St. Gregory Palamas. His definitive work on St. Gregory was published in 1938. Fr Staniloae succeeded in doing what many other men of deep thought don't: he wrote practical, though intellectually concentrated books based on the spiritual tradition of the Church. Such are his *Dogmatics*[2] and *Liturgics*. The Romanian *Philokalia* is also his work. Although the original Greek *Philokalia* consists of only five volumes, for the Romanian edition Fr. Dumitru added more patristic material, along with copious footnotes, to make 12 volumes.

For many years, Fr. Dumitru was Professor of Theology in Sibiu and Bucharest, where both in and out of the classroom he remained ever the humble, soft-spoken man of virtue and love described in the pages of this book. Well loved by his students and recognized by the Christians of many nations, he fell asleep in the Lord in 1993, at the age of 89. May his memory be eternal!

---

[1] *See*: "Romanian Orthodoxy and the Western Spirit," *Calendarul Credinta, The Faith*, Detroit, 1968, pp. 86-88; and "Orthodoxy and Modern Western Currents in Theology," in the same yearbook for 1969, pp. 67-68.

[2] Three volumes. Volume one, trs. by Ioan Ioniţa and Robert Barringer is two volumes in English and called *The Experience of God*.

Orthodox Spirituality was originally published in Romanian in Bucharest in 1981, when its author was already retired. Yet, at his advanced age, he still pondered the great truths of God and man. Now here is his *Orthodox Spirituality* in our own mother tongue, English. How did this come about, with the help of God?

Otilia Kloos of Stillwater, Minnesota, laid the conceptual foundation for this project. She had known Fr. Staniloae in her native Romania, and loved his many writings. When she immigrated to America in 1991, she came with the desire to see all of these writings available in the language of her new country. The hardships, however, of life in a new land, with a language new to her, prevented her from realizing her dream. So she turned for help.

In the end, the new work is basically a literal translation of the original Romanian into the common tongue of North America. One should say that Fr. Staniloae's expository style isn't always easy to understand; even so, there are beautiful passages in the book, and gold lies just underneath the surface. It was our desire to make the English text eminently readable, whatever this means in terms of altered syntax and vocabulary. We thus kept on working, editing the external form of textual exposition, but never editing his ideas. A note on the language: we have used some terminology, such as the concept "apophatic," that is yet not quite common in English. Maybe with time, with a rise of general familiarity with Orthodox theology, such concepts will become familiar to larger circles of readers.

The original text contains over 700 footnotes, and sometimes one note alone has several references. We had to check the notes against the sources, and make necessary corrections. Fortunately, we were able to locate most of Staniloae's original sources, although in a few cases we were unable to find the right references, which are so noted. Please forgive us for perhaps making new mistakes in correcting old ones. Quotations from ancient and modern writers, although translated for the most part from the original texts, when available, for the reader's convenience, are also referenced to modern translations when such exist.

Translators can't help but feel some emotion when a work is finished. It's not unlike watching your child graduate from college, or get married. You have spent a lot on him, invested heavily, but your life also has been enriched. Translating is like finding a hidden treasure, painstakingly digging it up with much time and expense, and then sharing it with others.

For several years, the translators have lived in the inner world of a master, following him word-by-word, chapter-by-chapter, experience-by-experience. They have found, sometimes with great difficulty, the books that he had read, and then studied them for themselves. Through these books, they came to know the saints that he loved and knew. At the same time, the master, constantly present with the translators in spirit, revealed to them, day by day, the contours of his own spiritual life, and also that of many others who had come before, even as they themselves had learned it from the Master Himself. In the process of work on this book, the translators finally realized that they were also getting to know Our Lord and Master better, too. Thus, they wanted to share their work with you.

Acknowledgements

Many good people have helped unearth this treasure of Orthodox theology, both when we started the project in Wisconsin and Minnesota some years ago, and when the project was resumed in Pennsylvania, and to all of them is due a debt of gratitude: to the staff of the Archbishop Ireland Memorial Library, the graduate theology library of University of St. Thomas and The Saint Paul Seminary School of Divinity, St. Paul, MN; John and Ingrid Larson; my beloved fellow clergy of the Minnesota Orthodox Clergy Association (MEOCA), especially Fr. Nick Kassemeotis; Fr. Nick Apostola, of Massachusetts; Dan and Roslyn Stark; Sergei Arhipov, the capable editor of this volume and also Head Librarian of The Patriarch St. Tikhon Library of St. Tikhon's Orthodox Theological Seminary; Hieromonk Juvenaly, Assistant Librarian; and to the numerous seminarians who helped along the way. We are grateful to Fr. Staniloae of blessed memory for his hearty endorsement and encouragement, to Archbishop Herman and the late Archbishop Victorin for everything they have done to assist and bring this project to fruition. God is to be praised for Fr. Archimandrite Tikhon and the entire brotherhood of St. Tikhon's Monastery. May He reward all those who quietly and humbly continue the work of St. Tikhon's Seminary and Monastery. A final thanks and acknowledgment to Lidia Ionescu-Staniloae, Fr. Staniloae's daughter, for her cooperation and permission to proceed after her father fell asleep in the Lord; and to all the others whom we might have unintentionally forgotten. May the Lord God remember us all in His Heavenly Kingdom, through the prayers of our holy father and patron, St. Nikolai of Zhicha, now and ever, and unto ages of ages, Amen.

Archimandrite Jerome

The Feast of the Nativity
December 25, 2001